REA

MBA'S
GUIDE TO

**The Essential Office Reference
for Business Professionals**

MICROSOFT®
OFFICE
XP

MBA'S GUIDE TO

**The Essential Office Reference
for Business Professionals**

MICROSOFT® OFFICE XP

Pat Coleman
Stephen L. Nelson
David B. Maguiness

**REDMOND
TECHNOLOGY
P R E S S**

MBA's Guide to Microsoft Office XP:
The Essential Office Reference for Business Professionals

Published by
Redmond Technology Press
8581 154th Avenue NE
Redmond, WA 98052
www.redtechpress.com

Library of Congress Catalog Card No: applied for

ISBN 1-931150-20-6

Printed and bound in the United States of America.

9 8 7 6 5 4 3 2 1

Distributed by
Independent Publishers Group
814 N. Franklin St.
Chicago, IL 60610
www.ipgbook.com

Product and company names mentioned herein may be the trademarks of their respective owners.

In the preparation of this book, both the author and the publisher have made every effort to provide current, correct, and comprehensible information. Nevertheless, inadvertent errors can occur and software and the principles and regulations concerning business often change. Furthermore, the application and impact of principles, rules, and laws can vary widely from case to case because of the unique facts involved. For these reasons, the author and publisher specifically disclaim any liability or loss that is incurred as a consequence of the use and application, directly or indirectly, of any information presented in this book. If legal or other expert assistance is needed, the services of a professional should be sought.

Contents at a Glance

Contents

Chapter 2   **Document Management** **33**

Chapter 3   **Word Basics** **59**

Chapter 4   **Excel Basics** **89**

Part 2   *Using Office in Business*   **267**

Chapter 9   **Formatting in Word** **269**

Chapter 15   Publishing an E-Mail Newsletter Using Outlook 419

Chapter 16   Setting Up a Web Site Using FrontPage 433

Chapter 20   **Performing Profit-Volume-Cost Analysis with Excel 537**

INTRODUCTION

You are unique among readers. Almost nobody reads the introduction to a book like this. However, you'll richly benefit by taking a few minutes to read through this introduction. Its purpose is to help you maximize your return on the investment you've made in this book—your investment in money and especially your even more costly investment in time.

Why This Book

Bookstore shelves are packed with guides to Microsoft Office. So why this book? Because although many fine books have been written about Office, there really isn't a book written specifically for business users of Office. Other books give you a great deal of information about Office and some useful information about how to access it, but don't (in our opinion) give the sorts of detailed commentary and advice useful to business people. Business users of Office benefit by having a reference that emphasizes, talks from the point of view, and focuses on the business aspects of using Office. In short, business users of Office need a book that talks about Office as a business tool.

MBA's Guide to Office XP is the only book that specifically describes how you can more easily, more productively, and more powerfully use Office in business.

Although this book's title references the popular business professional degree, MBA, this book will also be of use to people without MBAs. MBA students, for example, will find this book useful. People with graduate degrees in accounting, public administration, economics, and related fields will find this book useful as well.

In addition, anyone who's finished a good undergraduate program in business or a related field (like accounting) will feel comfortable and gain skills using this book as a desktop reference.

What's in This Book

The easiest way to see what's in this book is to turn to the table of contents. It lists each chapter and each chapter's contents in rich detail.

The chapters in this book fall into three categories:

Chapters 1 through 8 provide fast-paced but friendly tutorials on the programs in the Office suite of applications. In a nutshell, these eight QuickPrimers™ move you to professional proficiency in using Office—even if you're new to it. If you don't need this help, of course, you can easily skip these primers. If you're skilled in using one or two programs, but occasionally need to use one that you aren't familiar with, you can turn immediately to the primer for that application and find all the information you need to get started.

Chapters 9 through 13 provide rich, detailed coverage of topics of interest to business users of Office—topics that are shortchanged in books that have to be everything to everybody. Chapter 11, for example, explains how to create a chart for an Office document, and Chapter 13 shows you step-by-step how to use Word to do a mail merge.

Chapters 14 through 21 describe how to set up real-life business projects using Office—a contacts database, a Web site, a Web store, an e-mail newsletter, and a PowerPoint sales presentation. In addition, chapters in this part of the book discuss how to use Excel to create a business pro forma, to perform break-even analysis, and to perform capital expenditure analysis.

Conventions Used in This Book

In this book, the illustrations and the steps for processes assume the use of Office XP, the most recent release. If you have an earlier version of Office, the steps and what you see on the screen will be similar, but not identical. When you have a question, check out Help.

To identify screen elements, the first letter of each word in the description is capitalized. This convention may look a bit strange at first, but it makes it easier to understand an instruction such as, "Click the Print Table Of Links check box."

You'll also find Notes, Tips, and Warnings, which point out tidbits of useful information. Pay attention to Warnings; they help you avoid potential problems. A few sidebars are also scattered throughout the chapters. Sidebars contain helpful information that is not necessarily directly related to the topic at hand, or they may discuss in detail a subject that is mentioned in the running text but is not elaborated on.

Part 1

QuickPrimers™

In This Part

Chapter 1

COMMON OFFICE TOOLS

Featuring:

- Getting Help
- Using the Task Pane
- Checking Spelling
- Using AutoCorrect
- Using Speech Recognition
- Personalized Menus and Toolbars
- Using the Common Editing Tools
- Working with the Formatting Toolbar

One advantage of working with the Office suite of programs is that they share many common features and tools. Thus, when you learn how to use these features and tools in one program, you automatically know how to use them in the other programs. For example, if you know how to spell-check a Word document, you also know how to spell check an Excel worksheet, a PowerPoint presentation, a Web page you create with FrontPage, and an Access database.

This chapter introduces these features and tools, shows you how to use them, and points out the specific Office applications that share them.

Getting Help

Each of the Office programs includes a help system, and it works the same way in all of them, although each contains information that is specific to the program you are currently using. To open Help, click the Help menu, and then click Microsoft *program* Help. The first time you open Help in any Office program, you'll see a little character called the Office Assistant. When you click the Office Assistant, a balloon is displayed. To get help on a particular task, simply type a question and click Search. The Office Assistant will then typically display a list of topics; simply click a topic to view its contents.

The default Office Assistant character is Clippit. You can retain this character if you like using the Office Assistant, or you can select another character. If you find the Office Assistant more annoying than helpful, you can hide him. To do any of this, click the Options button in the Office Assistant balloon to open the Office Assistant dialog box, as shown in Figure 1-1. To hide the Office Assistant, click the Use The Office Assistant check box to clear it, and then click OK.

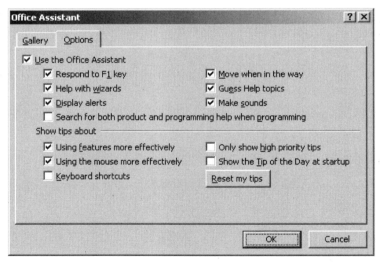

Figure 1-1   The Office Assistant dialog box.

To select another character as the Office Assistant, click the Gallery tab, as shown in Figure 1-2. Click Next to scroll through the selection of assistants. When you find one you like, simply click OK.

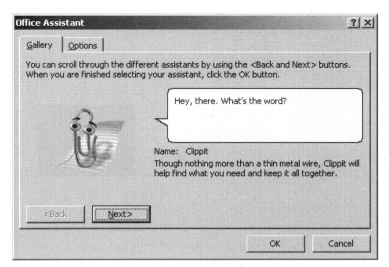

Figure 1-2 The Office Assistant dialog box, open at the Gallery tab.

You can also ask a question without using the Office Assistant. Simply enter it in the Type A Question For Help box, which is at the far right on the menu bar, and then press Enter.

If you are not displaying the Office Assistant, you open Help directly when you click the Help menu and then click Microsoft *program* Help. The Help window has three tabs: Contents, Answer Wizard, and Index. The Answer Wizard works similarly to the Office Assistant. You type a question to display a list of topics that answer the question, and then you click a topic to display its contents.

Figure 1-3 shows the Contents tab in Help in Excel. Double-click the book icon to display subtopics for a topic, and then double-click the topic to display its contents.

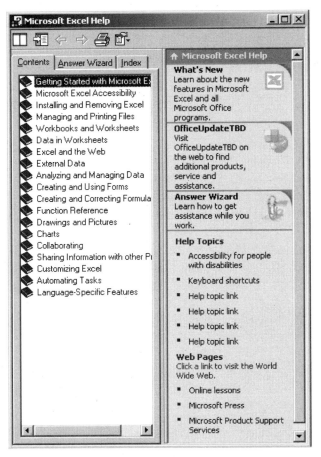

Figure 1-3   The Contents tab in Microsoft Excel Help.

Using the Index tab, however, is often the most efficient way to get information. In Figure 1-4, we entered *date* in the Type Keywords box, and Help displayed a list of 67 topics. To display the contents of a topic, simply double-click the topic.

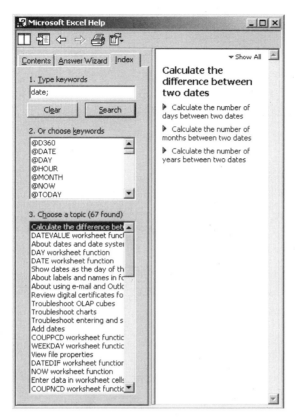

Figure 1-4 The Index tab in Microsoft Excel Help.

In many Office dialog boxes, you'll see a Help button next to the Close button. Click the button with question mark and then click an option in the dialog box to display help related to that option.

TIP   *To quickly open the Help window in any Office program, press the F1 key. If the task pane is open, you can also click the Help link near the bottom.*

Using the Task Pane

The *task pane* is a new feature in Office that is available in Word, Excel, Access, FrontPage, and PowerPoint. You use it to quickly open a new or an existing document and to format documents. The types of task panes depend on the application, and the QuickPrimers in Part 1 of this book will discuss these. Figure 1-5 shows the Slide Layout Task pane in PowerPoint. To use one of these layouts for the current slide, you simply click it.

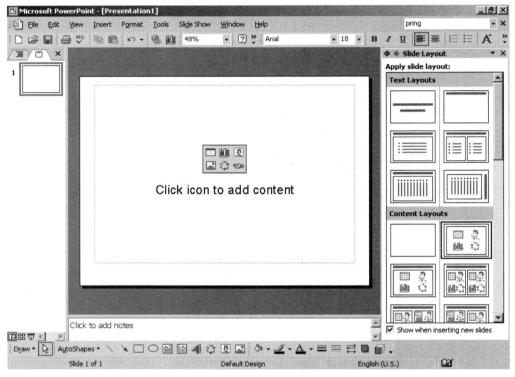

Figure 1-5   The Slide Layout task pane in PowerPoint.

If you prefer not to use the task pane (perhaps you need the screen area), you can disable it. Click the View menu, and then click Task Pane to remove the check mark.

Checking Spelling

Before you distribute a document of any kind in a business setting, you should check it for spelling and other errors. Communicating effectively involves paying attention to details such as punctuation, capitalization, spelling, word usage, writing style, and so on. But nothing detracts from your message quite like a glaring misspelling. A spelling checker is an indispensable tool, and you'll find this feature in all the Office applications. Although the basic procedure is the same in each application, all vary slightly, and so in this section, we'll look at each individually.

NOTE   *In any Office application, you can check spelling in a variety of languages. To change from the default, which is U.S. English, click the Dictionary Language drop-down list box in the Spelling or Spelling And Grammar dialog box, and select a language. You can also change the default dictionary language. In the Spelling or Spelling And Grammar dialog box, click the Options button to open the Options dialog box, select the language from the Dictionary Language drop-down list box, and click OK.*

Checking Spelling in Word

By default, Word checks spelling and grammar as you type, but you can disable this feature and check spelling and grammar manually whenever you want. We usually do disable this automatic checking feature and then do a thorough check when we've finished composing a document and right before we're going to distribute the document or submit it for publication. To disable the grammar and spelling check while you're typing, follow these steps:

1. Open the Options dialog box, as shown in Figure 1-6.

Click the Tools menu, and then click Options. In the Options dialog box, click the Spelling & Grammar tab.

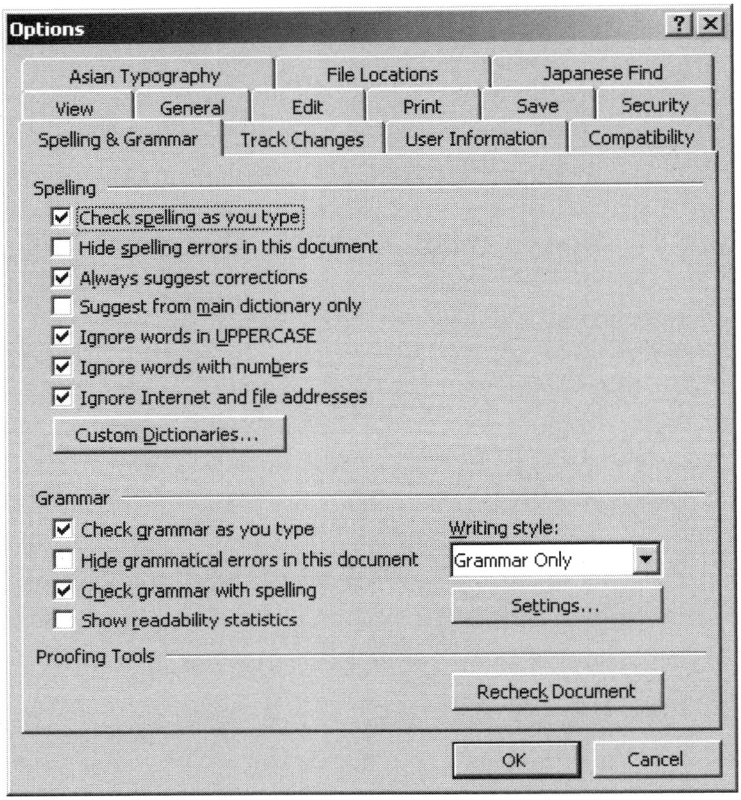

Figure 1-6 The Spelling & Grammar tab in the Options dialog box.

2. Disable checking as you type.

In the Spelling & Grammar tab, click the Check Spelling As You Type check box to clear it, and then click the Check Grammar As You Type check box to also clear it. Click OK.

To check spelling and grammar manually or to check only spelling manually, follow these steps:

1. Open the Spelling And Grammar dialog box, as shown in Figure 1-7.

Click the Tools menu, and then click Spelling And Grammar. Word now starts to check spelling and grammar. When it highlights a perceived mistake, you can choose an option from buttons on the right side of the dialog box.

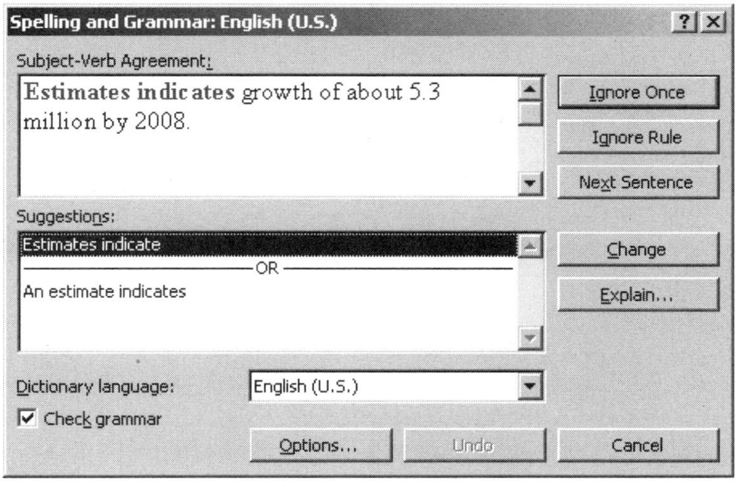

Figure 1-7   The Spelling And Grammar dialog box.

2. Tell Word to check only spelling.

Click the Check Grammar check box to clear it, and then continue to check only spelling.

Now let's look at the options available when you're checking spelling. Click the Tools menu, and then click Spelling And Grammar to start the spell check. When Word finds a perceived misspelling, it opens the Spelling And Grammar dialog box, as shown in Figure 1-8.

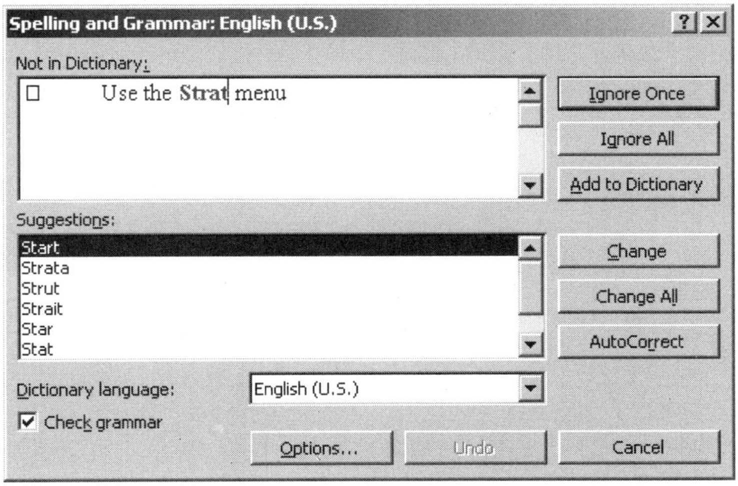

Figure 1-8   The Spelling And Grammar dialog box.

You have the following choices about what action to take:

- Ignore Once. When you click this button, Word does not change the highlighted word and continues to check the rest of the document. If Word finds the same spelling again in the document, it once again highlights it.

- Ignore All. When you click this button, Word does not change the highlighted word here or anywhere else in the document. You might click Ignore All when Word finds an unusual spelling that is correct and is used often in the document or when Word finds a proper name.

- Add To Dictionary. When you click this button, Word adds the highlighted word to the custom dictionary, which you can edit. We'll look at how to do so later in this section.

- Change. When you click this button, Word changes the highlighted word in the Not In Dictionary box to the word that is selected in the Suggestions box.

- Change All. When you click this button, Word changes the current highlighted word and other occurrences of the same misspelling throughout the document to the selected word in the Suggestions box.

- AutoCorrect. When you click this button, Word adds the spelling word and its correction to the AutoCorrect list. Word then corrects this misspelling every time you make it, if you have enabled Check Spelling As You Type in the Spelling And Grammar dialog box, which we'll look at shortly.

To check grammar and spelling at the same time, click the Check Grammar check box in the Spelling And Grammar dialog box. When Word finds what it considers a grammatical error, it opens the Spelling And Grammar dialog box. If you click the Explain button, Word displays a yellow balloon with an explanation of the rule.

If you agree with Word's suggested correction, click the Change button. As with the spelling check, you can click Ignore Once to retain the construction, or you can click the Ignore Rule to ignore the current construction and any other occurrence of it throughout the rest of the document. If you want to go back into the document and rewrite the sentence, click in the document, make the changes, and then click Next Sentence to continue the spelling and grammar check.

TIP   *If you have automatic spell checking turned off and want to check the spelling of an individual word in any application, simply select the word, click Tools, and then click Spelling And Grammar.*

Checking Spelling in Outlook

When you create a new message in Outlook, you are actually using Word and all the Word tools. Consequently, checking the spelling of an Outlook e-mail message works exactly the same as checking the spelling of a Word document. When you've finished creating the message, click the Tools menu, and then click Spelling And Grammar to start the spell check. When the spell checker finds a misspelled word, it will display the same dialog box with the same options that we discussed in the previous section.

You can tell Outlook to always check the spelling of a message before sending it. To do so, follow these steps:

1. **Open the Options dialog box.**

   Click the Tools menu, and then click Options.

2. **Tell Outlook to spell-check a message before sending it.**

   Click the Spelling tab, as shown in Figure 1-9, click the Always Check Spelling Before Sending check box, and then click OK.

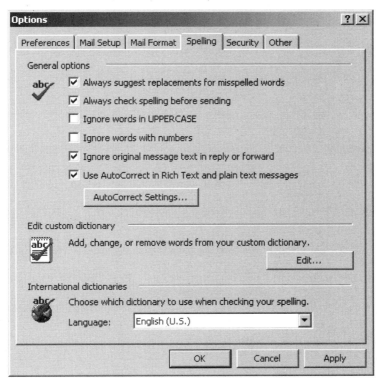

Figure 1-9 The Options dialog box open at the Spelling tab.

TIP
Popular practice notwithstanding, people judge the business presence of your e-mail messages just as they do printed documents or a Web page. An e-mail message full of typos and sloppy formatting implies that you may take that same approach to your accounting practices, your customer service, or the quality of the goods you manufacture. Take the time to see that your e-mail messages portray you and your organization in a professional manner.

Checking Spelling in PowerPoint

PowerPoint also checks spelling as you type. When you make a typo, you'll see a wavy green line appear beneath the misspelled word. As with Word, you can disable this feature. To do so, click the Tools menu, click Options to open the Options dialog box, and then click the Spelling And Style tab, as shown in Figure 1-10. Click the Check Spelling As You Type check box to clear it, and then click OK.

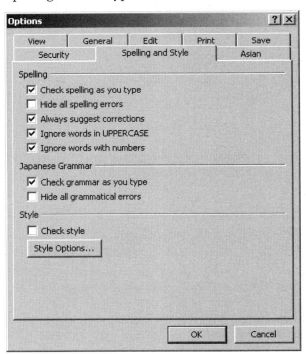

Figure 1-10 The Options dialog box open at the Spelling And Style tab.

When you're ready to check the spelling of a presentation, click the Tools menu, and then click Spelling And Grammar. When the spell checker finds a misspelled word, you'll see the dialog box shown in Figure 1-11. You use the options in this dialog box in the same way that you use the options when you spell-check in Word.

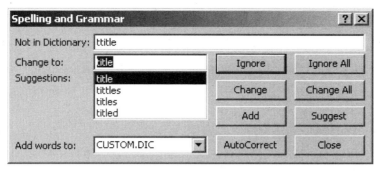

Figure 1-11 The PowerPoint Spelling And Grammar dialog box.

NOTE   *PowerPoint doesn't check the spelling in objects that you created in other applications and then inserted in a slide. It also doesn't check special effects such as WordArt. You'll need to check this spelling in the original application or very carefully yourself.*

Checking Spelling in FrontPage

In FrontPage, you can check spelling as you type, you can check the spelling on any open page, or you can check the spelling of an entire Web site. You take care of the first two tasks in the same ways that you do so in Word or PowerPoint. To check the spelling of a Web site, follow these steps:

1. **Open your Web site in Folders view.**

   Click the View menu, and then click Folders.

2. **Tell FrontPage which pages to check.**

   If you want to check certain pages, select those pages. Then click the Tools menu, and click Spelling. To check all pages, click Entire Web. To check only those pages you selected, click Selected Pages. To add a task for each page that contains misspelled words, click the Add A Task For Each Page With Misspellings check box. When your options are selected, click Start to begin the spell check.

When the spell check is complete, FrontPage will display a list of the pages that contain misspelled words. To correct the errors now, double-click a page to open it in Page view and follow the prompts to make corrections. When you are finished, save and close the page and continue with the next page.

If you selected to add a task for each page, click the Cancel button when FrontPage displays the list of pages that contain errors. When you are later ready to make corrections, switch to Tasks view (click the View menu, and then click Tasks). Double-click the Fix Misspelled Words task, and then click Start Task. When the page opens, follow the prompts to correct the misspellings.

Checking Spelling in Excel

Although Excel doesn't automatically check spelling as you enter information in cells in a worksheet, you can easily check a range of cells or the entire worksheet:

- To check the entire worksheet, click any cell in it, click the Tools menu, and then click Spelling.

- To check a range of cells, select the range, click the Tools menu, and then click Spelling.

When Excel finds a misspelled word, you'll see the Spelling dialog box, shown in Figure 1-12. You use the options in this dialog box in the same way that you use them in the other Office programs.

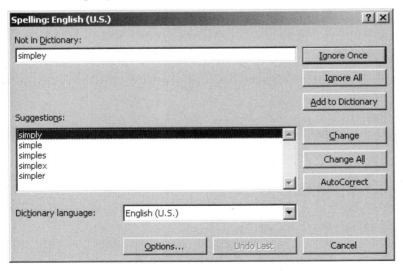

Figure 1-12 The Spelling dialog box in Excel.

In Excel, perhaps more than in the Office programs we've discussed so far, you are likely to include the names of products, trademarks, shoptalk, and industry buzzwords in a document. You'll want to add these terms to the dictionary that Excel uses to check spelling against. To do so, simply click the Add To Dictionary button when Excel comes across a word it doesn't recognize. When you add the word to the dictionary, Excel will not identify it as misspelled in the future.

Checking Spelling in Access

Spell checking in Access is almost identical to spell checking in Excel, with one exception. If your database contains fields such as product codes, companies, people, and other proper names or terms that Access won't find in its dictionary, you can tell Access to ignore these fields. To spell-check data in Datasheet view, in Form view, or in a database object in the Database window, click the Tools menu, and then click Spelling. When Access finds a word or phrase that is not in its dictionary, you'll see the Spelling dialog box, as shown in Figure 1-13. If you want Access to ignore the field, click the Ignore Field button.

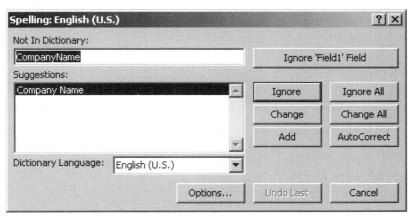

Figure 1-13   The Spelling dialog box in Access.

Finding Synonyms

When you're working in Word or FrontPage and find yourself at a loss for words, you can use the Thesaurus feature. A thesaurus is simply a file of synonyms. You'll find out soon enough, if you don't know already, that you can't always trust a thesaurus. If you blindly go about substituting synonyms, you can come up with some rather meaningless, convoluted sentences.

That said, when you're stuck, it may help to check out the thesaurus. First select the word for which you want a synonym. Then, in Word, click the Tools menu, click Language, and then click Thesaurus. In FrontPage, click the Tools menu, and then click Thesaurus. In either case, you'll see the Thesaurus dialog box:

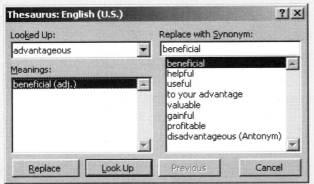

As you can see, the thesaurus also lists an antonym for the selected word. To use a word in the list instead of your original word, select the word and click Replace.

Using AutoCorrect

Word, Excel, Access, and PowerPoint also come to your spelling and typing aid with a feature called AutoCorrect. As you work along, AutoCorrect fixes common misspellings and typographical errors. For example, if you type *teh* instead of *the*, you'll see that the typo is corrected without your intervention.

To see a list of the changes that are made automatically, click the Tools menu and then click AutoCorrect Options to open the AutoCorrect dialog box. Figure 1-14 shows the AutoCorrect dialog box that opens in Excel. This dialog box will be similar, though not identical, in the other Office applications.

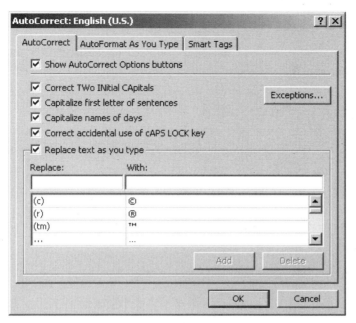

Figure 1-14 The AutoCorrect dialog box.

To see a list of the substitutions that the application will automatically make, scroll down the list at the bottom of the dialog box. To add a correction that you want the application to make, enter the misspelling or other characters in the Replace box, and then type the substitution you want the program to make in the With box. As you can see, the Office program substitutes some well-known symbols such as the trademark symbol and the copyright symbol when you type a string of certain characters. If you frequently type a certain symbol or a long proper name, for example, you can create your own shorthand of keystrokes and have the program substitute the symbol or long proper name, as long as that particular string of characters doesn't already represent something else. Even if it does, you can delete that substitution and use your own. Simply select the item in the list, and click the Delete button.

Using Speech Recognition

Speech recognition, also called voice recognition, is the capability of the computer or a program to understand the spoken word and transform it into the written word. In the past, speech recognition software was primarily available from third-party developers and was initially used in the scientific and medical community. Physicians, researchers, laboratory technicians, and others used it to describe and transcribe their observations and procedures while keeping their hands free to do the real work. Speech recognition is also an important assistive technology and has been used by those for whom keyboarding or clicking the mouse presented a physical challenge.

Now, however, speech recognition is available to all users of Word, Excel, Outlook, Access, FrontPage, and PowerPoint. To use this feature, you will need to install the Speech Recognition engine because it is not installed by default, and you'll need speakers and a microphone. You will also need to train the engine to recognize your voice and the peculiarities of your pronunciation.

Installing Speech Recognition

To install the Speech Recognition engine, click the Tools menu in any program that includes this feature, and then click Speech. You'll see a message that the feature is not installed and asking if you would like to install it. Click Yes. When asked to do so, insert your Office CD-ROM. As the installation proceeds, you'll see a progress indicator. When the installation completes, you'll need to restart your computer in order for the configuration changes to take effect. To do so, click Yes in the dialog box that asks if you want to restart now.

NOTE   *Once you install Speech Recognition in one program, it is installed and available in all the other programs that use it.*

If You Need to Acquire a Microphone...

The Speech Recognition feature will work best with a "close talk" microphone, such as the one that comes with a headset. In other words, a close talk microphone is very near to your mouth. You can find such microphones at your local computer store or office supply store, and, of course, you can purchase one over the Internet. They are not expensive—we recently bought one for about $15.00.

If you use a headset, you'll need to plug the microphone into the microphone jack on your computer and plug the headset speakers into the speakers jack.

Setting Up Your Microphone

You'll need to adjust the volume for your microphone before you begin training the speech recognition engine. To do so, you use the Microphone Wizard. Click the Speech icon in Control Panel to open the Speech Properties dialog box, as shown in Figure 1-15. Click the Configure Microphone button to start setting up your microphone and output speakers. Figure 1-16 shows the first screen of this wizard. Follow the onscreen instructions to set up your microphone.

Figure 1-15 The Speech Properties dialog box.

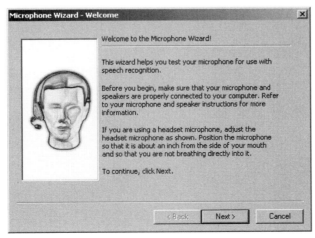

Figure 1-16 Using the Microphone Wizard.

Training the Speech Engine to Recognize Your Voice

After you set up your microphone, you will need to train the speech engine to recognize your pronunciation and speaking style. In the Speech Properties dialog box, click the Train Profile button to start the Microsoft Speech Recognition Training Wizard. Figure 1-17 shows the first screen of this wizard.

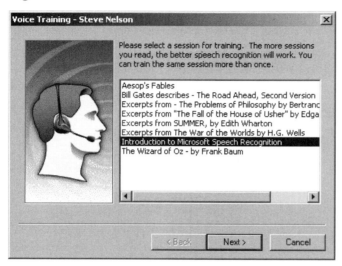

Figure 1-17 Starting to train the speech engine.

Follow the onscreen instructions, which involve reading phrases that the wizard displays on the screen. This will take some time, and you'll need to be in a quiet place so that outside noises don't interfere with the recognition process.

To start using Speech Recognition, click the Tools menu and then click Speech. You'll see a toolbar with buttons for activating the microphone, making corrections, and other options.

Personalized Menus and Toolbars

In the Office suite of programs, you can choose to use personalized menus and toolbars. A personalized menu or toolbar displays only those items you have most recently used rather than all the available items. For example, in Word the complete File menu contains 15 items as well as a list of most recently opened documents. If personalized menus are enabled, the Word file menu might include only half as many items when you click it and then display the rest of the items.

A personalized toolbar also includes only those tool buttons you have most recently used. To display the other buttons, you click the Toolbar Options button. In addition, you can choose to display the Standard and Formatting toolbars on one row or two rows. (Later in this chapter, we'll look at these toolbars.)

To specify how menus and toolbars are displayed, you use the Customize dialog box. Figure 1-18 shows the Customize dialog box open in Excel; it is similar in all the Office programs.

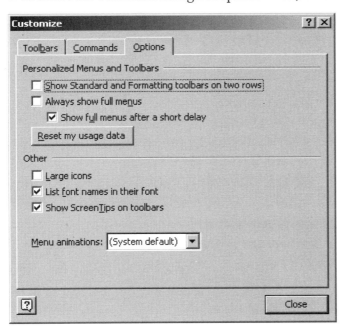

Figure 1-18 The Customize dialog box in Excel.

You have the following options in this dialog box as far as personalized menus and toolbars are concerned:

- If you want to always display all the items on every menu, click the Always Show Full Menus check box.

- If you want to display only the items you've most recently used, be sure that the Always Show Full Menus check box is cleared and that the Show Full Menus After A Short Delay check box is cleared.

- If you want to display the items you've most recently used first and then to display the full menu, be sure the Always Show Full Menus check box is cleared and that the Show Full Menus After A Short Delay check box is checked.

- To clear all the menu and toolbar settings and return them to their default state, click the Reset My Usage Data button.

Whether you use personalized or full menus is up to you. Some people find personalized menus and toolbars annoying, and others prefer them. Using one or the other changes nothing about the way an Office program basically works.

Using the Common Editing Tools

All Office programs include the Standard and Formatting toolbars, which you can display together on one row or separately on two rows. You can use the option in the Customize dialog box, which we looked at in the previous section, to specify one row or two, or you can click the Toolbar Options button (the one with the chevron and the down-pointing arrow). If both toolbars are currently displayed on one row, you'll see the Show Buttons On Two Rows option. If both toolbars are currently displayed on two rows, you'll see the Show Button On One Row option. Click the option to select your preference.

Figure 1-19 shows the toolbars on two rows in Word. The toolbar just below the menu bar is the Standard toolbar, and the Formatting toolbar is on the following row. In this section we'll look at some of the editing tools on the Standard toolbar that are common to all Office programs, and then in the next section we'll look at the Formatting toolbar.

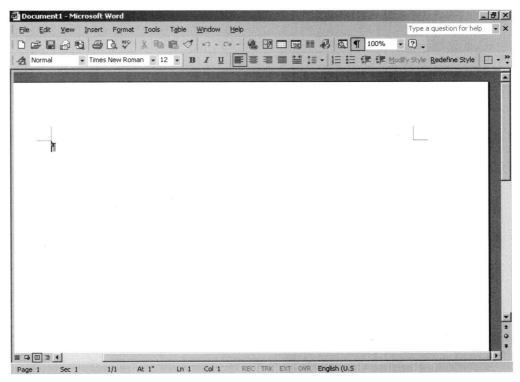

Figure 1-19 The Standard and Formatting toolbars shown on two rows in Word.

TIP   *To display a ScreenTip that describes a button, simply point to the button.*

Using Cut, Copy, and Paste

You use the Cut, Copy, and Paste buttons to move and copy a selection from one location to another within the same document or to a different document. The document can be in the same program or in another Office program. For example, you can copy a chart you create in Excel to a Word document, or you can move text you composed in Word to a Web page you are creating with FrontPage.

Before you cut or copy anything, you must select it. To select, you typically click and drag the mouse across some text or simply click within an object such as a chart or a picture. When you cut something, you remove it from its current location and insert it in another location. When you copy something, it remains in its current location, and a duplicate is places at the new location.

You can cut (or move) data in the following ways after you select it:

- Click the Cut button, place the insertion point in the new location, and then click the Paste button.

- Click the Edit menu, click Cut, place the insertion point in the new location, click the Edit menu, and then click Paste.

- Right-click your selection, choose Cut from the shortcut menu, right-click in the new location, and choose Paste from the shortcut menu.

- Press Ctrl+X, place the insertion point in the new location, and press Ctrl+V.

You can copy data in the following ways after you select it:

- Click the Copy button, place the insertion point in the new location, and then click the Paste button.

- Click the Edit menu, click Copy, place the insertion point in the new location, click the Edit menu, and the click Paste.

- Right-click your selection, choose Copy from the shortcut menu, right-click in the new location, and choose Paste from the shortcut menu.

- Press Ctrl+C, place the insertion point in the new location, and press Ctrl+V.

You can also cut, copy, and paste using the mouse, called dragging and dropping, but if you try to do so, you will see that this is a much less exact process than using any of the other four methods. To move, select the data, hold down the mouse, and then drag the data to the new location. To copy, select the data, hold down the Ctrl key, hold down the mouse, and then drag the data to the location where you want the copy placed.

Undoing and Redoing

When you are editing an Office document, the Undo and Redo buttons are often your best friends. For example, if you move something from one document to another and then change your mind, simply click the Undo button. What you cut from one document and placed in another is then back in its original location.

TIP   *The keyboard equivalent of clicking the Undo button is pressing Ctrl+Z.*

If you take an action and then want to repeat that action, clicking Redo can be a quick way to do so. For example, you create a table in Word and then decide you want to add several rows. Add the first row, and then click Redo (or press Ctrl+Y) to insert additional rows.

You can undo or redo the last action, or you can choose from a list to undo or redo an action that you took several steps back. Click the down arrow next to the Undo or Redo button, and then select an action from the list.

Copying Formatting

Just to the right of the Paste button on the Standard toolbar is the Format Painter button. You use this button to quickly apply formatting that you've specified for a selection. For example, if you've formatted an Excel worksheet with currency specifications, alignment, fonts, and so on, you can select the worksheet, click Format Painter button, open another worksheet, and drag the Format Painter button across an area to format it exactly like the original document.

Finding and Replacing

If you've ever worked on a long document and found upon completion that you had misspelled a person's name or some other term all the way through, you know how valuable the Find And Replace feature is. Not only is it quick, it's accurate. You can simply tell an Office program to find every instance of the word as it is now spelled and change it to the new spelling you supply. And, of course, you can also use the Find And Replace feature to replace a string of words, a sentence, a paragraph, and so on, or you can replace something with nothing, effectively deleting all instances of some offending word or term. In addition, you can replace formatting, special characters or symbols, spaces, tabs, graphics, and so on.

You can use Find And Replace in Excel, FrontPage, Access, PowerPoint, and Word, but the most complete implementation of the feature is that used in Word. Therefore, in this section, we'll show you how to use the Word Find And Replace feature. You can then easily apply these instructions to using Find And Replace in the other Office programs.

To use Find and Replace in Word, follow these steps:

1. **Open the Find And Replace dialog box.**

   Click the Edit menu, and then click Replace. The Find And Replace dialog box opens at the Replace tab, as shown in Figure 1-20. Click the More button to expand this dialog box.

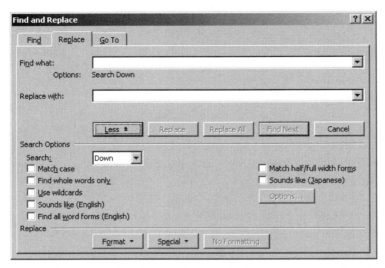

Figure 1-20   The Find And Replace dialog box open at the Replace tab.

TIP   *If you want only to find an item, click the Edit menu and then click Find. The Find And Replace dialog box will open at the Find tab.*

2. Tell Word what you want to find.

In the Find What box, enter the word or words you want to find. If you've done a previous search and want to repeat it, click the down arrow and select from the list that is displayed. Be sure to enter the term exactly as it appears in your document. Word is literal and will look for precisely what you enter, unless you tell it otherwise using the Search Options in the bottom of the dialog box. We'll look at those options shortly.

3. Tell Word what you want to replace the found item with.

In the Replace With box, enter the replacement text.

Now, you can simply click the Replace button to locate the next instance of what you want to find. Word begins searching from the location of the insertion point, so keep that in mind. You can begin a search anywhere, and when Word reaches the end of the document, it will ask if you want to continue by searching from the beginning of the document. To replace the found instance, click the Replace button again. Word makes the replacement and finds the next instance.

To replace all instances of the found text with its replacement, click the Replace All button. When you do so, Word automatically searches the entire document and makes the replacements without your intervention. If you want to verify that the replacement is valid before you make it, you can click the Find Next button and then click the Replace button to do the actual replacing.

As mentioned, Word takes whatever you enter in the Find What box quite literally, but you can override this by selecting some options in the lower part of the Replace tab. After you enter the term to look for, you can modify the search by selecting from the following:

- Match Case. If you click this check box, Word looks for a word that exactly matches what you enter in the Find What box. If you enter caps and lowercase, all lowercase, all capital letters, or any combination, Word finds only that exact match. If you leave the Match Case check box clear, Word finds all instances of the word no matter how it is capitalized.

- Find Whole Words Only. If you click this check box, Word finds only whole words. For example, if you enter *it,* Word finds only that word; Word does not find *its, it's, hit, sit,* and so on.

- Use Wildcards. A wildcard is a symbol that substitutes for a character or characters. For example, a question mark (?) stands for any single character, and an asterisk (*) stands for any string of characters. If you enter *min?,* Word will find *mind, mine, mint,* and the like. If you enter *min*,* Word will find *mind, mine, mint, minute, minuet, miniscule,* and so on. An easy way to employ wildcards is to place the insertion point where you want a wildcard, click the Special button at the bottom of the dialog box, and select from the list that is displayed.

- Sounds Like (English). If you click this check box, Word finds words that sound like the text in the Find What box but that are spelled differently, for example, *four* and *fore.*

- Find All Word Forms (English). If you click this check box, Word replaces all forms of the words in the Find What box with the appropriate forms of the words in the Replace With box. This option in unavailable if you've selected the Use Wildcards or the Sounds Like check box.

In addition, you can search for formatting and replace with formatting. To apply formatting to a Find What entry or a Replace With entry, click the Format button and select a format from the list. To remove formatting from an entry, select it and then click the No Formatting button.

Working with the Formatting Toolbar

You'll find the Formatting toolbar in Word, FrontPage, Excel, and PowerPoint. Some buttons are common to all these applications, and others are specific to the individual Office programs.

As this chapter has mentioned earlier, simply point to a button to display a ScreenTip that describes it. Figure 1-21 shows the Formatting toolbar in Word, which contains all the common buttons. Table 1-1 lists and describes these buttons. To apply formatting, select the text, and then click the appropriate button.

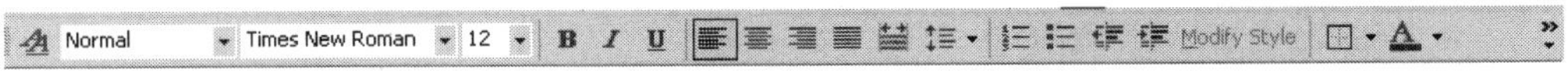

Figure 1-21   The Formatting toolbar in Word.

BUTTON	WHAT IT DOES
Style	Opens a drop-down list from which you can select a style.
Font	Opens a drop-down list from which you can select a font.
Font Size	Opens a drop-down list from which you can select a font size.
Bold	Boldfaces selected text.
Italic	Italicizes selected text.
Underline	Underlines selected text.
Align Left	Aligns selected text with the left margin.
Center	Centers selected text horizontally.
Align Right	Aligns selected text with the right margin.
Numbering	Turns selected text into a numbered list.
Bullets	Turns selected text into a bulleted list.
Decrease Indent	Reduces the left indention of selected text.
Increase Indent	Increase the left indention of selected text.
Font Color	Opens a drop-down list from which you can select a color for selected text.

Table 1-21   Common Formatting buttons.

Summary

This chapter has introduced you to the common Office tools, those tools that appear in all the Office applications and that work in basically the same way wherever you find them. Even if you use one or two Office programs often and use the others rarely, you'll know how to take care of basic tasks, such as getting help, checking spelling, or using Speech Recognition. This chapter has also shown you how to use the Task pane, AutoCorrect, personalized menus and toolbars, and the common editing tools. In addition, we looked at the formatting buttons you'll find in most Office programs.

Chapter 2

DOCUMENT MANAGEMENT

Featuring:

- Understanding How Windows Stores Your Documents
- Creating a New Document
- Saving Your Documents
- Understanding Document Properties
- Protecting Your Documents
- Opening Existing Documents
- Backing Up Your Documents
- Printing Your Documents

Obviously, the most important thing about the business documents you create and use is their content, but to work with them efficiently, you need to know how to use the Office programs to manage them. You also need to know what part Microsoft Windows plays in document management.

Managing your Office documents involves creating them, saving them, and organizing them in such a way that you can easily locate files when you need them. This chapter will look at how to take care of these tasks as well as how to protect your documents and print them.

Understanding How Windows Stores
Your Documents

The single most important tool for managing your Office documents is Windows Explorer. In our work as technical writers, editors, and consultants, we often find that many business users are quite skilled in the techniques of specific Office programs, but lack even a basic familiarity with Windows Explorer. Thus, we want to start the discussion in this chapter with a brief look at this tool.

Every document on your computer is a file, and Windows organizes these files into groups called *folders*. You can see this organizational scheme at work by opening Windows Explorer. From the desktop, right-click My Computer, and choose Explore from the shortcut menu. You'll see something similar to Figure 2-1.

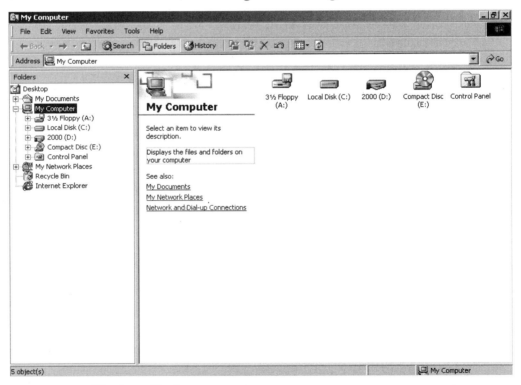

Figure 2-1   Windows Explorer.

In the Folders pane, select a folder to display its contents in the right pane. Click the plus sign (+) next to an item to display a list of what it contains. In the right pane, double-click a folder to display its subfolders or files. If you can't see all the items in the Folder pane, drag the horizontal scroll bar to the right, or drag the vertical scroll bar up or down.

To open any file or folder in Windows Explorer, simply double-click it. It will open in the application in which it was created in most cases.

Folders for Office Documents

When you save a file for the first time in Word, Excel, PowerPoint, and Access (and we'll look at how to do that shortly), Windows suggests that you save it in your My Documents folder, which was created during installation. When you save a file for the first time in FrontPage, Windows suggests that you save it in your My Webs folder, which was also created during installation. The My Documents folder and the My Webs folder are called default working folders.

Now you can create a folder just about anywhere in the folder hierarchy that you want, but we always suggest for starters that you keep your documents in subfolders of one of these folders. And if you are on a corporate network, these folders may be the only places you have permission to store documents, or your system administrator may have created a folder on a specific drive for you.

Creating Folders

You can create a folder from the desktop, from within Windows Explorer, and from within a Windows application.

Creating a Folder on the Desktop

To create a folder on the desktop, follow these steps:

1. **Open a shortcut menu.**

   Right-click an empty area on the desktop, click New, and then click Folder. You'll see a folder icon on the desktop and a box beneath it containing the words *New Folder*.

2. **Name the folder.**

   Click in the box, type a name for the new folder, and then click outside the box.

Your new folder will be stored in the desktop subfolder. You can leave it there or move it, as you'll see later in this section.

Creating a Folder from within Windows Explorer

To create a folder inside another folder in Windows Explorer, follow these steps:

1. **Locate the parent folder.**

Expand a folder or navigate to the folder inside which you want to create a new folder.

2. **Use the commands on the File menu to create the folder.**

Click the File menu, click New, and then click Folder. You'll see a folder icon in the right pane and a box beneath it that contains the words *New Folder,* as shown in Figure 2-2.

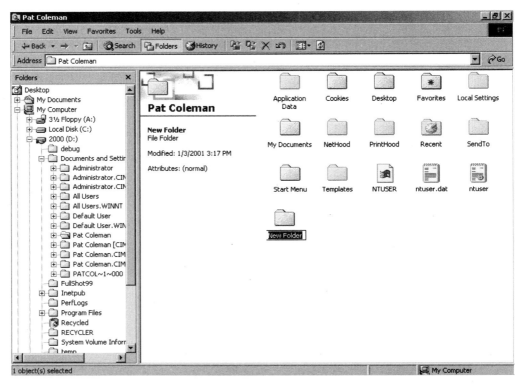

Figure 2-2   Creating a new folder in Windows Explorer.

3. **Give the folder a name.**

Click inside the box, type a name for the folder, and then click outside the box.

Creating a Folder from within an Office Application

We often find this the handiest way to create a folder. Here are the steps for creating a folder in Excel, but a similar procedure works in any Office application:

1. **Open Excel.**

Click the Start button, click Programs, and then click Microsoft Excel.

2. Open the Save As dialog box.

Click the File menu, and then click Save. Figure 2-3 shows the Save As dialog box.

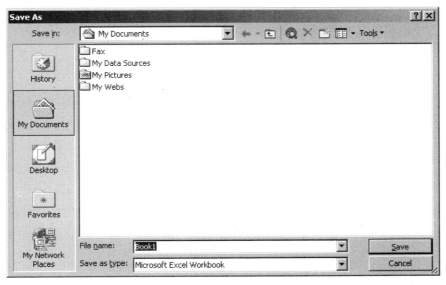

Figure 2-3   The Save As dialog box.

3. Create the folder.

Locate the folder in which you want to create the new folder, and then click the Create New Folder toolbar button. You'll see a new folder icon followed by a box that contains the words *New Folder*.

4. Name the folder.

Click in the box, type a name for your folder, and then click outside the box.

Changing the Default Working Folder

Although we recommend that you start out by saving files in the default working folders, you can select another folder as the default working folder. You might want to do so if you add a hard drive to your system, for example.

To change the default working folder in Excel, follow these steps:

1. Start Excel.

Click the Start button, click Programs, and then click Microsoft Excel.

2. Open the Options dialog box at the General tab, as shown in Figure 2-4.

Click the Tools menu, click Options, and then in the Options dialog box, click the General tab.

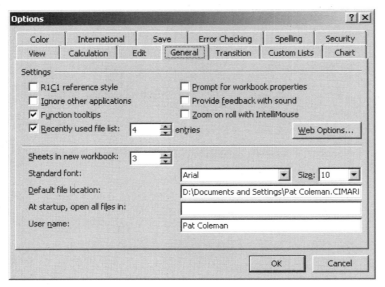

Figure 2-4   The Options dialog box in Excel, open at the General tab.

3. Tell Excel which folder you want to use.

In the Default File Location box, type the path to the folder, and then click OK.

NOTE   *The path consists of the exact route Windows must take when opening a file or a folder. For example, the file for this chapter is stored in the Chapter 2 folder in the MBA's Guide to Office folder, in the My Documents folder, in a user folder, in the Documents and Settings folder, on drive D. Therefore, its path is D:\Documents and Settings\Pat Coleman\My Documents\MBA's Guide to Office\Chapter 2\Chapter 2.doc.*

To change the default working folder in Word, follow these steps:

1. Start Word.

Click the Start button, click Programs, and then click Microsoft Word.

2. Open the Options dialog box at the File Locations tab, as shown in Figure 2-5.

Click the Tools menu, click Options, and then in the Options dialog box, click the File Locations tab.

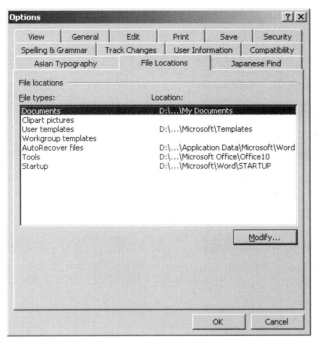

Figure 2-5   The Options dialog box in Word, open at the File Locations tab.

3. Open the Modify Location dialog box, as shown in Figure 2-6.

In the File Locations section, select the Documents file type, and then click the Modify button.

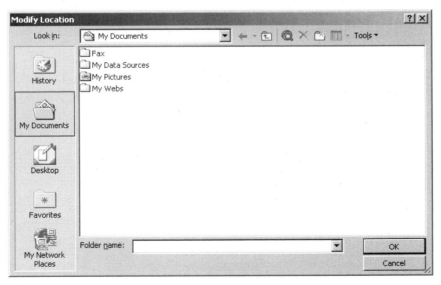

Figure 2-6   The Modify Location dialog box.

4. Tell Word which folder will be the default working folder.

In the Look In drop-down list box, browse to the folder you want to use, or click the Create New Folder toolbar button to open the New Folder dialog box, type a name for the folder, and click OK. When you've selected the new folder, click OK.

To change the default working folder in PowerPoint, follow these steps:

1. Open PowerPoint.

Click the Start button, click Programs, and then click Microsoft PowerPoint.

2. Open the Options dialog box at the Save tab, as shown in Figure 2-7.

Click the Tools menu, click Options, and then in the Options dialog box, click the Save tab.

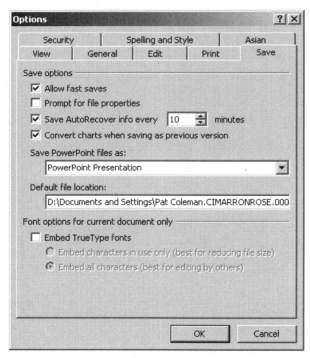

Figure 2-7   The Options dialog box in PowerPoint, open at the Save tab.

3. Tell PowerPoint which folder to use.

In the Default File Location box, type the path to the folder you want to set as the default, and then click OK.

To change the default working folder in Access, follow these steps:

1. **Open Access.**

   Click the Start button, click Programs, and then click Microsoft Access.

2. **Open the Options dialog box at the General tab, as shown in Figure 2-8.**

   Open a new or an existing database, click the Tools menu, and then click Options. In the Options dialog box, click the General tab.

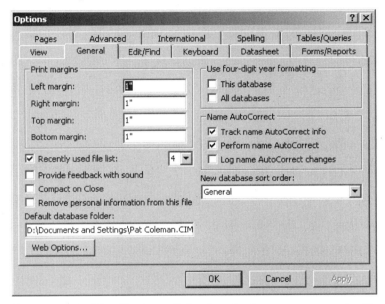

Figure 2-8   The Options dialog box in Access, open at the General tab.

3. **Tell Access which folder to use.**

   In the Default Database Folder box, type the path to the new folder, and then click OK.

NOTE   *You cannot change the default working folder in FrontPage.*

Naming Files and Folders

A filename or a folder name can contain a maximum of 255 characters, but since most programs can't deal with names of that length, it is recommended that you use fewer characters. The maximum practical number of characters for a filename is probably no more than 30 characters. Filenames and folder names can include spaces, commas, semicolons, equal signs, and square brackets and can be a combination of upper- and lowercase letters.

Be sure to give your files and folders names that are descriptive and that will make sense some time in the future when you're trying to locate something in particular.

The letters following the period (called a dot) in a filename constitute the *extension*. When you're naming or renaming a file in an Office program, don't type the extension. The Office program will supply the extension for you, and a specific extension identifies files created in each program. For example, a Word document has the extension .doc, and an Excel worksheet has the extension .xls.

Copying and Moving Files and Folders

As we mentioned earlier, regardless of where you create a file or a folder, you can always move it to another location. In addition, you can copy it to another location. When you move a file, you remove it from its current location and place it in another location. When you copy a file, the original remains in place, and a copy is placed in another location.

As with a number of tasks, you can move and copy a file or a folder in several ways:

- By dragging and dropping with the right mouse button
- By dragging and dropping with the left mouse button
- By copying and pasting or by cutting and pasting
- By using the Send To command

Which method you use depends on the situation and your personal preference.

Using the Right Mouse Button

To copy or move a file or a folder with the right mouse button, follow these steps:

1. **Open Windows Explorer.**

   Right-click My Computer, and click Explore.

2. **Drag the file to its new location.**

   Locate the file or folder, right-click it, and while holding down the mouse button, drag the file or folder to its new location.

3. **Choose whether to copy or move the file or folder.**

   Release the right mouse button, and choose Copy Here or Move Here from the menu.

If you change your mind in the middle of a copy or a move, press the Escape key.

Using the Left Mouse Button

If the source and destination for a copy are on different drives, left-click the file, and then drag it to its new location. If the source and destination are on the same drive, left-clicking and dragging the file or folder moves it. To move a file or a folder to a different drive, click the file or folder with the left mouse button and hold down the Shift key while you drag the item.

Using the Cut, Copy, and Paste Commands

To copy or move a file using the Cut, Copy, and Paste commands, follow these steps:

1. **Open Windows Explorer.**

   Right-click My Computer, and choose Explore from the shortcut menu.

2. **Locate what you want to copy or move.**

   Find the source file or folder.

3. **Open the shortcut menu.**

   Right-click the source file or folder, and choose Cut or Copy from the shortcut menu.

4. **Place the item in its new location.**

   Right-click the destination folder, and choose Paste from the shortcut menu.

Using Send To

A quick way to copy files and folders is to use the Send To command, which you'll find on the shortcut menu. Simply right-click the file or folder, choose Send To, and then select a destination. By default, you can send a file or a folder to a floppy disk, the desktop, a mail recipient, or the My Documents folder.

If you frequently want to copy files to a destination that's not on the Send To menu, you can add that destination. For example, you might want to back up your files on another computer's hard drive on your network. To add a destination to the Send To menu, follow these steps:

1. **Open Windows Explorer.**

   Right-click the Start button, and click Explore.

2. **Find your Send To folder.**

   Locate your user name folder, and then locate your Send To folder within it.

If you don't see your Send To folder, it's probably hidden. To display it, click the Tools menu and click Folder Options to open the Folder Options dialog box. Click the View tab, and in the Advanced Settings list, select the Show Hidden File And Folder option, and then click OK.

3. Find your Send To folder.

Locate your user name folder, and then locate and select your Send To folder within it.

4. Start the Create Shortcut Wizard, as shown in Figure 2-9.

Click the File menu, click New, and then click Shortcut.

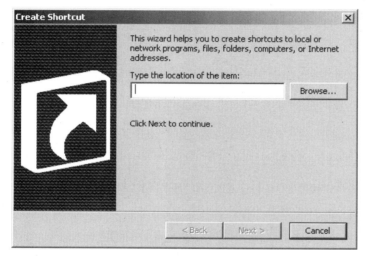

Figure 2-9   The Create Shortcut Wizard.

5. Enter the destination you want to add.

In the Type The Location Of The Item box, enter the filename for your new destination, or click Browse to locate it.

6. Enter a name for the destination.

Click Next, and in the Select A Title For The Program screen, type a name for the destination. Click Finish.

TIP   *You'll also find the Send To command on the File menu of all the Office programs except Outlook.*

Renaming Files and Folders

Renaming files and folders is a cinch. In Windows Explorer, right-click a file or a folder, choose Rename from the shortcut menu, type a new name in the box that appears, and then click outside the box. You can also rename a file or a folder from within an Office application. Open the Save As dialog box (click the File menu, and then click Save As), right-click the file or folder, choose Rename from the shortcut menu, type a new name, and click outside the box.

Deleting Files and Folders

When you delete a file or a folder, by default it goes to the Recycle Bin. It is not permanently deleted from your system until the Recycle Bin is emptied. You can delete a file or folder in several ways:

- In Windows Explorer, right-click the file or folder name, and choose Delete from the shortcut menu.

- In the Save As dialog box in an Office application, right-click the name of a file or a folder, and choose Delete from the shortcut menu.

- In Windows Explorer, left-click the file or folder name, and then press the Delete key or click the Delete button on the toolbar. (The Delete button has an X on it.)

- If the file or folder is visible on the desktop, click it, and then drag it to the Recycle Bin.

TIP *To bypass the Recycle Bin, hold down the Shift key while choosing the Delete command or pressing the Delete key.*

Creating a New Document

How you create a new document depends on the Office program you are using. When you open Word, Excel, FrontPage, and PowerPoint, a new document is automatically created for you. When you open Access, you'll see the New File task pane, from which you can choose the type of document you want to create.

You can also create a new document by clicking the New button on the Standard toolbar and then choosing a document type from the task pane.

Saving Your Documents

An important concept to understand is that whatever you enter in the document window is not automatically saved. You have to manually tell the Office program to save it—on your hard drive, on your network, or on some other medium. You can save the file when you first create it or when you finish working on it or at any time in between. A good practice in terms of organization is to create a file for the document and save it in a folder when you start to create the document.

To save a file for the first time, you can click the File menu and then click Save, or you can simply click the Save button on the toolbar. In either case, you open the Save As dialog box. Figure 2-10 shows the Save As dialog box in PowerPoint, but it is similar in all the Office applications.

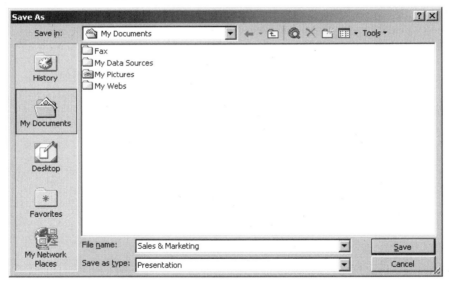

Figure 2-10 The Save As dialog box in PowerPoint.

After you select a folder, enter a name for the document in the File Name box. You also need to specify the type of file that you want to save. To see a list of file types, click the down arrow at the right of the Save As type box. When you've selected a file type, click the Save button to save the file.

After you save a file the first time, clicking the Save button saves your latest changes to the file but does not open the Save As dialog box. If you want to save the file with a different name or to a different folder, you'll need to click the File menu and then click Save As.

Earlier in this chapter we discussed how to manage documents using Windows Explorer. The Save As dialog box is really a Windows Explorer-like tool. You can use it to create folders (as you saw earlier); rename files; delete files; cut, copy, and move files and folders; share files and folders; view the properties of a file or folder; and in other ways take care of tasks relating to documents.

At the left of the Save As dialog box is the Places bar. To quickly save a document in any folder in the list, simply click it. You'll see its name appear in the Save In box.

At the right of the Save In box is a toolbar that has the following buttons, in order from left to right:

- My Documents. (In FrontPage, this button is called My Webs.) If you have navigated to another folder, clicking this button returns to the My Documents or My Webs folder and displays that folder name in the Save In box.

- Up One Level. Clicking this button takes you to the next level up in the folder hierarchy. Clicking the My Documents or My Webs button then takes you one level back down.

- Search The Web. Clicking this button opens the msn.Search page in Internet Explorer, if you are connected to the Internet. From this page, you can search by category or keyword.

- Delete. One way to delete a file or a folder is to select it and then click the Delete button on the toolbar.

- Create New Folder. Click this button to open the New Folder dialog box and create a new folder.

- Views. Click the drop-down arrow next to this button to display a list from which you can choose how to display items in the Save As dialog box. You can select Large Icons, Small Icons, List, and Details views, and you can choose to display the properties for a selected file or folder, a preview of the file or folder, or thumbnails. (This chapter will discuss properties in a later section.)

- Tools. Clicking the Tools button displays a drop-down list of actions you can take from this dialog box, including adding a file to your Favorites list, mapping a network drive, selecting save options, and so on. The options on this list depend on the application.

Understanding Document Properties

The properties of a document are simply its characteristics, such as size, location, date of creation or modification, title, author, and so on, and you view the properties of a document by opening its Properties dialog box. You can do this in several ways:

- In the Save As or Open dialog box, click the Tools button, and then click Properties.

- In Windows Explorer, the Save As dialog box, or the Open dialog box, right-click a file or a folder name, and then choose Properties from the shortcut menu.

- If a document is open, click the File menu, and then click Properties.

The Office program supplies some of the details in a Properties dialog box, and you can supply others. The information contained in a Properties dialog box can come in handy when you're searching for a document as well as be a valuable record about the document for future use. Figure 2-11 shows the Properties dialog box for an Excel worksheet that catalogs the books in our library. As you can see, it has five tabs, which each supply specific types of information. The number of tabs you see in a Properties dialog box depends on the kind of file and the application with which it is associated.

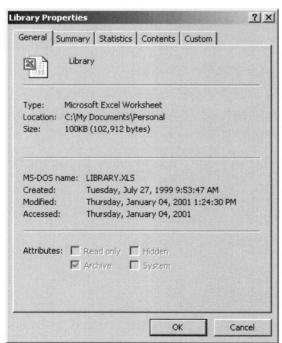

Figure 2-11 The Properties dialog box for an Excel worksheet.

The tabs contain the following types of information:

- The General tab primarily contains information supplied by the Office program—type of file, location, size, name, and dates the file was created, accessed, and modified. It also contains the file's attributes; for example, if you specified that the file was read-only, that is indicated in the Attributes section. (The next section will explain read-only.)

- The Summary tab contains primarily information that you supply, although the Office program can pick up your name from user information you entered during installation. If you enter terms in the Keywords box, you can search on them to locate the document.

- The Statistics tab contains some of the information that's also present on the General tab. All the information on this tab is supplied by the Office program.

- The Contents tab contains information that depends on which Office program is associated with the document. In a Word document, the Contents tab lists the document headings.

- The Custom tab is for use when you route a document.

Protecting Your Documents

If other people have access to your computer or if you work on a network, you may want to password-protect important or sensitive documents to prevent unauthorized users from reading or changing them. If you are using Windows 2000 Professional, as we are in this book, you can password-protect files at the operating system level, but you can also do so through Word, Excel, PowerPoint, and Access. The process is a bit different for each application, so we'll look at each one individually.

To password-protect an Excel worksheet, follow these steps:

1. **Open the Save As dialog box.**

   Click the File menu, and then click Save As.

2. **Open the Save Options dialog box, as shown in Figure 2-12.**

   Click the Tools button, and then click General Options.

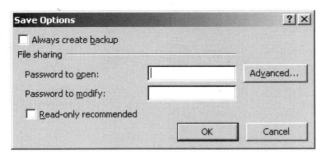

Figure 2-12 The Save Options dialog box.

3. Tell Excel how you want to share the file.

If you want to require a password to open the file, enter the password in the Password To Open box. In Excel, passwords are case sensitive and can contain a maximum of 15 characters, which can be any combination of letters, numbers, and symbols. If you want to require a password before anybody can change the file in any way, enter the password in the Password To Modify box. If you click the Read-Only Recommended check box, a user who opens the worksheet and changes it must save it under a different name. When you've selected your options, click OK.

WARNING *If you password-protect a file, be sure that you remember the password or make a note of it and keep the note in a secure place. If you forget the password, you will not be able to open the file.*

You can also password-protect Excel documents by clicking the Tools menu, clicking Protection, and then selecting one of the options on the submenu.

To password-protect a Word document, follow these steps:

1. Open the Save As dialog box.

Click the File menu, and then click Save As.

2. Open the Security dialog box, as shown in Figure 2-13.

Click the Tools button, and then click Security Options.

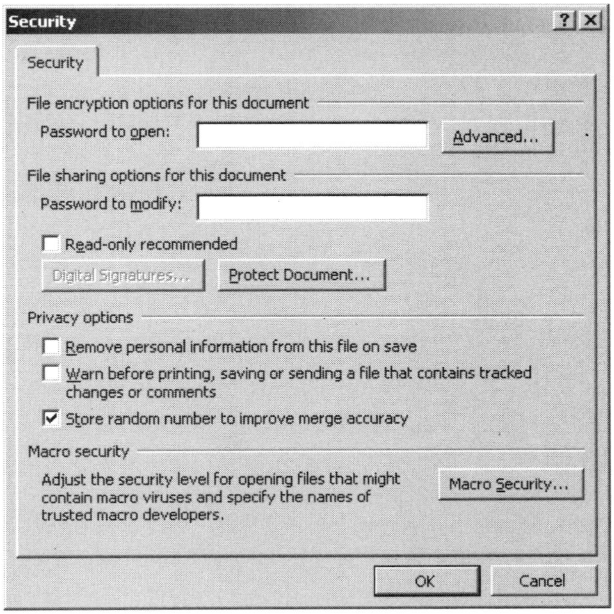

Figure 2-13   The Security dialog box in Word.

3. Tell Word how you want to share this document.

If you want to require a password to open the file, enter a password in the Password To Open box. If you want to require a password before someone can change the document, enter a password in the Password To Modify box. If you click the Read-Only Recommended check box, a user who opens the document and changes it must save it under a different name. If you want to protect the document for tracked changes, comments, or forms, click the Protect Document button to open the Protect Document dialog box, as shown in Figure 2-14.

Figure 2-14   The Protect Document dialog box.

Click the Tracked Changes option button if you want reviewers to be able to make changes but not to be able to turn off the Track Changes feature or accept or reject changes. Click the Comments option button if you want reviewers to be able to insert comments but not change the text of the document. Click the Forms option button if you want to prevent users from changing anything but form fields and unprotected sections. To protect or unprotect a section, click the Sections button. Type a password in the Password box if you want users to supply a password before doing anything you have previously prohibited, such as accepting or rejecting revision marks. When you've selected your options, click OK. Click OK again in the Security dialog box.

To password-protect a document in PowerPoint, follow the basic steps for doing so in Word. The only differences are that you won't have the Read-Only Recommended option or the options in the Protect Document dialog box.

To password-protect a database in Access, click the Tools menu, click Security, and then select from the options on the submenu.

NOTE   *You can't password-protect FrontPage documents.*

Opening Existing Documents

An Office program displays the filenames of the last four documents you save or open at the bottom of the File menu. To open one of these documents, simply click its filename. You can display more or fewer filenames in this list. To change the number of displayed filenames, open the Options dialog box, click the General tab, and select a number in the Recently Used File List spin box.

To open a document whose filename is not displayed, follow these steps:

1. Open the Open dialog box. Figure 2-15 shows the Open dialog box in Excel.

Click the File menu, and then click Open.

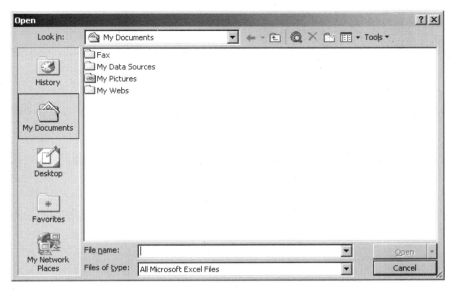

Figure 2-15 The Open dialog box in Excel.

2. Locate the file you want to open.

Click a folder in the Places bar, which is the area on the left side of the dialog box, or click the down arrow in the Look In box to browse for the file. When you locate it, double-click its name, or select it and click the Open button.

You can also choose the mode in which you open an existing document. Click the down arrow next to the Open button. You'll see that you can open a document in the following modes:

- As read-only, which means that you can view and read the document but not change it in any way.

- As a copy, which creates a duplicate of the original document that you can work on.

- In your Web browser, if you have saved the document in Web page format.

Choose the Open And Repair command from this list to tell an Office program to attempt to repair a corrupt document.

Backing Up Your Documents

Backing up means making a copy of your documents for safekeeping. It's said that there are only two kinds of computer users: those who have lost important files because the files weren't backed up and those who are going to lose important files because they aren't backed up. You can lose files because of a computer crash; because a hard drive fails; because of a power outage, spike, or dip; because someone trips over the power cord and disconnects your computer; because a virus invades your computer—for any of a number of reasons.

If you work on a corporate network, your network administrator no doubt has a backup schedule and process that includes the documents you save on a network server. The trick here is to remember to save them to the server rather than on your hard drive so that they do get backed up.

If you're working on a standalone machine, you can back up to various media, including a zip drive, a CD-ROM, a tape drive, even a floppy disk. What you back up to is not nearly as important as that you do create back-up copies of important documents and that you keep the backups in a safe place.

The easiest way to back up is to click the File menu and then click Save As. In the Save As dialog box, click the down arrow in the Save In field, and browse to the disk or medium where you want to create the backup. Click Save.

Printing Your Documents

If you know how to print in any Office program, you know how to print in all the others. To print quickly and easily, simply open a document and click the Print button on the Standard toolbar. When you print in this manner, however, you have no control over exactly what's printed, how many copies, and so on. To specify these sorts of options, you use the Print dialog box. Follow these steps:

1. **Open the Print dialog box.**

   Click the File menu, and then click Print. Figure 2-16 shows the Print dialog box in Word.

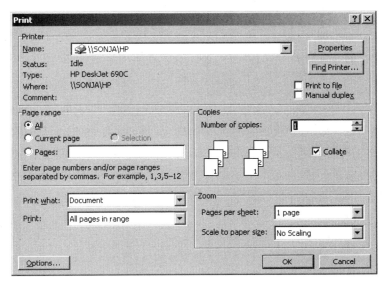

Figure 2-16 The Print dialog box in Word.

2. Select a printer.

If you have access to more than one printer, select the printer from the Name box in the Printer section.

3. Specify which pages to print.

In the Page Range section, click the All option button to print the entire document. Click the Current Page option button to print the page in which the insertion point is located. To print only certain pages, click the Pages option button and then enter the page numbers in the blank box. To print a selection, make the selection before you open the Print dialog box and then click the Selection option button.

4. Specify how many copies to print.

In the Number Of Copies box, click the spin arrow to display a number, or simply type the number in the box. If you are printing multiple copies of a multipage document, click the Collate check box so that each copy prints completely before another one starts to print.

5. Specify what to print.

In the Print What drop-down list box, select what to print. The default selection is the current document.

6. Specify how many pages to print on each sheet.

Use the Zoom section to tell Word how many pages to print on each sheet and whether to scale the pages to fit the type of paper on which you are printing.

7. Print the document.

When you've selected all your options, click OK to print.

NOTE   *To specify whether to print vertically or horizontally on the page, click the Properties button to open the Properties dialog box for your printer, click the Layout tab, and then click either the Portrait or the Landscape option button. Selecting Portrait prints vertically, and selecting Landscape prints horizontally. We'll look at other elements in the Properties dialog box in other chapters in this book. The options available in this dialog box depend on what kind of printer you are using and its features.*

You can check out how your document will appear on the printed page before you print in a couple of ways. One is to take a look at the document in Print Layout view. Another is to view the document in Print Preview. Click the Print Preview button on the toolbar, or click the File menu, and then click Print Preview to see a representation of your document in various percentages of resolution. Figure 2-17 shows the first six pages of a Word document in Print Preview.

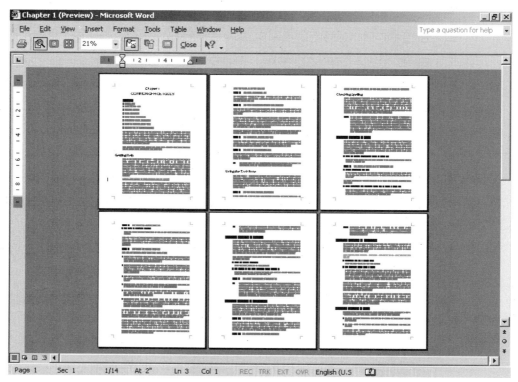

Figure 2-17   A document open in Print Preview.

The following options are available on the Print Preview toolbar in Word, in order from left to right:

- Print prints the document you are viewing in Print Preview.

- Magnifier zooms in or out on the document so that you can see more or less of the actual contents.

- One Page displays only one page of the document.

- Multiple Pages displays a grid from which you can select to display as many as six pages at one time.

- Zoom lets you select the magnification level by a percentage of the whole.

- View Ruler turns on and off the vertical and horizontal rulers.

- Shrink To Fit compresses the document by one page so that you won't have any straggling lines on the last page of a document.

- Full Screen displays Print Preview in Full Screen view.

- Close Preview closes Print Preview and returns you to the view you were using previously.

- Context-Sensitive Help opens Help for the next option you select.

- Toolbar Options opens the Add Or Remove Buttons menu so that you can customize the Print Preview toolbar.

NOTE   *Print Preview options in other Office programs will vary with the application.*

Regardless of which Office program is open when you're printing a document, Windows is really doing the printing. A program called the *print spooler* accepts the document and holds it on disk or in memory until the printer is free, and then the printer prints the document.

Tips for Printing in Specific Office Programs

Although the basic printing process is the same in all Office programs, printing an Excel worksheet is different from printing a Word document, which is different from printing a PowerPoint presentation or a FrontPage or an Access document. Here are some guidelines for setting up pages and printing the various kinds of documents:

- In Excel, use the Page Setup dialog box to precisely control how worksheets are printed (click the File menu, and then click Page Setup). Use the options in the Scaling section on the Page tab to reduce or enlarge the worksheet proportionally and to fit the worksheet onto the number of pages you specify.

- To print handouts in PowerPoint, open the Print dialog box (click the File menu, and then click Print) and select Handouts from the Print What drop-down list box. Indicate whether you are printing in grayscale or pure black and white. Describe the handouts in the Handouts section, and click OK. If you print three slides per page, PowerPoint includes lines that your audience can use to jot down notes about the slides.

- If you are printing a table in Word and the table will run over multiple pages, be sure that the column headings print at the beginning of every page. Select the heading row, click the Table menu, and then click Heading Rows Repeat.

- In Access, you can print selected records. Select the records first, open the Print dialog box (click the File menu, and then click Print), and be sure to click the Selected Record(s) option button.

Summary

This chapter has discussed the various ways you can organize your documents so that you can easily find them when you need them. It also looked at how to password-protect documents that you consider sensitive and important, at how to use Windows Explorer, the essential tool for organizing files and folders, and at how to print. In addition, it covered the basics of backing up your files and how to use the Properties dialog box as a valuable record of information about a document.

Chapter 3

WORD BASICS

Featuring:

- Starting Word
- Getting Help
- Using the Word Menus and Toolbars
- Entering Text
- Editing Text

What are the top three, most-used computer applications in your office? If you're like most business people, number one is your word-processing program. Number two might be a spreadsheet program, such as Excel, but if you think about it for a minute, you probably spend more time using your e-mail program and your Web browser than you do crunching numbers.

The ability to transform written, verbal, and recorded information into a printed format has always been key in the business world. The first true word processor was produced in 1964 by IBM, and it was called the Magnetic Tape/Selectric Typewriter. Using this relatively high-speed automatic typewriter, you could store data to and retrieve it from a magnetic tape. The development of the personal computer in the late 1960s and early 1970s, however, made possible computer word-processing systems.

The first such program was called the Electric Pencil, and it was developed in 1976 by a programmer so that he could write the documentation for programs on the same computer that he was programming. Other early word processors included WordPerfect, WordStar, Scripsit, and, the focus of this chapter, Word.

Word has come a long way since its introduction in 1983, when it ran under DOS and had no mouse support. During the intervening years, Word has become much more than a tool for entering and printing text. You can now use it to create a Web page, publish a brochure, create an organization chart, collaborate on a document online, and much more. This chapter looks at the parts and pieces of the Word application window and introduces the basic techniques for dealing with text.

Starting Word

To open Word, click the Start button, click Programs, and then click Microsoft Word. You'll see the *application window*, which is shown in Figure 3-1.

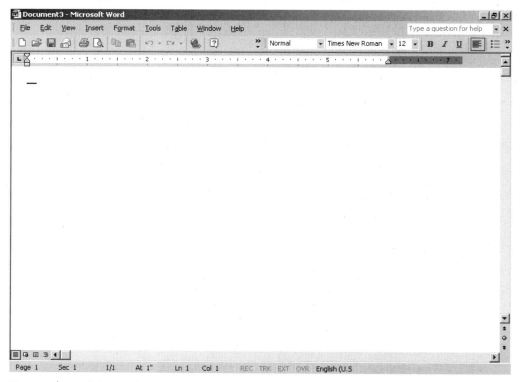

Figure 3-1   The Word application window.

TIP   *If you use Word often, you'll want to create a shortcut to the application on your desktop. To do so, simply right-click the Microsoft Word item on the Programs menu and then drag it to the desktop. From the shortcut menu that appears, select Create Shortcut(s) Here.*

At the very top of this window is the title bar. If we had already created and saved a document, its name would appear here instead of "Document*x*." The menu bar is immediately below the title bar. To see the items on a menu, simply click it. (We'll look at these items in detail in the next section.)

Beneath the menu bar is a toolbar that shows the icons for both the Standard and the Formatting tools. To display a ScreenTip for a tool, simply point to it with your mouse. (We'll look at these tools individually in a later section in this chapter.) Following the toolbar is the ruler, which you can use to set margins and tabs.

In the upper right corner of the application window are the Minimize, Restore, and Close buttons. To see which is which, point to a button with your mouse.

- Click the Minimize button to shrink the application window to an icon that appears in the task bar.

- Click the Restore button to display the application window in a smaller size. When the window is restored, the Restore button is replaced with the Maximize button. Click the Maximize button to display the window at its maximum size.

- Click the Close button to close the application window and Word.

When you create a new document or open an existing document, you work in the *document window,* and you can display a document in several views:

- Normal, which is best used for entering and editing text. Headers and footers, graphics, and certain kinds of formatting are not displayed in Normal view; thus, it is a faster way to move around in the document. To display a document in Normal view, click the View menu and click Normal; or click the Normal View button in the lower left corner of the document window.

- Web Layout, which shows how the document will display in your Web browser. To display a document in Web Layout view, click the View menu and then click Web Layout; or click the Web Layout View button in the lower left corner of the document window.

- Print Layout, which shows how the document will appear on the printed page. To display a document in Print Layout view, click the View menu and then click Print Layout; or click the Print Layout View button in the lower left corner of the document window.

- Document Map, which opens a task pane to the left of the document. If you have applied styles to your document's headings, the headings appear in the task pane, and you can simply click a heading to go to that portion of the document. (Chapter 9 discusses styles.) To display a document in Document Map view, click the View menu and then click Document Map.

- Full Screen, which clears everything from the screen but the document itself, including the menu bar, the toolbar, the scroll bars, the ruler, and so on. To display a document in Full Screen view, click the View menu and then click Full Screen. To return to the previous view, press the Escape key.

- Outline, which displays an outline of your document if it was created using styles. (Chapter 9 discusses styles.) To display a document in Outline view, click the View menu and then click Outline; or click the Outline View button in the lower left corner of the document window.

- Print Preview, which displays your document at various sizes as mocked-up printed pages. To display a document in Print Preview view, click the File menu and then click Print Preview.

To see the effect of selecting views, open an existing document and then display it in the various views. Figure 3-2 shows a document in Normal view, and Figure 3-3 shows that same document in Print Preview view.

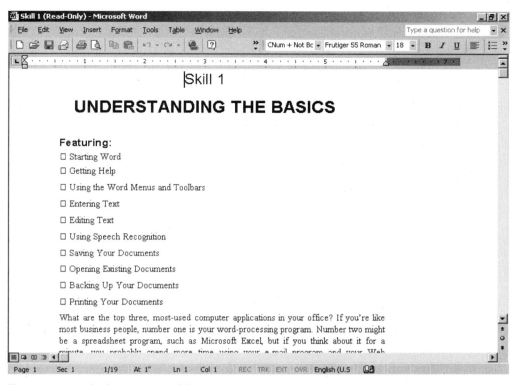

Figure 3-2   A document in Normal view.

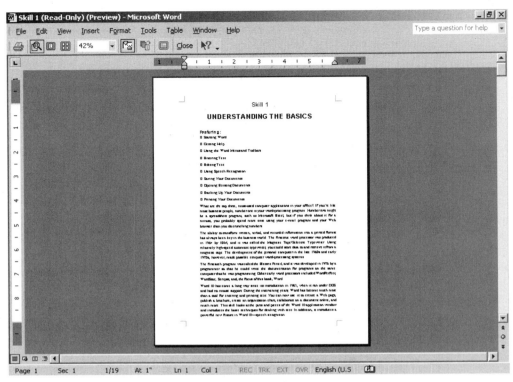

Figure 3-3   The document shown in Figure 3-2 in Print Preview view.

To move forward or backward in a document, you use the vertical scroll bar, located on the right side of the document window. Click the down or up arrow to move forward or backward one line at a time. Click and drag the marker on the vertical scroll bar to move large sections or pages at a time. As you drag the marker, Word displays the current page number in a small box on the screen. To move to the previous page of a document, click the double up-pointing arrow near the bottom of the vertical scroll bar. To move to the next page, click the double down-pointing arrow at the bottom of the vertical scroll bar.

To move right or left in a document, use the horizontal scroll bar at the bottom of the document window. It works in the same fashion as the vertical scroll bar.

The *task pane* appears on the right of the application window, as shown in Figure 3-4. To display the task pane, click the View menu and then click Task Pane.

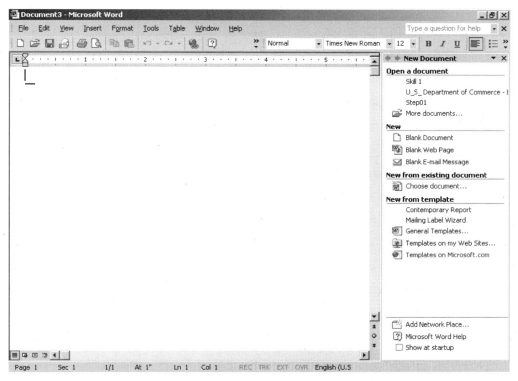

Figure 3-4   The task pane open in the application window.

By default, the task pane is open in New Document view, which you can use to quickly open an existing file, a new blank document, a blank e-mail message, a template, and so on. To close the task pane so that you have more of the window to work with, click its Close button. To open a task pane for other functions, click the Other Task Panes button (the down-pointing arrow) next to the Close button. You'll see that task panes are available for the following:

- The Clipboard
- Search
- Styles And Formatting
- Reveal Formatting
- Mail Merge
- Translate

Before leaving this tour of the basic Word interface, we need to look at one more navigation tool—the Select Browse Object toolbar. To open this toolbar, which is shown in Figure 3-5, click the little button that's between the double arrows on the vertical scroll bar. You can now use the buttons in this toolbar to select an object and move directly to it. Point to a button to display a description of what it does above the first row of buttons. Using this toolbar is a handy way to quickly move from table to table, from heading to heading, from one graphic to the next, and so on.

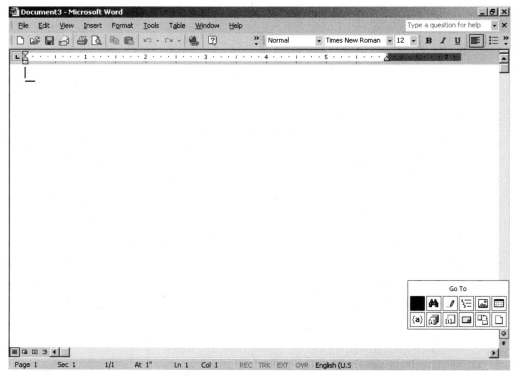

Figure 3-5   The Select Browse Object toolbar.

Getting Help

To get information about a task or a feature of Word, press the F1 key, or click the Help menu, and then click Microsoft Word Help. The first time you access Help, Clippit, the Office Assistant, will come to your aid. Click Clippit to display a box in which you can type a question, and then click Search. The answer will appear in a balloon on the screen.

You may or may not find the Office Assistant helpful. To be honest, just about the first thing we do after we install a new version of Word is to get rid of this creature. If you also find him more annoying than helpful, follow these steps to hide Clippit permanently (or until, for whatever reason, you want to use him again):

1. Open the Office Assistant dialog box, as shown in Figure 3-6.

Click Clippit, and then click the Options button.

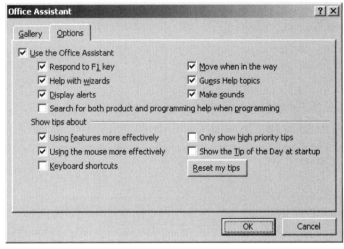

Figure 3-6 The Office Assistant dialog box.

2. Disable the Office Assistant.

Click the Options tab, if necessary, and click the Use The Office Assistant check box to clear it. Click OK.

Now when you click the Help menu and choose Microsoft Word Help, you'll open the window shown in Figure 3-7.

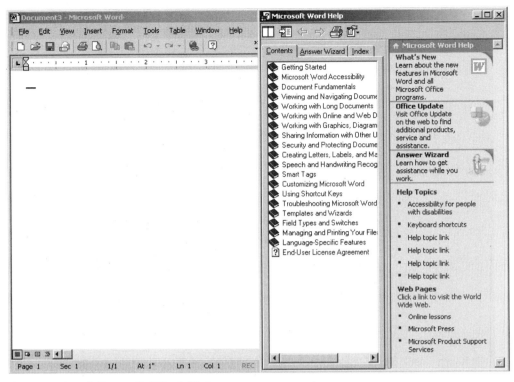

Figure 3-7   Microsoft Word Help.

You can search for information in three ways:

- Click the Contents tab, and then click the closed book next to a topic to open a list of subtopics. Click a subtopic to open it in a pane on the right.

- Click the Answer Wizard tab, type a question in the What Would You Like To Do? field, and then click Search. Click a topic from the list to display information about it in a pane on the right.

- Click the Index tab, enter a word in the Type Keywords field or select a topic from the Or Choose Keywords drop-down list, and then click Search. Click a topic from the Choose A Topic list to display information about it in a pane on the right.

NOTE   *If you find the Office Assistant helpful but just aren't overly fond of the Clippit character, you can select another character. In the Office Assistant dialog box, click the Gallery tab, and then click Next to browse through the choices. When you find a character you like, click OK.*

You can also get context-sensitive help from within any dialog box that displays a button with a question mark on it next to the Close button. Click the Help button, and then click the item for which you want information.

Using the Word Menus and Toolbars

A personalized menu initially displays only those items (commands) you have most recently used. After a short delay, all the items that any menu contains are displayed. You can also simply point to the More Buttons button (the chevron) at the bottom of any menu to display all items for a menu.

In Word, personalized menus are not enabled by default. In other words, when you click any menu, all the commands available on that menu are displayed. If you prefer to use personalized menus, follow these steps:

1. Open the Customize dialog box, as shown in Figure 3-8.

Click the Tools menu, and then click Customize.

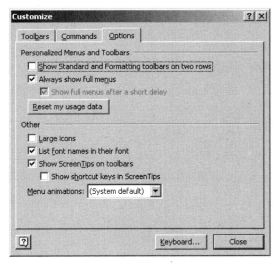

Figure 3-8 The Customize dialog box.

2. Tell Word to use personalized menus.

Click the Options tab, if necessary, click the Always Show Full Menus check box to clear it, and then click the Close button.

If you used Word 2000, you know that the toolbar just below the menu bar is really a combination of two toolbars—the Standard toolbar and the Formatting toolbar. In general, toolbar buttons are shortcuts to the functions of many menus and their commands. For example, if you wanted to italicize a word in a sentence, you could select the word, click the Format button, click Font to open the Font dialog box, select Italic from the Font Style list, and then click OK. Or you could simply select the text and click the Italic button on the toolbar.

You use the buttons on the Standard part of the default toolbar (the one you see when you first install Word) to take care of such tasks as saving a file, opening a new document, printing, undoing a previous action, and the like. The first (or left) half of the toolbar comprises the Standard section of the toolbar. You use the buttons on the Formatting toolbar, which comprises the second (or right) half of the toolbar, to take care of such tasks as aligning a paragraph, selecting a font, inserting a bulleted list, and the like. Because the toolbars are combined, not all buttons are visible. As it does with menu items, Word displays the buttons you've most recently used.

To see a list of the other buttons available for either toolbar, click the Toolbar Options button (the button with the chevron and the down arrow). You'll see something similar to Figure 3-9. To add a button, point to Add Or Remove Buttons, point to either Standard or Formatting, and then select a button from the list that appears on the right. Follow the same process to remove a button that is currently on the toolbar.

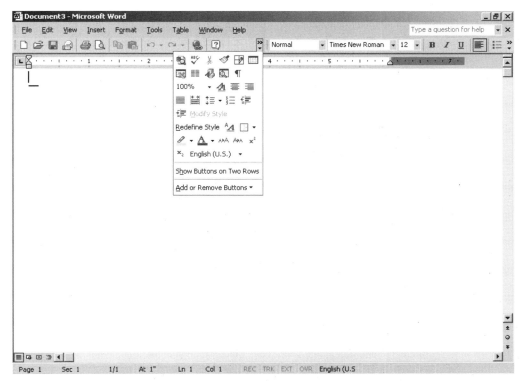

Figure 3-9 Additional toolbar buttons.

If you prefer two toolbars instead of the combined toolbar, click the Toolbar Options button and then click Show Buttons On Two Rows. To return to a single, combined toolbar, click the Toolbar Options button on the Standard toolbar and then click Show Buttons On One Row. Figure 3-10 shows the Word application window with the toolbar buttons on two rows.

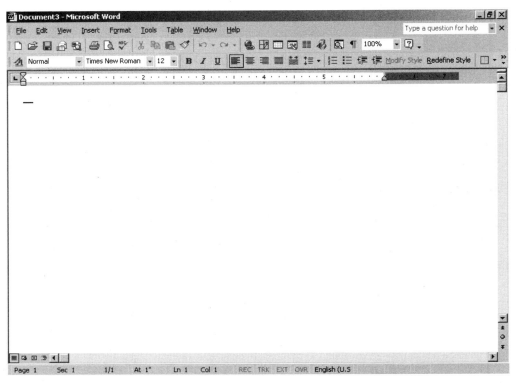

Figure 3-10 The Word application window displaying both the Standard and the Formatting toolbars.

You can right-click almost anywhere to display a shortcut menu containing commands that are relevant to the task at hand. For example, if you select some text and right-click, you'll see the shortcut menu shown in Figure 3-11. Experiment with right-clicking in Word. Even if you don't display a useful list of commands, you can never hurt anything.

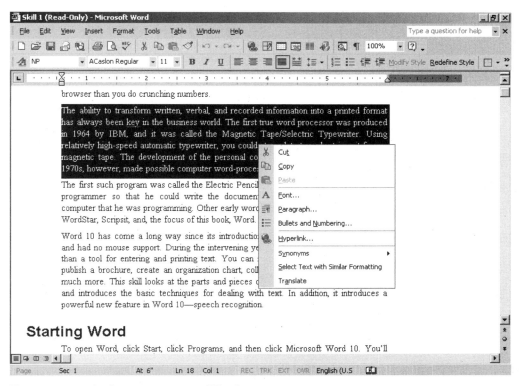

browser than you do crunching numbers.

The ability to transform written, verbal, and recorded information into a printed format has always been key in the business world. The first true word processor was produced in 1964 by IBM, and it was called the Magnetic Tape/Selectric Typewriter. Using relatively high-speed automatic typewriter, you could magnetic tape. The development of the personal co 1970s, however, made possible computer word-proce

The first such program was called the Electric Penci programmer so that he could write the documen computer that he was programming. Other early word WordStar, Scripsit, and, the focus of this book, Word.

Word 10 has come a long way since its introduction and had no mouse support. During the intervening ye than a tool for entering and printing text. You can publish a brochure, create an organization chart, coll much more. This skill looks at the parts and pieces and introduces the basic techniques for dealing with text. In addition, it introduces a powerful new feature in Word 10—speech recognition.

Starting Word

To open Word, click Start, click Programs, and then click Microsoft Word 10. You'll

Figure 3-11 A shortcut menu in Word.

Using Shortcut Keys

Do you typically use primarily the mouse, primarily the keyboard, or a combination? Most of us develop a style over time, and, in general, we find ourselves using a combination. Regardless of which style you prefer, you'll want to become familiar with at least some keyboard shortcuts. Often, even though you use your mouse primarily, you'll find that the fastest way to do something is to use a keyboard shortcut.

When you click a menu name, you'll see that many commands have associated keyboard shortcuts. For example, the New command on the File menu is associated with the keyboard shortcut Ctrl+N. That is you can simply hold down the Ctrl key and press the N key to open the New Document task pane, where you can select to create some type of new document.

To see a list of all the shortcut keys assigned in Word, follow these steps:

1. **Open the Macros dialog box.**

   Click the Tools menu, click Macro, and then click Macros.

2. **Open the List Commands dialog box.**

   In the Macros dialog box, type *ListCommands* in the Macro Name box, and then click Run. In the List Commands dialog box, select Current Menu And Keyboard Settings, and then click OK.

Entering Text

To enter text in Word, you can just simply open Word and start typing where you see the blinking insertion point. To be a bit more organized about it, however, follow these steps:

1. **Create a new document.**

   In the New Document task pane, click Blank Document in the New section. If the New Document task pane is not open, click the File menu and then click New. A new document window will open, and the task pane will close.

2. Enter some text.

Now, click the blinking insertion point, and start typing. You can type anything you want, of course, but the paragraph below is text that you can practice with. If you enter it, you can follow along with the instructions for editing text. The following is adapted from a recent report distributed by the U.S. Department of Labor:

```
The Bureau of Labor Statistics projects that between 1998 and 2008
the number of professional jobs will increase the fastest and will
add the most employment. Estimates indicate growth of about 5.3
million by 2008. Two-thirds of this job growth is expected among
educators and specialists in computer technology and health care.
```

As you type, notice that you don't have to press the Enter key or do anything else to indicate the ending of one line and the beginning of another. Word simply wraps the text to the next line when it encounters the right margin. You also don't need to place any extra space between the end of one sentence and the beginning of the next. We open documents all the time that have been created by professionals who've been using word processors for years, and we see two spaces between the punctuation that ends one sentence and the capital letter that starts the next one. Don't press the spacebar twice when you complete a sentence. Word accounts for this space automatically, and if you enter an extra space, your document will be formatted incorrectly and will not look professional either on the screen or when it's printed.

If you make mistakes while you're typing, you can easily correct them by pressing the Backspace key or the Delete key. Backspace erases characters to the left of the insertion point, including spaces, and Delete erases characters to the right, including spaces.

When you finish entering this paragraph, your screen should look similar to that in Figure 3-12. Now if you want to begin a new paragraph, press the Enter key.

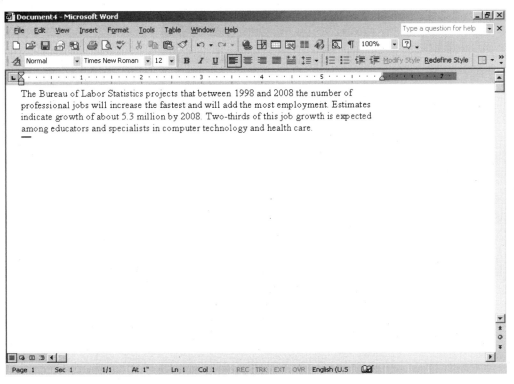

The Bureau of Labor Statistics projects that between 1998 and 2008 the number of professional jobs will increase the fastest and will add the most employment. Estimates indicate growth of about 5.3 million by 2008. Two-thirds of this job growth is expected among educators and specialists in computer technology and health care.

Figure 3-12 Entering some text in the Word document window.

Using Click-and-Type

As you have seen, you enter text at the insertion point, and when you create a new document the insertion point is blinking at the upper left corner of the document window. You can, however, use the Click-and-Type feature to move the insertion point to another location in your document. For example, you might want to create a title page for a report and center the title vertically and horizontally on the page. To do so, you use Click-and-Type, and you must be using either Web Layout or Print Layout view.

Simply double-click in the center of a blank page. The insertion point will then display over a formatting pointer, which in this case will look like the Center button on the toolbar. Type your text, and it is centered on the page. If you then want to left-align or right-align another paragraph, double-click at the right or left margin.

Editing Text

Did you make any mistakes as you were typing? Did Word automatically correct them? All of them? Rather than correcting some mistakes, did Word instead place a wavy red line under them? By default, Word uses the AutoCorrect feature to fix many typing mistakes. To see a list of the changes Word automatically makes, click the Tools menu and then click AutoCorrect Options to open the AutoCorrect dialog box, which is shown in Figure 3-13.

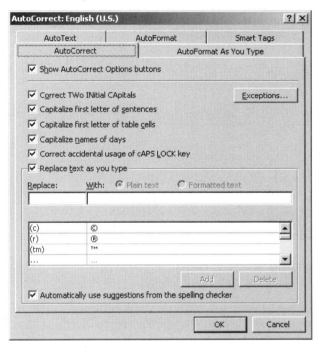

Figure 3-13 The AutoCorrect dialog box.

Do you see a wavy green line beneath any words or phrases? If so, the grammar checker is at work. Right-click the suspect word or phrase to display a shortcut menu that lists possible corrections. If you want more information about the grammar rule that's being invoked, click the Grammar button to open the Grammar dialog box and then click the Explain button. The explanation will appear in a balloon over the Office Assistant, as shown in Figure 3-14. In this case, *Estimates indicates* was typed instead of *Estimates indicate,* and so we have a disagreement between subject and verb. To close the Grammar dialog box and the explanation, click the Cancel button in the Grammar dialog box.

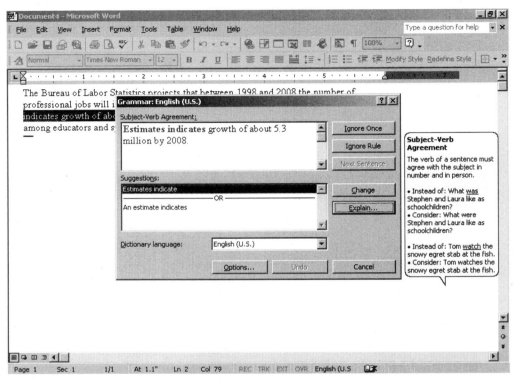

Figure 3-14 An explanation of a grammatical correction.

By default, Word checks spelling and grammar as you type, but you can disable this feature and check spelling and grammar manually whenever you want. We usually do disable this automatic checking feature and then do a thorough check when we've finished composing a document and right before we're going to distribute the document or submit it for publication. To disable the grammar and spelling check while you're typing, follow these steps:

1. Open the Options dialog box, as shown in Figure 3-15.

Click the Tools menu, and then click Options. In the Options dialog box, click the Spelling & Grammar tab.

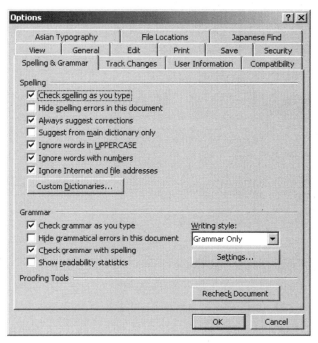

Figure 3-15 The Spelling & Grammar tab in the Options dialog box.

2. Disable checking as you type.

In the Spelling & Grammar tab, click the Check Spelling As You Type check box to clear it, and then click the Check Grammar As You Type check box to also clear it. Click OK.

To check spelling and grammar manually or to check only spelling manually, follow these steps:

1. Open the Spelling And Grammar dialog box, as shown in Figure 3-16.

Click the Tools menu, and then click Spelling And Grammar. Word now starts to check spelling and grammar. When it highlights a perceived mistake, you can choose an option from buttons on the right side of the dialog box.

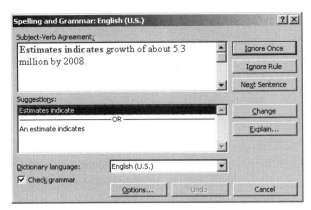

Figure 3-16 The Spelling And Grammar dialog box.

2. Tell Word to check only spelling.

Click the Check Grammar check box to clear it, and then continue to check only spelling.

WARNING *Never distribute or release a document for publication without spell-checking it, but don't totally trust this spell check if you want an error-free document. For example, Word's spelling checker won't alert you if you have typed the correctly spelled word* four *instead of* for. *Read over every document carefully before you circulate it for others to read, and if your spelling/punctuation/grammatical skills leave something to be desired, ask a colleague or coworker who's known to have these skills to check the document for you.*

Selecting Text

Editing a document in Word can involve some copy-editing or some content editing, but we are not necessarily talking about copy-editing or content editing in this context. Editing text in Word involves the mechanics of selecting text; correcting spelling; deleting words, phrases, or sentences; moving a sentence, a paragraph, or a group of paragraphs to another location in a document or even to another document; and other similar tasks.

Before you can edit, though, you need to know how to select. Before you can delete text, move it, copy it, or do anything else with it, you must select it. Basically, you can drag the mouse to select, but as you will learn, if you haven't tried this already, dragging the mouse to select is not the most precise method. Here are some techniques that you can use to select quickly and exactly:

- To select a single word, double-click anywhere in the word.

- To select an entire sentence, hold down the Ctrl key and click anywhere in the sentence.

- To select an entire paragraph, simply triple-click anywhere in the paragraph.

- To select a single line, point in the left margin. When the pointer becomes a right-pointing arrow instead of a left-pointing arrow, point to the line and click.

- To select the entire document, click the Edit menu and then click Select All.

- To select multiple consecutive lines, point in the left margin. When the pointer becomes a right-pointing arrow, point to the first line, hold down the mouse button, and drag to the last line.

- To select multiple words, sentences, or lines, click the first element, hold down the Shift key, and click the last element.

If you make a selection and change your mind, click anywhere in the document outside the selected area to deselect it.

Copying and Moving Text

When you're editing text, you'll obviously correct typos, fix punctuation errors, and correct any grammatical mistakes, but after that the most common changes you'll make will probably involve copying or moving text. To copy or move text from one location to another, you use the Cut, Copy, and Paste features:

- When you cut text (or a graphic or any other object, for that matter), the material is placed on the Office Clipboard and removed from its current location.

- When you copy something, it remains in its original location and is also placed on the Office Clipboard.

- When you paste something, it is placed in a new location but also remains on the Office Clipboard, whether it was originally cut or copied.

This may sound confusing, but it's really a rather straightforward process that you can see by opening the Clipboard task pane. If the task pane is already open, you can display the Clipboard by clicking the Other Task Panes button (the down arrow next to the Close button) and choosing Clipboard. If the task pane is not already open, click the Edit menu and then click Office Clipboard.

You can cut, copy, and paste in several ways. Let's start by looking at how to do so with the mouse. If you entered the sample paragraph used earlier in this chapter, you can practice by following along. To copy or move the first line to the end of the paragraph using drag-and-drop, select the line, right-click the selection, and drag the mouse to the end of the paragraph. When you release the mouse button, you'll see the shortcut menu shown in Figure 3-17. Click either Move Here or Copy Here, and the line is inserted in the document. It is not, however, placed on the Office Clipboard. Word also places a Paste Options button next to the insertion, as you can see in Figure 3-18.

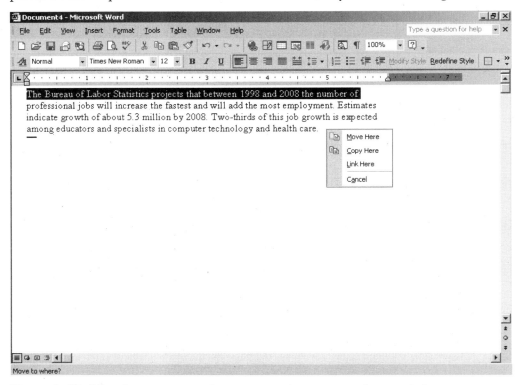

Figure 3-17 The shortcut menu that appears when you use drag-and-drop to move or copy.

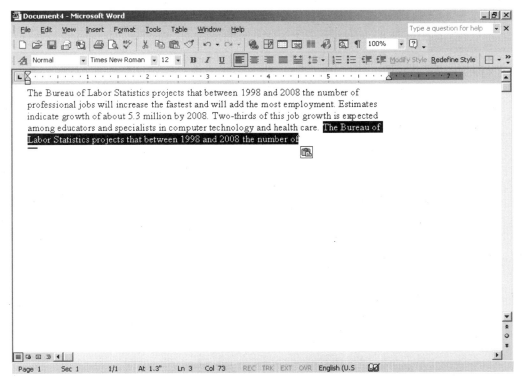

Figure 3-18 The Paste Options button appears when you move or copy an item.

TIP   *You can also left-click and drag an item to a new location. In this case, the item is moved, and the shortcut menu is not displayed. To use this method to copy an item, hold down the Ctrl key while dragging and dropping.*

Using drag-and-drop to move or copy is fairly easy if the source and the destination are both visible and if the distance between the source and the destination is reasonably small. An easier way to copy or move an item long distances is to select it, right-click it, and then choose Cut or Copy from the shortcut menu. Right-click where you want the item placed, and then choose Paste from the shortcut menu. When you use this method, the item is also placed on the Office Clipboard.

The Office Clipboard can hold a maximum of 24 objects (text, graphics, and so on), and it retains all objects until you close all Office programs that are running on your computer. If you attempt to place a 25th object on the Office Clipboard, you'll receive a message asking if you want to remove the first item or not copy the current item.

As long as an item remains on the Office Clipboard, you can paste it repeatedly into other locations. Simply place the insertion point where you want to paste the item, point to it on the Office Clipboard, click the down arrow that appears, and click Paste. You can paste all items on the Office Clipboard at once by placing the insertion point where you want them in a document and clicking the Paste All button on the Clipboard task pane.

When you copy or move an item, any formatting associated with it travels along. If you click the Paste Options button, you'll see that the Keep Source Formatting option is selected by default. If you want the copied or moved material to take on the formatting of the new location, click Match Destination Formatting. Click Keep Text Only if you want to get rid of any formatting. To apply a new style or format, click the Apply Style Or Formatting option to open the Styles And Formatting task pane, from which you can select a style to apply. (Chapter 9 discusses styles.)

If you don't really need the Paste Options button, follow these steps to prevent its display:

1. **Open the Options dialog box, as shown in Figure 3-19.**

    Click the Tools menu, and then click Options.

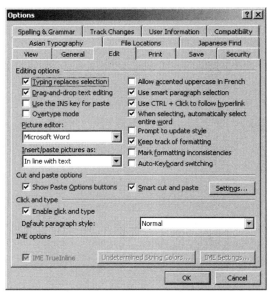

Figure 3-19   The Options dialog box.

2. Tell Word not to display the Paste Options button.

Click the Edit tab, and then in the Cut And Paste Options section, click the Show Paste Options Buttons check box to clear it.

Before leaving this discussion of how to edit by using Cut, Copy, and Paste, we need to mention two more methods. The first is rather laborious: make a selection, click the Edit menu, and click either Cut or Copy. Now move the insertion point to the new location, click the Edit menu, and then click Paste. When you opened the Edit menu, did you notice the shortcut keys associated with the commands? We tend to use the mouse a lot when we're writing and editing, but we almost always use these shortcut keys to cut, copy, and paste. To cut and paste, we select with the mouse, press Ctrl+X, click the mouse to move the insertion point to the new location, and press Ctrl+V.

As you can see, you can copy and move text or any other object in a document in many ways. It doesn't really matter which you use as long as it gets the job done, and if you use Word often in your business, you'll soon establish a preference.

Copy-Editing and Content Editing

Earlier in this skill, we mentioned that the mechanics of editing a Word document were not necessarily the same as copy-editing or content editing (also referred to as developmental editing), although you certainly use all the editing mechanics discussed here to do either in Word. Word includes some rather sophisticated editing features that let you identify the changes that multiple people can make when reviewing a document.

In the publishing world, copy-editing and content editing are important steps in the process. And, even if you don't compose or develop documents that will be "published" in a magazine, in a newspaper, in a book, on a Web page, or in some other medium, your documents will be distributed to others (unless you're keeping a personal journal) and in that sense are "published." Especially in a business situation, you want any communications you create to inspire confidence and to present you and your work in a professional light. That's where copy-editing and content editing come in.

When we submit a manuscript to a publisher, it often goes first to a content editor. This person reviews it asking some or all of the following questions:

- Is the reading level appropriate for the intended audience?

- Is the organization of material on target? Does information flow in a logical manner?

- Are all the important, pertinent areas about the topic discussed?

- Are paragraphs and sections well constructed?

- Given the size and scope of the project, is it likely that the author can do what he or she set out to do and meet the schedule?

- Is the information factually and/or technically correct?

- Do any topics deserve further discussion or do they need to be fleshed out with more detail?

- Is the writing clear and concise? Does the author seem to know his or her subject but seem unable to construct strong, dynamic sentences and paragraphs?

A good content editor will query the author in all these areas and will request that the author make another pass if the manuscript is deficient. A good content editor will also point out the places where the author excels, perhaps including a note that says something to the effect, "Good point; well put," "Excellent description," or "Great idea—I'm glad you included this." You get the idea.

Although the copy editor is also responsible for pointing out any content issues that the author needs to deal with, his or her primary job is to take a more granular approach. The copy editor's tasks are numerous. Here are some of the more important:

- Ensure that the manuscript adheres to a house style, if there is one, or to the guidelines of some other authoritative source such as *The Chicago Manual of Style*. In this sense, style refers to capitalization (for example, is it web page or Web page?), punctuation (do you use the serial comma or not?), spelling (is it encyclopedia or encyclopaedia?), special treatment of terms (do you italicize book titles or put them in quotation marks?), and so on.

- Correct any grammatical mistakes, and if there is room for misinterpretation, query the author.

- Correct typos.

- Correct punctuation.

- Impose the rules of good writing. For example, change almost any sentence that begins with "There is" to a sentence that begins with a precise noun and a strong verb. Recast sentences in the passive voice to active voice. Point out any repetition of words, phrases, ideas, and so on.

- Call the author's attention to anything that just plain doesn't make sense.

We're including this information to make a point, which is that "editing" involves a lot more than running a spell checker and using the Cut, Copy, and Paste features. When you're composing a memo, you certainly won't put it through the process that we describe here. But when you're creating an annual report, a document that will be published on your company's Web site, or any other publication that will be widely distributed, you need to take the time or obtain the resources to ensure the editorial integrity of the document. You do that by following the steps outlined here.

Summary

In this chapter, we've looked at the basic skills and information you need to work with Word. Some of these skills apply to any Office application, but, of course, entering and editing text are skills that are especially important in a word-processing application. You no doubt noticed that in Word you can take care of a single task in many ways. As you work with Word, you'll decide which you prefer to use.

Chapter 4

EXCEL BASICS

Featuring:

- Anatomy of a Workbook
- Moving Around a Workbook
- Entering Data
- Formatting Data and Worksheets
- Inserting and Deleting Cells, Rows, Columns, and Worksheets
- Copying, Cutting, and Pasting

Before computerized spreadsheet programs, financial and accounting spreadsheets were created by hand with a lot of care, time, and tedium. Workbooks were (usually) massive covers with multiple sheets for multiple usages. Today, it is all so much easier. Excel is a powerful business tool for any job that requires the compilation, processing, and analysis of data.

Anatomy of a Workbook

When you start Excel, it automatically opens an empty *workbook* file called Book1. In reality, an Excel workbook is not too different from the old massive binder and multiple sheets. It is far easier to handle and does all the math for you, but it looks somewhat the same.

Worksheets

A *worksheet* is very much like a page from an old-fashioned binder. It is made up of columns and rows but holds far more data than a columnar page ever did. By default, new Excel workbooks open with three worksheets, indicated by the sheet tabs at the bottom of the screen. However, spreadsheets may be added to a maximum of 256 and may be deleted until there is only one. The Excel spreadsheet appears in the area between the formula bar and the status bar.

Columns

In a spreadsheet, *columns,* which run vertically through the length of the sheet, are indicated by letters of the alphabet. Each spreadsheet in a workbook contains 256 columns.

Rows

Numbers identify *rows,* which run horizontally through the width of the spreadsheet. There are 65,536 rows in each spreadsheet.

Cells

The intersection of a column and row is called a *cell.* Each cell has an address, called a *reference,* consisting of the column letter and row number. For example, the cell in the top left corner of the worksheet is cell A1.

A dark outline called the *cell selector* identifies the active cell. Figure 4-1 shows the cell selector in cell C8. If you type a number and press the Enter key, Excel places the number in the active cell.

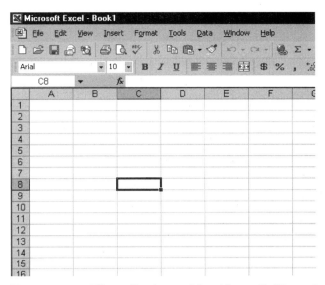

Figure 4-1   The cell selector identifies cell C8 as the active cell.

Name Box

The reference of the active cell appears in the *Name box,* which is on the left side of the line immediately above the column indicators.

Formula Bar

On the same line as the Name box is the *formula bar*. The formula bar displays the data you enter in your worksheet

Moving Around a Workbook

With three (or more) sheets, 256 columns, and 65,536 rows, an Excel workbook is so large that only a small area is visible onscreen at one time. Not surprisingly, Excel provides several ways for you to view different portions of the workbook displayed in the program window:

- With the mouse, you can use the vertical and horizontal scroll bars along the right and bottom edges of the document window to move through your worksheet. Just click inside the scroll bars to move one screen at a time. Click the scroll bar arrows to move one row or column.

- With the mouse, click a sheet tab to move to that worksheet in the workbook.

- The standard navigation keys, Page Up and Page Down, move through your worksheet one screen at a time. When you hold down the Ctrl key and press Page Up or Page Down, you move to the previous or next worksheet.

- The arrow keys move up and down, right and left one cell at a time. You can also move to the right one cell by pressing the Tab key and to the left one cell by holding down the Shift key while pressing Tab.

TIP   *To move directly to a specific cell, you can enter that cell's reference in the Name box and press the Enter key. You can also click the Edit menu and click Go To. When you choose this command, Excel displays the Go To dialog box. You can enter a cell reference in its Reference text box and then click OK to move to the cell.*

Entering Data

Excel worksheets can contain four kinds of data: labels, values, formulas, and functions.

NOTE   *Although functions are really a type of formula, they have a specific format and usage. Therefore, we are discussing them independently.*

Entering Labels

Labels are simply any information entered in a worksheet that you don't want to manipulate arithmetically. They often identify the values that are subject to calculation, so you normally enter them as the first stage in setting up a worksheet. Usually, labels are pieces of text, such as the expense categories in a budgeting worksheet or the employee names in a payroll worksheet. However, they can also be numbers that won't be used arithmetically, such as telephone numbers or part or project ID numbers.

To enter a label, follow these steps:

1. **Move the cell selector to the desired location.**

   You can do this by clicking the cell, using the navigation keys to move the cell selector, or using the Name box.

2. **Type the label.**

   As you do, Excel displays what you type in the formula bar. It also adds the Enter button (the one that looks like a check mark) and the Cancel button (the one that looks like an X) to the formula bar.

3. **Set the label in the cell.**

   You can do this by pressing the Enter key, clicking the Enter button on the formula bar, or moving to another cell.

Figure 4-2 shows a simple workbook fragment with just a handful of labels. Notice that Excel aligns text to the left edge of each cell and allows long labels to spill over into adjacent cells if they are unoccupied.

	A	B	C	D	E	F	G
1	Budget 2002						
2			January	February	March	Totals	Averages
3	Mortgage						
4	Power						
5	Telephone						
6	Transportation						
7	Insurance						
8	Recreation						
9							
10							

Figure 4-2   A worksheet with labels entered.

Entering Values

Values are numbers you want to add, subtract, multiply, divide, or otherwise manipulate in formulas. In a budgeting worksheet, for example, you would enter the budgeted amounts as values. Figure 4-3 shows the values, or amounts, entered beside each of the worksheet labels.

	A	B	C	D	E	F	G
1	Budget 2002						
2			January	February	March	Totals	Averages
3	Mortgage		1000	1000	1000		
4	Power		235	235	175		
5	Telephone		75	75	75		
6	Transportation		375	375	375		
7	Insurance		895				
8	Recreation		2500	200	1500		

Figure 4-3   A budgeting worksheet with labels and values.

To enter values, use the 10 number keys either on the main keyboard or on the numeric keypad. To use the numeric keypad, the Num Lock key must be selected. Use the period key to show decimal places and the hyphen key to identify negative values.

To enter values, use the same three-step process as you do to enter labels. For example, to enter the value *1000* shown in cell C3, follow these steps:

1. **Move the cell selector to the desired cell.**

   In Figure 4-3, for example, you move the cell selector to C3 to enter the first value. You do this by clicking in cell C3.

2. **Type the value.**

   As you do, Excel displays the number in the formula bar. It also adds the Enter and Cancel buttons to the formula bar.

3. **Set the value in the cell.**

   As with setting a label, you can do this by pressing the Enter key, clicking the Enter button on the formula bar, or moving to another cell.

To enter the rest of the values shown in Figure 4-3, repeat the steps above for each value.

Entering Formulas

Excel's power stems from its ability to perform calculations on the values you have stored in a workbook—something you do with *formulas* and *functions*. Excel calculates formulas automatically. You enter them in a worksheet cell in the same way as you do with labels and values. In the cell, however, Excel displays not the formula, but its result. For example, if you enter a formula that says to add 4 and 2, Excel retains the formula and displays it in the formula bar when the cell is selected, but Excel displays the result, 6, in the worksheet itself.

Formula Fundamentals

Formulas must begin with the equal sign (=); that is how Excel distinguishes them from values and labels. You can construct formulas that add, subtract, multiply, divide, and exponentiate. The plus sign (+) means addition, the minus sign (−) means subtraction, the asterisk (*) means multiplication, the slash (/) means division, and the caret (^) means exponential operation. Table 4-1 shows the different mathematical operators and the results they return.

FORMULA ENTERED	RESULT DISPLAYED IN CELL
=4+2	6
=4-2	2
=4*2	8
=4/2	2
=4^2	16

Table 4-1   A list of simple formulas illustrating the standard arithmetic operators.

Figure 4-4 shows a simple budgeting worksheet built from Figure 4-3. The formula used in cell C9 appears in the formula bar and the result is displayed in the worksheet.

	C9	▼	f_x =1000+235+75+375+895+2500				
	A	B	C	D	E	F	G
1	Budget 2002						
2			January	February	March	Totals	Averages
3	Mortgage		1000	1000	1000		
4	Power		235	235	175		
5	Telephone		75	75	75		
6	Transportation		375	375	375		
7	Insurance		895				
8	Recreation		2500	200	1500		
9	Totals		5080				

Figure 4-4   A budgeting worksheet with a formula entered and the result displayed.

To build more complicated formulas, you need to recognize the standard rules of operator precedence: Excel first performs exponential operations, then multiplication and division operations, and finally, addition and subtraction.

For example, in the equation =1+2*3^4, Excel first raises 3 to the fourth power to get 81. It then multiplies this value by 2 to get 162. Finally, it adds 1 to this value to get 163.

To override these rules, you must use parentheses. You can use multiple sets of parentheses in a formula as need be. Excel first performs the function in the innermost set of parentheses. Take the following formulas in Table 4-2 as an example:

FORMULA ENTERED	RESULT DISPLAYED IN CELL
=1+2*3^4	163
=(1+2)*3^4	243
=((1+2)*3)^4	6561

Table 4-2   A list of formulas that show how parentheses override operator procedure.

Using Cell References

In the budgeting worksheet, you could total the budgeted expenses by entering the formula *=1000+235+75+375+895+2500* in cell C9. There is, however, a practical problem with this approach: You would need to rewrite the formula each time any of the values changed. Because this approach is unwieldy, Excel also allows you to use *cell references* in formulas. When a formula includes a cell reference, Excel uses the value that cell contains. For example, to add the budgeted amounts on your budgeting worksheet using a formula with cell references, follow these steps:

1. **Move the cell selector to C9.**

   You can do this by clicking cell C9. Or you can use the arrow keys.

2. **Type** *=C3+C4+C5+C6+C7+C8.*

   If you make a mistake entering this formula, you can edit it in the same way that you edit any label or value.

3. **Press the Enter key, or click the Enter button.**

   Excel enters your formula in the cell, calculates the formula, and then displays the formula result, as shown in Figure 4-5.

	C9	▼	*fx*	=C3+C4+C5+C6+C7+C8		
	A	B	C	D	E	F	G
1			Budget 2002				
2			January	February	March	Totals	Averages
3	Mortgage		1000	1000	1000		
4	Power		235	235	235		
5	Telephone		75	75	75		
6	Transportation		375	375	375		
7	Insurance		895	0	0		
8	Recreation		2500	200	1500		
9	Totals		5080	1885	3185		

Figure 4-5   A worksheet with cell references used in a formula.

To reference a cell on the same worksheet as the formula, you need to supply only the column-letter-and-row-number cell reference. To reference cell C3 on the same worksheet, for example, you enter *C3*.

You can also reference cells on other worksheets. To reference a cell on another worksheet in the same workbook, however, you need to precede the cell reference with the name of the worksheet and an exclamation point (!). To reference cell C1 on the worksheet named Sheet2, for example, you enter *Sheet2!C1*.

You can reference cells in other workbooks, too. To do this most easily, open the other workbooks, begin building your formula as described earlier in this chapter, and then click the other workbook cell you want to reference at the point you want to include the reference. Excel then writes the full cell reference for you, which includes the workbook name. An external reference to cell C3 on the worksheet named Sheet2 in the workbook named Budget might be written as =[Budget.xls]Sheet2!$C$3.

Understanding Worksheet Recalculation

As you build and edit your worksheet, Excel automatically updates the formulas and recalculates their results. For example, in the budgeting worksheet, if you change the value in cell C3 from 1000 to 1500, Excel recalculates any formulas that use the value stored in cell C3. As a result, the formula in cell C9 returns the value 3400—an increase of 500.

In simple worksheets such as the one shown in Figure 4-5, recalculation takes place so quickly you won't even be aware it is occurring. In larger worksheets with hundreds or even thousands of formulas, however, recalculation is much slower. The mouse pointer changes to the hourglass symbol when Excel is busy recalculating.

If you don't want Excel to automatically recalculate formulas as you are working, click the Tools menu, click Options, and then click the Calculation tab. Click the Manual option button under Calculation, and click OK. The word *Calculate* appears on the status bar when your worksheet needs to be recalculated. You can force recalculation by pressing the F9 key.

Formula Errors

It is possible to build an illogical or unsolvable formula. When you do, Excel displays an error message in the cell rather than calculating the result. The error message, which begins with the number sign (#), describes the error. Suppose, for example, that you enter the formula =1/0 in a cell. Because division by zero is an undefined mathematical operation, Excel can't solve the formula. To alert you to this, Excel displays the error message #DIV/0!.

Another common error is a circular reference. This occurs when two or more formulas indirectly depend on one another to achieve a result. For example, if the formula in cell A1 is =A2 and the formula in cell A2 is =A1+A3+A4, A1 depends on A2 and A2 depends on A1. Excel displays a warning and the Circular Reference toolbar when you create a circular reference. Excel identifies circular references by displaying the word *Circular* on the status bar and showing the address of the cell whose formula completed the "circle." It also draws arrows between the cells causing the circle.

To fix a formula error, edit the erroneous formula using the same techniques as with label and value editing. Move the cell selector to the cell holding the formula, click the formula bar, and edit the formula. When the formula is correct, set it by moving the cell selector and pressing the Enter key or clicking the Enter button.

NOTE   *When a formula refers to a cell that contains an erroneous formula, both formulas return the error message. For example, if cell A1 attempts to divide by zero and cell A2 refers to cell A1, cell A2 returns the error message #DIV/0! as well.*

Using Functions

Excel provides several hundred prebuilt formulas, called *functions,* that provide a shortcut to constructing complicated or lengthy formulas. In general, a function accepts *input values,* or *arguments,* and then makes some calculation and returns a result.

Excel provides financial, statistical, mathematical, trigonometric, and even engineering functions. Each function has a name that describes its operation. The function that adds values is named SUM, for example, and the function that calculates an arithmetic mean, or average, is named AVERAGE.

Most functions require arguments, or input values, which you enclose in parentheses. The ROUND function, for example, rounds a specific value to a specified number of decimal places. To round the value 5.75 to the nearest tenth, you could use the function shown below:

=ROUND(5.75, 1)

Even if a function doesn't require arguments, you still need to include the parentheses. For example, the function PI returns the mathematical constant pi. The function needs no arguments, but you still need to enter it as =PI().

Functions can use values, formulas, and even other functions as arguments. If entered in the budgeting worksheet shown in Figure 4-5, for example, each of the following functions returns the same result, 5080:

=SUM(C3:C8)

=SUM(C3,C4,C5,C6,C7,C8)

=SUM(1000,235,75,375,895,2500)

=SUM(SUM(C3),SUM(C4),SUM(C5),SUM(C6),SUM(C7),SUM(C8))

NOTE   *Because summing is such a common spreadsheet operation, Excel provides an AutoSum button on the toolbar; you can use it to enter an =SUM function in the active cell of a contiguous range of cells. If cell C9 in the worksheet shown in Figure 4-5 were empty, for example, and you selected the range C3:C8, you could click the AutoSum toolbar button to direct Excel to place the formula =SUM(C3:C8) in cell C9.*

TIP   *To identify a toolbar button, point to the button. Excel displays the button name in a small box called a ScreenTip. If you point to the button that shows the Greek sigma character, for example, Excel displays a ScreenTip box identifying the button as the AutoSum button.*

To most easily insert complicated functions and reduce your chance of error, click the Insert Function button to the left of the formula bar (identified by *fx*) or click the Insert menu and then click Function. This displays the Insert Function dialog box, as shown in Figure 4-6. Type a brief description of what you want to do in the box provided, or select a category from the drop-down list box. Because some of the functions are a little difficult to recognize or distinguish by name, Excel describes what the selected function does at the bottom of the Insert Function dialog box. After you have found the function you want to use, click OK.

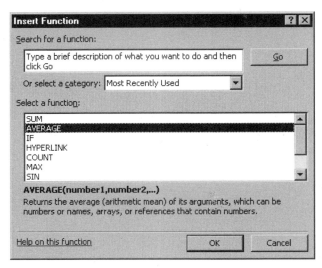

Figure 4-6   The Insert Function dialog box.

Excel displays the Function Arguments dialog box with text boxes you can use to identify or supply the arguments required for the function, as shown in Figure 4-7. If you know the cell reference or the range you need for the argument, type it in the appropriate argument box.

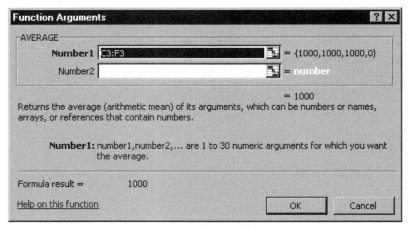

Figure 4-7   The Function Arguments dialog box.

However, if you need to look back at your spreadsheet, Excel provides a convenient way to do so. To the right of each argument box is a Collapse/Expand button that allows you to temporarily collapse the dialog box, leaving just the argument box showing, as shown in Figure 4-8. This provides access to the data. (You can drag the argument box to another location on your screen, if necessary.) Click the cell or drag through the appropriate range and the data is entered in the argument box. Then click the button to the right of the argument box to expand the dialog box back to your screen. Do the same for any other arguments that may be required by the function. Click OK when you are finished. Excel pastes the function in the cell.

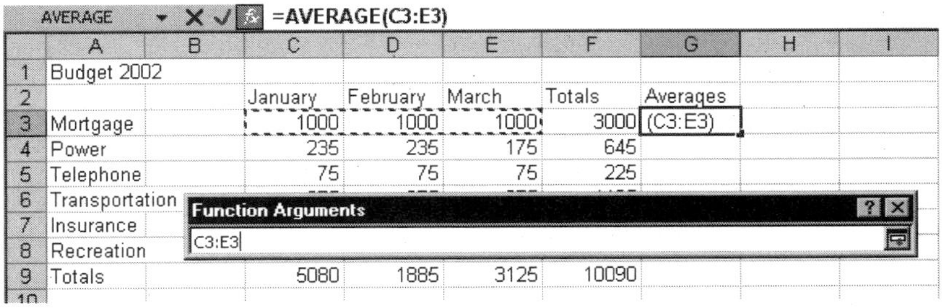

AVERAGE	▾ ✕ ✓ ƒx	=AVERAGE(C3:E3)						
	A	B	C	D	E	F	G	H	I
1	Budget 2002								
2			January	February	March	Totals	Averages		
3	Mortgage		1000	1000	1000	3000	(C3:E3)		
4	Power		235	235	175	645			
5	Telephone		75	75	75	225			
6	Transportation	Function Arguments						? ✕	
7	Insurance	C3:E3							
8	Recreation								
9	Totals		5080	1885	3125	10090			

Figure 4-8   Selecting data required for a function.

NOTE *A range is simply any group of cells of the worksheet. It can consist of only two cells or several hundred. Excel uses opposite corner cell references and a colon (:) to define ranges. For example, the range of cells from C1 and up to and including C5 is written as C1:C5. And the range of cells from C1 to D2 is written as C1:D2.*

You'll need to repeat the process for each formula or function needed to complete your worksheet, as shown in Figure 4-9. Although functions shorten the time it would take to think through and write out complicated formulas, re-creating functions or formulas over and over again can be time consuming, particularly in a very large worksheet. In the section on "Copying, Cutting, and Pasting," later in this chapter, you'll learn how to repeat functions and formulas quickly and easily.

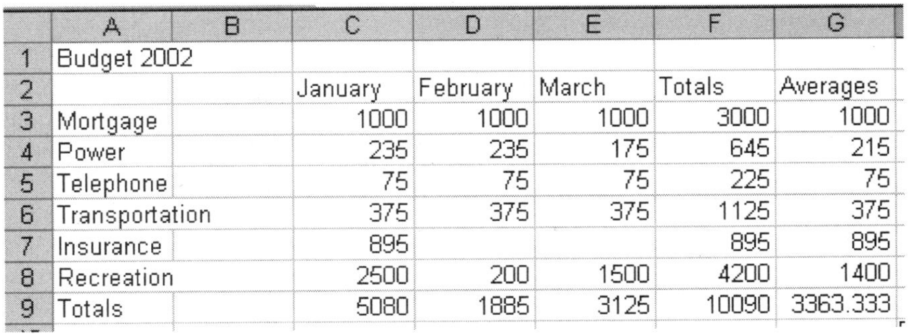

	A	B	C	D	E	F	G
1	Budget 2002						
2			January	February	March	Totals	Averages
3	Mortgage		1000	1000	1000	3000	1000
4	Power		235	235	175	645	215
5	Telephone		75	75	75	225	75
6	Transportation		375	375	375	1125	375
7	Insurance		895			895	895
8	Recreation		2500	200	1500	4200	1400
9	Totals		5080	1885	3125	10090	3363.333

Figure 4-9   The completed budgeting worksheet.

Formatting Data and Worksheets

When you first enter data in a worksheet, it is unformatted. Labels are entered in the default font and font size (Arial, 10 pt), and values are shown without commas, currency symbols, or even decimal places, unless you enter decimal places with the data. This leaves the appropriate formatting up to you.

This section describes many of the ways in which you may alter the appearance, and even the structure, of a worksheet.

Aligning Labels and Values

Excel normally aligns numbers against the right edge of a cell and text against the left edge. You can override these default alignments by using the Left Align, Center, Right Align, and Merge And Center buttons on the Formatting toolbar.

The Left Align, Center, and Right Align toolbar buttons work as you might expect. For example, to left-align the contents of selected cells, click the Left Align button.

The Merge And Center toolbar button is a little more complex. It lets you center a label across a selection of cells. For example, you can enter a label in cell A1 of the budgeting worksheet and then center it across the range A1:G1. To do so, first select the range and then click the Merge And Center toolbar button. Figure 4-10 shows the worksheet after this alignment.

A1		*fx*	Budget 2002			
A	**B**	**C**	**D**	**E**	**F**	**G**
1			Budget 2002			
2 Mortgage		January	February	March	Totals	Averages
3 Mortgage		1000	1000	1000	3000	1000
4 Power		235	235	175	645	215
5 Telephone		75	75	75	225	75
6 Transportation		375	375	375	1125	375
7 Insurance		895			895	895
8 Recreation		2500	200	1500	4200	1400
9 Totals		5080	1885	3125	10090	3363.333

Figure 4-10   A label centered across the range A1:G1.

Formatting Numbers

You can assign numeric formats such as dollar signs, percentage symbols, and commas. To quickly assign these specific, common formats, select the cell or range you want to format and click the Currency Style, Percent Style, or Comma Style buttons on the Formatting toolbar, as shown in Figure 4-11.

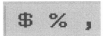

Figure 4-11 The Currency Style, Percent Style, and Comma Style buttons from the Formatting toolbar.

Using the Format Cells Command

You can access a more sophisticated array of formatting features by selecting the cell or range you want to format, clicking the Format menu, clicking Cells, and then clicking the appropriate tab.

On the Alignment tab, the Horizontal drop-down list box lets you align cell contents in the same ways as the Left Align, Center, Right Align, and Merge And Center buttons do, as shown in Figure 4-12. The Vertical drop-down list box allows you to align cell contents at the top, center, or bottom of the cell. The Orientation box allows you to rotate the cell contents.

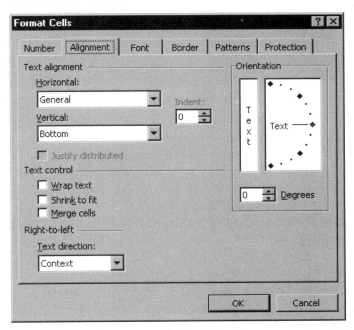

Figure 4-12 The Format Cells dialog box open at the Alignment tab.

The Text Control check boxes provide you with several more specialized alignment options. The Wrap Text check box allows you to wrap a long line of text into multiple lines in a single cell. The number of lines varies depending on the amount of text and the width of the cell. The Shrink To Fit check box allows you to decrease the size of the numbers or letters in a cell so that they fit in the current size constraints of the cell. The Merge Cells check box allows you to combine cells into larger, single cells.

To assign numeric formats other than those on the Formatting toolbar, follow these steps:

1. **Open the Number tab of the Format Cells dialog box.**

   Click the Format menu, click Cells, and then click the Number tab of the Format Cells dialog box, as shown in Figure 4-13.

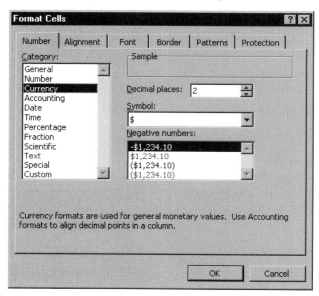

Figure 4-13 The Format Cells dialog box open to the Number tab.

2. **Select a numeric-formatting category from the Category list box.**

   In a budgeting worksheet, you would probably choose the Accounting category.

3. **Use the boxes and buttons for the category you chose to specify the exact formatting.**

   In a budgeting worksheet, for example, you might need to select a different currency symbol from the Symbol drop-down list box.

4. **Click OK.**

Changing Font and Font Size

Excel offers a wide variety of choices for changing a selected font's appearance, such as by adding boldfacing or underlining, for changing a font, and for specifying a different size.

To add effects such as boldfacing, italics, and underlining, you can use the Bold, Italic, and Underline font buttons on the Formatting toolbar. To use any of these buttons, simply select the worksheet range you want to format and then click the button.

NOTE *If you are creating an Excel worksheet that you intend to publish on the World Wide Web, you probably don't want to use underlines in your formatting. Underlines are usually reserved for hyperlinks.*

To change the font of text, click the down arrow next to the Font toolbar button and select a font from the list. If you open the Font drop-down list box, Excel displays the font's name using the font itself, so you can preview it, as shown in Figure 4-14. Fonts listed with a TT icon next to them are TrueType fonts. Fonts built into your printer have a printer icon next to them. If you use a TrueType font, the font you see on your screen will be the same one that the printer prints. If you use a scalable printer font and the printer you use doesn't support your selection, the printer uses the closest matching font.

Figure 4-14 The Font drop-down list box.

To change the size of text, click the down arrow next to the Size toolbar button. Fonts are measured using points. One point is 1/72 of an inch. So a point size of 18 means that the font is ¼ inch tall. Excel's default point size is 10. You probably don't want to use fonts smaller than 10 points for legibility.

Modifying Column and Row Size

As you reformat the labels and values in your worksheet, you may need to modify the standard column and row sizes to accommodate your formatting changes. To quickly increase the column width to accommodate all text in the column but include no extra white space, double-click the right border of that column heading. Normally, Excel automatically increases row height when you increase point size, but you can perform the same trick on rows by double-clicking the lower border of a row heading. This expands the row to the smallest height possible that still fits all entries within that row.

To specify exact column width, select any cell in that column, click the Format menu, click Column, and then click Width. Enter the width in characters in the Column Width text box, as shown in Figure 4-15, and click OK.

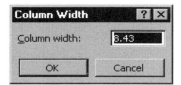

Figure 4-15 The Column Width text box.

To specify exact row height, select any cell in that row, click the Format menu, click Row, and then click Height. Enter the height in points in the Row Height text box, and click OK.

To hide a row, select any cell in the row, click the Format menu, click Row, and then click Hide. To redisplay a hidden row, select a range that includes cells in the rows above and below the hidden row. Then click the Format menu, click Row, and click Unhide.

To hide a column, select any cell in the column, click the Format menu, click Column, and then click Hide. To redisplay a hidden column, select a range that includes cells in the columns to the left and right of the hidden column. Then click the Format menu, click Column, and click Unhide.

Excel attempts to adjust the cell references and range definitions used in formulas for row and column insertions and deletions. For example, if a formula uses values in column C and you delete column B so that column C becomes the new column B, Excel adjusts the formulas to read column B. If you delete a cell referenced in a formula, however, Excel replaces the formula's reference with the error message #REF, indicating that the formula originally referenced a now-deleted cell.

Using AutoFormat

Excel's AutoFormat feature performs many standard formatting tasks in a single operation: setting fonts, aligning labels, setting column width and row height, establishing numeric and date/time formats, and adding borders and rules.

To use AutoFormat, you first enter worksheet labels, values, and formulas, as shown in Figure 4-16.

	A	B	C	D	E	F	G
1			Budget 2002				
2			January	February	March	Totals	Averages
3	Mortgage		1000	1000	1000	3000	1000
4	Power		235	235	175	645	215
5	Telephone		75	75	75	225	75
6	Transportation		375	375	375	1125	375
7	Insurance		895			895	895
8	Recreation		2500	200	1500	4200	1400
9	Totals		5080	1885	3125	10090	3363.333

Figure 4-16 The budgeting worksheet before an AutoFormat is applied.

To use the AutoFormat command, follow these steps:

1. Select the worksheet range you want to format.

In Figure 4-16, you would select the range A1:G9.

2. Open the AutoFormat dialog box.

Click the Format menu, and click AutoFormat, as shown in Figure 4-17.

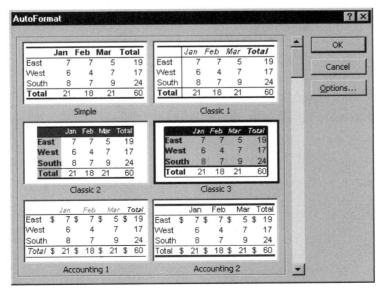

Figure 4-17 The AutoFormat dialog box.

3. **Select the AutoFormatting options you want to use.**

Click the Options button if you want to specify which AutoFormatting options should be applied to your worksheet selection. When you do this, Excel adds Options check boxes to the AutoFormat dialog box. Click to check or clear these check boxes to selectively apply individual components of an AutoFormat.

4. **Select an AutoFormat by clicking it.**

The AutoFormat pictures show roughly what the AutoFormat formatting looks like.

5. **Click OK to apply the format to the range you selected.**

Figure 4-18 shows what the budgeting worksheet looks like after the AutoFormat selected in Figure 4-17 is applied.

	A	B	C	D	E	F	G
1	Budget 2002						
2			January	February	March	Totals	Averages
3	Mortgage		1000	1000	1000	3000	1000
4	Power		235	235	175	645	215
5	Telephone		75	75	75	225	75
6	Transportation		375	375	375	1125	375
7	Insurance		895			895	895
8	Recreation		2500	200	1500	4200	1400
9	Totals		5080	1885	3125	10090	3363.333333

Figure 4-18   A worksheet range with an AutoFormat applied.

Inserting and Deleting Cells, Rows, Columns, and Worksheets

Excel lets you insert and delete cells, rows, columns, and worksheets in your workbook with speed and efficiency. You can easily delete what you no longer need or insert new items between existing entries when you need more space.

Using the Insert Command

To insert a row, click any cell in the row below where you want a row inserted. Then click the Insert menu, and click Rows.

To insert a column, click any cell in the column to the right of where you want a column inserted and click the Insert menu and click Columns.

To insert a cell in a column or row, right-click the cell where you want the new cell to appear. Excel displays the Insert dialog box, as shown in Figure 4-19. Click the Shift Cells Right option button to insert a new cell in a row, or click the Shift Cells Down option button to insert a new cell in a column. Then click OK.

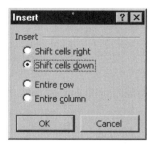

Figure 4-19 The Insert dialog box.

To insert a worksheet, display the worksheet tab in front of which you want to create a new worksheet, click the Insert menu, and click Worksheet.

Using the Delete Command

To delete a cell, range, row, or column, select the specific cell or range or any cell in the row or column you want to delete, click the Edit menu, and click Delete. Excel displays the Delete dialog box, as shown in Figure 4-20. Specify whether you want to shift the remaining cells up or to the left, or whether you want to delete the entire row or column, and click OK.

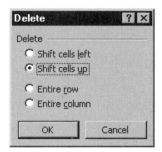

Figure 4-20 The Delete dialog box.

Naming Cells and Cell Ranges

In a small worksheet it's not too difficult to remember that cell C3 contains January's mortgage expense, C6 contains transportation costs, and so on. In the real world, however, Excel worksheets can be much more complex, and keeping track of what each cell represents becomes correspondingly more difficult. In this way, instead of referring to cell C3 in a formula, you could refer to JanMortgage if you first name the individual cell. For example, if you named cells C3, C4, C5, C6, C7, and C8 JanMortgage, JanPower, JanTelephone, JanTransportation, JanInsurance, and JanRecreation respectively, the following two formulas would be identical:

=C3+C4+C5+C6+C5+C8

=JanMortgage+JanPower+JanTelephone+JanTransportation+JanInsurance+JanRecreation

To name a cell or range, select the cell or range of cells to be named and then type the cell or range name in the Name box.

Copying, Cutting, and Pasting

You can copy or cut the contents of cells and ranges and then paste them into other locations. This means you don't have to repeatedly type a label, value, or formula. You can type the entry just once and then copy or move it.

TIP *With most programs, when you copy or cut something, the program places it on the Windows Clipboard. The only catch with the Windows Clipboard is that it can hold only one copied or cut piece of information at a time. So if you copy or cut another piece of information, the program replaces what the Clipboard previously stored. Office programs like Excel provide a nifty feature called the Clipboard toolbar that allows you to store up to 24 pieces of copied or cut information at a time. To use the Clipboard toolbar, click the View menu, click Toolbars, and then click Clipboard.*

Copying Labels and Values

Suppose, for example, that the numbers shown in the first four rows of column C of the budgeting worksheet represent the unchanging budgeted expenses for January, February, and March, as shown in Figure 4-21. Rather than reenter the same values, you could copy the values already stored in column C.

	A	B	C	D	E
1			Budget 2002		
2			January	February	March
3	Mortgage		1000		
4	Power		235		
5	Telephone		75		
6	Transportation		375		
7	Insurance		895	0	0
8	Recreation		2500	200	1500
9	Totals		5080		

Figure 4-21 The simple budgeting worksheet.

To copy the labels and values for such an operation, follow these steps:

1. Select the cell or range to be copied.

In Figure 4-21, this would mean you select the range C3:C6. The easiest method for selecting a specific cell or range is by clicking or clicking and dragging the mouse.

2. Click the Copy toolbar button, or click the Edit menu and click Copy.

When you do this, Excel places a copy of the labels and values on the Clipboard and indicates the copied cells with a scrolling marquee.

NOTE   *The scrolling marquee will remain around the range until you remove it or place another range on the Clipboard. To remove the scrolling marquee, press the Esc key.*

3. Select the destination cell or the cell in the upper left corner of the destination range.

If you want to duplicate the selected cells more than once, select the multiple destination ranges in their entirety. For the worksheet shown in Figure 4-21, for example, you would select the range D3:E6.

NOTE   *If you paste a copy of a single cell into a multiple-cell range, the contents of the cell are duplicated in each cell in the destination range.*

4. Click the Paste toolbar button, or click the Edit menu and click Paste.

When you do this, Excel copies the worksheet range from the Clipboard into the specified worksheet range, as shown in Figure 4-22.

	A	B	C	D	E
1			Budget 2002		
2			January	February	March
3	Mortgage		1000	1000	1000
4	Power		235	235	235
5	Telephone		75	75	75
6	Transportation		375	375	375
7	Insurance		895	0	0
8	Recreation		2500	200	1500
9	Totals		5080		

Figure 4-22 A worksheet with two copies of C3:C6 pasted in D3:E6.

TIP *You can also copy a cell or range with the mouse. Just select the cell or range, hold down the Ctrl key, point to the black border around the cell or range so that the mouse pointer changes from a cross to an arrow, and then drag the cell or range to a new location.*

Copying Formulas

When you copy labels and values, Excel duplicates the contents of the copied cell or cells and pastes the data into the selected range. When you copy a formula, however, Excel adjusts any cell references used in the formula. This important difference can be illustrated by copying the formula in cell C9 of Figure 4-22, =C1+C2+C3+C4+C5, into cells D9 and E9. To do this, follow these steps:

1. **Select the cell or range with the formula(s) you want to copy.**

   In the example of the worksheet shown in Figure 4-22, you would select cell C9.

2. **Click the Copy toolbar button.**

   Excel moves a copy of the formula in cell C9 to the Clipboard.

3. **Select the destination range D9:E9.**

   In the example of the worksheet shown in Figure 4-22, you would select the range D9:E9.

4. **Click the Paste toolbar button.**

   Excel adjusts the formulas for the column in question and pastes the formula =D3+D4+D5+D6+D7+D8 into cell D9 and the formula =E3+E4+E5+E6+E7+D8 into cell E9. Figure 4-23 shows the worksheet after copying the formula.

	A	B	C	D	E
1			Budget 2002		
2			January	February	March
3	Mortgage		1000	1000	1000
4	Power		235	235	235
5	Telephone		75	75	75
6	Transportation		375	375	375
7	Insurance		895	0	0
8	Recreation		2500	200	1500
9	Totals		5080	1885	3185

Figure 4-23 The budgeting worksheet after copying the formula in cell C9 into cells D9 and E9.

The formula changes that Excel makes aren't a mistake. Excel assumes—unless you tell it otherwise—that the cell references in your formulas are *relative*. When Excel copies and pastes a formula with relative cell references, it adjusts them.

To prevent Excel from automatically adjusting the relative references of copied formulas, you can make them *absolute*. Simply place a dollar sign ($) in front of the part or parts you don't want Excel to adjust. For example, to tell Excel not to adjust the formula at all, place a dollar sign in front of both the column letter and row number, like this: $A$1. To allow Excel to adjust row numbers but not column letters, put a dollar sign in front of the column letter but not the row number, like this: $A1. And to allow Excel to adjust column letters but not row numbers, put a dollar sign in front of the row number but not the column letter, like this: A$1.

Special Pasting Options

If you want to specify pasting options, instead of just clicking the Paste toolbar button after copying or cutting, click the Edit menu and click Paste Special. Excel displays the Paste Special dialog box, as shown in Figure 4-24. To paste a row of cells as a column of cells or vice versa, click the Transpose check box. To paste only a portion of the copied or cut cells' contents, click a Paste option button other than All. For example, to paste only the comments in a cell, click the Comments option button in the Paste section. To add, subtract, multiply, or divide the values in the copied range with the values in the destination range, click the Add, Subtract, Multiply, or Divide option button in the Operation section. To tell Excel it shouldn't paste blank cells over values, click the Skip Blanks check box.

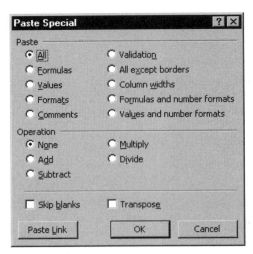

Figure 4-24 The Paste Special dialog box.

Moving Labels, Values, and Formulas

To move, rather than copy, a selected range, follow the same procedure, but click the Cut toolbar button or click the Edit menu and click Cut instead of Copy. Excel removes the selected contents from their original location and allows you to paste them in a new location.

NOTE *When you move a formula, Excel doesn't adjust the relative references used in the moved formula.*

You can also move a cell or range with the mouse by selecting the cell or range and pointing to the black border around the cell or range so that the mouse pointer changes from a cross to an arrow. Then drag the cell or range to a new location.

AutoFill

To continue a pattern you have begun, use the fill handle in the lower right corner of a cell or range. For example, if you begin the pattern 0, 5, 10 and want to continue it down a column, select the cells holding these values and click the little black square in the lower right corner of the range. The mouse pointer changes from a white outlined cross to a black cross. Now drag the mouse down the column as far as you want the pattern to go. This procedure also works for easily identifiable patterns of labels, such as months of the year and days of the week.

Summary

The proficient use of Excel is one of the most important skills to have in today's business world. Just about any number-crunching process can be efficiently performed on an Excel worksheet. From extremely complex corporate accounting to simple budgets, Excel provides you with the tools you need to get the job done.

In this chapter, we introduced you to Excel worksheets with a discussion of the essential elements and their functions. Then we led you through the core of Excel, working with the four types of data you can enter into a worksheet: labels, values, formulas, and functions. We also looked at ways to format Excel data for clarity and presentation and discussed techniques that increase Excel's efficiency and productivity.

Chapter 5

POWERPOINT BASICS

Featuring:

- PowerPoint Terminology
- Creating Your Presentation
- Enhancing Your Presentation
- Polishing Your Slide Show
- Guidelines to Effective Presentations

Consider this scenario: The CEO calls you in and compliments you on the work you did on a recent hurry-up project. And, because you did such a great job, he wants you to present it to the stockholders meeting next month. No holds barred; it needs to be a knock-their-socks-off presentation. Where to go? What to do? You know the subject inside and out, but how do you make the stockholders stand up and say "Wow!"?

Never fear, PowerPoint is the application you need and with the techniques you learn in this skill, you can create the presentation that makes the impression you want.

PowerPoint Terminology

PowerPoint is an easy application to learn, but first you need to understand some basic PowerPoint terms:

- The *slide* is the essential element of a presentation, as shown in Figure 5-1. Although most PowerPoint presentations today are presented electronically with a computer connected to other computers or a projector, most presentations used to use 35mm slides and slide projectors. The terminology has carried through. You can still have 35mm slides prepared, if you choose, or overhead transparencies; but whatever your delivery medium, each screen you create is called a slide.

Figure 5-1   A PowerPoint slide.

- The *title slide* is usually the first slide that you have in your presentation. It frequently has a slightly different arrangement of text and graphics from the regular slides so that it stands out, much like the title page of a book or report.

- The *Master Slide* is the plan for how your slides look. Any text or graphic that is placed on the Master Slide, by default, is shown on all slides in a presentation. On the Master Slide, you set text font, size, and color. You set the arrangement of text objects for all slides. In addition to the Slide Master, which is the plan for all regular slides, you may have a Title Master, which sets the parameters for your title slide (or slides).

- The *presentation* is the completed product, the collection of all the slides put together in an organized, informative manner. You can print a presentation on paper, on transparency stock to use with an overhead projector, on 35mm slides for use in a slide projector, or you can run a presentation from a computer to other computer screens or to a LCD projector.

- An *object* is any single component of a slide. You can have a text object, a clip art object, an AutoShape object, and so on.

- *Animation* in PowerPoint is an attention-getting way to enhance your presentation. Remarkable animations are included within PowerPoint, such as text or clip art flying onto the screen or following a motion path around the screen. Of course, animation works only with onscreen presentations, but with it you can add pizzazz to any computer slide show.

- *Transition* is a type of animation, but transitions specifically govern the way one slide changes into the next. Transitions may be very simple (sliding in from the right or left) or may be very dramatic (eight-spoke wheel spinning to reveal new slide).

Defining PowerPoint Views

A view is one of the several ways of looking at your presentation within the PowerPoint program. To change a view, choose a different view from the View menu. The following three views are used the most:

- Normal view places one slide at a time in the PowerPoint window with toolbars and the Outline/Preview pane to the left side of the screen, as shown in Figure 5-2. In this view you can edit text and apply graphics.

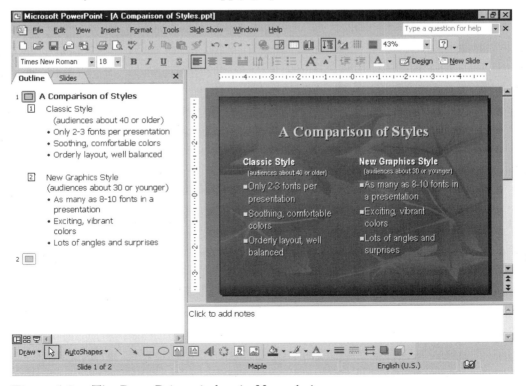

Figure 5-2   The PowerPoint window in Normal view.

- Slide Sorter view places all the slides, in miniature, in the PowerPoint window, as shown in Figure 5-3. You cannot edit individual slides in this view, but you can easily reorder them by dragging them from one place to another with the mouse.

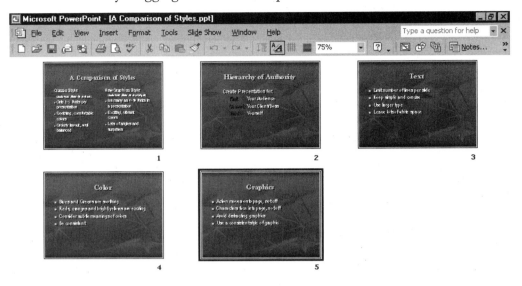

Figure 5-3   The PowerPoint window in Slide Sorter view.

- Slide Show view shows the presentation, one slide at a time, on the computer screen all by itself. This is the view that you use to show the final product to your audience if you are preparing a computer display presentation. You can use the mouse or the keyboard to control it manually, or you can set it to run automatically with predetermined timings.

Creating Your Presentation

PowerPoint provides three ways of approaching the creation of your presentation. First, you can use the AutoContent Wizard that is part of the PowerPoint program. The AutoContent Wizard asks you some questions, lets you make some choices, and produces a presentation for you. All you need to do is enter text and fine-tune it to your specifications. Second, you can outline what you want to say in the Outline pane and let it determine the slides that you want to use. You can also create an outline in Word and open it in PowerPoint to have a presentation created from your outline. Third, you can build your presentation one slide at a time, manually entering text and layout. In this section, we take a look at all three of these ways to create a presentation.

Using the AutoContent Wizard

By far the easiest way to jump-start your presentation is to use the AutoContent Wizard, because the wizard does most of the work for you. Not all presentations are suited to the use of the wizard, but for those that are, it is a powerful tool. To use the wizard, follow these steps:

1. Select From AutoContent Wizard from the New Presentation task pane.

If you have just started PowerPoint, the New Presentation task pane is displayed to the right of your screen. If you do not see the New Presentation task pane, click the File menu, click New, and the pane appears. Then click From AutoContent Wizard link in the New section. The AutoContent Wizard Start screen is displayed, as shown in Figure 5-4.

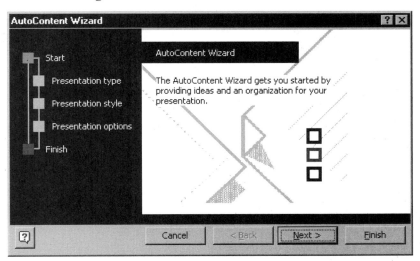

Figure 5-4   The Start screen of the AutoContent Wizard.

2. Click Next.

The Start screen provides information on the AutoContent Wizard. Click Next and the Presentation Type screen is displayed, as shown in Figure 5-5.

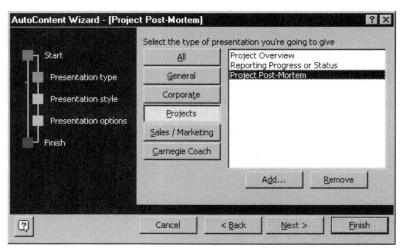

Figure 5-5 The Presentation Type screen of the AutoContent Wizard.

3. Select the type of presentation you are going to give.

The Presentation Type screen provides numerous presentation types divided into categories. Click a button to select a category, and then click the presentation type in the box to the right. (For our scenario, we select the Projects category and the Project Post-Mortem type.) After making your selection, click Next to move to the Presentation Style screen, as shown in Figure 5-6.

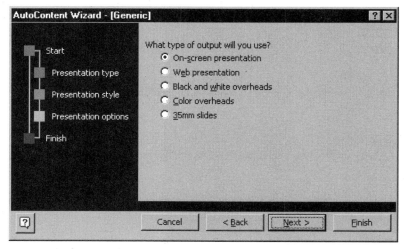

Figure 5-6 The Presentation Style screen of the AutoContent Wizard.

4. Select the type of output you will use.

To properly configure your presentation to the final output medium, select one of the styles listed in the Presentation Style screen by clicking the appropriate option button. Then click Next to move to the next step in the wizard, the Presentation Options screen, as shown in Figure 5-7.

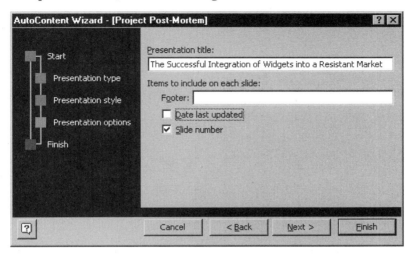

Figure 5-7   The Presentation Options screen of the AutoContent Wizard.

5. Enter the necessary data.

Type the presentation title in the box provided. Also, consider what information you want to show on every slide, such as date last updated, slide number, or other footer information. Make the appropriate selections, and click Next to display the Finish screen, as shown in Figure 5-8.

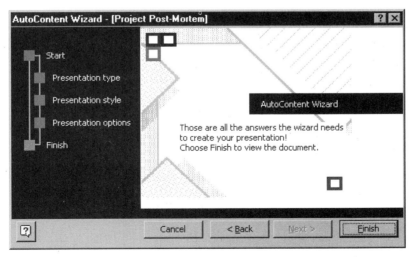

Figure 5-8   The Finish screen of the AutoContent Wizard.

6. Click Finish.

Clicking Finish displays your completed presentation, as shown in Figure 5-9. Notice that the author's name is displayed on the title slide. The computer pulls this information from user data established at the installation of Office. If the name that is displayed is not accurate, you can change it by highlighting the text in either the Outline pane or on the slide itself and entering the correct information.

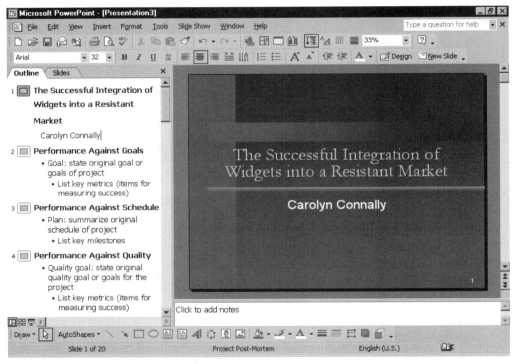

Figure 5-9 The presentation completed by AutoContent Wizard.

7. Edit the presentation.

The text of the presentation is composed of suggestions of appropriate data to include in the presentation. Quite obviously, you need to use your own text in its place. Additionally, the presentation may be enhanced using techniques discussed later in this chapter.

Using the Outline Pane

Although the AutoContent Wizard is the fastest way to create a presentation, many people prefer to work from an outline. PowerPoint provides a powerful outline tool that you can use to create your presentation. To do so, follow these steps:

1. **Open the Outline pane, as shown in Figure 5-10.**

   By default, the Outline pane appears in your PowerPoint window to the left of the slide display. If the Outline pane is not displayed, click the View menu, click Normal, and the Outline pane appears. There are two tabs on this pane: one showing the outline of your presentation, the other showing previews of the slides that currently make up the presentation. Click the Outline tab.

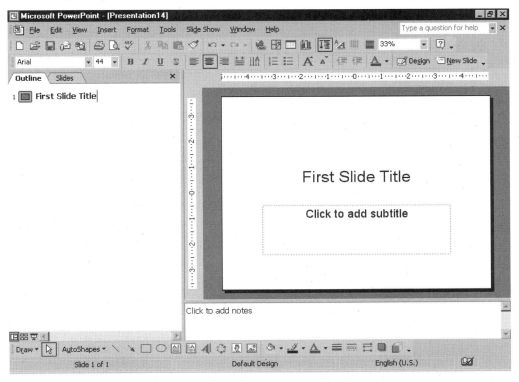

Figure 5-10 The PowerPoint window displaying the Outline pane.

2. **Compose your outline.**

   In the Outline pane, create an outline with the exact text you want in your presentation using these guidelines:

   - The first level of text is a slide title; subsequent levels of text are bullet points on that slide.

   - Subordinate levels can be achieved by pressing the Tab key.

   - To reverse that action and make a line of text a higher level, press Shift+Tab.

- You can create as many levels as you need, but keep in mind that more than three may confuse your audience.

- Keep each slide's text to a minimum.

- Notice that your outline text is being placed on a slide in the Slide Display window.

3. Edit or enhance your presentation.

Fine-tuning your presentation can take place in the Outline pane or on the slides themselves. In the Outline pane, edit text using standard word-processing techniques. To change text on the slides, just click the text first to select the text box, as shown in Figure 5-11, and then use word-processing techniques.

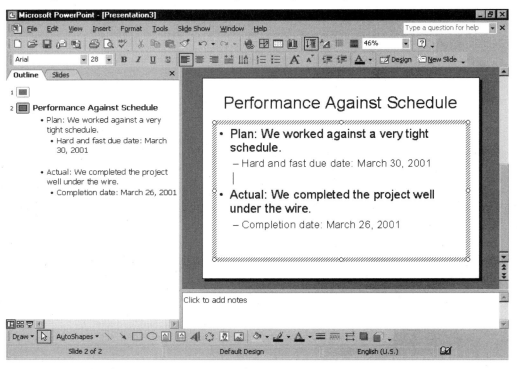

Figure 5-11   Clicking selects the text box.

To further augment your work, see the section "Enhancing Your Presentation."

Importing an Outline from Word

If you have an outline already developed in Word, there is no need to re-create it. In PowerPoint, just click the File menu, click Open, locate the folder, and double-click the outline file. A new presentation is created in PowerPoint based on the Word document. Here, too, the first level of the outline becomes a slide; subsequent levels are the text on that slide. Use the same techniques discussed above to adjust the text levels.

Enhancing Your Presentation

The effectiveness of a presentation is increased by the layout of the slides. Although you should keep the adornments appropriate to your audience and subject matter, clip art, graphics, and layout design are usually a good way to add punch to your presentation and keep audience attention. The following sections describe some of the techniques you can use to do so.

Applying a Design Template

Although you may create a background design yourself (see the section "Customizing the Master Slide," below), PowerPoint comes packed with numerous design templates that you can apply to your presentation. You want to do this for sure if you created your presentation from an outline, because no design will be applied automatically. When you use the AutoContent Wizard to create your slide presentation, however, a design template is automatically applied, although it can be changed. To apply a design template to your presentation, follow these steps:

1. **Display the Slide Design task pane, as shown in Figure 5-12.**

   Click the Format menu, and click Slide Design.

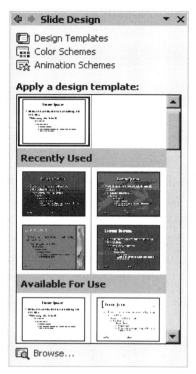

Figure 5-12 The Slide Design task pane.

2. Select Design Templates.

The design templates may already be displayed at the bottom of the pane (see Figure 5-12). If not, click the Design Templates link.

3. Select a design template.

You can have fun with this. When you click a design template from the previews in the Slide Design task pane, the design is automatically applied to your slide, as shown in Figure 5-13. If you are considering a change to a presentation with a template already applied, don't hesitate to try a new look. If you don't like the results, you can find the original design under the Recently Used category at the top of the display.

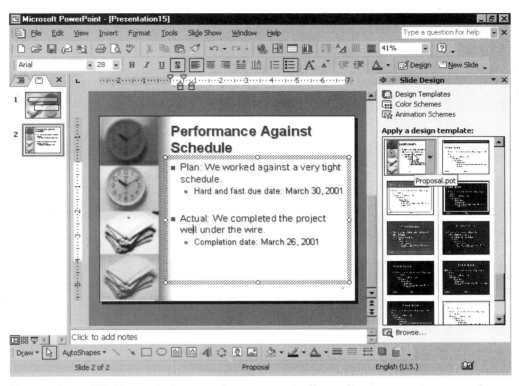

Figure 5-13 Clicking a design template automatically applies it to your presentation.

4. Save your presentation.

After you have applied a design template to your presentation, it is important to save that change. Just click the Save button on the toolbar. If you have already named and saved the presentation, the save occurs in the background. If your presentation has not yet been saved, of course, you are asked to name it and save it to the desired folder.

Adding Clip Art and AutoShape Graphics

Even for the most reserved and conservative of audiences, adding graphics to your presentation helps break up the monotony of text alone. You can use the clip art that comes with PowerPoint, you can use clip art from anywhere on your hard drive, or you can create graphics using PowerPoint's AutoShape feature.

Inserting Clip Art from Media Gallery

To insert a clip from the software that comes with PowerPoint, follow these steps:

1. Display the slide.

Start by displaying the slide where you want the clip art to appear.

2. Open the Insert ClipArt task pane.

Click the Insert menu, click Picture, and then click Clip Art. The Insert Clip Art task pane appears to the right of your slide.

3. Enter text, and start the search.

In the Search text box, enter a descriptive word or phrase for the graphic you want to find. Then click Search.

TIP   *The Media Gallery is capable of holding an unlimited amount of graphics, photos, sound files, and videos, so you can add files you have acquired through outside sources. Although you can add clips and other media to your presentation from anyplace on your hard drive, the Media Gallery offers you an excellent location for sorting and locating the files you want.*

4. Select the clip.

From the clip art displayed in the Insert Clip Art task pane, select the graphic that is most suited to your presentation. The clip art is placed on your slide, as shown in Figure 5-14.

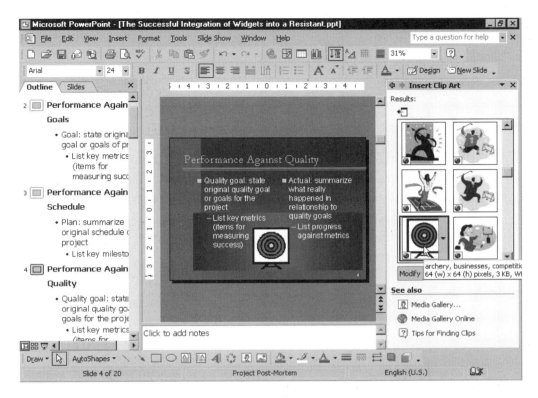

Figure 5-14 Selecting a graphic from the Insert Clip Art task pane places that graphic on your slide.

5. Arrange the graphic.

After the graphic is located on your slide, you can size it or arrange it for the best result by using the following methods:

- Move a graphic. When you place your mouse pointer over the graphic, it changes into a four-pointed arrow. Just click and drag the graphic to place it in the best location.

- Size a graphic. When you click once on the graphic to select it, sizing handles (little round dots) appear along the sides, top, and bottom of the clip. With your mouse, grab one of the handles and drag to enlarge or reduce the graphic. Dragging one of the corner handles enlarges or reduces the picture proportionately. Using one of the side handles stretches the picture and distorts it from its original proportions.

- Arrange the graphic's order. When clip art is first inserted into a slide, it is, by default, placed as the top layer of all the other items on the slide. If you want the graphic to be tucked in behind another layout element, you can change its level. From the Drawing toolbar, as shown in Figure 5-15, choose Draw, choose Order, and then choose Send To Back (which puts it at the very bottom of all of the layout elements) or Send Backward (which places the picture one layer further down each time you select it). If you want to bring a picture forward among the layers, use the Bring To Front or Bring Forward commands.

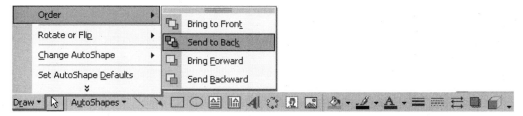

Figure 5-15   The Drawing toolbar displaying the Order menu.

NOTE   *The Drawing toolbar, by default, is located at the bottom of the screen. However, if your Drawing toolbar is not visible, right-click any toolbar and choose Drawing from the shortcut menu.*

Inserting Clip Art from a File

Clip art that you have stored on your hard drive in folders other than Media Gallery is just as easily incorporated into your slides. To insert a clip from a file, follow these steps:

1. **Display the slide.**

   Start by displaying the slide where you want the clip to appear.

2. **Open the Insert Picture dialog box, as shown in Figure 5-16.**

   Click the Insert menu, click Picture, and then click From File.

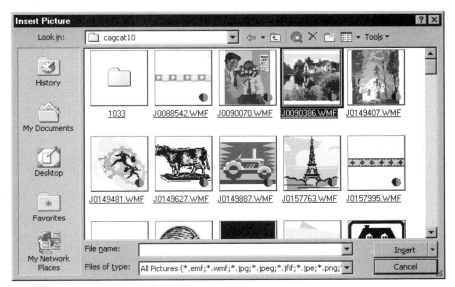

Figure 5-16 The Insert Picture dialog box.

3. **Select the graphic file.**

   Using the list, locate the file that you want to insert into your slide. Double-click or click to select it, and then click Insert. The graphic is inserted into the slide.

4. **Arrange the graphic.**

   After the graphic is located in your slide, you can move it by dragging, size it by dragging the sizing handles, or arrange it by using the Drawing toolbar (see Figure 5-15).

Adding AutoShape Graphics

If you are speaking to a conservative or sophisticated audience, such as a Board of Directors, you want to keep your graphics as simple as possible. Sometimes PowerPoint's AutoShape graphics are just what you need.

AutoShape graphics are simple forms that you choose from a menu and drag to create, making them the size and proportion that is right for you. To use this convenient PowerPoint feature, follow these steps:

1. Open the AutoShape menu, as shown in Figure 5-17.

Click the AutoShape button on the Drawing toolbar.

Figure 5-17 The AutoShape menu.

TIP   *The AutoShape menu can float freely on your screen. This is particularly useful if you are going to be using it a lot. Floating it saves you from having to click the Drawing toolbar when you want to choose from the AutoShapes.*

2. Select an AutoShape category.

From the seven AutoShape categories, click the category that would most likely contain the shape you are looking for.

3. Select an AutoShape.

From the pop-up menu, select the AutoShape of your choice. The pop-up menu and the AutoShape menu close, leaving your mouse pointer in the shape of a cross, as shown in Figure 5-18.

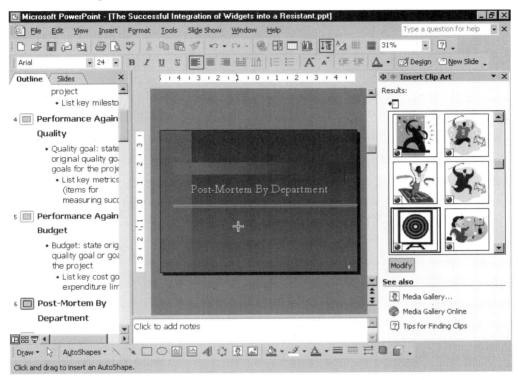

Figure 5-18 The mouse pointer prepared to insert an AutoShape graphic.

4. Insert the AutoShape.

Place your mouse pointer on your slide where you want the shape to be located. Click and drag to insert the shape, adjusted to the proportions you want, as shown in Figure 5-19.

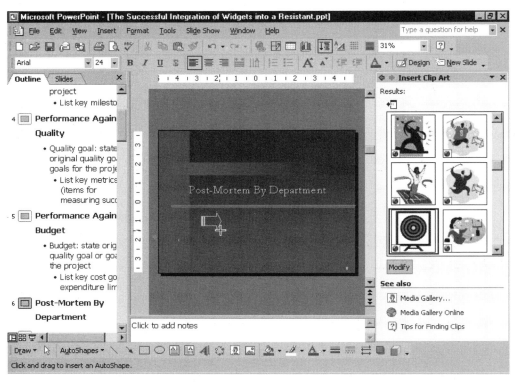

Figure 5-19 Drawing the AutoShape on a slide.

5. Adjust the AutoShape.

AutoShapes can be moved or sized like any other graphic: click and drag to move; click and drag a sizing handle to enlarge or reduce.

6. Add color to your AutoShape.

If you have a slide design applied to your slide, the AutoShape will automatically be filled with a color complementary to your color scheme. To change the color or fill in a noncolored AutoShape, select the graphic, click the Fill Color button on the Drawing toolbar, and select a color. The graphic is filled with the selected color, as shown in Figure 5-20.

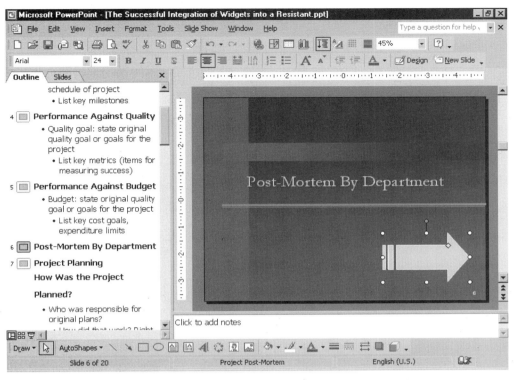

Figure 5-20 The AutoShape graphic filled with color.

Using Applets to Add Objects

PowerPoint comes with several *applets,* or mini applications, that allow you to insert certain objects into your slides. Using the applet is a far simpler job than trying to create the object yourself.

WordArt

WordArt is a remarkable program that allows you to create artistic shapes with text. To insert a WordArt object into your slide, follow these steps:

1. Start the WordArt program.

Click the WordArt button (it looks like a large, tilted, blue A) on the Drawing toolbar to open the WordArt Gallery, as shown in Figure 5-21.

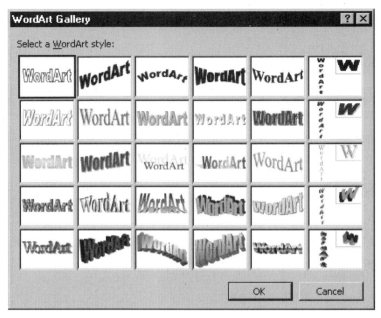

Figure 5-21 The WordArt Gallery.

2. Select a WordArt style.

From the many styles presented in the WordArt Gallery, select the one that most closely meets your needs. It can be adjusted if it is not exactly right. Then click OK. The Edit WordArt Text dialog box is displayed, as shown in Figure 5-22.

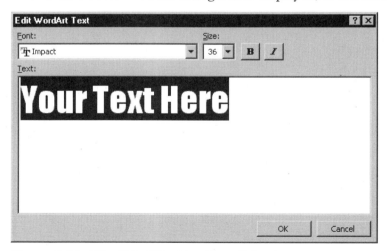

Figure 5-22 The Edit WordArt Text dialog box.

3. Enter WordArt text.

The words *Enter Text Here* are already highlighted in the Edit WordArt Text dialog box. All you have to do is type in the text you want, and click OK. The WordArt object is placed on the slide, as shown in Figure 5-23.

Figure 5-23 A WordArt object placed on a slide.

4. Adjust the WordArt object.

Just like other graphics, you need to adjust a WordArt object to the size and position that works best in the presentation. Click the object to display the sizing handles; drag one of the handles to resize your WordArt. Click and drag the object with your mouse to reposition it.

In addition to the sizing handles, a WordArt object can have other handles (colored bright yellow) that otherwise adjust the shape of the WordArt. For example, a WordArt object in which the letters are slanted may have a yellow handle that adjusts the degree of the slant. Just click and drag the yellow handle to see the effect.

Diagram

The Diagram applet allows you to choose one of six diagram formats:

- Organization Chart, which is used to show hierarchical relationships.

- Cycle diagram, which is used to demonstrate process with a continuous cycle.

- Radial diagram, which shows the relationships of a core element.

- Pyramid diagram, which portrays foundation-based relationships.

- Venn diagram, which shows areas of overlap between elements.

- Target diagram, which shows steps toward a goal.

To place one of these helpful diagrams in your presentation, follow these steps:

1. Display the slide.

Make sure that the slide on which you want to insert the diagram is active.

2. Open the Diagram Gallery, as shown in Figure 5-24.

Click the Insert menu, and click Diagram. The Diagram Gallery displays graphics representing the six diagrams from which you may choose.

Figure 5-24   The Diagram Gallery.

3. Select the diagram.

Clicking a diagram identifies the function of that diagram in the lower portion of the Diagram Gallery window. Select the diagram that best meets your needs, and click OK. The diagram is inserted into your slide.

4. Adjust the diagram.

Like any graphic, a diagram can be moved and sized. It can also be altered to reflect the data you are presenting. Here's how:

- Move the diagram. Place your mouse pointer over the graphic. The mouse pointer turns into a four-headed arrow. Then click and drag the diagram to a new location.

- Size the diagram. When you click the diagram once with your mouse, sizing handles appear. However, these sizing handles are configured differently from other graphics. Instead of little dots, they are lines reflecting the sides (straight lines) and the corners (bent lines). Any one of these lines can be grasped with the mouse and dragged to increase or decrease the size. Using the side handles stretches the size of the box in which the diagram is displayed, but does not distort the graphic itself.

- Add labels. Each of the diagrams has provision for labeling its elements, but each does this in its own way. For example, to label the Target diagram, click any of the callout lines and a box appears for you to enter the label data. In the Venn diagram, each of the overlapping circles has a box for labeling, but it cannot be seen until you click it. Just click around, and when you see the box, then type, as shown in Figure 5-25.

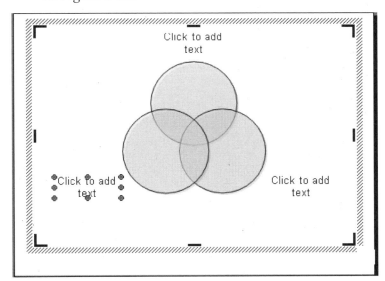

Figure 5-25 A Venn diagram with a label box selected.

- Add shapes. The diagrams are fully adjustable to represent any number of data series. Just right-click in the diagram area, and choose Add Shape from the shortcut menu.

Chart

Chart is an applet that is very similar to the chart function in Excel. You can use it to insert a chart or graph into your presentation, or you can create one in Excel and copy and paste it into PowerPoint. To use Chart, follow these steps:

1. Display the slide.

Make sure that the slide on which you want to insert the graph is active.

2. Insert a chart into the slide.

Click the Insert menu, and click Chart. A sample chart is placed in your slide and a data sheet is opened on top, as shown in Figure 5-26. The data sheet contains sample data.

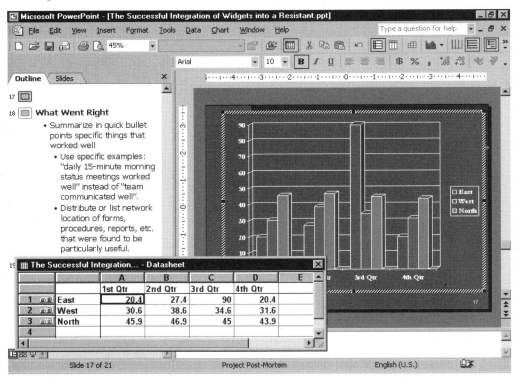

Figure 5-26 A sample chart opened with a sample data sheet on top of it.

3. Edit the data sheet.

Replace the information in the data sheet with labels and values of your own, adding or subtracting columns or rows as necessary. Notice that the chart changes as you edit the data, as shown in Figure 5-27. Also notice that the Standard toolbar changes to a Chart toolbar.

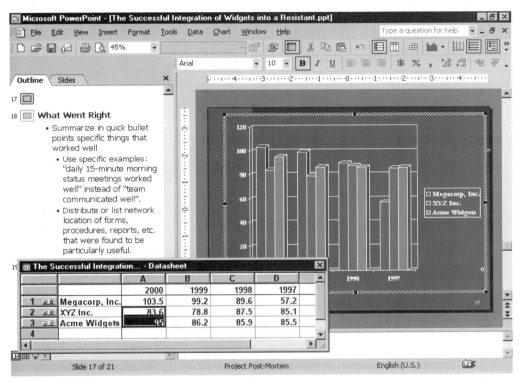

Figure 5-27 Editing the data sheet also changes the chart.

4. Turn off Chart.

Click off of the chart area within the slide. Chart is turned off, and the data sheet closes, as shown in Figure 5-28. To reposition your chart, drag it to a new location on the slide with the mouse.

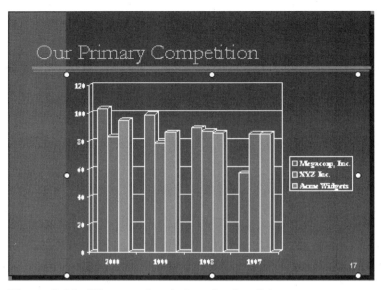

Figure 5-28 The completed chart in the slide.

Customizing Your Master Slide

A Master Slide is the blueprint for all of the slides based on it in the presentation. Objects that show on every slide are held there. A good example would be a company logo that you want to appear on each slide. The Master Slide also dictates the arrangement of text as well as the font face, size, and color.

There are, by default, two Master Slides. One is the Slide Master, the other the Title Master. If you want to change an object on your title slide, you would use the Title Master. All other slides would be affected by the Slide Master. The techniques of editing both Master Slides are the same. To edit the Slide Master or Title Master, follow these steps:

1. Access the Master Slide.

Click the View menu, click Master, and then click Slide Master. The Master view is displayed, as shown in Figure 5-29.

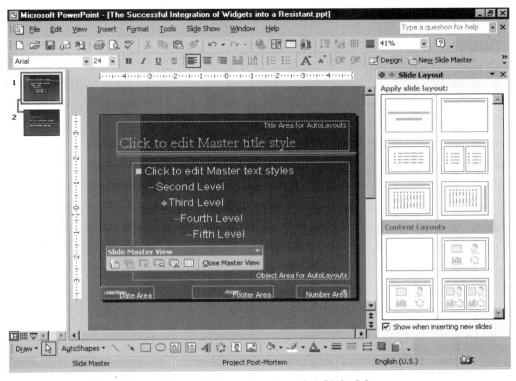

Figure 5-29 The Master View window showing the Slide Master.

2. Select the Slide Master or Title Master.

From the Preview pane to the left of the window, select the Slide Master or the Title Master. The Slide Master is usually the top one with the Title Master below it. To be certain which is which, click on one preview and its name appears in the status bar at the bottom of the screen. The selected Master also appears in the main window.

3. Edit the Master.

After the Master appears in the PowerPoint window, you can select and edit any of the elements on it. Just keep in mind that anything you place on the Master affects all of the slides that are based on it. Here are some of the areas you may want to adjust:

- Date area. This area, found in the lower left of the Master Slide, allows you to place a date on your slides. This is probably not as important for an onscreen slide show as it is for a printed presentation. Click where it says <Date/Time>, and enter the appropriate date.

- Footer area. Found in the center of the lower edge of the Master Slide, the footer allows you to place any text that needs to be on all slides. An example might be the company name or the word *Confidential*. Click the <footer> text, and enter your information.

- Number area. It is sometimes helpful to have slides numbered. This area adds a number to your slides automatically. In our example, we chose to have the pages numbered during the AutoContent Wizard. If this is not turned on, however, you can do so by clicking the Insert menu and clicking Slide Number.

- Text face, size, and color. To establish the text scheme for the presentation, click the text block you want to format. Using the Formatting toolbar, select the type face, size, and color you want to use.

- Bullets for levels. In the lower text box on the Master, the bullets that are used for five levels of bulleted points are shown. If you want to edit this list (change the bullets), click the level you want to edit, click the Format menu, and then click Bullets And Numbering. Click the Bulleted tab, if necessary, and then select the bullet you want from the list. Click OK.

- Graphics and background. In addition to the elements mentioned above, you can change the slide design by selecting any design object, including clip art, and editing it as you wish. To add new graphics to the Master, click the Insert menu, click Picture, and then either click Clip Art to take you to the Media Gallery or click From File to allow you to locate the graphic on your hard drive or from a floppy disk.

4. **Close the Master view.**

   After you have edited the Master Slide to your satisfaction, click the Close Master View button on the Slide Master toolbar. Or click the View menu, and click Normal. If the slides don't look like you want them to, just repeat the process and edit the Master Slide again.

Polishing Your Slide Show

You've created your presentation. All the data is shown in the most effective way. Now you need to jazz up the onscreen presentation (also called the Slide Show in PowerPoint) with special effects to make it even more memorable. The following Slide Show effects do just that.

Adding Transitions

A transition is the way one slide leads into another. This can be as simple as one slide disappearing and another taking its place or it can be a very elaborate transition, such as the old slide dissolving into the new one or an eight-spoke wheel turning to reveal the next slide. Transitions are easy to affix to individual slides or to the entire presentation. To affix transitions, follow these steps:

1. **Open the Slide Transition task pane, as shown in Figure 5-30.**

   Click the Slide Show menu, and click Transition.

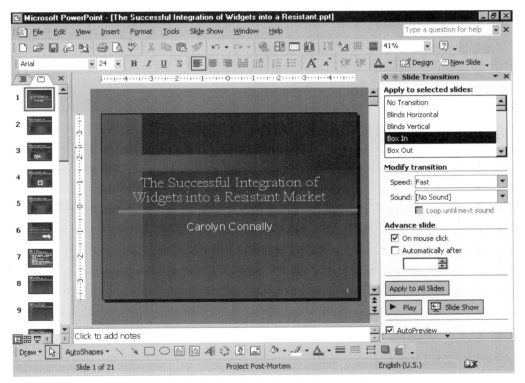

Figure 5-30 The PowerPoint window displaying the Slide Transition task pane.

2. **Select a slide.**

   From the Preview pane to the left of your screen, click the slide to which you want to apply a transition. If you want to apply the transition to all slides in the presentation, it doesn't matter which slide is selected.

3. **Select a transition.**

In the Slide Transition task pane, select a transition from the Apply To Selected Slides section. As you click a transition, its effect is demonstrated on the selected slide.

4. **Modify the transition.**

Here is where you establish how quickly you want to transition from one slide to another and what sounds you want to be associated with it. From the Speed drop-down list box, select Slow, Medium, or Fast. The effect and speed is demonstrated on the slide.

From the Sound drop-down list box, select the sound you want from the sounds available on your computer. This is demonstrated, as well. If you want to keep the sound looping until the next sound, select the check box. This is briefly demonstrated but is cut short.

5. **Choose slide advance settings.**

If you want to control when the slide advances, click the On Mouse Click check box. If you want to set a time for the slide to advance, click the Automatically After check box. If both are selected, the slide is advanced by a mouse click or after the determined number of seconds or minutes have elapsed.

6. **Add transitions to the remainder of your presentation.**

If you want to set the same transition for all slides, click the Apply To All Slides button. Otherwise, select another slide and repeat the process.

Adding PowerPoint Animation

PowerPoint animation is not as sophisticated as Mickey Mouse marching and singing across the screen. However, it is a clever way to maintain attention, emphasize points, and dress up your presentation. For best results, use in restraint.

Animation Schemes

Animation schemes are sets of animation already configured by PowerPoint that are available for you to apply to a slide or your entire presentation. These schemes include transitions, so you do not need to set transitions on those slides to which you are applying animation schemes. To apply an animation scheme, follow these steps:

1. **Open the Slide Design task pane, as shown in Figure 5-31.**

Click the Slide Show menu, and click Animation Schemes. The Slide Design task pane appears with Animation Schemes selected.

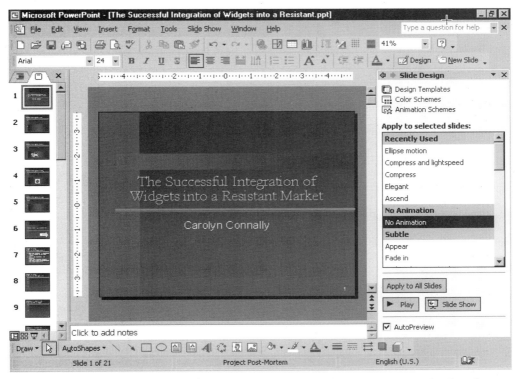

Figure 5-31 The PowerPoint window with the Slide Design task pane displayed.

2. Select a slide.

From the Preview pane to the left of your screen, click the slide to which you want to apply an Animation Scheme. If you want to apply the same animation to all slides in the presentation, it doesn't matter which slide is selected.

3. Select an animation scheme.

Select an animation scheme from the Apply To Selected Slides section in the Slide Design task pane. As you click a scheme, its effect is demonstrated on the selected slide. The schemes are grouped by the following categories: Recently Used, No Animation, Subtle, Moderate, and Exciting. Consider your audience, and select a scheme accordingly

4. Add animation to the remainder of your presentation.

If you want to set the same transition for all slides, click the Apply To All Slides button. Otherwise, select another slide and repeat the process.

Custom Animation

Custom animation allows you to set specific actions to specific objects on a slide. These settings are set slide by slide. Because individual objects must be selected on each slide, there is no Apply To All Slides command. To apply custom animation, follow these steps:

1. Open the Animation Schemes task pane, as shown in Figure 5-32.

Click the Slide Show menu, and click Custom Animation.

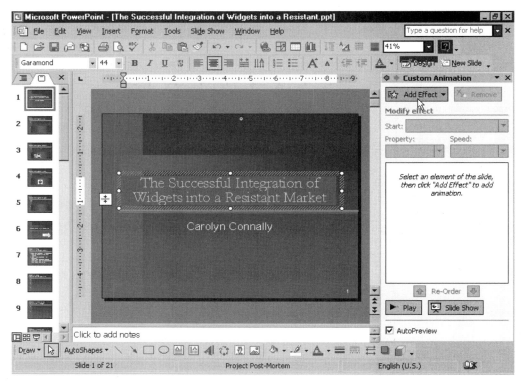

Figure 5-32 The Custom Animation task pane.

2. Select a slide.

From the Preview pane to the left of your screen, click the slide to which you want to apply an Animation Scheme. The selected slide appears in the PowerPoint window.

3. Select an object.

Select a text or graphic object on your slide by clicking it.

TIP *If you cannot select an object, it may be on your Master Slide. To apply animation to that object, you must open the Master Slide, as described above, and apply animation from there.*

4. Select an effect.

From the Add Effect menu, as shown in Figure 5-33, select whether you want the animation to provide an Entrance or an Exit, an Emphasis or a Motion Path. Then select a specific effect from the submenu.

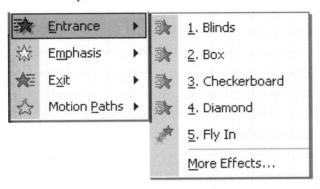

Figure 5-33 The Add Effect menu.

5. Modify the effect.

Depending upon the effect you choose, you are asked to modify the effect with your choices. For example, if you selected the Fly-In Entrance effect for the slide's title, you need to specify when the effect starts, what direction the title flies-in from, and whether you want the animation to be Very Slow, Slow, Medium, Fast, or Very Fast. To remove an effect, select the effect where it is listed in the center of the Custom Animation task pane and then click the Remove button.

6. Preview your work.

Although PowerPoint demonstrates the animation effect with each setting, you can initiate all of the animations on the selected slide by clicking the Play button.

To run the entire slide show to get the full effect of your animation choices, click the Slide Show button. The slide show starts from the selected slide. If you want it to run from the beginning, select the first slide before running the show. To end a running slide show, right-click and choose End Show from the shortcut menu.

NOTE   *With some effects, Motion Path for example, the path appears on your screen. This is for your information and it does not appear in your slide show.*

Setting Slide Show Timing

If you want the presentation to run without your control, you can set timings for each slide and each effect on the slide. This is done by running the slide show and clicking when you want an effect or a transition to take place. PowerPoint times each command and saves it so that the presentation runs automatically.

1. **Start timing.**

   Click the Slide Show menu, and click Rehearse Timings. A timing meter, showing total time elapsed for the current effect and the total for the presentation at that point, is displayed. The slide show timing begins immediately, as shown in Figure 5-34.

Figure 5-34 The Slide Show Rehearsal Meter.

2. **Set timings.**

   Run through the presentation, clicking your mouse to forward slides and effects, allowing an appropriate time for your audience to view the slides. Continue until you reach the end of the slide show. At the end of the show, right-click the screen and select End Show.

3. **Accept or reject timings.**

   When the slide show has ended, a dialog box is displayed asking if you want to save the timings, as shown in Figure 5-35. Click Yes if you are satisfied with the settings. If you want to try it again, click No.

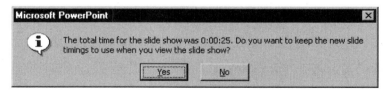

Figure 5-35 The Slide Show Timings Acceptance box.

When the slide show runs, it automatically progresses using the timings you set for it.

Guidelines to Effective Presentations

Although PowerPoint provides remarkable tools for building an effective presentation, using those tools is just a part of the knock-their-socks-off presentation that you want. So we are including this section to give you some simple guidelines to keep in mind as you work with PowerPoint.

Know Your Audience

- Write your presentation for the audience you will present it to, rather than for yourself or even someone else.

- If your audience is highly conservative and/or sophisticated, leave out cute graphics and keep animation sedate.

- If your audience averages 40 to 50 years of age or even older, limit the typefaces to three at the most and use soft, complementary colors. (This has less to do with actual age, by the way, than the style that was considered acceptable when they were forming opinions.)

- If your audience is 30 or younger, use lots of action, lots of color, and a larger variety of fonts. Set items on an angle. Use unusual shapes to back text.

- If your audience is between 30 and 40, use a combination of the latter two styles.

- Keep in mind that just because you *can* do something in PowerPoint does not necessarily mean you *should* do it.

Text

- Keep presentation text short and to the point. Use only brief descriptions. Save longer explanations for your verbal accompaniment.

- Use no more than three levels of bullet points.

- Use fewer than eight bullet points per slide (three or four is actually better). If you have more information than that, separate it into additional slides.

- Use a *minimum* font size of 24 points. Larger is better.

- Use font colors that are easily read against the background color.

- Absolutely do not fill your slide up with text. Leave lots of white space (blank area) around the text so it can breathe.

Colors

- Blues and greens are soothing. Reds, oranges, and bright yellows are exciting. Consider the result you want from your presentation and choose colors accordingly.

- Use a consistent color scheme throughout.

- Consider the impact of colors on your audience. For example, red means deficit in the financial world. A presentation with red text would not come across as positive to an audience of bankers.

- Understand cultural interpretations of colors as well. Red is a color denoting good fortune in many Asian cultures, for example.

Graphics

- Avoid cute or cartoon graphics in presentations to conservative audiences.

- If a graphic denotes action, the action should move into the slide, not off of it.

- If a graphic has a face (as in a person or caricature) it should face into the slide, not off of it.

- Use graphics that augment your text, not distract from it.

- Use a consistent style of graphic throughout. In other words, do not mix cartoons with line drawings; modern styles with old-fashioned ones.

Making Your Presentation

- Smile. Let the audience know that you are glad to be there.

- Introduce yourself. Explain why you are the one making this presentation.

- Explain your objectives for the presentation.

- Speak slowly. Do not rush.

- Don't worry about making mistakes. If you know your subject, the audience will easily forgive slight mix-ups.

- Don't read the slide to your audience. Elaborate on it. Explain it. But let the audience do the reading themselves.

- Be sure to give enough time to each slide and each point on the slide for its meaning to be absorbed.

- Allow time for questions. State up-front whether you welcome questions during the presentation or want them to be held to the end.

- If you want to elicit some action from your audience, be sure to request that they do so. Call for them to take an action, make a change, work toward a goal, or otherwise follow your suggestions. A frequent mistake of presenters is to assume that the audience knows what they want them to do; therefore, they never ask for the action to take place. Always end by making an appropriate call for action.

Summary

PowerPoint is more important to the business individual than any presentation software ever before. Today's technology is making a PowerPoint computer slide show the standard for business presentations of all types.

In this chapter we discussed ways in which to create a presentation and then enhance it. Although there are many ways to present PowerPoint slides other than a computer slide show (print, color or black-and-white transparencies, and 35mm slides), the slide show is rapidly becoming the most used. Therefore, we looked at animation, transitions, and predetermined timings. And because the success of a presentation is not only based on the outline and graphics you create, we included guidelines for making the actual presentation.

Chapter 6

OUTLOOK BASICS

Featuring:

- Understanding Outlook
- Exploring the Outlook Application Window
- Managing Tasks
- Using Calendar
- Taking Notes
- Using Outlook to Send and Receive E-Mail
- Printing in Outlook

It's always been important in the business world to have a system for managing your contacts, your schedule, and your to-do list as well as for staying on top of personal information. Several years ago, the organizer notebook appeared on the scene, and many corporations provided organizers to their employees as well as seminars on how to use them to be more productive. In an organizer loose-leaf notebook, you could keep contact information, credit cards, a scheduling calendar, a to-do list, a calculator, and all sorts of other items—all in one place. Lots of business professionals viewed the organizer notebook as a lifesaver, carrying it with them wherever they went.

Today, it's still not uncommon to sit down in a meeting and see several of the participants pull out their organizers, but a new class of software, called *personal information managers (PIM),* is quickly replacing the loose-leaf notebook as well as all the other scraps of paper that cover the desks of many of us. Commonly a PIM includes an address and phone book, a scheduler, a to-do list manager, and the ability to keep notes and track interactions with contacts. The ideal PIM has been described as an intelligent desk drawer, into which you could scoop all the scraps of paper on your desktop. The PIM would then retrieve exactly the scrap you wanted whenever you ask for it.

Today, PIMs are available at many Web sites, and they are available for handheld computers as well as desktop computers. All the major productivity applications suites include a PIM, and in this chapter we'll look at Outlook, the PIM that's included with Office.

Understanding Outlook

When you install Office, the Setup program places a shortcut to Outlook on your Microsoft Windows desktop. Simply double-click the shortcut to open the program. By default, Outlook opens at your Inbox, the Outlook source for sending and receiving electronic mail. But as you can see in Figure 6-1, Outlook is much more than an e-mail program. You use different parts of the application, called *modules,* to track your appointments, create and maintain a contacts database, keep your to-do lists, and take notes.

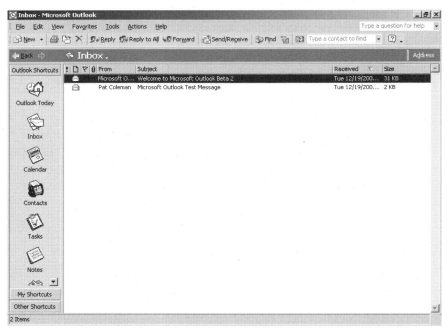

Figure 6-1   Outlook open at the Inbox.

This chapter discusses the basics of using the Inbox, Calendar, Tasks, and Notes modules. Chapter 14 discusses in detail how to create a Contacts database.

Exploring the Outlook Application Window

Figure 6-2 shows the Outlook window as it appears when you click the Outlook To-day icon in the Outlook bar, the area that runs vertically on the far left side of the screen. At the top of the window is the title bar, which identifies the application and the currently running module. At the far right on the title bar are the standard Windows Minimize, Restore, and Close buttons.

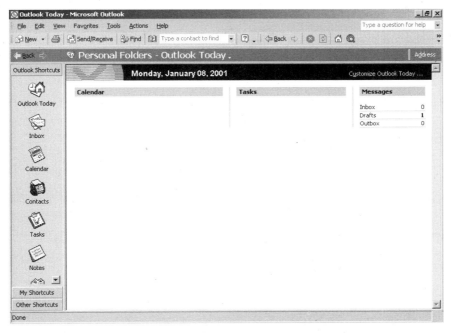

Figure 6-2 The Outlook application window.

Beneath the title bar are the menu bar and the combined Standard and Web toolbar. At the very bottom of the window is the status bar, which displays messages and information, such as how many items are in the current module. The large area to the right of the Outlook bar is called the Information Viewer. You can use the scroll bars to the right of the Information Viewer to see any information that does not appear in the display.

Every record in Outlook is an *item*—every e-mail message, appointment, note, or task. Items are stored in folders in the module in which the item was created.

The commands on the menus and the buttons on the toolbar depend on which module you are currently using. Point to a button on the toolbar to display a ScreenTip that describes the function of the button.

To open a module, simply click its icon in the Outlook bar.

Managing Tasks

In Outlook, you create and manage your to-do list using the Tasks module. In addition to the usual list-making, you can track the progress of a task, assign a task to someone else, set reminders for tasks, schedule time to complete tasks, and evaluate your progress. To open the Tasks module, click Tasks in the Outlook bar. If you haven't yet added any items, you'll see the screen shown in Figure 6-3.

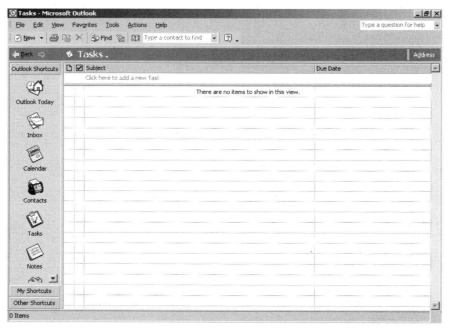

Figure 6-3   The Tasks module in Outlook.

To add a task to the list, click Click Here To Add A New Task. Enter the task in the Subject box, and then press the Tab key to move the insertion point to the Due Date box. You can type a date in any form, or click the down arrow to select a date from a calendar. Click the left- or right-pointing arrow to move to the previous or next month. After you enter the date, press the Enter key.

In most cases, you'll want to enter some details about the task, to take advantage of all the task management features in Outlook. Double-click the task in the list to open the Task form, as shown in Figure 6-4.

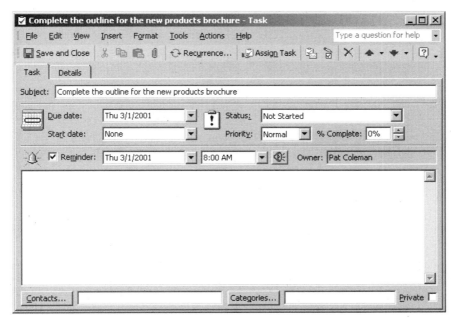

Figure 6-4   Filling in details about a task.

You can use the Task tab on the Task form to change the subject or the due date, to indicate the task's status and priority, and to set a reminder. Simply click any of the drop-down lists and make a selection.

Sometimes tracking the progress of a task is easier if you break the steps into categories. To do so, click the Categories button to open the Categories dialog box, as shown in Figure 6-5. You can use the preexisting categories in this dialog box or create a new category. To create a new category, click in the Item(s) Belong To These Categories box and then click the Add To List button.

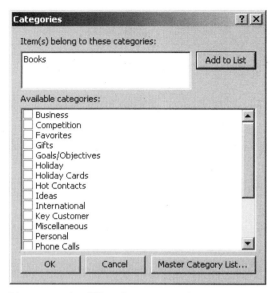

Figure 6-5   The Categories dialog box.

If you work on a network and share Outlook files, you may not want everybody in the office to see every task on your to-do list. In such a case, click the Private check box on the Task form.

Setting Up a Recurring Task

Most likely you have work-related tasks that must be tended to periodically, for example, writing a monthly report, compiling sales figures, or reviewing employees' compensation. In Outlook, you can enter the task once, and then specify how frequently it should recur. After you enter the task and due date initially, click the Recurrence button on the toolbar to open the Task Recurrence dialog box, as shown in Figure 6-6.

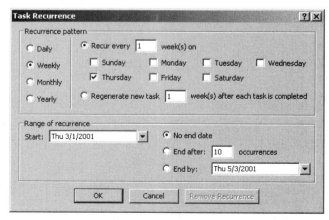

Figure 6-6   The Task Recurrence dialog box.

In the Recurrence Pattern section, indicate whether the task will occur daily, weekly, monthly, or yearly. The options in the right-hand portion of the Recurrence Pattern section will reflect your choice of pattern. Use these options to further refine how often the task will occur and to tell Outlook how long to wait after the completion of the task before generating the next one.

In the Range Of Recurrence section, indicate when Outlook should start entering the task and when to stop. After you've made your choices, click OK.

Assigning a Task to Someone Else

You can assign a task to another person if that person is running Outlook and has access to e-mail. Enter the task and due date on the Task form, and then click the Assign Task button on the toolbar to open a message window, as shown in Figure 6-7.

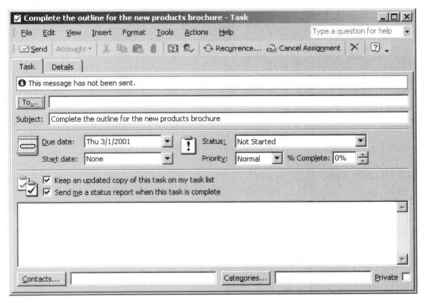

Figure 6-7   Assigning a task.

Enter the person's e-mail address in the To box, and add a message if you want. You can keep the task on your list and receive updates when the new owner updates the status of the task, or you can tell Outlook to send you a status report. Click the Keep An Updated Copy Of This Task On My Task List check box, or click the Send Me A Status Report When This Task Is Complete check box.

Your recipient is notified that his or her workload has increased when he or she receives an e-mail message labeled Task Request. The recipient can accept or decline the assignment by clicking the appropriate button on the form (though if you are the recipient's boss, it seems unlikely that he or she would summarily click the Decline button).

When the recipient clicks the Accept button, the task is automatically added to that person's task list. When the new owner of the task indicates that the task is completed, Outlook will notify you, and the task will be marked as complete on your task list.

Completing a Task

When you finish a task, click the check box next to the Subject box in the Tasks list. Outlook draws a line through the task and the due date, effectively crossing it off your list. If you want to record further information about the completed task, double-click the task to open the Task form, and click the Details tab, as shown in Figure 6-8.

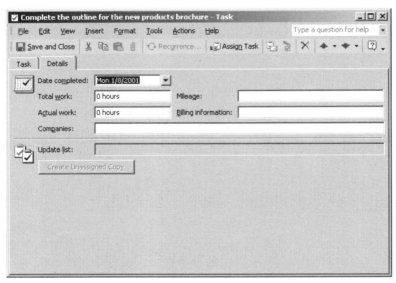

Figure 6-8   The Details tab in the Task form.

Use this tab to record the planned number of work hours in the Total Work box and to record the actual number of hours in the Actual Work box. If appropriate, you can enter mileage data, billing information, and so on.

Using Calendar

As we mentioned earlier, Calendar is the Outlook module you use to schedule appointments. To open Calendar, click its icon in the Outlook bar. You'll see something similar to Figure 6-9. This view shows a daily calendar, a monthly calendar in the Date Navigation area, and the TaskPad, which display all active tasks.

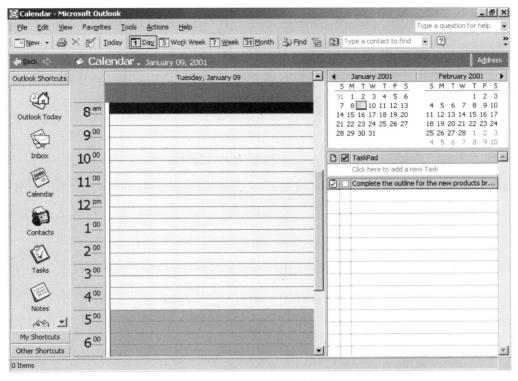

Figure 6-9   The Calendar in day, month, and TaskPad view.

You can also view Calendar by the workweek, by the calendar week, and by the month. To change the view, click the corresponding button on the toolbar (Day, Work Week, Week, or Month). If you prefer to display only one month instead of two in the Date Navigation area, point to the left border of the Date Navigation area. When the pointer changes to a resize arrow, drag the border to the right until only one month is visible. To change which months are shown, click the left- or right-pointing arrow.

TIP   *In the previous section, we entered tasks directly in the Tasks module, but you can also enter tasks in the TaskPad that's shown in the Calendar module.*

Scheduling an Appointment

To schedule an appointment in Day view, follow these steps:

1. Tell Calendar the date.

Click the date on the calendar in the Date Navigation area. That date will then appear at the top of the daily calendar.

2. Enter the appointment on the daily calendar.

Click in the time slot, and then type the notation for the appointment. If the appointment will last longer than one-half hour, click the lower border of the time slot and drag it to the end time of the appointment. Figure 6-10 shows a meeting that is scheduled to start at 10:00 A.M. and last until noon.

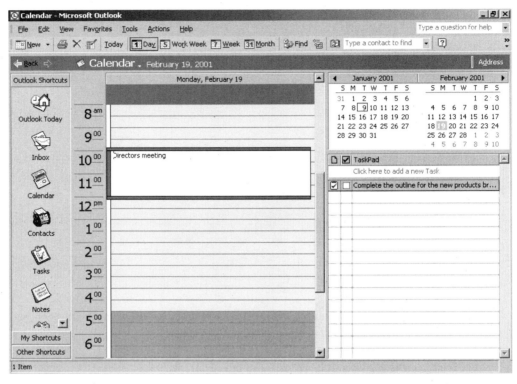

Figure 6-10   An appointment in the daily calendar.

As we all know, appointments have a way of changing. Here are some ways you can reschedule an appointment after you enter it in the daily calendar:

- To delete an appointment, right-click it, and then choose Delete from the shortcut menu.

- To move an appointment to another date, display the month in the Date Navigation area, select the appointment, and drag it to the new date. In the Appointment form that opens, fill in any details about the appointment, and then click the Save And Close button.

- To change the start or ending time of an appointment, drag the upper or lower border until the appropriate time slot is selected.

Adding Details About an Appointment

If you want to add details about an appointment, such as what you need to take to a meeting or any other preparation that will be necessary, double-click the appointment to open the Appointment form, as shown in Figure 6-11. You use this form in much the same way that you use the Task form. When you've finished adding details, click the Save And Close button to save the information.

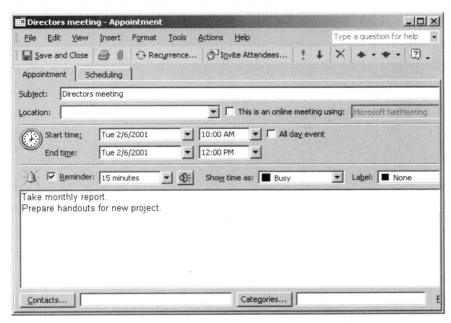

Figure 6-11   The Appointment form.

Setting a Reminder

When you schedule an appointment in Calendar, you'll be automatically reminded 15 minutes ahead of time if Outlook is running. A message dialog box will appear in whatever application you are using, accompanied by a sound, and you can then close the dialog box, ask to be reminded again, or open the Appointment form so that you can review details about the appointment.

You can also change the time when the reminder will appear or choose not to be reminded. To change the time, click the Reminder drop-down list box and select a time. If you don't want to be reminded, clear the check box next to the Reminder drop-down list box. To change the sound associated with the reminder, click the loudspeaker icon to open the Reminder Sound dialog box, as shown in Figure 6-12. Enter the path to the sound you want to use or browse for it, and then click OK. If you want to be reminded about an appointment but don't want to hear any sound, clear the Play This Sound check box.

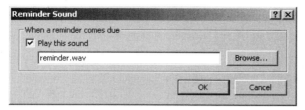

Figure 6-12   The Reminder Sound dialog box.

Scheduling a Recurring Appointment

If an appointment will occur repeatedly at regular intervals, click the Recurrence button on the toolbar in the Appointment form to open the Appointment Recurrence dialog box. You use the options in this dialog box almost exactly as you use those in the Task Recurrence dialog box, as shown in Figure 6-13. The only difference is that in the Appointment Time section, you need to enter a start time, an end time, and a duration for the appointment.

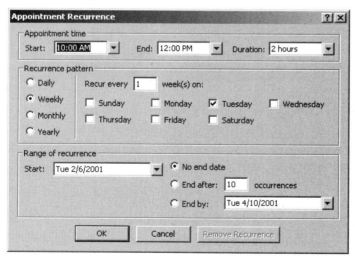

Figure 6-13   The Appointment Recurrence dialog box.

Scheduling an Event

Outlook distinguishes between an appointment and an event. An *appointment* has a start time and an end time and may last less than a day or more than a day. An *event* does not have a start time or an end time and can last an entire day or several days. A vacation, for example, is an event. To schedule an event, in Calendar click the Actions menu and then click New All Day Event to open the Event form, as shown in Figure 6-14.

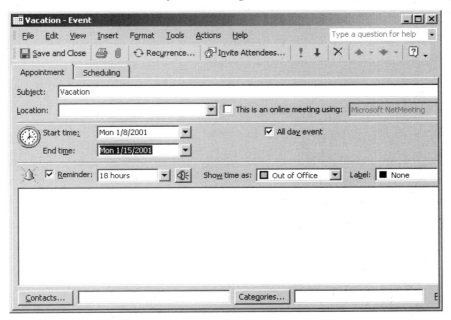

Figure 6-14 The Event form in Calendar.

Enter a title for the event in the Subject box, enter start and end dates, specify a reminder if you want one, and specify how to show the time on your calendar by selecting from the Show Time As drop-down list box. When you've completed the details, click the Save And Close button. The event will now be identified at the top of the daily calendar for each appropriate day.

Taking Notes

Outlook extends the "all in one place" feature to include a module for keeping track of odd bits of information, Notes. To enter a note, click the Notes icon on the Outlook bar, and then double-click in the Notes window to open the equivalent of a yellow sticky note. Type your note, and then click the Close button. You'll see an icon for the note in the Notes window, as shown in Figure 6-15.

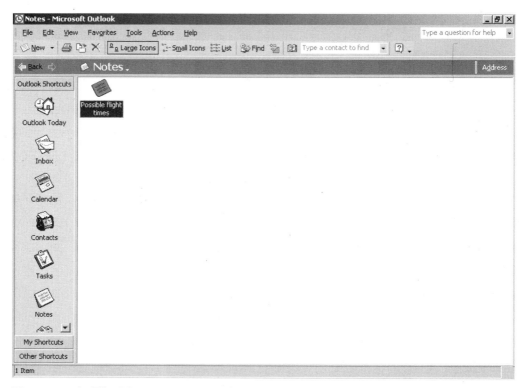

Figure 6-15 The Notes window.

When you enter a note and then close it, it is automatically date- and time-stamped and saved, and the entire contents of the note appear in the Notes window under its icon. Create a title for a note if you'd rather the entire contents not be displayed. Type a title as the first line, press the Enter key, and then type the rest of the note. Now only the title is displayed beneath the icon.

To read a note, double-click it. To dispose of a note in some way, right-click it and choose an option from the shortcut menu. Using this menu you can delete the note, print it, forward it to someone, change the color of the note, and place it in a category.

Using Outlook to Send and Receive E-Mail

Although Outlook is much more than a tool for e-mail communication, that is, of course, its primary purpose. Outlook is the parent application of Outlook Express, the e-mail application that is included with Windows.

Reading and Processing Messages

From the Outlook bar, click the Inbox icon to open your Inbox folder and read messages. Figure 6-16 shows the Inbox folder in Preview Pane view. Message headers appear in the upper pane, and you select a message to open it in the lower pane. To view messages in a separate window rather than using the Preview pane, click the View menu, and then click Preview Pane.

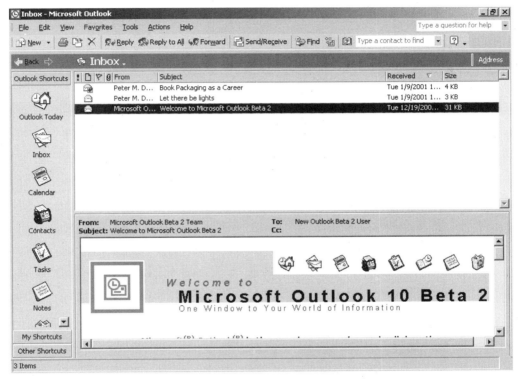

Figure 6-16   Reading a message in Preview Pane view.

If you are connected to the Internet, Outlook will automatically check the mail server for new messages and download them to your Inbox folder when you click the Send/Receive button on the toolbar. Depending on your network configuration (if you work on a corporate network), you can specify that Outlook check for new messages at regular intervals as along as you are connected to the Internet. To specify this interval, follow these steps:

1. **Open the Options dialog box at the Mail Setup tab, as shown in Figure 6-17.**

   Click the Tools menu, and then click Options. In the Options dialog box, click the Mail Setup tab.

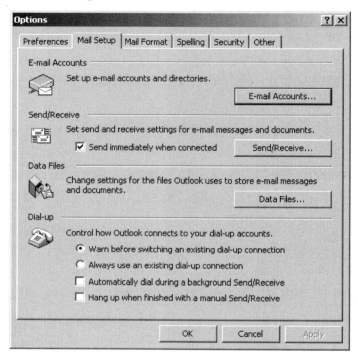

Figure 6-17 The Options dialog box open at the Mail Setup tab.

2. **Open the Send/Receive Groups dialog box, as shown in Figure 6-18.**

   Click the Send/Receive button.

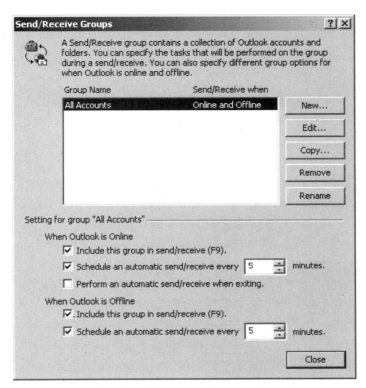

Figure 6-18 The Send/Receive Groups dialog box.

3. Change the time interval.

In the When Outlook Is Online section, click the Schedule An Automatic Send/Receive Every *x* Minutes check box, and then select the number of minutes in the spin box. In the When Outlook Is Offline section, click the Schedule An Automatic Send/Receive Every *x* Minutes check box, select the number of minutes in the spin box, and then click the Close button.

By default, Outlook plays a sound when new messages arrive in your mailbox. If you prefer silence, click the Preferences tab in the Options dialog box, and then click the Advanced E-Mail Options button to open the Advanced E-Mail Options dialog box, as shown in Figure 6-19. In the When New Items Arrive section, clear the Play A Sound check box, click OK, and then click OK twice again.

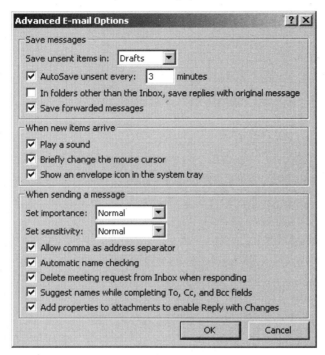

Figure 6-19 The Advanced E-Mail Options dialog box.

If you'd like a message displayed when new messages arrive, in the E-Mail Options dialog box, click the Display A Notification Message When New Mail Arrives check box, and then click OK.

Saving Messages

You can save messages in Windows Explorer folders or in Outlook folders, and you can also save attachments to messages. We'll look at attachments later in this chapter.

To save messages in Windows Explorer folders, open the message or select its header, and follow these steps:

1. Open the Save As dialog box, as shown in Figure 6-20.

Click the File menu, and then click Save As.

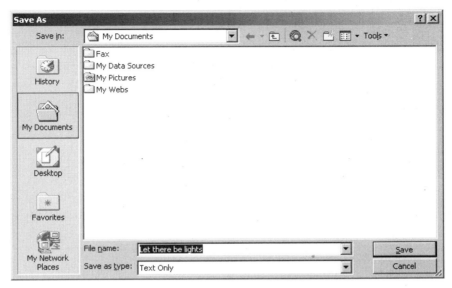

Figure 6-20 The Save As dialog box.

2. Select a folder.

Select a folder, and then accept the filename that's suggested, or type a new filename.

3. Select a file type.

In the Save As Type drop-down list box, choose how to save the message, and then click Save.

You can also create your own folders. For example, you might want to create a folder for a project and then place all correspondence related to that project in that folder. Or you might want to create a folder for a person and place all messages from that person in that folder. To create a new Outlook folder, follow these steps:

1. Open the Create New Folder dialog box, as shown in Figure 6-21.

Click the New drop-down list, and then click Folder.

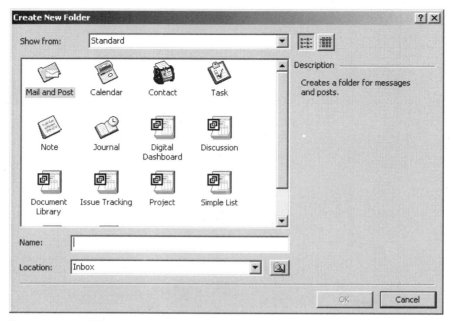

Figure 6-21 The Create New Folder dialog box.

2. Name the folder.

In the Name box, enter a name for the folder.

3. Select a folder in which to place the new folder.

Click the Select Folder button next to the Location list to open the Select Folder dialog box, as shown in Figure 6-22. Select a folder, and then click OK. Click OK again in the Create New Folder dialog box.

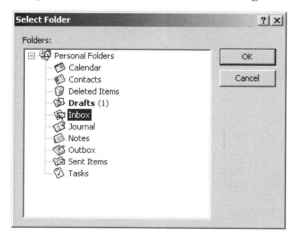

Figure 6-22 The Select Folder dialog box.

Marking Messages

You don't need to read and process every message as it arrives in your Inbox. When you're checking mail, you can mark messages so that when you have time you can go back and deal with them. If you've read a message but want to read it again later and respond, you can mark it as unread. Select the message header, click the Edit menu, and then click Mark As Unread. Now instead of an open envelope preceding the header, you'll see a closed envelope, and the header is in boldface.

You can also flag a message so that you can deal with it later. Select the message header, click the Actions menu, and click Follow Up to open the Flag For Follow Up dialog box. Select an action from the Flag To drop-down list box, assign a date and time by which to follow up, and click OK.

Replying to Messages

To reply to a message from a single sender, you simply click the Reply button on the toolbar. If the message was sent to multiple recipients, you can reply to them as well as the sender by clicking the Reply To All button.

By default, Outlook Express includes the text of the original message in your reply. Sometimes this can be helpful, and at other times it can be a real nuisance, especially if you have to wade through several replies to get to the essence of the message. You have a couple of alternatives if you don't want the original message included in the reply. You can click the Reply button, place your cursor in the body of the message, click the Edit menu, click Select All to highlight the message, and press the Delete key. Or you can follow these steps to tell Outlook never to include the original message in the reply:

1. **Open the Options dialog box.**

   Click the Tools menu, and then click Options.

2. **Open the E-Mail Options dialog box.**

   In the Options dialog box, click the Preferences tab, and then click the E-Mail Options button.

3. **Tell Outlook not to include the original message.**

   In the On Replies And Forwards section, click the When Replying To A Message drop-down list, and select Do Not Include Original Message. Click OK.

Forwarding Messages

Sometimes it's very handy to forward a message, and you can include your own comments in the forwarded message as well. As is the case with passing along anything that was created by somebody else, be sure that forwarding a message will not infringe on the original sender. Of course, some people maintain that you should never put anything in an e-mail message that you wouldn't want to see on the front page of the newspaper—but that's probably a topic for discussion at happy hour.

To forward a message, open it, click the Forward button, enter an e-mail address, add your comments if you want, and click the Send button.

Deleting Messages

You can delete a message in the following ways:

- Select the message header, and press the Delete key.
- Open the message, and press the Delete key.
- Right-click the message header, and choose Delete from the shortcut menu.

By default, deleted messages are placed in the Deleted Items folder, and they stay there until you manually delete them. To do so, click the Tools menu, click Empty "Deleted Items" Folder, and then click Yes when you're asked if you want to delete these items.

To automatically clear the Deleted Items folder when you close Outlook Express, follow these steps:

1. **Open the Options dialog box.**

   Click the Tools menu, and then click Options.

2. **Click the Other tab, as shown in Figure 6-23.**

   Click the Other tab, click the Empty The Deleted Items Folder Upon Exiting check box, and then click OK.

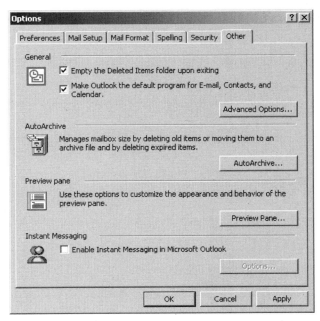

Figure 6-23   The Options dialog box open at the Other tab.

Creating and Sending Messages

You can create a message in three formats:

- HTML (HyperText Markup Language), which creates a message as a Web page.

- Rich text, which is a format originally developed to transfer documents between applications running on different operating systems.

- Plain text, which includes no formatting and is a document in the basic ASCII character set.

By default, Outlook uses HTML. As you'll see in the next section, not all e-mail programs can deal with HTML messages, so you'll want to use that with caution.

Creating a Plain Text Message

To compose and send a message in plain text, follow these steps:

1. Open the Message window, as shown in Figure 6-24.

Click the New button on the toolbar.

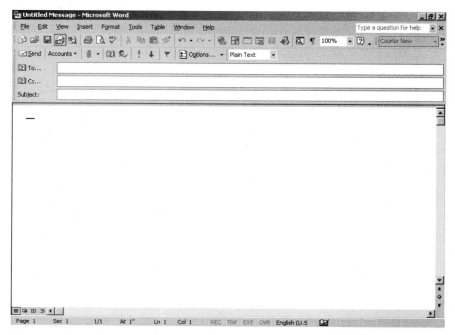

Figure 6-24 The Message window.

2. Specify plain text format.

Click the Message Format drop-down list box, and choose Plain Text.

3. Address and compose your message.

In the To line, enter an e-mail address, or click the icon to open your Address Book or Contacts list and select the address. Follow the same procedure to copy someone on the message. To send a blind carbon copy of the message, click the Cc icon to open the Select Names dialog box, select a name from the list, and click the Bcc button. Enter a subject in the Subject line, place the cursor in the message body, and type your message.

4. Send the message.

Click the Send button.

NOTE   *To create a message in rich text format, follow these same steps, but in step 2, select Rich Text.*

By default, messages are sent immediately if you are connected to the Internet. If you prefer to wait and send a message later or send all your messages at one time when you click the Send/Receive button, follow these steps:

1. **Open the Options dialog box.**

   In the main Inbox window, click the Tools menu, and then click Options.

2. **Tell Outlook not to send messages immediately.**

   Click the Mail Setup tab, and then in the Send/Receive section, clear the Send Immediately When Connected check box, and click OK.

Using HTML

When you use HTML to create a message, you are essentially creating a Web page, and you can include several neat effects, such as a background color or image, sound, and so on. The drawback, as I mentioned earlier, is that not all e-mail programs can deal with these Web pages. In most cases, these programs will convert the message to plain text, and all your careful formatting will be lost.

When you open the Message window, you are essentially working in Word. All the Word formatting tools are available, and you can use them to do the following, among other things, in your message:

- Insert a bulleted list.

- Add effects such as boldface, italics, underline, and font color.

- Insert a numbered list.

- Format paragraphs as flush left, flush right, or centered.

- Insert a horizontal line.

- Insert a picture.

- Insert a table.

- Specify a font and font size.

Sending Files with Messages

Earlier in this chapter, we mentioned that you can save files that are attached to messages. Obviously, you can also attach files to messages. Before getting into the details, though, we need to remind you that some rather serious computer viruses make the rounds via attachments to e-mail. Many businesses would cease to function these days if they couldn't e-mail files to colleagues and clients, so abandoning the use of file attachments is not an option. To be on the safe side, we recommend not opening an attachment if you don't know the source; just select the message header, and press the

Delete key. And I'd say to be particularly wary of an attachment that appears to have been forwarded, and forwarded, and forwarded.

When you receive a message that has a file attached to it, you'll see a paper-clip icon preceding the header. When you open the message, you'll see the filename of the attachment in the Attach line. If the file is in a format that a program on your computer can read, simply double-click the filename of the attachment to open it. To save the attachment, follow these steps:

1. Open the Save Attachments dialog box.

Click the File menu, and choose Save Attachments.

2. Save the file.

In the Save In box, specify a folder into which to save the file, and click Save.

To attach a file to a message you are composing, follow these steps:

1. Open the Insert File dialog box, as shown in Figure 6-25.

Click the Insert menu, and choose File.

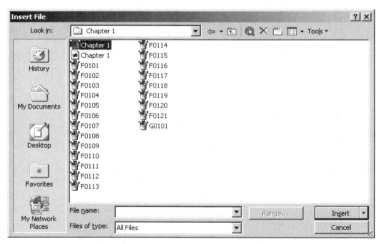

Figure 6-25 The Insert File dialog box.

2. Attach the file.

Enter the filename in the File Name box or browse to find it, and then click Insert.

Your message now contains the name of the file in the Attach line.

Creating a Signature

Many people never bother to sign their e-mail messages. After all, their name appears in the From line. Others create elaborate signatures that are automatically appended to all messages. Your business or organization may, in fact, have guidelines about what you should include in a signature. It's common to include your name, title, the name of your organization, perhaps its physical address, and your phone number.

To create a signature that is automatically appended to all your messages, follow these steps:

1. **Open the Options dialog box at the Mail Format tab, as shown in Figure 6-26.**

   Click the Tools menu, click Options, and then click the Mail Format tab.

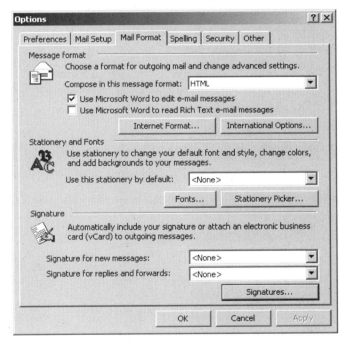

Figure 6-26 The Options dialog box open at the Mail Format tab.

2. **Open the Create Signature dialog box, as shown in Figure 6-27.**

   Click the Signatures button.

Figure 6-27   The Create Signature dialog box.

3. Open the Create New Signature dialog box, as shown in Figure 6-28.

Click the New button.

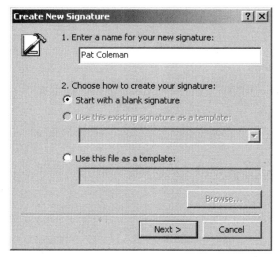

Figure 6-28   The Create New Signature dialog box.

4. Create a signature.

Enter your name in the first text box. If you have a file that contains the information you want in your signature, click the Use This File As A Template option button, and then click Browse to locate the file. If you are creating a signature from scratch, click the Start With A Blank Signature option button, and then click Next to open the Edit Signature dialog box, as shown Figure 6-29. Enter the text for your signature in the box, and then format it using the buttons underneath, just as you would format any Word document. When you're satisfied with your signature, click Finish. Close the Create Signature dialog box, and then click OK to close the Options dialog box.

Figure 6-29   The Edit Signature dialog box.

Organizing Messages

You are not at the mercy of your Inbox. You can automatically delete mail from certain senders, and you can route mail from other senders directly to a folder. You can also color-code your messages. To take care of these and other organizational tasks, click the Organize button on the toolbar to open the Ways To Organize Inbox window at the top of the Inbox, as shown in Figure 6-30. As you can see, this window has four tabs: Using Folders, Using Colors, Using Views, and Junk E-Mail.

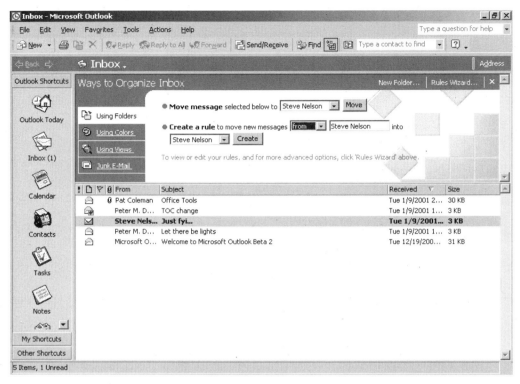

Figure 6-30 The Ways To Organize Inbox window.

Moving Messages

Earlier, this chapter looked at how to move messages into a particular folder and at how to create a new folder. You can also move messages and create folders using the Using Folder tab in the Ways To Organize Inbox window. Select the message, click the Move Message Selected Below To drop-down list box to select a folder, and then click the Move button. To create a new folder for the message, select Other Folder from the drop-down list to open the Select Folder dialog box (see Figure 6-22).

If you always want to move new messages from certain recipients into certain folders, select a message from that recipient in your Inbox, and select From from the Create A Rule To Move New Messages drop-down list. That recipient's name will appear in the next text box. Click the Into drop-down list to select a folder, and then click the Create button to create the rule. Now all messages from this recipient will be placed in the folder you selected when they arrive in your Inbox. To change this rule, click the Rules Wizard button to open the Rules Wizard, as shown in Figure 6-31. Click the appropriate button to delete this rule, create a new rule, copy the rules, change the rule, or rename or delete it.

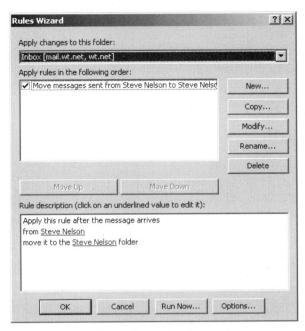

Figure 6-31   Using the Rules Wizard.

Color-Coding Messages

If you send and receive a lot of messages, color-coding message headers according to who sent them, who you sent messages to, and whether you were the only recipient might well help you prioritize your handling of them. To color-code message headers, you use the Using Colors tab, as shown in Figure 6-32. Select a message header, click the Using Colors tab, select From or Sent To in the Color Messages drop-down list, select a color in the In drop-down list, and click Apply Color.

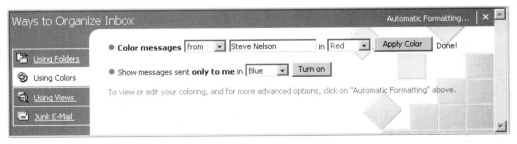

Figure 6-32   The Using Colors tab.

To apply a color to messages sent only to you, that is, you are not part of a distribution list or multiple recipients, select a color from the Show Messages Sent Only To Me In drop-down list, and then click the Turn On button. The Turn On button then becomes the Turn Off button, and you can click it to restore these messages to the original color.

To add or modify any color-coding rules you apply, click Automatic Formatting to open the Automatic Formatting dialog box. You can use the options in this dialog box to apply more elaborate formatting.

Changing Your Inbox View

By default, your Inbox displays in Messages view. To select another view, click the Using Views tab, as shown in Figure 6-33. Choosing a different view from the Change Your View list displays your Inbox in that view immediately. To see the possibilities, scroll through the list and click the various views. Figure 6-33 shows the Message Timeline view.

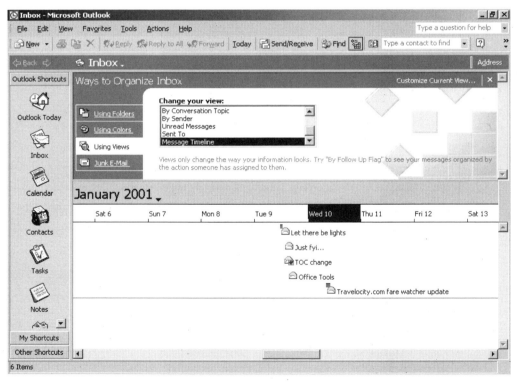

Figure 6-33 The Inbox in Message Timeline view.

Handling Junk and Adult-Content E-Mail

Though by its own admission, Outlook is not perfect at identifying junk and adult-content messages, it does a passable job. The filters that Outlook applies look for certain keywords and phrases. You can find a list of all of them in the filters.txt file in the folder in which Outlook is installed. Outlook searches for terms in both message headers and in the body of messages.

You can identify junk or adult-content messages by color-coding their headers, or you can simply get rid of them by specifying that they go straight to your Deleted Items folder. To color-code junk and adult-content messages, click the Junk E-Mail tab, as shown in Figure 6-34. Select a color in the same ways that you've done so in the other tabs, and then click the Turn On button to apply your color choices.

Figure 6-34 The Junk E-Mail tab.

To move junk or adult-content messages to your Deleted Items folder or to any other folder, in the Automatically drop-down list, select Move. Then in the Junk Messages To or the Adult Content Messages To drop-down list, select the folder, and click Turn On.

For tips about other ways to handle these types of messages, click the Click Here link.

Printing in Outlook

To print from any of the Outlook modules, display what you want to print on the screen, and then click the Print button on the toolbar. As is the case with all Windows applications, though, if you want more control over what's printed, click the File menu, and then click Print to open the Print dialog box, as shown in Figure 6-35.

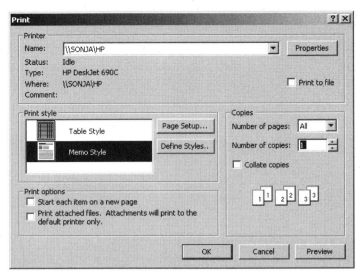

Figure 6-35 The Print dialog box in Outlook.

Many of the options in the Print dialog box are the same as those in most Windows applications. However, the options in the Print Style section depend on the module from which you are printing. The Table style and the Memo style are available in all modules:

- In Table style, data is formatted in rows and columns.

- In Memo style, data is formatted as a traditional memorandum.

Use the items in the Print Options section to tell Windows whether to start each item on a new page and whether to print attached files.

To see the setup options available in each module, open the module, click the File menu, and then click Page Setup.

Summary

This chapter has introduced you to some of the ways you can use Outlook as your personal information manager—to schedule appointments, to maintain a calendar, to create and manage to-do lists, and, of course, to send and receive e-mail messages. You can choose to use all or only some of the modules. As you begin to use the modules, you will also see how they are integrated, adding yet another tool to your organizational bag of tricks.

Chapter 7

ACCESS BASICS

Featuring:

- Access Terminology
- The Wonder of Wizards
- Creating a Blank Database
- Creating a Table
- Entering Data with a Form
- Analyzing Data with a Simple Query
- Publishing Your Data with an Access Report
- Sending a File to Excel
- Importing a File from Excel

Access is a highly sophisticated relational database management program that is included in the Office suite. Access stores and organizes an unlimited amount of data and provides the tools you need to analyze it. Use Access to find answers, share information, and make better decisions.

If you're an experienced database user, moving to Access from another program is an easy transition. If you're new to the world of databases, you have a somewhat steeper learning curve, but this chapter is here to get you started. In this chapter, we discuss the essential elements of an Access database: tables, forms, queries, and reports. First, however, let's begin with some terminology.

Access Terminology

Because Access approaches database management a little differently than some database programs you may have used, we need to define some basic Access terms:

- In Access, the word *database* is defined as the entire collection of data that is gathered together in one group. That means you can have several separate tables in Access, all within the same database, as well as queries and reports. As a whole, they are named and saved as a database.

- A *table* is a collection of data on one topic, for example, Customers' Orders Table. This table may overlap with other tables, such as Customers Accounts Receivable Table or Customers Mailing List. Separating customer information out in this manner keeps tables from being unwieldy and makes analysis workable.

- A *field* is a single data point. For example, First Name, Address, and SS# are each a field.

- A *record* is the total collection of data on one item or individual within a table. For example, the First Name, Last Name, Address, Address1, City, State, and Postal Code of a specific customer is that customer's record.

- A *query* is a question you ask of the database. Queries can be set up to run on fields from more than one table at a time. A query is the way to determine information about the data in the database. Queries can be simple or extremely complicated. (We will be dealing with simple queries in this chapter.) An example would be a query established to list all the customers who live in Austin, Texas.

- A *form* is a tool that can be used to simplify data entry. Using a form to enter a record takes you step-by-step through all the fields in that record.

- A *report*, of course, is a presentation of data arranged to provide certain information. Access reports are easily configured using the Report Wizard.

The Wonder of Wizards

More than any other program in the Office suite, Access uses wizards to create elements and tools, and to produce results. A *wizard* is a small program that produces a specific end-result after asking for information and preferences.

In Access, wizards save time by designing tables, queries, forms, and reports. All of these can be designed without the use of wizards, but wizards can save a lot of time and frustration, particularly if Access is new to you. In describing the development of Access elements and tools, we will be using the many wizards at our disposal.

Creating a Blank Database

Before you can create a table, you must create a database to store it in. To get started in Access, follow these steps:

1. Click the Blank Database link.

When you start the application, Access opens to a blank window with the New File task pane to the right. Click the Blank Database link, as shown in Figure 7-1, to open the File New Database dialog box.

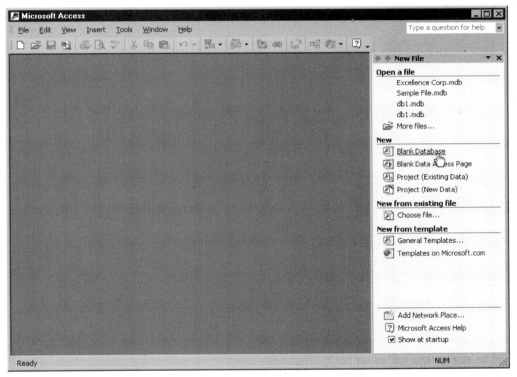

Figure 7-1   The New File task pane and the Blank Database link.

2. Name the new database.

Locate the folder in which you want to store the new database. Then name the new database, and click Create. The Database window appears. Although blank at this time, this is where all your tables, forms, queries, and reports are stored.

NOTE   *While working in Access, the Database window is shown as a separate button on your taskbar for easy activation.*

Creating a Table

While a field is the essential building block of Access, a table is the collector that holds the data together. For ease of use, an Access table should supply one essential group of information, such as customer contact information. To create a new, blank table, follow these steps:

1. **Start the Table Wizard.**

   In the Database window, click the Tables button on the Objects bar, if necessary. Then start the Table Wizard by double-clicking Create Table By Using Wizard, as shown in Figure 7-2.

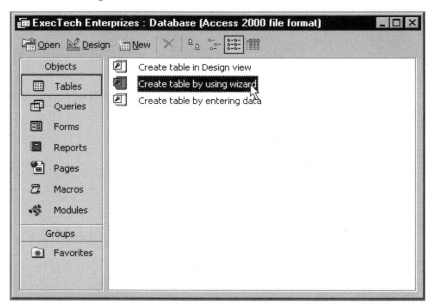

Figure 7-2   Starting the Table Wizard.

2. **Select the table type.**

   In the first screen of the Table Wizard, choose the type of table you're going to create. Access divides sample tables into two categories, Business and Personal. Each category provides a large number of sample tables from which to choose. Select a category, and then select a table type from the Sample Tables drop-down list box, as shown in Figure 7-3.

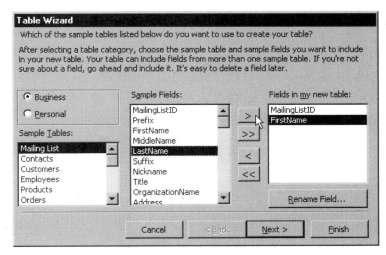

Figure 7-3   Selecting table options in the first Table Wizard screen.

3. Select table fields.

Each sample table has numerous fields typical to that kind of table. Move a field from the Sample Fields list to the Fields In My New Table list by selecting the field and clicking the top button with a right-pointing chevron. If you want to select all the fields in a sample table, click the second button with a right-pointing double chevron. Figure 7-3 shows fields being selected. Select the ID field in every table, because this field automatically provides a unique number for each record in the table.

If you want to remove fields from your table, click the left-pointing chevron to remove selected fields and click the left-pointing double chevron to remove all fields.

If you want to rename a field (for example, PostalCode to ZipCode), move the field to the list for the new table and then click the Rename Field button. In the Rename Field dialog box that appears, enter a new name and click OK. Click Next.

NOTE   *Be certain that the field you're renaming will serve in its new capacity. The sample fields are created with specific criteria (all numbers, for example, for PostalCode) so you could not use a PostalCode field for, say, County Name. PostalCode can successfully be changed to ZipCode because they are the same things. However, Canadian postal codes contain letters and cannot be entered in the PostalCode field as it first appears.*

4. Name your table, and set the primary key.

The second Table Wizard screen asks you to name the table you're creating and set a unique field called a *primary key*, as shown in Figure 7-4. Just type the name in the What Do You Want To Name Your Table? text box. Then click an option button below.

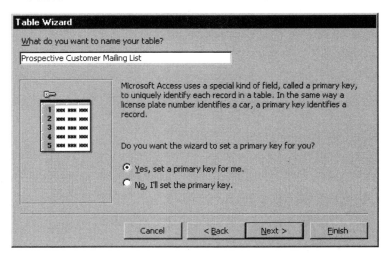

Figure 7-4   Naming your table and creating a primary key.

Until you're more familiar with the application, allow Access to set the primary key. (If you selected an ID field for your new table, it will probably serve as the primary key because it is truly unique. With the ID field automatically generating ID numbers for records, there are never two records with the same ID.) Then click Next.

5. Finish the wizard.

In the final screen of the Table Wizard, you're asked what you want to do next, as shown in Figure 7-5. After you're more familiar with Access, you may want to try your hand at altering a table's design, but for now we recommend that you click the Enter Data Directly Into The Table option button. (We discuss the use of forms in the next section.)

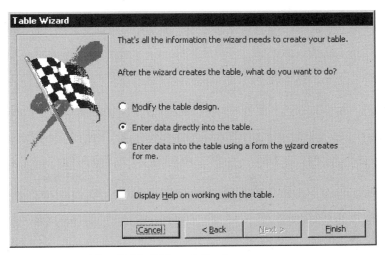

Figure 7-5   The Table Wizard final screen.

Click Finish. The wizard closes, and the empty table is displayed on your screen. Only one row (for one record) is available, but once you begin that record another row is created.

6. Enter data.

All that remains is to enter data in the table. You can do this right in the table, tabbing from one field to the next, as shown in Figure 7-6. Or you can create a form.

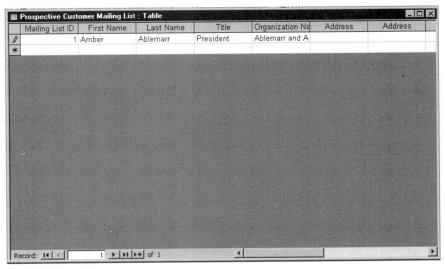

	Mailing List ID	First Name	Last Name	Title	Organization Na	Address	Address
	1	Amber	Ablemarr	President	Ablemarr and A		

Figure 7-6   Entering data in a new table.

Entering Data with a Form

Although it is a matter of personal preference, many people feel that entering data by using a form keeps the process on track and is much easier than entering data into the table. If you find that you, too, prefer the use of a form, clicking the Enter Data Into The Table Using A Form The Computer Creates For Me option button on the final Table Wizard screen causes a form to be automatically created for you.

To enter data using a form, click in the second field (the first is the ID and is automatically filled once you begin entering data) and enter the appropriate data. Press the Tab key to move from one field to the next. When you want to begin a new record, press the Enter key.

To create a form, follow these steps:

1. Select the form object.

In the Database window, click Forms on the Objects bar.

2. Start the Form Wizard.

Double-click Create Form By Using Wizard, as shown in Figure 7-7, to start the Form Wizard.

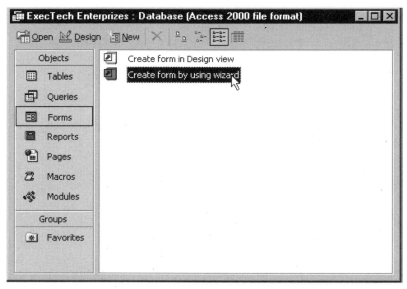

Figure 7-7   Starting the Form Wizard.

3. Select the fields.

In the first Form Wizard screen, select the fields that you want to appear on your form, as shown in Figure 7-8. To select all the fields, click the button with the right-pointing double chevron. When you're finished, click Next.

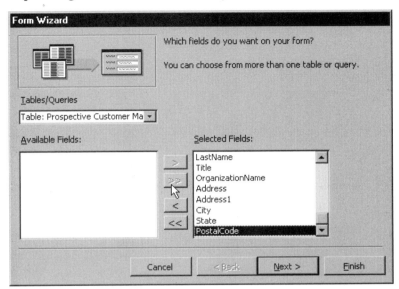

Figure 7-8   Selecting fields for the form.

4. Select a form layout.

The second Form Wizard screen asks you to choose how you want your form to look. Click one of the option buttons and view the preview, as shown in Figure 7-9. When you're finished, click Next.

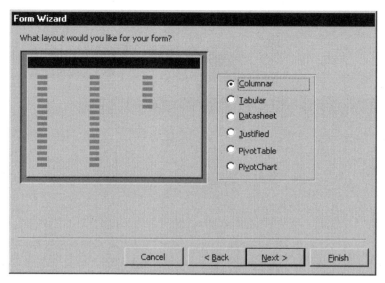

Figure 7-9 Choosing the form's layout.

5. Select a form style.

In the third Form Wizard screen, click one of the styles and view the preview. The Standard selection creates a simple form with a gray background; the others offer some interesting backgrounds, as shown in Figure 7-10. When you're finished, click Next.

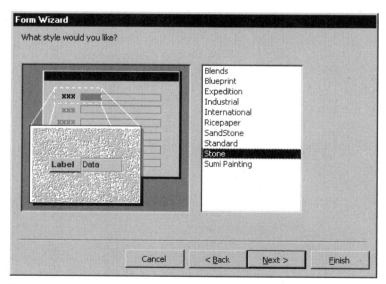

Figure 7-10 Selecting the form's style.

6. Name the form.

In the final Form Wizard screen, enter a name for your form in the box provided, as shown in Figure 7-11. Choose a name that identifies the table for which it was created.

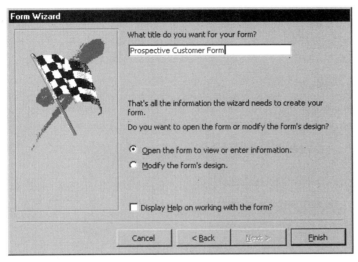

Figure 7-11 Entering a name for your form.

7. Finish the wizard.

Click the Open The Form To View Or Enter Information option button, and click Finish. Your new form opens, as shown in Figure 7-12. You can begin entering data, or close it until you're ready to do so.

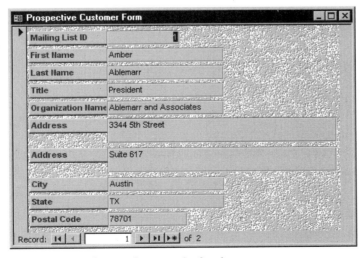

Figure 7-12 A new form ready for data entry.

Analyzing Data with a Simple Query

The purpose of a database is to store data. The purpose of a query is to retrieve that data in a fashion that provides you with information. For example, if we want to do a special mailing to our prospective customers who live in the states of Louisiana and Texas, we would design a query to run against our Prospective Customers Mailing List which would find and display those specific customers and their addresses. To do this, follow these steps:

1. Start the Query Wizard.

In the Database window, click Queries on the Objects bar, as shown in Figure 7-13. Then double-click Create Query By Using Wizard to open the Query Wizard.

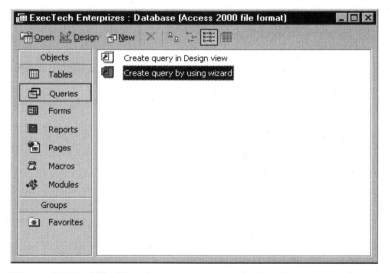

Figure 7-13 The Database window with the Queries object selected.

2. Select the tables or queries on which you want to base your query.

The first Query Wizard screen displays the name of a table and the fields located within that table, as shown in Figure 7-14. The Tables/Queries drop-down list box displays all tables and queries that have been created for your database. If the table name that is shown is not a table on which you are basing your query, click the drop-down arrow to display the list and select the appropriate table or query.

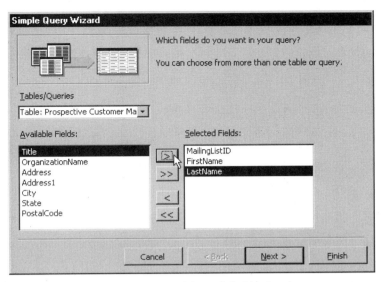

Figure 7-14 Selecting the table and fields for the query.

3. Select the fields for your query.

The fields that are contained in the selected table are displayed in the Available Fields list (see Figure 7-14). Select the fields you want shown in your completed query and move them into the Selected Fields box using the right-pointing chevron button. If you want all fields, use the button showing a right-pointing double chevron. Use the left-pointing chevron buttons to remove one field or all fields.

After your selection is complete, click Next.

TIP   *The fields that you choose should show all the information that you need. For example, if we are pulling all records with a Texas or Louisiana address so that we can send out a mailing, we would want the query to pull just those records but show ID, FirstName, LastName, Address, Address1, City, State, and PostalCode so that we would have the names and addresses for the mailing. It is better to pull too many fields than not enough.*

4. Name the query.

In the Query Wizard's final screen, enter a name for your query in the What Title Do You Want For Your Query? text box, as shown in Figure 7-15.

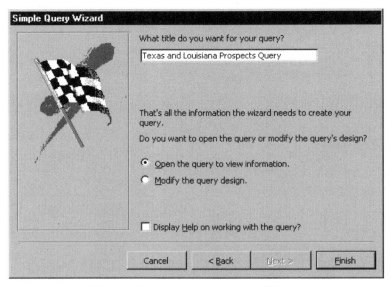

Figure 7-15 The final screen of the Query Wizard.

5. Finish the wizard.

Click the Open The Query To View Information option button, and click Finish. The basic query is displayed in Datasheet view, as shown in Figure 7-16.

Mailing List ID	First Name	Last Name	Title	Organization Na	Address	Address
1	Amber	Ablemarr	President	Ablemarr and A	3344 5th Street	Suite 617
2	Betty	Biedermeyer	Regional Direct(	Excellence Cor|	5391 Maple Stre	Building 5, Suite
3	David	Dattwieler	CEO	The Widget Sto	23456 Main Stre	
4	Ernest	Eagleman	Account Manag	Fix-it-uppers, In	63987 Harmony	Suite 159
5	Freida	Feinbinder		Feinbinder's	203 Central	
6	George	Garrison	Account Manag	XYZ Corp.	4596 Symphon|	
7	Heidi	Harrison	Sales Manager	Widgets for Les	23418 Grand P;	Suite 610
8	Ira	Inglebrecht		Progressive, Inc	19573 Military [	Suite 1269
9	Enrique	Bourdelon	Account Manag	Harbinger Parts	2936 Spicewoo(	
10	Jenny	Jensen	Vice-President !	Heath Health Pr	5666	125th Street
11	Karsten	Kellmann	Owner	Uptown Industri(	15986 Redwood	Suite 23
12	Noe	Hebert	Account Manag	Baton Rouge St	25698 Lightning	
13	Lucida	Lockridge		Best's Place	12368 Uptown E	
14	Marvin	McAllister	President	McAllister and F	1459 Overlook	Suite 652
15	Marjorie	McGivney		Table Rock Mar	116 Station Stre	
16	Nathan	Neighbors		Adams and Zett	459 Central Par	Suite 1259

Record: 14 ◄ | 1 | ► | ►| | ►* | of 16

Figure 7-16 The query in Datasheet view.

NOTE *Notice that the result is really just the original table reproduced with only the fields that you have chosen. Because we have not yet applied any criteria to the query, all records for all states are shown.*

6. Display the query in Design view.

With the query open on your screen, the Access toolbar has changed to the Query Design toolbar. Clicking the first button on that toolbar changes the view of the query from Datasheet view to Design view, as shown in Figure 7-17.

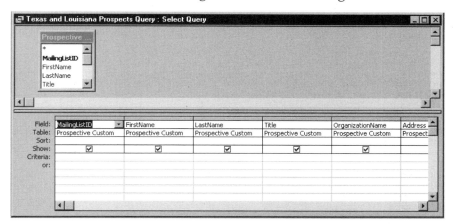

Figure 7-17 The new query in Design view.

7. Enter criteria.

In this example, we set the criteria of Texas or Louisiana. In the lower half of the Design View window, locate the row identified as Criteria. In that row, under the State field, enter TX or LA, as shown in Figure 7-18.

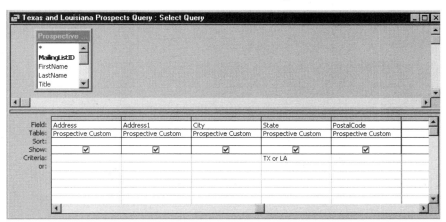

Figure 7-18 Setting query criteria.

We are using the U.S. Postal Service abbreviations because that is how the records were entered, and we are using *or* so that records from both states appear in the results.

(*And* would have told Access to show any records that had both TX and LA in the State field and we would have had zero results.)

8. **Run the query against criteria.**

Located about midway on the Design Query toolbar is the Run button, shown with a large red exclamation point. Clicking the Run button runs the query against the criteria and the results show only the records we designated, Texas and Louisiana, as shown in Figure 7-19. Save your resulting query.

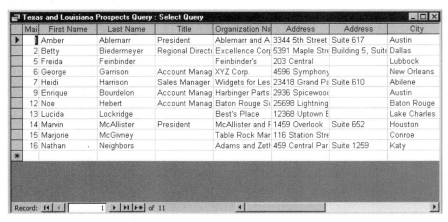

Mai	First Name	Last Name	Title	Organization Na	Address	Address	City
1	Amber	Ablemarr	President	Ablemarr and A	3344 5th Street	Suite 617	Austin
2	Betty	Biedermeyer	Regional Directc	Excellence Corp	5391 Maple Str	Building 5, Suitc	Dallas
5	Freida	Feinbinder		Feinbinder's	203 Central		Lubbock
6	George	Garrison	Account Manag	XYZ Corp.	4596 Symphony		New Orleans
7	Heidi	Harrison	Sales Manager	Widgets for Les	23418 Grand Pa	Suite 610	Abilene
9	Enrique	Bourdelon	Account Manag	Harbinger Parts	2936 Spicewooc		Austin
12	Noe	Hebert	Account Manag	Baton Rouge Su	25698 Lightning		Baton Rouge
13	Lucida	Lockridge		Best's Place	12368 Uptown E		Lake Charles
14	Marvin	McAllister	President	McAllister and F	1459 Overlook	Suite 652	Houston
15	Marjorie	McGivney		Table Rock Mar	116 Station Stre		Conroe
16	Nathan	Neighbors		Adams and Zeth	459 Central Par	Suite 1259	Katy

Record: 1 of 11

Figure 7-19 The completed query.

Publishing Your Data with an Access Report

Access offers a quick and easy way to publish your data: an Access report. A report may be based on any combination of tables and queries in your database. Additionally, Access offers several formats and styles from which to choose.

1. **Start the Report Wizard.**

In the Database window, click Reports on the Objects bar, as shown in Figure 7-20. Then double-click Create Report By Using Wizard to open the Report Wizard.

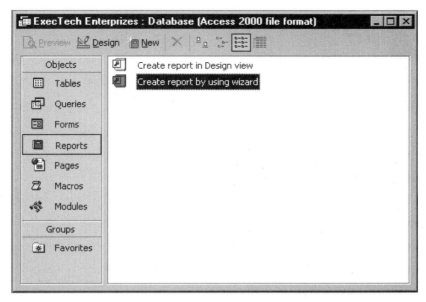

Figure 7-20 The Database window with the Reports object selected.

2. Select the tables or queries on which you want to base your report.

The first Report Wizard screen displays the name of a table and the fields located within that table, as shown in Figure 7-21. The Tables/Queries drop-down list box displays all tables and queries that have been created for your database. If the table name that is shown is not a table or query on which you are basing your report, click the drop-down arrow to display the list and select the appropriate table or query.

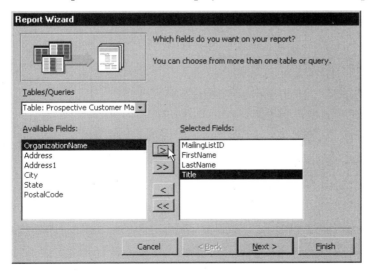

Figure 7-21 Selecting the table or query and fields for the report.

3. Choose the fields for your report.

The fields that are contained in the selected table are displayed in the Available Fields list (see Figure 7-21). Select the fields you want shown in your completed report and move them into the Selected Fields area using the right-pointing chevron button. If you want all fields, use the button showing a right-pointing double chevron. Use the left-pointing chevron buttons to remove one field or all fields.

You can pull fields from other tables or queries as well. Simply select a new table or query from the Tables/Queries list, and move the desired fields into the Selected Fields box.

After your selection is complete, click Next.

4. Select grouping and set priorities.

In the second Report Wizard screen, you're given the opportunity to rearrange the fields into the order you want and to set priorities, as shown in Figure 7-22. Because our data is already in a usable form for a mailing list, we won't make any changes here. Click Next to continue.

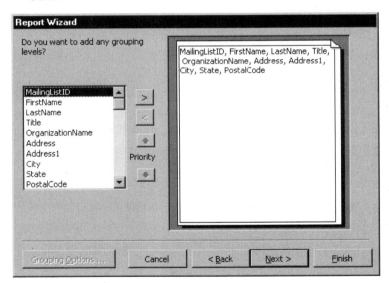

Figure 7-22   Establishing field order and priority.

5. Set sorting order.

In the finished report, you want your data organized so that all records in each state are together, as well as cities and zip codes. We want to establish the sort keys so that the finished report is organized.

In the third Report Wizard screen, click the drop-down arrow for the first sort key box. In that list, all fields in the report are listed. We want the records sorted by State so that is the sort we selected. In the following three sort key boxes, we chose City, PostalCode, and LastName, respectively, as shown in Figure 7-23. Click Next to continue.

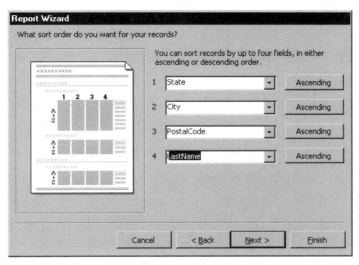

Figure 7-23   Setting the sort keys.

6. Select report layout.

The fourth Report Wizard screen asks you to select the layout for your report, as shown in Figure 7-24. When you select a layout on the right, the preview is shown on the left. When you're finished, click Next.

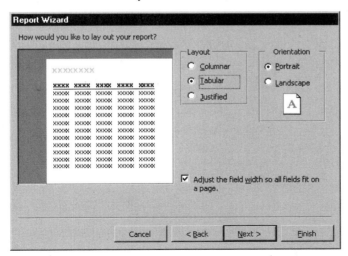

Figure 7-24   Selecting a report layout.

7. Select a report style.

In the fifth Report Wizard screen you select a report style. Click one of the choices on the right to see the preview on the left, as shown in Figure 7-25. When your selection is made, click Next.

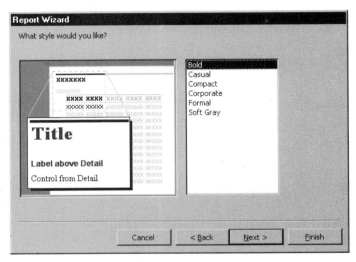

Figure 7-25 Selecting a report style.

8. Name the report.

In the final Report Wizard screen, enter the name you want for your report, as shown in Figure 7-26.

Figure 7-26 Finishing the report.

9. **Finish the wizard.**

Click the Preview The Report option button, and click Finish. Your completed report appears, as shown in Figure 7-27.

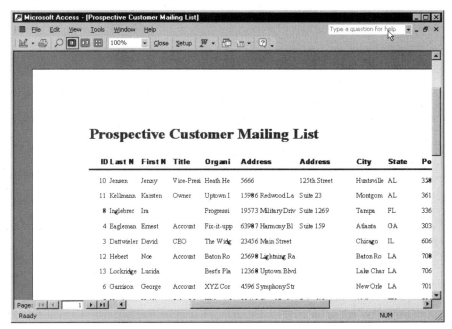

Figure 7-27 The completed report.

Sending a File to Excel

Although there is a vast difference in the purpose of Excel and Access, there may be times when you want to move an Access table to Excel for use in a spreadsheet. The process of doing so is simple. Follow these steps:

1. **Select a table to export to Excel.**

In the Database window, click Tables on the Objects bar and select the table that you want to send to Excel, as shown in Figure 7-28.

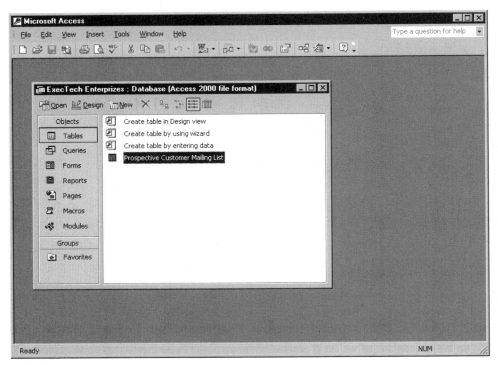

Figure 7-28 The Database window with the Prospective Customer Mailing List table selected.

2. Open the Export Table dialog box.

Click the File menu, and click Export. The Export Table dialog box appears.

3. Select a version of Excel.

In the Export Table dialog box, click the drop-down arrow next to the Save As Type box, as shown in Figure 7-29, and select the version of Excel to which you want to send the file.

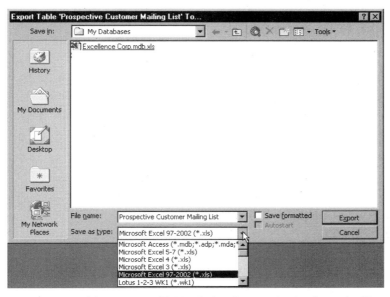

Figure 7-29 The Export Table dialog box with the Save As Type list displayed.

4. Save the file.

Using the list in the Export Table dialog box, locate the folder where you want to store the table as an Excel file. Then click Export.

After the export process is complete, a copy of the table is saved in the new location as an Excel file. The original table remains in your Access database.

Importing a File from Excel

You may occasionally want to copy a file from Excel and place it into an Access database. To do this, follow these steps:

1. Open the Import dialog box.

In the Database window, click the File menu, click Get External Data, and then click Import. The Import dialog box appears.

2. Import an Excel file.

Set the Files Of Type to Microsoft Excel. Using the list in the Import dialog box, locate the Excel file you want to import into Access. Click Import. The Import Wizard starts.

3. **Select worksheet or named ranges to import.**

The Import Spreadsheet Wizard helps you select and configure the Excel file you want to import. If you have more than one worksheet in the workbook selected, you need to tell Access which worksheet it is. Or, if you have named ranges within the selected workbook, you can select one of the named ranges for import, as shown in Figure 7-30. Select the appropriate worksheet or file, and click Next.

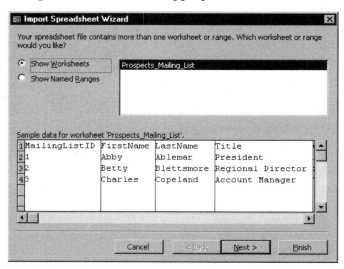

Figure 7-30 Selecting a worksheet for import.

4. **Identify column headings.**

If the first row of the Excel range contains column headings, click the First Row Contains Column Headings check box. Click Next to continue.

5. **Enter storage criteria.**

The third Import Spreadsheet Wizard screen asks whether you want to import the Excel range as a new table or place the data in an existing table, as shown in Figure 7-31. If you choose to place it in an existing table, tell Access which table to place it in. Click Next to continue.

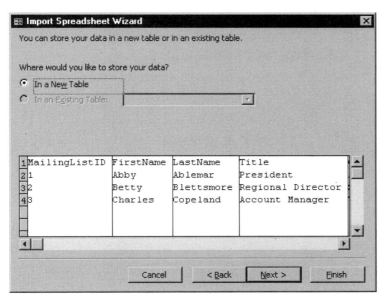

Figure 7-31 Making the selection to import as a new table.

6. Configure fields for new table.

In the fourth Import Spreadsheet Wizard screen, select each field, one by one, and rename it (if you want) and indicate whether it is okay for the field to contain duplicates, as shown in Figure 7-32. In our scenario of the Prospective Customer Mailing List, the one field that should not have duplicates is the ID field. All others could possibly have duplication. If you do not want a field in the Excel range to appear in your Access table, click the Do Not Import Field (Skip) check box. When you're finished, click Next.

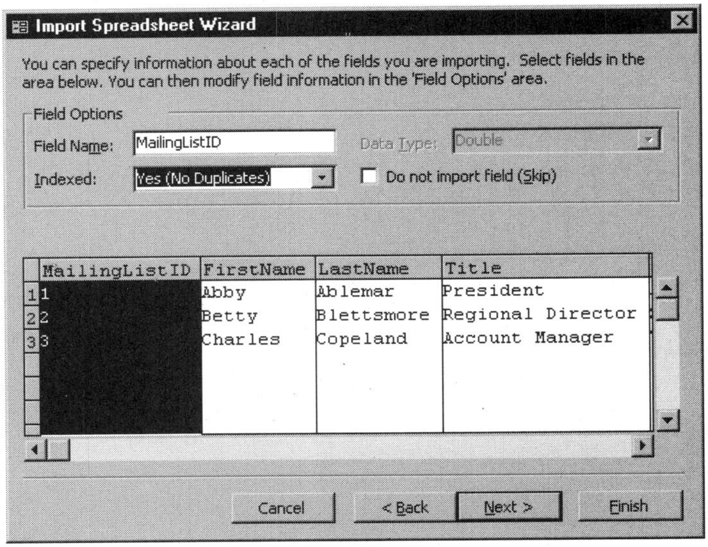

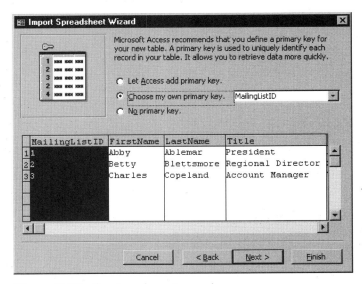

Figure 7-32 Configuring fields.

7. Set the primary key.

The fifth Import Spreadsheet Wizard screen allows you to set the primary key or allows Access to add a field to be used as the primary key, as shown in Figure 7-33. Since we already have an ID field, we can use it as the primary key. Therefore, we would click the Choose My Own Primary Key option button. However, if you're importing a table from Excel that does not contain a unique field, allow Access to add that field. Click Next to continue.

Figure 7-33 Setting the primary key.

8. Finish the import.

In the final Import Spreadsheet Wizard screen, give the new Access table a name by entering it in the Import To Table text box. Then click Finish. A copy of the Excel range has been placed in Access as a new table, as shown in Figure 7-34.

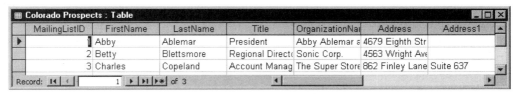

Figure 7-34 The newly created table.

Summary

Businesses today are more dependent upon the use of database technology than ever before, and Access is an application that provides powerful, sophisticated database management.

In this chapter, we looked at the four essential elements of an Access database—tables, forms, queries, and reports—and we discussed the creation and use of those essential elements. Because Access data is frequently interfaced with data in Excel, we also looked at ways to import data from Excel into Access and export Access data to Excel.

Chapter 8

FRONTPAGE BASICS

Featuring:

- Reviewing the FrontPage Interface
- Creating a FrontPage Web
- Creating Your Pages
- Adding Interactivity to Your Web Site

Many flavors of the Office suite come with the popular FrontPage Web-authoring program. FrontPage makes it easy to create attractive, professional Web sites. If you already have the content you want to publish to a Web site, you can literally create a simple site with a few dozen pages in a morning.

Reviewing the FrontPage Interface

Before you begin work on creating a Web site, you'll want to become familiar and comfortable with the FrontPage interface.

FrontPage consists of several areas, as shown in Figure 8-1, some of which will be familiar and some of which may be new to you. At the top of the window is a familiar menu bar—where the File, Edit, and other menus are located. Immediately below this is one or more toolbars, where the most frequently accessed features and functions of FrontPage are located.

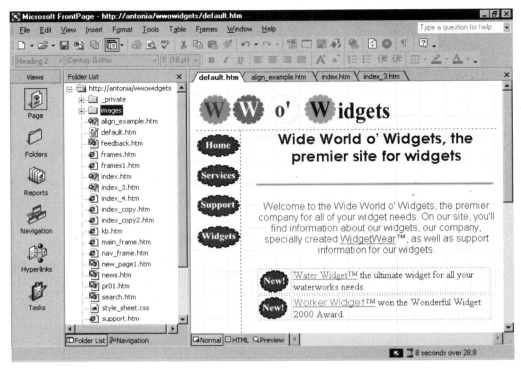

Figure 8-1 The FrontPage interface in Page view.

Below the menu bar and toolbars is the heart of the FrontPage interface—the tri-pane display. The three panes are the Views bar (similar to Outlook's Outlook bar), the Folder List (similar to Windows Explorer's Folder List), and the page or information pane, which typically displays a Web page for editing.

Using Views to View Your Web Site

The Views bar provides six different views that you can use to view and work with your Web site: Page view, Folders view, Reports view, Navigation view, Hyperlinks view, and Task view.

- Page view is what you use for most of your work in FrontPage. With Page view you can edit pages as well as manipulate files in the Folder List.

- Folders view is a more specialized view for working with files. It uses the pane in which you would normally edit a Web page and instead displays the contents of the currently selected folder.

- Reports view is where you can quickly find out the vital statistics of your site: how much server space it takes, how many broken links you have, what tasks and pages are assigned to the various people working on your site, and whether any pages take too long to download.

- Navigation view is where you control the structure of your Web site for the purposes of automatically created navigation bars; only pages that are in the Navigation view appear on navigation bars.

- Hyperlinks view graphically displays all the hyperlinks in the selected page, as well as all the pages that link to the selected page.

- Tasks view is useful for keeping track of Web site tasks that must be completed. It's a view that you'll probably want to become familiar with, especially if you need to coordinate work with many people.

TIP   *To open a particular view, click its icon on the Views bar.*

Viewing Your Web Pages

When you're editing in Page view, there are several ways that you can change your view. If you have more than one Web page open, each page is shown as a tab at the top of the Web page. Click a tab to display the corresponding page. At the bottom of each page are three different tabs: the Normal tab, the HTML tab, and the Preview tab.

Each tab shows a different representation of the currently open Web page, and each has a different use. Use the Normal tab to create or edit your Web page visually, as if in a word processor, as shown in Figure 8-2. Use the HTML tab to work with color-coded, true HyperText Markup Language (HTML) code. Use the Preview tab to view how your Web site would look in a browser.

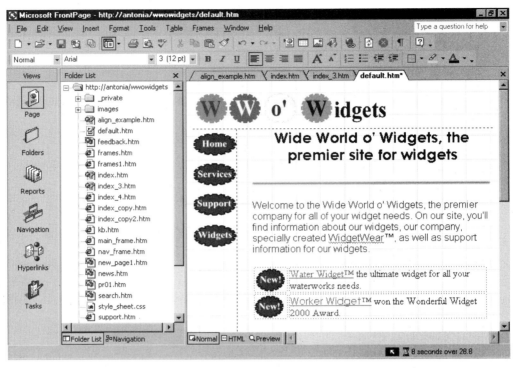

Figure 8-2 Editing a page using the Normal tab.

Creating a FrontPage Web

The first thing you need to do when actually creating your Web site is to create or open your FrontPage web, the local version of your Web site. You perform all Web site work on the FrontPage web.

Setting Up the Empty Web

FrontPage provides several templates and wizards to help you create a web. To create a Web site using FrontPage, follow these steps:

1. Start FrontPage.

Click the Start button, click Programs, and then click Microsoft FrontPage. This opens the FrontPage window with the New Page Or Web task pane displayed on the right, which you can use to quickly open or create new Web pages or Web sites.

2. Create a new web.

To do this, in the New From Template section of the task pane, shown in Figure 8-3, click the Web Site Templates link. To create an empty web, click the Empty Web link under the New heading of the task pane.

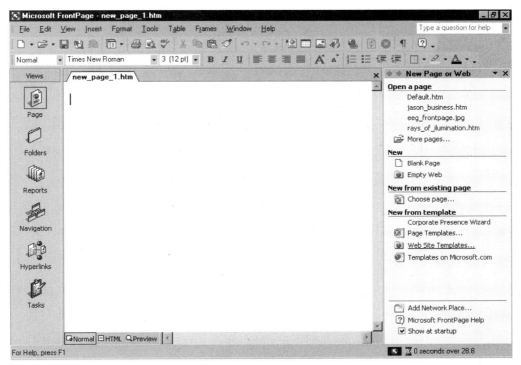

Figure 8-3   FrontPage with the New Page Or Web task pane visible on the right.

3. Choose a template or wizard.

Select the template or wizard you want to use to create your Web site, as shown in Figure 8-4. Click the One Page Web icon or click the Empty Web icon if you don't want or need to have pages created for you.

- *Templates* create a Web site filled with predesigned pages that you can fill in with your own content.

- *Wizards* take you through a series of dialog boxes that ask you questions, and then create pages for you using the information you provided.

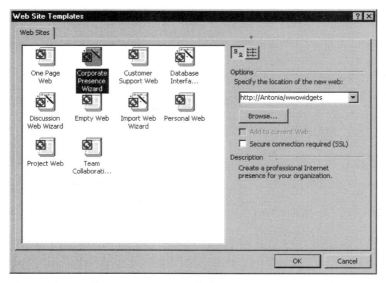

Figure 8-4   Creating a new web from a template or wizard.

4. Choose the location where your web should be stored.

Type the location where you want to store your web in the Specify The Location Of The New Web text box. You get the most bang for your buck if you store your FrontPage web on a local computer running a Web server program. Typically, this will be a Windows 2000 computer running Internet Information Services (IIS), but Windows NT 4 computers can also work well for this task. If a local Web server is already configured, you may be able to simply enter the Web server's address in the Specify The Location Of The New Web text box, followed by your web's name, for example, *http://wks2/mycompany*.

5. Click OK, and proceed through the wizard, if chosen.

Click OK. If you chose a wizard, follow the instructions provided, as described in the next section.

Using FrontPage Web Wizards

Using FrontPage's Web wizards is an efficient way to rapidly create a Web site, and it is especially useful for companies or organizations that don't have a clear idea of how their site should be structured.

When you use a FrontPage wizard, FrontPage creates many of the essential pages for your web, based on the information you type into the various screens. Although these

Web pages will need some modifications and you'll still need to insert your own content, they can streamline the process of creating your initial pages.

To use a wizard such as the Corporate Presence Web Wizard (as discussed here; other wizards are similar), follow these steps:

1. Start the wizard.

Start FrontPage, and click the icon for a Web site wizard. In the first screen of the wizard, click Next.

TIP *If you decide that you want to change something you previously entered, click the Back button.*

2. Select which pages to create using the wizard.

Click the check boxes corresponding to the Web pages you want in your web, as shown in Figure 8-5, and then click Next.

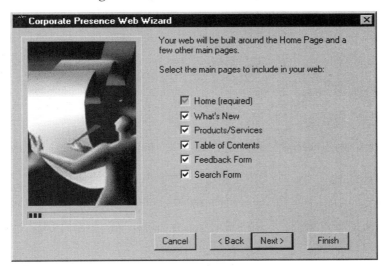

Figure 8-5   Selecting pages to include in your web.

3. Select the content to include on your home page.

Click the check boxes corresponding to the sections you would like on your home page (the first page of your Web site), as shown in Figure 8-6, and then click Next.

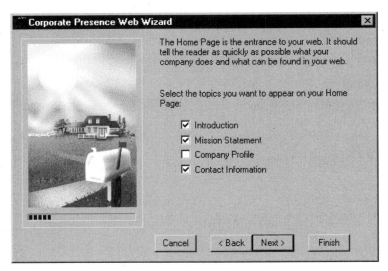

Figure 8-6   Specifying which sections to include on your home page.

4. Specify the sections to include on other pages.

FrontPage asks which sections you'd like to include on each of the pages you chose to include in your web. Click the check boxes corresponding to the sections you would like (you can add more later), and click Next after each screen.

TIP   *If you chose to include a Feedback form on your Web site, you'll be asked what fields to include and whether to use a Tab-Delimited Format for collected data. Choose the fields you think you want, and don't worry too much about the format question—it's easily changed later. See the later chapter section, "Adding Interactivity to Your Web Site" for more information on creating and modifying Web page forms.*

5. Specify the content to include on other pages.

The wizard will ask what other content you want included on the Web pages—typically using check boxes. Click to check and clear check boxes to make your choices, and then click Next to continue.

6. Enter your company information.

Enter your company's name and address, click Next, and then enter your company's telephone numbers and e-mail addresses and click Next again.

7. Choose a theme for your site.

Click the Choose Web Theme button, and select a coordinated look for your Web site. Select a theme from the list at the left to see the selected theme in the Preview pane on the right, as shown in Figure 8-7. Click OK when you're finished.

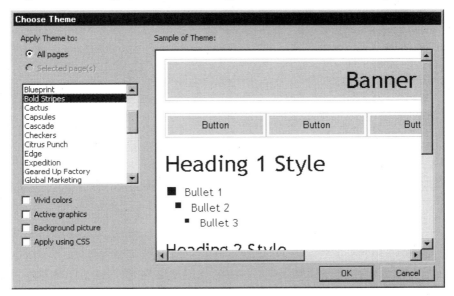

Figure 8-7   Choosing a theme for your web.

TIP   *As with every other decision you make when creating a Web site using a wizard, the theme you choose can easily be changed after the wizard is finished.*

8. Finish the wizard.

Click Next, and then click Finish to create your web. If you want to immediately view the Web site tasks you need to accomplish (such as replacing sample content with original content), leave the Show Tasks View After Web Is Uploaded check box checked; otherwise, clear it.

TIP   *Once you create a web, you can later open it by clicking the File menu and clicking Open Web. When FrontPage displays the Open Web dialog box, select the folder containing the web from the Look In drop-down list box or by using the Places bar. When you find the web you want to open, select it and then click Open. If prompted, enter your username and password in the dialog box provided, and click OK. To close a web, click the File menu and click Close Web.*

Managing Files in FrontPage

FrontPage makes it easy to work with files:

- To add a new Web page or folder to your web, right-click the folder in the Folder List to which you would like to add a page or folder, choose New from the shortcut menu, and then choose Page or Folder.

- To import files, open Windows Explorer, select the files you want to import, and drag them into the appropriate folder in the FrontPage Folder List (make sure you can view both Windows Explorer and FrontPage at the same time).

- To move a file to another folder, click the file in Folders view or in the Folder List of Page view and drag it to the desired folder in the Folder List.

- To copy a file, drag the file to the desired folder by pressing the right mouse button instead of the left mouse button. When you release the button, choose Copy from the shortcut menu.

- To rename a file, right-click a file in the Folder List and choose Rename from the shortcut menu. Type in a new filename or edit the existing one. (Don't change the file's three-letter extension or you won't be able to properly view or use the file.)

- To delete a file or folder, simply right-click the file or folder you want to delete and choose Delete from the shortcut menu. Or select the file or folder and press the Delete key on your keyboard.

- To delete an entire FrontPage web, right-click the highest-level directory in your web and choose Delete from the shortcut menu. (Files that are deleted in FrontPage do NOT go to the Recycle Bin. After you respond to FrontPage's confirmation, the files you deleted are immediately and permanently gone, so be careful.)

NOTE *If you move or rename a file using FrontPage, all hyperlinks to that file are automatically updated.*

Creating Your Pages

Creating and working with Web pages in FrontPage is remarkably similar to using Word to create documents. You can create and edit text, insert images and tables, and perform other common tasks the same in FrontPage as you would in Word. This makes creating Web pages relatively easy if you're already comfortable with Word.

Opening Pages

Creating new pages in FrontPage is just like creating new documents in any other Office program. You can create a blank page or choose from a variety of templates and wizards.

After creating a new page, it appears open in FrontPage ready for you to add your own content or modify the sample content if you chose a Web page template.

Saving and Exporting Pages

After you've created your Web page in FrontPage, you need to save it. Although you probably haven't added anything to the page yet, saving it immediately establishes the title of the page and also allows you to easily create hyperlinks to the page. Once the page has been created and saved, you can also postpone adding content, or delegate this task to someone else.

You save Web pages in FrontPage the same way that you save documents in other Office applications. To save or export your Web page, click the Save toolbar button. When the Save As dialog box appears, use its boxes to choose a folder and name the page.

Working with Text

Text is still the heart of most good Web pages, providing a clear and concise means of communicating to your visitors. Web pages that consist largely of text also download quickly, and search engines can index the content easily and efficiently. (Images don't index well in search engines.)

Importing Text

If you already have text ready to be inserted into a Web page, follow these steps:

1. **Position the cursor where you want to insert the text.**

   FrontPage will insert the entire contents of the file you specify at the current location of the cursor, so place the cursor somewhere suitable.

2. **Click the Insert menu, and click File.**

   Use the Select File dialog box to find the file from which you want to import text, as shown in Figure 8-8.

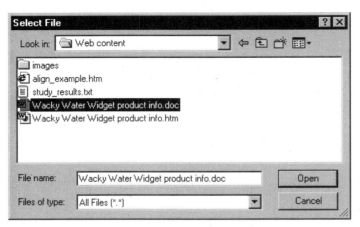

Figure 8-8   Inserting text into a Web page using the Select File dialog box.

3. Locate the folder that contains your text.

Select the drive where your folder is located from the Look In drop-down list box. Navigate to the folder by double-clicking folders to open them. When you find it, double-click it to view the contents of the folder. (If the file is located elsewhere, open the appropriate folder.)

4. Choose the file type you're looking for.

Select the type of file you want to import from the Files Of Type drop-down list box, or select All Files from this box if you're unsure.

5. Select the file you want to import, and click Open.

FrontPage converts the document into HTML code and imports the text into your Web page. The text you import appears as normal text in FrontPage, although you can view the actual HTML code using the HTML tab if you want.

Entering Text

Entering text in FrontPage works much the same as it does in a normal word processor. Click in the location where you want to add text and enter the text.

NOTE   *Pages created with a wizard will often have comments in them telling you to write an introductory paragraph. To replace the comment with your own text, select the comment and start typing.*

Shared Borders

If you created your Web site using one of FrontPage's templates or wizards, you've probably noticed that your Web pages have a few different sections in them, separated by dashed lines. These sections are called *shared borders*.

Shared borders allow you to place the same content on all pages in your web, without using frames and without manually inserting the content into every page. Simply place the content in a shared border once, and FrontPage automatically inserts the content into all other pages in the web.

To edit content in a shared border, click inside the shared border section and enter your text, image, or other content, as shown below.

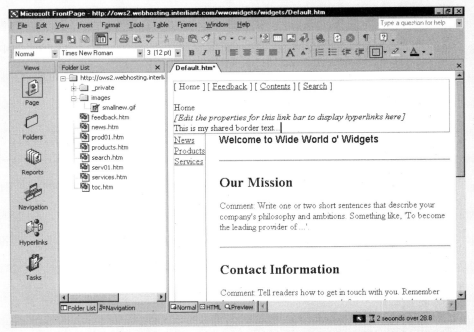

Shared borders are typically used for page titles, navigation bars, and copyright information. For information onhow to use shared borders, see the later section "Using Shared Borders."

Reusing Information on Web Pages

You can use FrontPage's Parameters feature to keep a list of often-used information in your FrontPage web that may change, for example, your company's telephone numbers or your Webmaster's e-mail address. Instead of entering this information on every page, you insert a Substitution Web Component that inserts the current value for the parameter. If you used a Web wizard to create your Web site, FrontPage already did this for you on some pages.

When you need to change your information, simply change the value of the parameter and FrontPage automatically updates all pages with that parameter. To modify your web's parameters, click the Tools menu and click Web Settings. When FrontPage opens the Web Settings dialog box, click the Parameters tab. Then use the Parameters tab, shown in Figure 8-9, to modify the web's parameters. For example, to create a new parameter, click Add, enter a name for the parameter, such as *CopyrightInfo*, and then enter the value, such as your company's copyright statement. Or, to modify an existing parameter, select it from the list, click Modify, and change the parameter's name or value in the next dialog box.

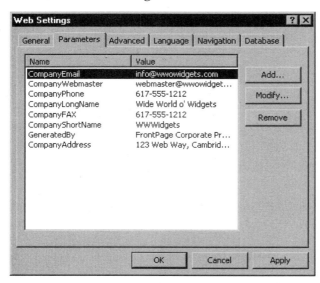

Figure 8-9   Modifying the parameters for a FrontPage web.

To insert a parameter in a Web page, click the Insert menu and click Web Component. When FrontPage opens the Web Component dialog box, select Included Content from the Component Type list. Next, select Substitution from the list on the right. And then select the parameter from the drop-down list box, and click OK.

Formatting Text

Just as is the case with other Office programs, FrontPage allows you to format your text almost any way you want. To apply formatting, select a block of text and use the appropriate Formatting toolbar button or Format menu command.

Creating Hyperlinks

A *hyperlink* is a piece of text or an image that when clicked takes the visitor to another page, image, or file. Hyperlinks are one of the most useful features of Web pages. They allow visitors to easily access information they're seeking and also provide a way for visitors to access related information they may not have otherwise sought out.

Linking to Another Page

To create a hyperlink, follow these steps:

1. **Open the Insert Hyperlink dialog box, as shown in Figure 8-10.**

    Select the text or image, and click the Insert Hyperlink toolbar button.

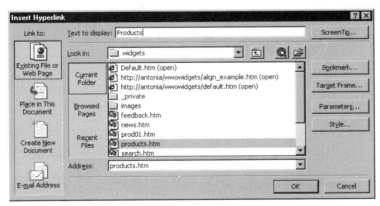

Figure 8-10   Creating a hyperlink.

TIP   *Creating effective hyperlinks can be an art unto itself, but in general, all you need to do is make the linking text short and descriptive. No need to include the words* click here—*this instruction is implicit. For example, use* <u>widgets</u> *instead of* <u>click here for widgets</u>.

2. **Select the page to link to.**

    If you can't find the page, use the Look In drop-down list box to open a different folder, click Recent Files, or use the shortcuts in the Places bar to find the appropriate page.

To make a hyperlink to an e-mail address, click the E-Mail Address icon in the Places bar and then enter the e-mail address and subject in the boxes provided.

3. Verify the linked text, or change the text.

In the Text To Display box, enter the text you want to hyperlink. Changing this affects the text you originally selected on your Web page.

4. Create a ScreenTip for the link.

Click the ScreenTip button to enter text that pops up when a visitor moves his or her mouse over the link.

5. Click OK.

The linked text now appears underlined.

TIP   *To make the page you linked to (the target page) open in a different window or frame (if you're using frames), click the Target Frame button. Select New Window from the Common Targets list to open the link in a new browser window—a good idea if the link is to a page outside your Web site.*

Linking Within a Web Page

To create a hyperlink that points to another location in the same page, called a *bookmark*, follow these steps:

1. Place the cursor where you want to bookmark.

This will most likely be immediately before a key heading on your page or at the top of the page (so that visitors can quickly get to the top of the page without scrolling up).

2. Open the Bookmark dialog box, as shown in Figure 8-11.

Click the Insert menu, and click Bookmark.

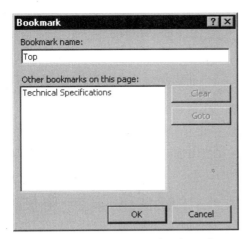

Figure 8-11 Creating a bookmark.

3. Name the bookmark.

In the Bookmark dialog box, enter a short name for the bookmark in the Bookmark Name text box, and then click OK.

4. Highlight the text you want to make into a link.

Enter some descriptive text at the top of your page, and select it.

5. Click the Insert Hyperlink toolbar button.

6. Click the Place In This Document icon in the Places bar.

In the screen that's displayed, select the bookmark you want to link to, and click OK.

Working with Images

Along with the standard image capabilities available in other Office applications, FrontPage has a few special abilities that help make your use of images in Web pages more effective.

Inserting Images

The easiest way to insert an image into a Web page is to find the image in the Folder List and then drag it to the spot where you want it in your Web page. FrontPage converts the image into a JPEG or GIF file if the image is in another format.

Frequently check the Estimated Time To Download indicator on the right side of FrontPage's status bar. If the indicator shows that your page will take longer than 30 seconds to download over a 28.8 connection, reduce image sizes or remove some images. You can also create thumbnail images, as described later in the section "Creating Thumbnail Images."

Scanning Images

If you have a scanner or a digital camera, you can also insert pictures directly from your device. To do so, follow these steps:

1. Open the Insert Picture From Scanner Or Camera dialog box.

To do so, click the Insert menu, click Picture, and then click From Scanner Or Camera.

2. Select the device to use from the Device drop-down list box.

3. Select the appropriate resolution.

Click the Web Quality option button unless you have some need for a high-resolution image (perhaps you want to allow visitors to download a high-quality sample), as shown in Figure 8-12.

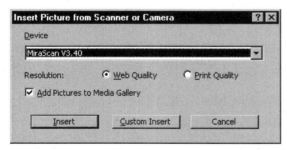

Figure 8-12   Inserting an image from a scanner or digital camera.

TIP *To insert a simple horizontal line—a visual divider used to separate content elements—position the cursor where you want to place the horizontal line and then click the Insert menu and click Horizontal Line. To modify the horizontal line's properties, double-click it.*

4. Click Insert.

The image is scanned or transferred from your camera and inserted into your Web page at the current cursor location. If the Add Pictures To Media Gallery check box is checked, the image(s) are added to the Media Gallery so that you can use them as if they were clip art.

TIP   *To manually scan or import images, click the Custom Insert button.*

NOTE   *FrontPage, like other Office programs, lets you insert clip art and create drawings to enhance your Web pages. For information on how to do this, refer to Chapter 12.*

Resizing Images

Some images you come across just won't be the right size for your Web page. You can still make use of these images, though, by resizing them using either FrontPage or a standalone image editor. For most uses, FrontPage generally does a fine job.

NOTE   *You might want to use a standalone image editor, such as Microsoft PhotoDraw, instead of FrontPage's built-in tools to resize images with transparency (usually GIFs) or JPEG images that you notice degrade in quality when resized and resampled by FrontPage.*

The easiest way to resize an image in FrontPage is to click it to select the image, move the mouse over one of the sizing handles until the cursor turns into a dual-sided arrow, and then drag the outline of the image in or out to make the image smaller or larger.

TIP   *Keep in mind that you can only discard image information, not gain it; so avoid increasing the size of images by much. An image that is enlarged too much looks pixilated and ugly, something that doesn't reflect well on a Web site.*

To precisely resize an image, right-click the image and choose Picture Properties from the shortcut menu. Click the Specify Size check box, and then adjust the width and height in pixels to the new size. Clear the Keep Aspect Ratio check box if it's okay to distort the image by adjusting the height and width nonproportionally.

NOTE   *In general, images shouldn't be sized by percent because they'll end up strangely distorted, the wrong size, or pixilated. Some exceptions are images used as horizontal lines and images used as visual dividers.*

Adjusting Image Layout

To adjust how text is laid out with an image—for example, how text lines up with the image and how much space is in between the image and the text, follow these steps:

1. **Open the Picture Properties dialog box.**

   To do so, right-click the image and choose Picture Properties from the shortcut menu.

2. **Specify the wrapping style.**

   To allow multiple lines of text to "wrap" around your image, choose either the Left or Right picture in the Wrapping Style section of the dialog box, as shown in Figure 8-13.

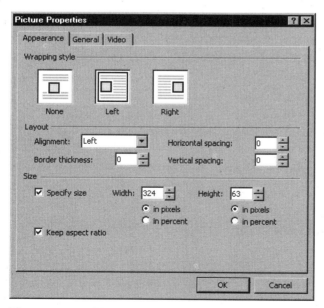

Figure 8-13   Changing the layout options for an image.

3. **Specify the alignment.**

   If you choose not to specify a wrapping style (it's unnecessary with only a single line of text) select an option from the Alignment drop-down list box to specify how you want to align text adjacent to your image.

4. **Set the image spacing.**

   To control how much space there is between the image and whatever it's next to, use the Horizontal Spacing and Vertical Spacing boxes to control the amount of spacing (in pixels) on all sides of the image.

5. **Set the border thickness.**

   To add a border around the image, enter a border thickness (in pixels) in the Border Thickness box. Most of the time you should leave this blank.

Creating Thumbnail Images

You can use FrontPage's Auto Thumbnail tool to create a *thumbnail image,* or a small version of an image that is hyperlinked to the full-size version. When you use thumbnail images, visitors can quickly load and read your pages. If they want to view a specific full-size image, they can click that one image and wait for it to load—without waiting for a whole page of full-size images.

To create a thumbnail out of an image, click the image and then click the Auto Thumbnail toolbar button on the Picture toolbar.

To change the way FrontPage creates Auto Thumbnails, click the Tools menu, click Page Options, and then click the Auto Thumbnail tab. Change the width of the thumbnail image, the border thickness, or bevel the edges of the image, and then click OK, as shown in Figure 8-14.

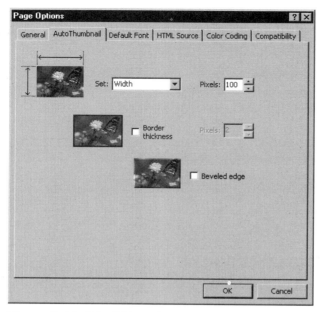

Figure 8-14 Modifying the way FrontPage creates thumbnail images.

Using Shared Borders

One of the best ways to implement a navigational aid for a Web site is to use shared borders. Shared borders are Web page margins that are shared among all pages in a FrontPage web. Content that is placed in a shared border is automatically inserted into all other pages in the web, making it easy to create a navigation bar or Web site banner that appears on all pages, for example.

To set up shared borders in your FrontPage web, you first need to tell FrontPage where you want to place them. For example, you might want to create a left-margin border for navigation links, a top border for page titles and your company logo, and a footer for copyright information and contact information.

Creating a Shared Border

To create new shared borders or modify the layout of existing borders, follow these steps:

1. **Open the Shared Borders dialog box, as shown in Figure 8-15.**

    Click the Format menu, and click Shared Borders.

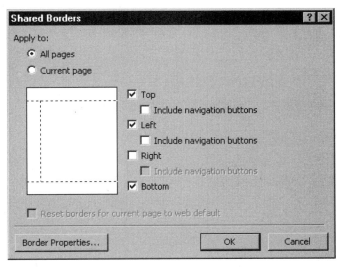

Figure 8-15   Using the Shared Borders dialog box to select which borders to add to your pages.

2. Select the pages you want to have borders.

Click the All Pages option button to apply the borders to your entire web, or click the Current Page option button to use the borders only on the current page (most likely you'll want to apply the shared borders to your entire Web site).

3. Select the borders you want to use.

Click the check boxes corresponding to the borders you want to add. If you want to add navigational buttons to a border, click the appropriate Include Navigation Buttons check box.

4. Change the Border background.

Click the Border Properties button and use the Border Properties dialog box to optionally specify a different color or background picture for a shared border. Click OK when you're finished.

5. Click OK to implement changes.

FrontPage may notify you that it's about to overwrite any existing content in your shared borders. Click Yes to do so.

Working with Page Banners

If you create a shared border across the top of your Web pages, it usually works out well to include a page banner, which is an automatically created heading that displays the title of the page, as shown in Figure 8-16.

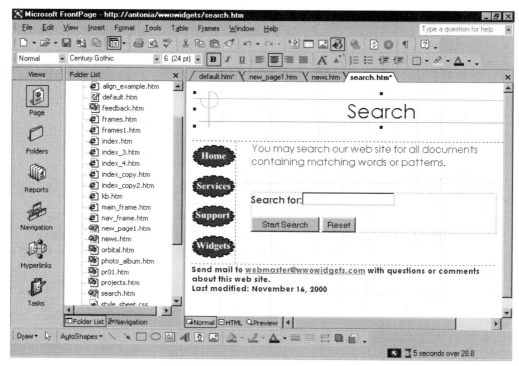

Figure 8-16 A Web page with a page banner in the top shared border.

To add a page banner to a shared border, follow these steps:

1. Position the cursor inside the shared border in the appropriate location.

This will probably be in the top shared border. It doesn't have to be in a shared border, but placing it in a shared border permits FrontPage to automatically generate different page banners for each page.

2. Open the Insert Web Component dialog box.

Click the Insert menu, and click Web Component.

3. Select Included Content from the Component Type list.

Then select Page Banner from the Choose A Type Of Content pane, and click Finish.

4. Specify whether to create a picture or text page banner.

In the Page Banner Properties dialog box, shown in Figure 8-17, click an option button to specify whether you want the banner to appear as a picture with a graphic (which looks nice if you have a theme applied to the Web page) or as plain text.

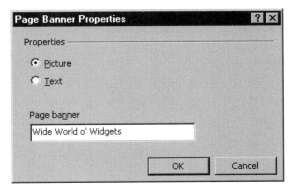

Figure 8-17 The Page Banner Properties dialog box.

5. Enter the banner's text, and click OK.

TIP   *The information for each shared border is stored in a Web page located in the hidden _borders folder of your FrontPage web. To view these pages, click the Tools menu, click Options, click the Advanced tab, and then click the Show Documents In Hidden Directories check box.*

Using Themes

FrontPage includes a number of themes, which are professionally designed groups of colors, graphics, and fonts that you can apply to individual Web pages or your entire web. Themes are a convenient way to apply a consistent look to the pages in your Web site, although they do lack a certain amount of uniqueness. If uniqueness is important, consider purchasing a third-party theme or modifying an existing theme.

Using themes to change Web page colors and fonts is preferable to doing it manually for the following reasons:

- Themes can be applied consistently to all pages in your site.

- Theme colors are all "Web safe," which means that they display properly across computing platforms (such as Mac, PC, and UNIX) and are discernable to people with color-blindness.

- Fonts are specified with alternatives in case visitors don't have the specified font.

To apply a theme to an individual page or your entire web, follow these steps:

1. **Open the page you want to modify, or select multiple pages in the Folders view.**

   To apply a theme to a single page or all pages in the FrontPage web, open a single page. To apply a theme to only certain pages, switch to the Folders view and select pages by holding down the Ctrl key and clicking pages.

2. **Open the Themes dialog box.**

   Click the Format menu, and click Themes to open the Themes dialog box, which you can then use to select a theme, modify a theme, or create a new one.

3. **Specify whether to apply the theme to all pages or only selected pages.**

   Click the All Pages option button to apply the theme to your entire web, or click the Selected Page(s) option button to apply the theme to only the currently selected pages, as shown in Figure 8-18.

Figure 8-18 Using the Themes dialog box to choose and modify themes.

4. **Select a theme.**

   Select a theme from the list, and examine the preview in the Sample Of Theme box on the right.

5. **Select any minor theme options.**

   Click the Vivid Colors and Active Graphics check boxes to make the colors and graphics stand out more. Click the Background Picture check box to include the Theme's background picture in your pages. Click the Apply Using CSS check box to use Cascading Style Sheets to create the theme. (This feature allows you to manually edit the CSS file if you want to, but it is generally not recommended because of compatibility issues with Netscape Navigator 4.5 or earlier.)

6. **Modify or create a new theme.**

   To modify the theme or create your own theme, click the Modify button, and then use the Colors, Graphics, and Style buttons and dialog boxes to modify the theme. To save your theme, click the Save As button.

7. **Click OK to apply the theme.**

   FrontPage will inform you that applying a theme erases all custom font colors, background information, and fonts. Click OK to continue. Depending on how many pages to which you applied the theme, FrontPage may take a bit of time to apply the theme. The theme won't be visible on your pages during this process.

TIP   *To remove a theme, select No Theme from the list of Themes, click OK, and then click the Refresh button to update your display.*

Using Tables

Tables are tremendously useful for creating advanced layouts in a Web page, and they are used much more often than most people realize. Besides their obvious use for creating tables of text and graphics, tables are frequently used to make more precise text and graphic layouts than can be accomplished with standard techniques.

FrontPage supports creating and modifying tables in almost the same way that Word does, so if you're a Word user, you'll find it easy to work with tables in FrontPage.

Creating Tables

To create a table using the Insert Table toolbar button, position the cursor where you want to insert the table, click the Insert Table toolbar button, highlight the number of cells you want the table to have, and then click the lower rightmost cell to create the table, as shown in Figure 8-19.

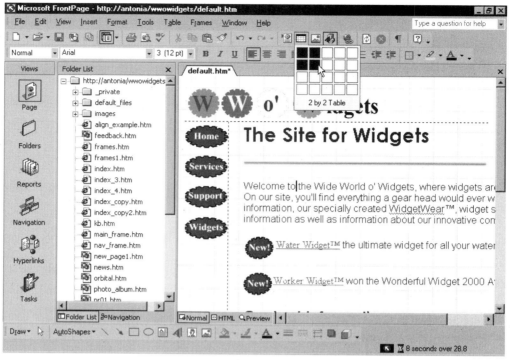

Figure 8-19   Inserting a table using the Insert Table toolbar button.

NOTE   *You can also draw a table freehand by using the Draw Table tool. Click the Table menu and click Draw Table to display the Table toolbar. The cursor changes to a pencil you can use to draw the table outline and dividers. If you make a mistake, click the Eraser button. To resize columns or rows, move the mouse over a divider until the cursor turns into a dual-sided arrow and then drag the divider.*

Modifying Table Properties

The tables that FrontPage creates usually require a little tweaking before they can be put to use on a Web site. For example, if you're using the table to position text more precisely, you'll probably want to make the table invisible (by eliminating the table borders). Or you may need to adjust the sizing of the table, how it's aligned on the page, or the colors or background image used. To do so, follow these steps:

1. **Open the Table Properties dialog box, as shown in Figure 8-20.**

   Right-click the table, and choose Table Properties from the shortcut menu.

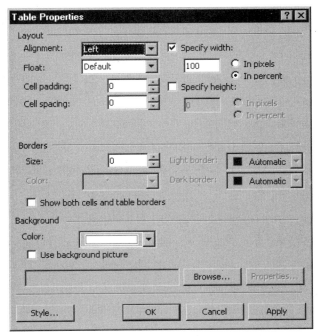

Figure 8-20 Using the Table Properties dialog box to change a table's appearance.

2. **Specify how the table should be aligned on the page.**

   Select an entry from the Alignment drop-down list box to specify how the table should be aligned on the page.

3. **Choose on which side of the table the text should wrap.**

   To allow text and other objects on your page to be displayed next to the table, select an entry from the Float drop-down list box to specify on which side of the table that text and images should be allowed.

4. **Specify the cell padding and spacing.**

   In the Cell Padding box, specify how many pixels you want between the contents of a cell and the cell border. In the Cell Spacing box, enter the width in pixels of the table border. (Note that this is different from the thickness of the table's lines.)

5. **Manually specify the width and height of the table.**

   To manually control the width and height of the table, select the Specify Width and/ or Specify Height check boxes and then enter the width or height of the table in percent or in pixels.

Specify the width of your table in percent rather than in pixels if you want your table to scale well to a different window size or screen resolution. The Table menu's AutoFit command is also a useful way of creating a table that sizes perfectly to your content and also appears properly at different screen resolutions.

6. Specify the thickness of the table's lines.

In the Size box of the Borders section, enter the thickness in pixels of the table's dividing lines. You can also use the Color, Light Border, and Dark Border boxes to change the colors used to draw the dividing lines.

TIP
To hide all lines in a table so that only the contents show, set the border thickness to zero.

7. Optionally, select a background color or image for the table.

Select a background color for your table from the Color drop-down list box in the Background section, or click the Use Background Picture check box and type the name of the image you want to use in the text box provided. Click OK when you're finished.

NOTE
Only Internet Explorer 3.0 and newer versions support using background pictures in a table. Currently Netscape Navigator and WebTV don't support this feature.

Specifying Cell Properties

You can change the properties of individual cells or a group of cells, such as a column or row, separately from the rest of the table. This is useful if you want the contents of particular cells to be aligned differently, or perhaps if you want to visually set some cells apart by giving them a different colored background. (This feature can also be used with invisible tables to create a visual divider in a page, without the actual table showing up.)

To change the appearance of an individual cell, follow these steps:

1. Select the cell(s) you want to modify, and open the cell properties.

Right-click inside the cell you want to modify, and then choose Cell Properties from the shortcut menu.

TIP
To select multiple cells, position the cursor in a cell, click the Table menu, click Select, click Cell, and then click any other cells you want to select.

2. Modify the cell properties.

The properties of a cell are no different from those of the table as a whole (see the previous section) except for a couple of special options, as shown in Figure 8-21. Click the Header Cell check box if the cell is a header for the table. (This makes the cell's contents boldface.) Click the No Wrap check box to force all the text inside a cell to remain on one line, no matter how small the window size gets. (This is useful for text that absolutely cannot wrap, but use it sparingly.) Click OK when you're finished.

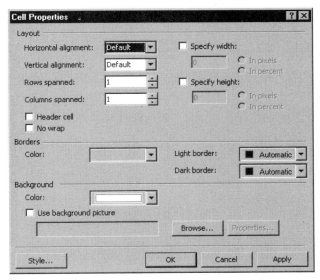

Figure 8-21 Using the Cell Properties dialog box to specify how a cell should appear.

Adding Interactivity to Your Web Site

The most effective method of obtaining information from visitors is through a form on your Web site. In the past, creating forms was an arduous task, requiring HTML coding and special CGI scripts. You can now avoid this hassle and easily create forms visually within FrontPage, provided that your Web host supports FrontPage Server Extensions.

Creating Form Pages

FrontPage comes with a couple of form page templates and a Form Page Wizard to help you get started creating forms. To create a new page with a form, click the down arrow next to the Create A New Normal Page toolbar button and then choose Page from the pop-up menu. Choose the Form Page Wizard or a form page template from the list box, and then click OK, as shown in Figure 8-22. Use the wizard to create your form.

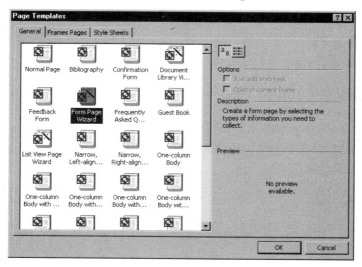

Figure 8-22   Choosing the Form Page Wizard to create a new page containing a form.

TIP   *If your Web server supports the latest Office Server Extensions, you can add a survey form to your Web site. To do so, click the File menu, click New, and then click Survey. Select the New Survey Wizard and click OK to start the wizard, which walks you through creating the survey.*

Inserting Form Fields

To insert a new form field (such as a drop-down menu or a check box) into your form, place your cursor where you want to add the form field, click the Insert menu, click Form, and then choose the type of field you want to insert from the submenu, as shown in Figure 8-23.

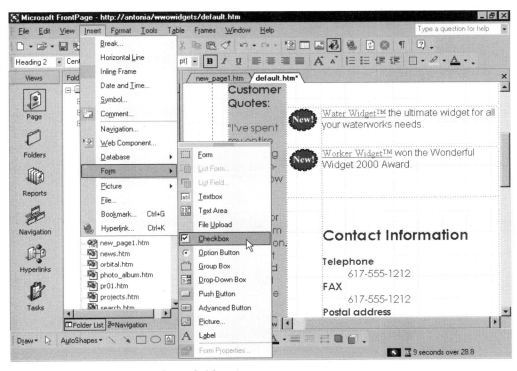

Figure 8-23 Choosing a form field to insert.

TIP *You can insert a form field into any page. When you insert a form field outside of a form, FrontPage automatically constructs a form for the field to go in. You can then work with the form like any other form.*

Modifying Form Field Properties

Form fields you insert are functional without any further tinkering; however, you will probably want to modify the fields to more accurately reflect the specific information your business needs to gather.

Although each form field's properties are slightly different, the following procedure will help you understand most of the properties of each form field type that you can change. To modify a form's properties, follow these steps:

1. **Open the form field's properties.**

   Right-click the field you want to modify, and then choose Form Field Properties (not Form Properties) from the shortcut menu.

2. **Name the field or group.**

   Enter a short but descriptive name for the field in the Name box, as shown in Figure 8-24. If you created an option button (also known as a radio button), enter the name you want to use for the group of buttons in the Group Name box. Since option buttons are intended to represent options that a visitor can select, they must be placed in a group, and only one button in a group can be selected at a time. Therefore, enter the same group name for each button you want to belong to the same group.

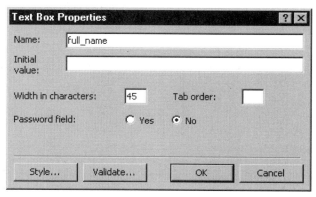

Figure 8-24 Naming a text box form field.

TIP *Field names must start with a letter and can contain upper- and lowercase letters, numbers, and the underscore character. All other characters, including spaces, are prohibited.*

TIP *The names and values you choose will not usually appear on the forms themselves (except for button and drop-down menu values); however, they will appear on the confirmation page that visitors see after they submit a form. If you change FrontPage's names and values to reflect the actual meaning of the form field, visitors can better understand what they submitted when they read the confirmation page.*

3. **Enter a value for the field.**

   Enter a short and descriptive value for the field. For example, you might use the no_mail value for a check box, allowing visitors to request not to receive any e-mail from you. For text boxes, optionally enter any text you want to be initially present in the box (visitors can change it as they choose). A button is a little different because its value doubles as the button's label.

NOTE   *Check boxes, option buttons, and buttons are all binary form fields—they're either on or off. When they're on (selected or pushed), they send the contents of the Value box to the* form handler *(the software that gathers data from the form). The form handler displays this information on the confirmation page and in the form results (which you'll view by Web page, text document, or e-mail). For text boxes, the visitor enters the value when he or she types in the text box, although you can set an initial value if you want.*

4. Choose the initial state of the field.

If the form field has two states (selected or not selected), use the Initial State options or check boxes to select the way you want the form field to initially appear to a visitor.

NOTE   *Drop-down menus work a little differently from the other form fields. To add a choice to a drop-down menu, click the Add button in the Drop-Down Menu Properties dialog box. Then enter the text (value) you want to appear as a choice on the menu in the Add Choice dialog box and choose whether the choice should be initially selected or not. You can then use the Drop-Down Menu Properties dialog box to move choices around on the menu and control whether to allow multiple menu selections or not.*

5. Enter the tab order for the field.

Visitors can switch between form fields by using the Tab key on their keyboard. To control the order in which form fields are reached by using the Tab key, enter a unique number in the Tab Order box for each form field. Pressing the Tab key will cycle through the form fields, starting with the field containing a 1 in the Tab Order box. If you leave the Tab Order boxes empty, the fields will be accessed in the order in which they appear on the page.

TIP   *To exclude a form field from the tab order, enter −1 in the Tab Order box.*

6. Optionally, validate the form field.

If you want to require that the form field is used, or if you want to validate the data the visitor entered, click the Validate button in the form field's Properties dialog box. This is especially useful for text boxes, where you may want to ensure that the visitor entered the correct type of data. For example, if you have a telephone number field, set up the field to validate that the visitor entered text in the Digits format, as shown in Figure 8-25. This allows numbers and dashes, but no letters or other characters.

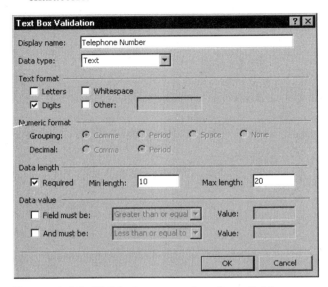

Figure 8-25   Validating a text box form field.

TIP   *If you require visitors to enter their phone number, specify a minimum Data Length of 10 characters so you're assured that they will enter their area code in addition to their phone number.*

Modifying Form Properties

Besides modifying the properties of individual form fields, you'll probably find it useful to change the way that the form handles submitted data. For example, you might want to automatically e-mail submitted information to a certain e-mail address or write it to a text file for eventual data analysis in a spreadsheet or database program.

To modify the properties for a form, follow these steps:

1. Open the form's properties.

Right-click anywhere in your form, and then choose Form Properties from the shortcut menu to display the Form Properties dialog box.

2. Enter the filename of the location where you want to store form results.

Enter the filename where you want form results stored in the File Name text box, as shown in Figure 8-26.

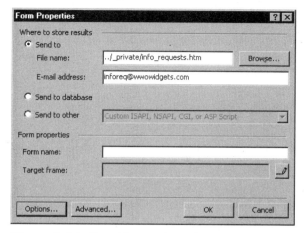

Figure 8-26 Specifying where FrontPage should store the results from your form.

NOTE   *If you don't want visitors to be able to access the form results, you should specify a file located in the _private directory.*

3. Optionally, specify an e-mail address where form results can be sent.

To automatically send all form submissions to an e-mail address, enter the e-mail address where you want form results sent in the E-Mail Address text box.

4. Modify options, if desired.

Click the Options button to modify the form's advanced options. For example, to change the file format for the form results file, select an option from the File Format drop-down list box in the Saving Results dialog box. Click the E-Mail Results tab to modify the e-mail format and the subject line for results that are e-mailed to someone, as shown in Figure 8-27. Click the Saved Fields tab to specify what form fields should be saved and to specify additional information to save, such as browser type.

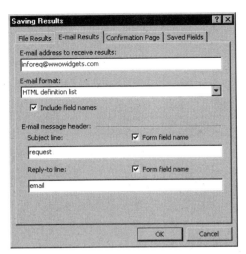

Figure 8-27 Changing the settings for e-mail results.

TIP *If you're not using a Web server to locally host your Web site, FrontPage will ask if it should remove the e-mail address you specify. Assuming you're publishing your FrontPage web to an Internet Web server that's set up to handle e-mail, you can safely click No.*

Automatically Processing Form Data

We live in an instant gratification world, and nowhere is this truer than the Web. Visitors will come to your Web site with expectations, but if they can't find what they need, they should be able to receive a prompt reply via e-mail.

The best way to help visitors when they have questions or can't find what they're looking for on your Web site is to set up a form that sends results to your e-mail program, which in turn processes the results and takes appropriate action automatically.

For example, depending on the visitor's request, you might create a message rule to forward the message to a different e-mail account, and send a standard e-mail message with a list of frequently asked questions and boilerplate telling the visitor that someone will get back to them in the next 24 hours.

In order to automatically process form data via e-mail, you need to modify the form's properties to e-mail results to the proper e-mail account, and then set up your e-mail program to process the form results.

Preparing a Form for Automatic Processing

To modify a form's properties to properly send its results to your e-mail program, follow these steps:

1. **Open the Form Properties dialog box.**

   Right-click the form, and choose Form Properties from the shortcut menu.

NOTE   *The form you created must collect the visitor's e-mail address in addition to any other information. You may also want to use a drop-down list box or other multiple-choice field on the form to divide responses into categories, which your mail program can then process differently.*

2. **Click the Options button, and then click the E-Mail Results tab.**

3. **Specify the appropriate e-mail address for the results.**

   Enter the e-mail address where you want to send the form results in the E-Mail Address To Receive Results box. You might want to create a special e-mail account or alias just to handle form results.

4. **Set up the message header.**

   Click the Form Field Name check box next to Reply-To Line, and enter the field name the form uses to collect a visitor's e-mail address in the box provided, as shown in Figure 8-28. Use the Saved Fields tab to see a list of fields for which the form saves results.

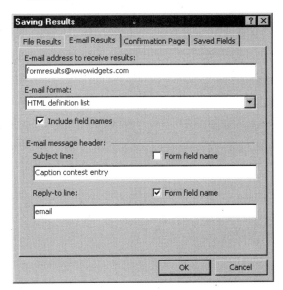

Figure 8-28   Setting up form results for automatic processing via e-mail.

If you want to automatically reply to information requests with information pertaining to each type of request, set up the subject line with the form field name that collects the type of information request. This information request might be a drop-down list box with options for Troubleshooting, Customer Service, and so forth. By using the field name as the subject line, the visitor's selection becomes the subject of the e-mail, which your mail program can then use to respond with a list of troubleshooting procedures or customer service information.

Using Outlook to Process Form Data

After you modify the form to properly e-mail form results to the appropriate e-mail account, create an e-mail message rule to process the form result e-mails. To process the results using Outlook, follow these steps:

1. Create a new message in Outlook.

Click the New Mail Message toolbar button and compose the message you want to automatically send to visitors using your form (but don't address the message), as shown in Figure 8-29.

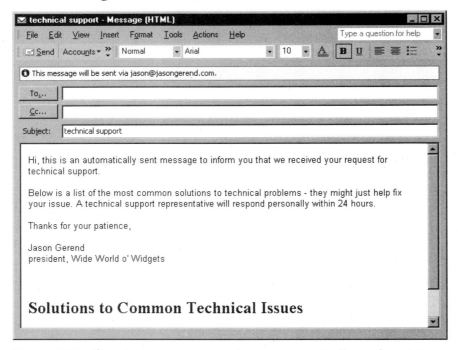

Figure 8-29   Creating a message template to automatically send to visitors.

2. Save the message as a template.

Click the File menu, click Save As, select Outlook Template from the Save As Type drop-down list box as shown in Figure 8-30, enter a name for the template in the File Name box, and click Save.

Figure 8-30   Saving the message as an Outlook template.

NOTE   *If the Outlook template file format isn't available, you need to disable Word as your e-mail editor. To do this, close the message (but allow Outlook to save a copy to the Drafts folder), click the Tools menu, click Options, click the Mail Format tab, and clear the Use Microsoft Word check boxes. Then open your message from the Drafts folder and continue from step 2.*

3. Click the Tools menu, and click Rules Wizard.

4. Click New.

5. Click the Start From A Blank Rule option button, and click Next.

6. Select the conditions to process.

Click the With Specific Words In The Subject check box, and click the Through The Specified Account check box, as shown in Figure 8-31. Click OK when Outlook warns that this rule won't work with previous versions of Outlook.

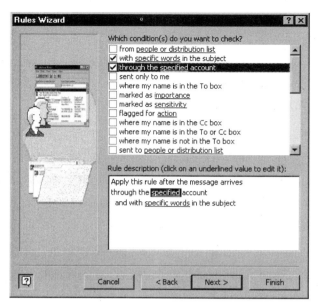

Figure 8-31 Creating a message rule to process form results.

NOTE *If you don't have a separate e-mail account for form results, create an e-mail alias for the results, create a contact in Outlook for this e-mail address, and click the Sent To People Or Distribution List check box instead of the Through The Specific Account check box. Then select the contact you created for the alias. If you don't want to do this, you can set up the form to say "form results" as the subject and use that phrase to identify form results from other e-mail, but this method isn't as powerful or reliable.*

7. Specify the e-mail account and subject line to process.

Click the underlined words at the bottom of the dialog box to specify the e-mail account form results are received with and to specify the subject line to process. If you want to send different responses based on the subject field, enter only a single term or phrase in the Search Text box, as shown in Figure 8-32. When you're done creating this rule, create another rule, but specify a different subject, and a different action to take. Click Next.

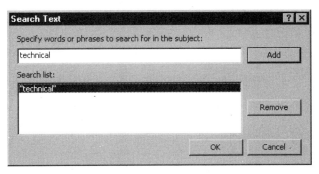

Figure 8-32 Specifying which word(s) to look for in the Subject field of the messages.

8. Select the action(s) to take.

Click check boxes to select actions you might want to perform on the received message, as shown in Figure 8-33. Click Next when you're finished.

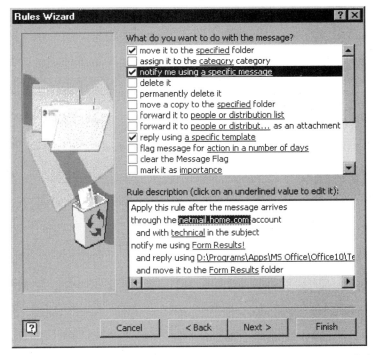

Figure 8-33 Specifying which actions to take with received form results.

The following list describes some typical actions you might want to select for your rule:

- To automatically reply to the message, click the Reply Using A Specific Template check box, select User Templates In File System from the Look In drop-down list box, select the appropriate template, and click Open.

- To forward the message to a different e-mail account, click the Forward It To People Or Distribution List check box and click the underlined term to specify the appropriate contact.

- To move the message to a specific folder in Outlook, such as a Form Results folder, click the Move It To The Specified Folder check box and click the underlined term to specify the appropriate folder.

- To display a dialog box informing you that form results have arrived, click the Notify Me Using A Specific Message check box and click the underlined term to enter the text you want to display.

9. **Add any exceptions.**

   Click the check boxes corresponding to any exceptions you want to make—perhaps to single out important customers, for example. Click Next to move on.

10. **Name and review the rule.**

    Enter a descriptive name for the rule in the Please Specify A Name For This Rule box, and review the rule description displayed below, as shown in Figure 8-34. To make any changes, click the underlined words or click the Back button. Click Finish to save the rule.

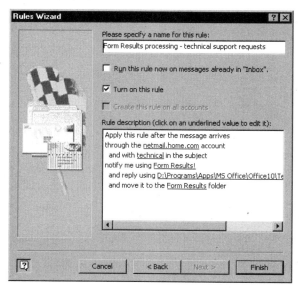

Figure 8-34 Using the last dialog box to name and review the rule.

11. **Create additional rules as necessary.**

Select the rule you created in the list of rules, and click the Copy button to use the previous rule as a start for your new rule (which will probably differ only in the subject words to look for and the e-mail template used to reply to the message).

Creating a Search Form

Search forms are a special type of form that allows visitors to search for information on your Web site. Usually search forms are complicated to create and involve a certain amount of scripting, but FrontPage provides a special Search Form component that you can use to quickly and easily create a working search form on your site.

NOTE   *To use FrontPage's search form component on your Web site, your Web hosting company's Web server needs to support FrontPage Server Extensions. Also, its server needs to be set up to properly search your site, which may require some additional configuration on the part of the Web host. Consult with your Web hosting provider for more details.*

To insert a form that visitors can use to search for a particular page on your site, follow these steps:

1. **Insert the Search Form component.**

Position the cursor where you want to insert your search form, click the Insert menu, click Web Component, select Web Search from the list, and click Finish, as shown in Figure 8-35.

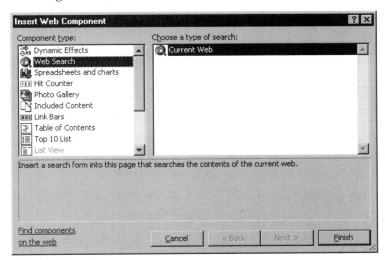

Figure 8-35 Inserting a search form.

TIP *You can create a dedicated search page by creating a new page using the Search Page template.*

2. Create a label for the search form.

Type a label for the search form in the Label For Input text box, as shown in Figure 8-36.

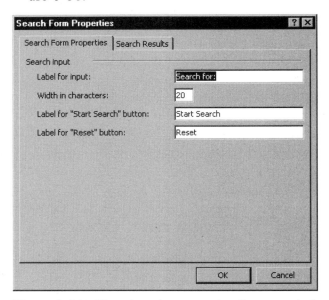

Figure 8-36 Changing the properties for a search form.

3. Specify the width of your search field.

Use the Width In Characters text box to specify how many characters that visitors are allowed to enter in the search field.

4. Label the Start Search and Reset buttons.

If you want to change the Start Search and Reset buttons for your search form, enter new labels in the next two text boxes.

5. Specify where the search form should look for pages.

Click the Search Results tab, as shown in Figure 8-37, and then specify what parts of the Web site the search form should search. You will probably want your entire site searched, although if the search form is in a subweb, you might want to search only the subweb by clicking the This Web option button. To search a particular directory, click the Directory option button and enter the directory name in the box provided.

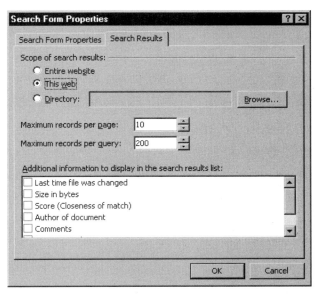

Figure 8-37 Specifying how you want search results displayed.

6. Modify how search results are displayed.

Use the Maximum Records Per Page and Maximum Records Per Query boxes to specify how many matching pages should be listed per page and the maximum number of matching Web pages the search form should locate. Use the check boxes at the bottom of the dialog box to display additional information about matching pages, and click OK when you're finished.

Summary

FrontPage makes is easy to set up a professional-looking, productive Web site. You need to learn how to work with the FrontPage interface—but that's easy enough, especially if you've already been using other Office programs. After learning your way around the interface, you'll find it easy to use one of FrontPage's wizards to set up an empty web and then use FrontPage's tools to fill it with pages of text, images, and hyperlinks. If you want, you can even add interactivity to your Web site by using forms.

Part 2

USING OFFICE IN BUSINESS

In This Part

Chapter 9

FORMATTING IN WORD

Featuring:

- Creating Tables
- Formatting Columns
- Adding Headers and Footers
- Inserting Section Breaks, Page Breaks, and Page Numbers
- Enhancing a Page with Borders
- Adjusting Hyphenation
- Taking Care of Widows and Orphans

The good news and the bad news about today's word-processing programs is that you can use them to impose spectacular formatting on any document. In a matter of minutes, you can create a document that looks like a graphic designer's spread for the world's most popular magazine. The problem arises when format becomes more important than content, and that's the bad news part. On the other hand, when you neglect the visual aspects of communication, readers may react negatively to its content or even just ignore it altogether.

The trick, of course, is to learn to use the tools that Word provides to become a better writer and to use the formatting features of Word that enhance your message. In this chapter, we'll take a look at some specifics—which formatting options are best for which kind of content and the mechanics involved in creating those formats. In addition, we'll look at the steps for putting a document in final form. How the pages of a document are laid out determines to a large extent how accessible the document is to your readers and whether your readers are drawn to your content and continue to turn the page (or click the Page Down button).

Creating Tables

Information that is arranged in rows and columns forms a *table,* and tables are excellent for presenting the following kinds of data:

- Statistical information

- Content that intends to compare and contrast

- Content that would otherwise require long-winded and possibly confusing verbal information

- A body of information that the reader needs to see at a glance and possibly refer to repeatedly

For example, take a look at Table 9-1 and think about how unwieldy it would be to present this information in any other format:

AMOUNT	PORTRAIT	EMBELLISHMENT ON THE BACK
$1	Washington	Great Seal of the United States
$2	Jefferson	Signers of the Declaration of Independence
$5	Lincoln	Lincoln Memorial
$10	Hamilton	U.S. Treasury
$20	Jackson	White House
$50	Grant	U.S. Capitol

Table 9-1   Denominations of U.S. currency.

Inserting a Table

You can insert a table in a document in three ways:

- Click the Insert Table button on the toolbar, and then drag to highlight the number of rows and columns you want in your table. When you release the mouse button, the table is inserted in your document.

- Click the Tables And Borders button on the toolbar to display the Tables And Borders toolbar, as shown in Figure 9-1. The Draw Table button (the one with the pencil) is selected by default. Drag it to draw a rectangle about the size of the table you want. Release the mouse button and then drag the pencil again to draw in columns and row borders.

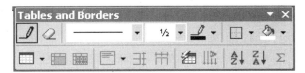

Figure 9-1   The Tables And Borders toolbar.

- Click the Table menu, click Insert, and then click Table to open the Insert Table dialog box.

You'll find that drawing a table takes some practice. Of the three methods, using the Insert Table dialog box is the most exact. You can quickly specify the number of rows and columns and column width. To insert a table using the Insert Table dialog box, follow these steps:

1. **Open the Insert Table dialog box, as shown in Figure 9-2.**

    Click the Table menu, click Insert, and then click Table.

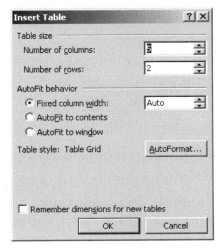

Figure 9-2   The Insert Table dialog box.

2. **Specify the number of columns and the number of rows.**

   In the Number Of Columns spin box, click the arrow to select the number of columns you want. In the Number Of Rows spin box, click the arrow to select the number of rows.

3. **Adjust column width and specify how the table fits on the page.**

   In the Fixed Column Width spin box, click the arrow to select a dimension in inches, or accept the default of Auto, which creates columns of equal width to fit the width of the page from the left to the right margin. Click the AutoFit To Contents option button if you want to adjust the width so that each column adjusts to accommodate the longest cell contents in a column. Click the AutoFit To Window option button if you want the table to fit in the window of a Web browser, even if the size of the browser's window changes.

4. **Tell Word to use the dimensions for other new tables.**

   If you want to use the dimensions you established for other new tables that you insert, click the Remember Dimensions For New Tables check box. Click OK.

NOTE   *We'll look at the AutoFormat option in the Insert Table dialog box later in this section.*

To delete a table, click anywhere in it, click the Table menu, click Delete, and then click Table.

Entering Information in a Table

To enter information in a cell, simply click in the cell and start typing. Text wraps to the next line when you reach the cell border on the right. If you want to create paragraphs in a cell, simply press the Enter key. To move to the next adjacent cell, press the Tab key. To move back one cell to the left, press the left arrow key. To move down one cell, press the down arrow key, and to move up one cell, press the up arrow key. Of course, you can also simply click in a cell to move the insertion point to it.

When you press the Tab key at the end of a row, you move to the first cell in the next row. Or, if there is no next row, a new row is added. Table 9-2 describes how to select in a table.

TO SELECT	DO THIS
A cell	Move the insertion point to the left border of the cell until it turns into an angled, up-pointing arrow, and then click.
Multiple cells	Select the first cell as described above, and then drag to select other adjacent cells.
A row	Move the insertion point to the left margin, point to the row, and then click.
Multiple rows	Select the first row as described above, and then drag to select other adjacent rows.
A column	Move the insertion point above the column until it turns into a down-pointing arrow, and then click.
Multiple columns	Select the first column as described above, and then drag to select other adjacent columns.
The entire table	Click in the table, click Table, click Select, and then click Table.

Table 9-2   Selecting in a table.

You can cut, copy, and paste the contents of a table just like you cut, copy, and paste elsewhere in a document.

Formatting Text in a Table

You can format text in each cell in a table in all the ways you can format text elsewhere in a document. You can use boldface, italic, small caps, all caps, the alignment options (centered, right- or left-aligned, or justified), and so on. In addition, you can rotate text in a cell. To do so, select the text and then click the Change Text Direction button on the Tables And Borders toolbar. Or, right-click in the cell, choose Text Direction from the shortcut menu to open the Text Direction dialog box, select an orientation, and then click OK. When you select an orientation, the Preview box displays how text will look in that orientation.

Modifying a Table

You can easily add and delete rows and columns, add and delete cells, merge and split cells, and further modify a table after you create it. Earlier this chapter mentioned that pressing the Tab key at the end of a row adds another row if one doesn't already exist. But you can also add rows at the beginning of a table or elsewhere within the table:

- To add a row at the beginning of a table, select the row, click the Table menu, click Insert, and then click Rows Above. To insert additional rows, press Ctrl+Y.

- To insert a row in the midst of other rows, select a row, click the Table menu, click Insert, and then click either Rows Above or Rows Below.

To delete a row, select it, right-click, and then choose Delete Rows from the shortcut menu.

You can also insert and delete columns:

- To insert a column to the left of the first column, place the insertion point in the first column, click the Table menu, click Insert, and then click Columns To The Left.

- To insert a column after the last column in the table, place the insertion point in the last column, click the Table menu, click Insert, and then click Columns To The Right. You can insert a column anywhere in the table using either of these methods.

- To delete a column, place the insertion point in it, click the Table menu, click Delete, and then click Columns. You can delete the table, rows, or cells in this manner also. Deleting a column or a row also deletes all data in the row or column.

As you work with tables, you will find that merging and splitting cells comes in handy. Merging cells means combining two or more cells into one cell. Splitting cells means dividing a single cell into two or more cells. You might want to merge cells, for example, to create a heading midway down a column or a title across the top row of a table, and you might want to split cells to include a further breakdown of data.

You can merge selected cells in the following ways:

- Click the Table menu, and then click Merge Cells.

- Right-click the selected cells, and choose Merge Cells from the shortcut menu.

- Click the Merge Cells button on the Tables And Borders toolbar.

- Click the Eraser button on the Tables And Borders toolbar, and then click the borders between the cells that you want to merge.

To split a selected cell, follow these steps:

1. Open the Split Cells dialog box, as shown in Figure 9-3.

Click the Table menu, and then click Split Cells.

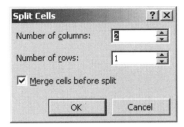

Figure 9-3   The Split Cells dialog box.

2. Tell Word how many columns and rows into which to split the cells.

In the Number Of Columns spin box, click the arrow to select the number of columns. In the Number Of Rows spin box, click the arrow to select the number of rows. You could, for example, split a single cell into three columns and two rows, or any other combination, thus creating a block in which you can place a long text passage, a graphic, and so on. If you want to merge cells before you do the split, click the Merge Cells Before Split check box. (This box is grayed out if you have selected only one cell.) Click OK.

You can now treat the split cells just as you'd treat any other cells in the table.

TIP   *You can also split tables. Place the insertion point where you want to divide the table, click the Table menu, and then click Split Table.*

Changing Width and Height

The easiest way to change the width of a cell or the height of a row is to click the border and drag it. You can also specify exact measurements for the width of a column or the height of a row using the Table Properties dialog box. To change the height of a row, select the row and then follow these steps:

1. Open the Table Properties dialog box.

Click the Table menu, and then click Table Properties. The Table Properties dialog box opens at the Row tab, as shown in Figure 9-4.

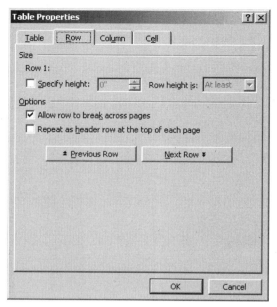

Figure 9-4   The Table Properties dialog box open at the Row tab.

2. Specify the row height.

Click the Specify Height check box, click the arrows in the spin box to select a dimension in inches, and in the Row Height Is spin box, select At Least or Exactly.

3. Tell Word how to treat the row.

If the row contains a lot of text, you can click the Allow Row To Break Across Pages check box if you want the row to end on one page and continue at the top of the next page. This is generally not a good solution because it is difficult to read and you lose the continuity of the table. Select this option only if you are really pressed for space. If you want the selected row to be used as a header row, click the Repeat As Header Row At The Top Of Each Page check box. If you are adjusting the first row in a table to accommodate a larger type size, it's handy to have this option in this tab. If you want to adjust the height of the previous row or the next row, click the Previous Row or the Next Row button. Click OK.

TIP   *If a table will span multiple pages, always include a header row on each page. The header row typically contains the column titles. For example, Table 9-2 in this chapter contains the column titles "To Select" and "Do This." If this table were long and spanned more than one page, you'd want to repeat this row at the top of each page. To specify this, simply select the row, click the Table menu, and then click Heading Rows Repeat.*

To change the width of a column, select the column, and then follow these steps:

1. **Open the Table Properties dialog box.**

   Click the Table menu, and then click Table Properties. The Table Properties dialog box opens at the Column tab, as shown in Figure 9-5.

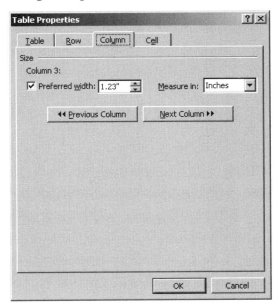

Figure 9-5   The Table Properties dialog box open at the Column tab.

2. **Specify the width of the column.**

   Click the Preferred Width check box, and in the spin box, click the arrows to select a dimension. By default, measurement is in inches. If you prefer a measurement as a percentage, click the Measure In spin box and select Percent. To adjust the width of a previous or next column, click the corresponding button. Click OK.

You can adjust the width of a single cell or selected cells using the Cell tab in the Table Properties dialog box, as shown in Figure 9-6. In addition, you can specify the vertical alignment of the text in a cell on this tab. To adjust the width, follow the procedure for adjusting column width. To select an alignment, click Top, Center, or Bottom, and then click OK. To adjust the top and bottom margins of a cell, click the Options button in the Cell tab to open the Cell Options dialog box.

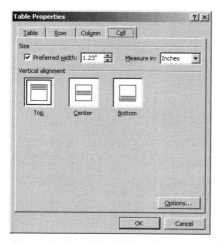

Figure 9-6   The Table Properties dialog box open at the Cell tab.

Formatting a Table

The easiest way to format a table is to use the AutoFormat feature, which gives you a number of predefined table designs. To check out these designs and apply one of them to a table, follow these steps:

1. Open the Table AutoFormat dialog box, as shown in Figure 9-7.

Click in the table, click the Table menu, and then click Table AutoFormat.

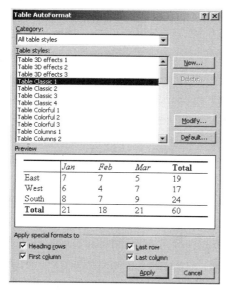

Figure 9-7   The Table AutoFormat dialog box.

2. **Check out the available designs.**

In the Category drop-down list, be sure that All Table Styles is selected. In the Table Styles list, click a style to see what it looks like in the Preview box.

TIP   *Notice that some table styles are in black and white, some are shaded, and some are in color. If you will be printing your document in black and white, not all the colored styles will be readable. Of course, if you are printing in color or will be displaying the document on the screen, the colored styles will look great.*

3. **Select a style for your table.**

When you find a style that's to your liking, simply click the Apply button to apply it to your table. You can modify the style by checking or clearing the check boxes in the Apply Special Formats To section. Clear and then check these check boxes to see that effect on the style in the Preview box.

You can modify an existing style even further, and you can also use these basic styles to develop a custom style of your own. To further modify a style, click the Modify button to open the Modify Style dialog box and select the options you want to change. To create a new style based on an existing style, click the New button to open the New Style dialog box. Give the style a name, and then select the options you want to change. When you click OK, the name of your style will appear in the Table Styles list. To make it the default style for all tables you insert, select it, click the Default button to open the Default Table Style dialog box, click the All Documents Based On The Normal Template option button, and click OK.

You can also format your table in some other ways. You can specify its overall width, you can specify its alignment on the page, and you can even wrap text around it. Click in the table, and then follow these steps:

1. **Open the Table Properties dialog box.**

Click the Table menu, and then click Table Properties. If necessary, click the Table tab, as shown in Figure 9-8.

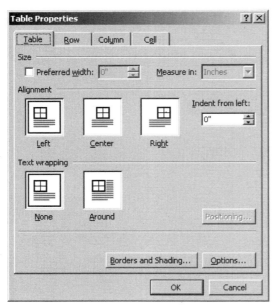

Figure 9-8   The Table Properties dialog box open at the Table tab.

2. Specify the overall width.

Click the Preferred Width check box, and in the spin box, select a measurement. By default the measurement is in inches. If you want to specify a percentage instead, click the Measure In drop-down list, and select Percent.

3. Specify the alignment.

In the Alignment box, click Left, Center, or Right. If you select Left, you can specify the distance from the left margin by using the Indent From Left spin box.

4. Specify text wrapping.

If you have a small table, wrapping text around it is often an effective touch. Select Around in the Text Wrapping box, and then click Positioning to open the Table Positioning dialog box to specify vertical and horizontal position, distance from the surrounding text, and so on.

5. Add borders and shading.

Click the Borders And Shading button to open the Borders And Shading dialog box, as shown in Figure 9-9. When you've selected all your options, click OK.

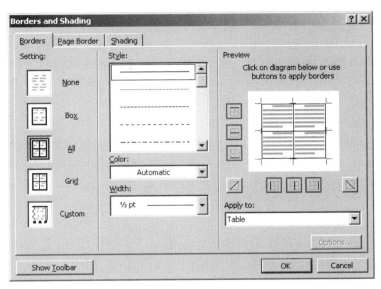

Figure 9-9   The Borders And Shading dialog box.

TIP   *Always call out a table in the paragraph that precedes it. For examples, check the paragraphs that precede tables in this book.*

Using Other Table Features

You can use a Word table as a mini-worksheet in which you can calculate. For example, if you want to total a column of figures, click in an empty cell at the bottom of the column, click the Table menu, click Formula to open the Formula dialog box, and click OK.

You can convert text to a table and a table to text. To convert text to a table, select the text, click the Table menu, click Convert, and then click Text To Table to open the Convert Text To Table dialog box. Specify the number of columns and rows, the column width, and whether to separate at paragraphs, tabs, commas, or some other delimiter, and then click OK. To convert a table to text, select the table, click the Table menu, click Convert, and then click Table To Text to open the Convert Table To Text dialog box. Specify whether to separate text with paragraph marks, tabs, commas, or something else, and click OK.

You can use the table sorting feature to rearrange items in a table in various orders. For example, if you have a table that includes dates and amounts, you might want to sort by date from earliest to latest or by amount from smallest to largest. Select the table, click the Table menu, and then click Sort to open the Sort dialog box, and then specify your options. You can also use the Sort feature on regular text in a document. For example, if you have a bulleted list that you want to arrange in alphabetic order, simply select the list, click the Table menu, click Sort to open the Sort dialog box, specify Ascending, and click OK.

Seven Tips for Constructing Great Tables

1. Tables with several columns often work better when they run sideways on the page. Although you can't turn a table on the screen, you can print it in landscape orientation, and you can view it in landscape orientation in Print Layout view.

2. Some tables communicate more effectively without gridlines or with only vertical or only horizontal gridlines. For example, the tables in this book have only horizontal gridlines. To turn off gridlines entirely, click in the table, click the Table menu, and then click Hide Gridlines. To use only vertical or horizontal gridlines, open the Table Properties menu, click the Borders And Shading button to open the Borders And Shading dialog box, and click to remove certain borders from the diagram in the Preview box.

3. Be sure that column heading and cell contents are grammatically and syntactically parallel. For example, the cell contents in Table 9-2 in this chapter complete the thought begun in the column heading. All cells in the To Select column contains noun phrases, and all cells in the Do This column begin with a verb.

4. If a table contains statistical data, that is, numbers, be sure that all numerals are consistent in the number of decimal places and the use of the comma and are of like quantities. For example, if the column is giving percentages, be sure that each cell in the column is a percentage. If the column heading doesn't indicate the quantity, add a parenthetical statement under the heading that does so, for example, "(in millions of dollars.)" If you are using decimals, align the decimal points in all cells in the column, and if a quantity is less than zero, precede the decimal with a zero, for example, 0.49. In addition, always carry every figure out to the same number of decimal places. If one cell contains 0.49 and the next cell contains 0.50, for example, be sure to include the zero following the 5.

5. If any cell contains a complete sentence, follow it with a period, and end the contents of other cells with a period even if they do not contain complete sentences.

6. Be consistent with capitalization. Always begin the first letter of text in a cell with a capital letter. Obviously, if the terms are proper nouns, such as a person's name or the official trade name of a product, you will capitalize accordingly. If the terms are not proper nouns, you can decide whether to capitalize each word, use title case, or use sentence case. But be consistent. Don't use title case in one cell and sentence case in another.

7. Each table needs a table number and a caption, which can precede or follow the table. Select a numbering scheme and use it consistently throughout your document. For example, in this book all tables include the chapter number and a table number, and tables are numbered consecutively throughout a chapter.

Formatting Columns

Traditionally, the text of many publications is formatted in *columns*—newspapers, magazines, newsletters, phone directories, and brochures, for example. One reason for formatting in columns is that you can get more text on a page by using a smaller font size. A small type size that would be very difficult to read when set at full-page width is quite legible in a two- or three-column format. And sometimes you can enhance the visual communication of your document by setting, say, the first half of the page full measure and then breaking out a portion of the page into columns.

Although you can enter text in a multicolumn format, it's much easier to compose in one column and then format text into multiple columns. (One column is not necessarily a narrow column of text, but rather any text on a page that is not formatted into multiple columns. For example, the text on this page is in a one-column format.) Enter your text, turn on Print Layout view, and then format your columns.

To quickly format text into multiple columns, you can select the text, click the Columns button on the toolbar, and then drag to select the number of columns you want. When you use this method, though, you have no control over the width of the columns or the space between. To specify the details about how columns are arranged, select the text that you want to format into columns and then follow these steps:

1. **Open the Columns dialog box, as shown in Figure 9-10.**

   Click the Format menu, and then click Columns.

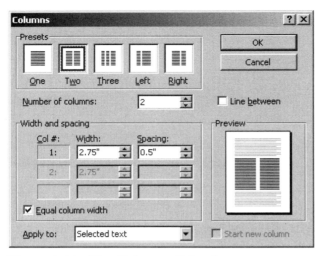

Figure 9-10 The Columns dialog box.

2. Specify the number of columns.

In the Presets box, click One, Two, or Three, or select the number of columns from the Number Of Columns spin box. If you select one of the presets, the default dimensions of the column widths and the spacing between the columns are displayed in the Width And Spacing section. You can also select a preset of unequal column widths by clicking Left or Right.

3. Specify column width and spacing.

If you don't want to use a preset, select the number of columns in the Number Of Columns spin box, and then specify the column width and spacing in the Width And Spacing section. If you want to separate the columns with a vertical line, click the Line Between check box. The Preview box shows how your options affect the appearance of the columns. Click the Equal Column Width check box if you want both columns to be the same width. Click OK.

If you want to format an entire document in multiple columns, click the Apply To drop-down list in the Columns dialog box, and select Whole Document.

Balanced columns are columns of the same length, and if at all possible, you want balanced columns. If balanced columns are not possible, the last column should be shorter than the first or preceding columns. To create balanced columns, place the insertion point at the end of the text of the next-to-last column, click the Insert menu, click Break to open the Break dialog box, click Continuous, and then click OK.

To manually insert a column break, place the insertion point where you want a column to break, and in the Break dialog box, click Column Break, and then click OK.

TIP *To convert multiple columns back into a one-column format, select the columns, click the Columns button on the toolbar, and select one column.*

Figure 9-11 shows a portion of this chapter formatted in two columns with a heading centered over the two columns.

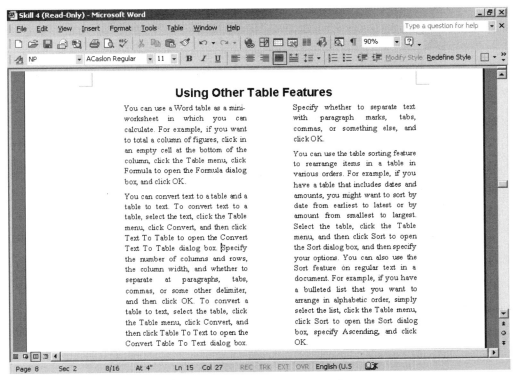

Figure 9-11 A portion of this chapter in a two-column format.

Adding Headers and Footers

A *header* is the information displayed at the top of pages, and a *footer* is the information displayed at the bottom of pages. Some publications have headers and footers, and others have only one or the other. This book has only footers. Footers on the left-hand page (also know as the *verso*) contain the page number and the title of the book. Footers on the right-hand page (also known as the *recto*) contain the chapter number, the title of the chapter, and the page number. Another book might contain only headers. For example, the verso header could contain the page number and the part title, if the book is divided into parts (large sections of chapters). The recto header might contain the chapter number and title and the page number.

Typically, you'll want a page number on every page of your document except for perhaps the title page and some other front matter regardless of whether you place it in the header or the footer. The date and the author's name are also frequently included in a header or a footer. You can also include a graphic, such as a company logo.

To add a header or a footer, follow these steps:

1. **Open the Header box and display the Header And Footer toolbar, as shown in Figure 9-12.**

   Click the View menu, and then click Header And Footer. To display a ScreenTip description of a button on the toolbar, simply point to it.

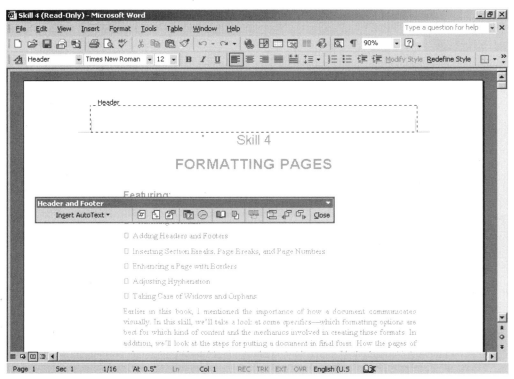

Figure 9-12   The Header box and the Header And Footer toolbar.

2. **Enter your text.**

   You can type text directly in the Header box, or you can click the Insert AutoText button to display a drop-down list of items. Select an item to insert it. You can also use the other buttons on the toolbar to enter header or footer content. To switch between the header and the footer, click the Switch Between Header And Footer button. Press the Tab key to space between items in a header or a footer.

You can format a header in all the ways that you can format regular text in a document. Click the Close button when you're finished.

Now, in Normal view, headers and footers are not displayed, but in Print Layout view, you'll see them in position but grayed out.

If you want different headers or footers for verso and recto pages, follow these steps:

1. Open the Page Setup dialog box, as shown in Figure 9-13.

Click the View menu, and then click Header And Footer to open the Header box and the Header And Footer toolbar. Click the Page Setup button on the toolbar. The Page Setup dialog box opens at the Layout tab.

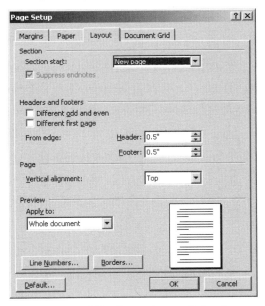

Figure 9-13 The Page Setup dialog box open at the Layout tab.

2. Tell Word that you want different headers or footers for odd pages (recto pages) and even pages (verso pages).

Click the Different Odd And Even check box, and then click OK. Back in your document, you'll see that the Header box now reads Odd Page Header (or Even Page Header, depending on the page you are viewing).

3. Enter header or footer information.

Enter the information for the Odd Page Header, and then click the Show Next button on the toolbar to display the Even Page Header box. Enter the information you want on those pages, and then click Close.

If you don't want header or footer information on the first page of your document, and often you don't, click the Different First Page check box in the Layout tab of the Page Setup dialog box. Then back in your document click the Show Previous button until the First Page Header box is displayed. Leave it blank.

NOTE   *Headers are also known as* running heads, *and footers are also known as* running feet.

Inserting Section Breaks, Page Breaks, and Page Numbers

In Word, a section break defines a part of a document that can have its own page size or header or footer. When you create multiple columns or headers and footers, Word automatically inserts a section break for that portion of the document. You may also need to manually insert a section break occasionally. For example, if you have a single document that is divided into chapters, you will want to vary the headers or footers according to the chapters. To do so, you need to insert a section break between the chapters. To insert a section break, follow these steps:

1. **Open the Break dialog box, as shown in Figure 9-14.**

   Position the insertion point in the document where you want the break, click the Insert menu, and then click Break.

Figure 9-14   The Break dialog box.

2. **Specify the type of break.**

   In the Section Break Types list, click the Next Page option button to start a new section at the beginning of the next page. Click the Continuous option button to insert a section break but not a page break. Click the Even Page option button to start the new section at the beginning of the next even-numbered page. If you insert this type of break on an even-numbered page, the following page will be blank. Click the Odd Page option button to start the new section at the beginning of the next odd-numbered page. If you insert this type of break on an odd-numbered page, the following page will be blank. Click OK.

You can view section breaks in Normal view. To delete a section break, place the insertion point on it, and press the Delete key.

To insert a page break, place the insertion point where you want the break, open the Break dialog box, click the Page Break option button, and click OK.

You can insert page numbers using the Header and Footer boxes, or you can use the Page Numbers dialog box by following these steps:

1. Open the Page Numbers dialog box, as shown in Figure 9-15.

Click the Insert menu, and then click Page Numbers.

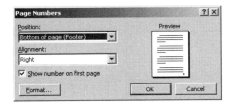

Figure 9-15 The Page Numbers dialog box.

2. Specify the page numbers' position and alignment.

In the Position drop-down list, tell Word whether you want the page number at the top or the bottom of the page. In the Alignment drop-down list, tell Word whether you want to center the page number horizontally or place it at or outside the left or right margin. The position and alignment you select is reflected on the Preview pages. If you don't want the page number to appear on the first page of your document, clear the Show Number On First Page check box.

3. Format the page number.

Click the Format button to open the Page Number Format dialog box, as shown in Figure 9-16. Select a format from the Number Format drop-down list. If your document has chapters and you want to include the chapter number with the page number, click the Include Chapter Number check box. Now in the Chapter Starts With Style drop-down list, select the style you have used for the chapter headings in your document. If you want a separator character between the chapter number and the page number, select it from the Use Separator drop-down list.

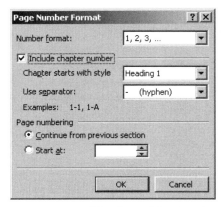

Figure 9-16 The Page Number Format dialog box.

4. Tell Word where to start numbering.

Click the Continue From Previous Section option button to start numbering the document with 1 and continue consecutively. Click the Start At option button and select a number from the spin box if you want to begin with a number other than 1. Click OK, and then click OK again in the Page Numbers dialog box.

TIP   *When we're working with long documents, we like to use the format* Page 1 of 50. *This format is not available in the Page Numbers dialog box, but it is available on the Header And Footer toolbar. Click the Insert AutoText button, and select Page X Of Y to set this up.*

Enhancing a Page with Borders

To give your documents a special, finished look, you can add borders. For example, you might want to add a border only to the title page of a document, as shown in Figure 9-17.

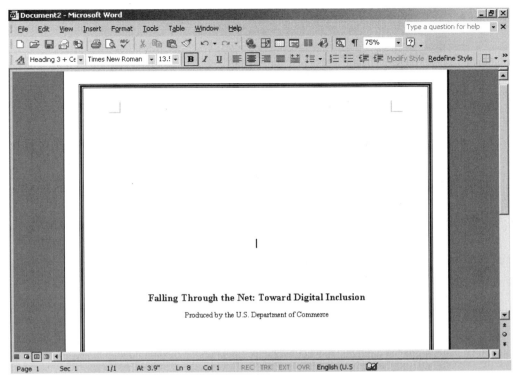

Figure 9-17 The title page of this document is surrounded by a border.

To add a border, follow these steps:

1. Open the Borders And Shading dialog box.

Click the Format menu, and then click Borders And Shading. Click the Page Border tab, as shown in Figure 9-18.

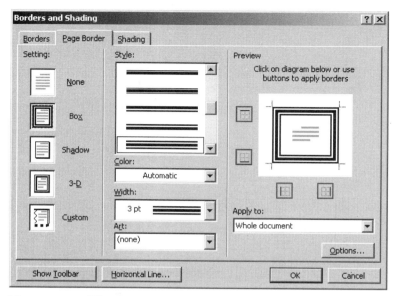

Figure 9-18 The Borders And Shading dialog box open at the Page Border tab.

2. Select a setting.

In the Setting section, choose from Box, Shadow, 3-D, and Custom. If you have already added a border and want to remove it, click None.

3. Select a line style, color, and width.

From the Style list, select a line style. Then, from the Color drop-down list, select a color, and choose a line width from the Width drop-down list. The Preview box shows the result of your selections. If you want an artsy border, click the Art drop-down list and select from a number of little graphics that can be combined into a border.

4. Specify the distance of the border from the edge of the page or from the text.

Click the Options button to open the Border And Shading Options dialog box, as shown in Figure 9-19. In the Margin section, select the top, bottom, left, and right margins, and then in the Measure From drop-down list, select Text or Edge Of Page. Click OK. Click OK again in the Borders And Shading dialog box.

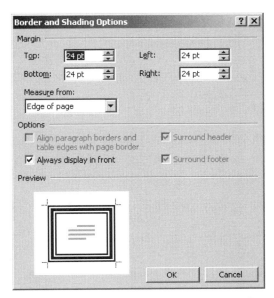

Figure 9-19 The Border And Shading Options dialog box.

To create a custom border, select the Custom setting and then click the border buttons in the Preview box to selectively include borders.

Adjusting Hyphenation

One of your very last tasks before printing and distributing a document is to check hyphenation. The long-established rule is not to allow more than two consecutive lines to end with a hyphen. In addition, a hyphenated word should not break across a page. The reasons for these rules involve aesthetics and readability. Several consecutive hyphens at the end of lines look ugly from a typographical point of view, but they also make it difficult for the eye to pick out the correct next line of type.

Don't bother adjusting hyphenation until editing and formatting is complete. Adding or deleting a single character can change the end-of-line hyphenation.

If you want, you can turn hyphenation off completely, and this is sometimes done if you are formatting paragraphs with a ragged right edge. Even then, you can end up with very short lines and a lot of unsightly white space.

You can tell Word to hyphenate automatically, and Word does an excellent job in most cases. To be entirely professional about it, however, you need to double-check Word's work. Some words are spelled the same but pronounced differently and therefore are hyphenated differently, and Word doesn't necessarily distinguish. For example, Word hyphenates the word *desert* as *de-sert,* which is correct if the sense is "to desert." However, the noun *desert* should be hyphenated as *des-ert,* and Word doesn't catch this sort of difference. In these cases, verify hyphenation in *Merriam Webster's Collegiate Dictionary,* which you'll find on the Internet at *http://www.m-w.com.*

To use automatic hyphenation, follow these steps:

1. Open the Hyphenation dialog box, as shown in Figure 9-20.

Click the Tools menu, click Language, and then click Hyphenation.

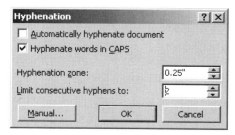

Figure 9-20 The Hyphenation dialog box.

2. Specify what to hyphenate.

Click the Automatically Hyphenate Document check box, and if you want to hyphenate words in all capital letters, click the Hyphenate Words In CAPS check box. In general, you don't want to hyphenate words that are in all caps.

3. Specify how to hyphenate.

In the Hyphenation Zone spin box, specify the maximum distance between the end of the last word on a line and the right margin. In the Limit Consecutive Hyphens To spin box, select 2. Click OK.

NOTE   *Not all publications observe the best hyphenation rules. Newspapers are an example. But if you want a professional-looking business document, you'll do well to follow the guidelines in this section.*

You can also hyphenate manually. To do so, follow the previous steps for automatic hyphenation, but instead of clicking OK, click the Manual button. When Word finds a word that needs to be hyphenated at the end of a line, you'll see the Manual Hyphenation dialog box, as shown in Figure 9-21.

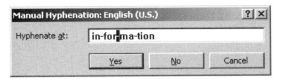

Figure 9-21   The Manual Hyphenation dialog box.

You now have the following options:

- Click the Yes button to accept the proposed hyphenation.

- Click elsewhere in the word to change the hyphenation, and then click the Yes button.

- Click the No button to reject the proposed hyphenation and continue the manual hyphenation process.

- Click Cancel to end manual hyphenation.

Taking Care of Widows and Orphans

Although the terminology here is unfortunate, it has long been used in the publishing world, and so we seem to be stuck with it. A *widow* is a single last line of a paragraph that becomes separated from the related text and lands at the top of a printed page or a column. An *orphan* is the first line of a paragraph that appears by itself as the last line of a printed page or a column. Both are considered aesthetically unpleasing in the typographical world.

Left to its own devices, Word will not take care of widows and orphans, but you can tell it to do so. Select the paragraphs or document for which you want to prevent widows and orphans, and then follow these steps:

1. **Open the Paragraph dialog box.**

   Click the Format menu, and then click Paragraph. Click the Line And Page Breaks tab, as shown in Figure 9-22.

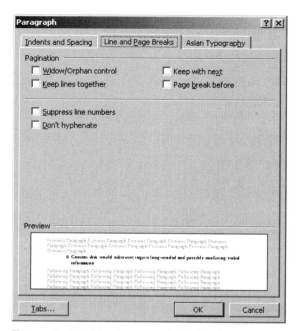

Figure 9-22   The Paragraph dialog box open at the Line And Page Breaks tab.

2. Tell Word to control widows and orphans.

Click the Widow/Orphan Control check box, and then click OK.

Summary

Putting a document in final form by using the techniques and features discussed in this chapter is key to producing a professional-looking business publication. Many business publications can benefit from the use of tables, columns, artwork, headers and footers, and borders. Taking the time to hyphenate your document properly and to control widows and orphans may not be the most exciting tasks in document preparation, but the results are not only helpful to your reader. The finished document sends a message that you and your business pay attention to detail and creates a professional image for you and your company.

Chapter 10

USING MACROS

Featuring:

- Understanding VBA
- Creating Macros
- Running Macros
- Editing Macros
- Sharing Macros
- Macro Examples

This chapter introduces you to Excel macros by showing you how to create simple macros using Excel's Macro Recorder and how to run them. You'll also get acquainted with Microsoft Visual Basic for Applications (VBA), the language that is used by Excel for macros. Finally, several macros are presented to help you with common worksheet tasks.

NOTE   *Although this chapter describes the basics of creating and running Excel macros, you'll find that the process of creating and running macros in other Office applications is very similar.*

Understanding VBA

All Office applications rely on VBA for their macro language. VBA is a version of the Visual Basic programming language designed specifically for Office applications. Visual Basic itself is descended from the BASIC programming language.

You can create simple *macros* using the Macro Recorder, which records your actions and allows you to play them back later. More complex macros require that you use the Visual Basic Editor to create them. Similar to the Macro Recorder, the Visual Basic Editor is available from any Office application, as displayed in Figure 10-1.

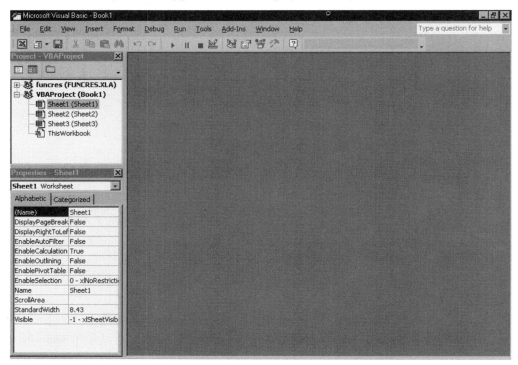

Figure 10-1   The Visual Basic Editor.

The Visual Basic Editor contains a title bar, a menu bar, and toolbars similar to Office applications. The Visual Basic Editor also contains the following three windows:

- Project Explorer window
- Properties window
- Code window

The Project Explorer window displays the projects that are currently open in the application. Projects consist of the VBA code and forms, if any, you created, and objects of the application. In Excel, a project consists of VBA code, any forms, and Excel objects, such as worksheets and charts. Note that a workbook always has a project even if you have not created a macro. You navigate the Project Explorer window in a way similar to that of the left pane of Windows Explorer.

The Properties window displays information about the currently selected item in the Project Explorer window. For example, if you have a worksheet selected in the Project Explorer window, attributes about the worksheet are displayed in the Properties window, such as whether the worksheet has been saved. Depending on the property, you can change the property's value.

The Code window displays the macro code contained in the modules of all open workbooks. To display the code, open a Module folder in the Project Explorer pane and select a module. Its associated code is displayed in the Code window.

If you have a programming background or are familiar with Visual Basic, you'll feel right at home with VBA. If you are new to programming and your macro needs go beyond those created by using the Macro Recorder, you may want to consider learning how to program and then apply those skills to the VBA language. One effective way to learn how to program is to take a beginning course at a local college. In this manner, you learn good programming techniques. Another way is to learn one-on-one from a programmer who is willing to work with you on developing your programming skills.

Whether you are an experienced programmer or a newcomer who wants to learn more about VBA, you can view and print the online programmer's reference to VBA at the following address:

http://msdn.microsoft.com/library/default.asp?URL=/library/officedev/odeopg/deovroffice2000visualbasicprogrammersguide.htm.

Creating Macros

You can create macros by using the following methods:

- Using the Macro Recorder
- Copying the macro from another workbook
- Typing the macro directly

Let's look at each of these alternatives.

Using the Macro Recorder

If you are new to programming or Excel macros, the Macro Recorder can help you create macros quickly. The Macro Recorder records your actions, such as choosing commands and selecting cells and ranges. You then play them back when you need a process repeated. To automate repetitive tasks, the Macro Recorder may be all that you need. The Macro Recorder is also a good way to begin learning VBA. Practicing the sequence of actions you want recorded as a macro before you use the Macro Recorder is a good habit to develop. The Macro Recorder records *all* your actions, including those that are unintended.

TIP   *If you prefer using toolbar tools rather than menu commands, click View, click Toolbars, and then click Visual Basic. You can perform many of the actions in the following sections using the Visual Basic toolbar.*

To create a macro using the Macro Recorder, follow these steps:

1. Display the worksheet where you want to record your actions.

2. Open the Record Macro dialog box, as shown in Figure 10-2.

Click the Tools menu, click Macro, and then click Record New Macro.

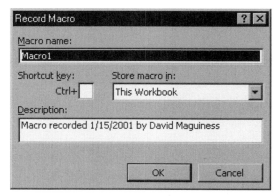

Figure 10-2   The Record Macro dialog box.

3. Name the macro.

Type a name in the Macro Name box. Use a name that describes the purpose of the macro and that will be easy to remember.

4. **If you want the option of using a shortcut key to run the macro, type a letter in the Shortcut key box.**

Each time you press a Ctrl key and the shortcut key, the macro will run. If you use Shift and a letter to enter your shortcut key, you use Ctrl+Shift and the shortcut key to run the macro.

5. **From the Store Macro In list, select where you want the macro stored.**

You have three options: Personal Macro Workbook, This Workbook, or New Workbook. Select Personal Macro Workbook if you want to use the macro with any workbook. (The macros in the Personal Macro Workbook are always available.) Select This Workbook to store the macro in the active workbook because you want to use the macro with that workbook. Select New Workbook to direct Excel to open a new workbook to store the macro—presumably the workbook where you'll use the macro.

6. **Optionally, describe the macro in more detail.**

If you want to include information about the macro, type it in the Description box, or accept the default information. If you do not want to include a description, select and delete the default information.

Macro descriptions appear in the Macro dialog box as well as in the Visual Basic Editor. Omitting a description results in less cluttered code in the Visual Basic Editor, but a description can provide important documentation about your macros.

7. **Click OK.**

Recording appears next to Ready on the Status Bar, and the Stop Recording toolbar appears. If the Visual Basic toolbar is displayed, the Stop Recording tool is highlighted.

8. **Type the keystrokes you want to record.**

To follow along with the example we're discussing here, type the information shown in Figure 10-3. If you were creating your own macro, of course, you would type the actual keystrokes you wanted to record.

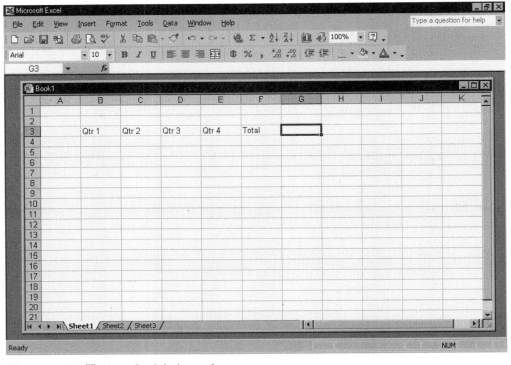

Figure 10-3 Typing the labels as shown.

9. Tell the Macro Recorder to stop recording.

From the Stop Recording toolbar or Visual Basic toolbar, click Stop Recording so that the Macro Recorder stops recording. You can run your macro from the Macro dialog box or by using a shortcut key if you assigned one.

Viewing Your Macro Code

You can view the macro the Macro Recorder created using the Visual Basic Editor. To do so, follow these steps:

1. Open the Visual Basic Editor, as shown in Figure 10-4.

Click the Tools menu, click Macro, and then click Edit.

TIP   *You can also display the Visual Basic Editor by clicking the Visual Basic Editor tool on the Visual Basic toolbar or by pressing Alt-F11.*

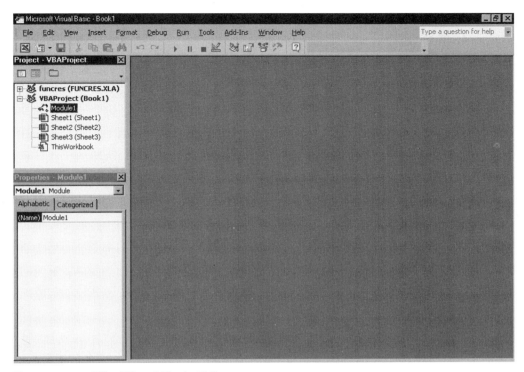

Figure 10-4 The Visual Basic Editor.

2. Select the VBA project.

From the Project window, select the name of the VBA project that represents the workbook that contains the macro.

3. Select the macro, as shown in Figure 10-5.

From the Module1 folder, double-click the module that contains the macro. The macro appears in the Code window.

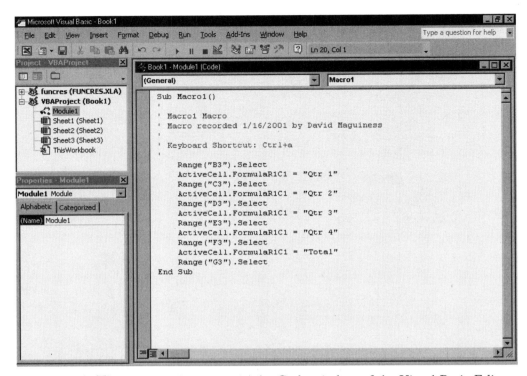

Figure 10-5 The macro as it appears in the Code window of the Visual Basic Editor.

Understanding Relative and Absolute References

When you copy a function or formula to other cells, Excel automatically adjusts cell references in functions and formulas. Excel uses *relative cell references* in functions and formulas. In macros, however, Excel does the opposite—the Macro Recorder records actions using *absolute cell references*—cell references that do not change. In Figure 10-5, for example, the macro always places the labels in range B3:F3. If you want your macro to use relative cell referencing, you must specify this before you begin recording your keystrokes.

To create a macro using relative cell references, first open and make active the worksheet where you want to record your actions. Then follow these steps:

1. Open the Record Macro dialog box, as shown in Figure 10-6.

Click the Tools menu, click Macro, and then click Record New Macro.

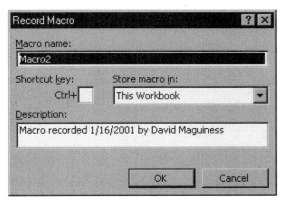

Figure 10-6 The Record Macro dialog box.

2. Name the macro.

In the Macro Name box, type a name for the macro.

3. Optionally, provide a shortcut for the macro.

If you want the option of using a shortcut key to run the macro, type a letter in the Shortcut Key box.

4. Indicate where to store the macro.

From the Store Macro In list, select where you want the macro stored.

5. Optionally, describe the macro.

If you want to include information about the macro, type it in the Description box or accept the default information. If you do not want to include a description, select and delete the default information.

6. Begin recording.

To begin recording your keystrokes, click OK.

7. Tell Excel to assume relative cell references.

From the Stop Recording toolbar, click the Relative Reference tool. Note that Excel doesn't record clicks and keystrokes you may using the Stop Recording toolbar.

8. Type the keystrokes you want to record.

Once you tell Excel to assume relative cell references, type the keystrokes you want to record. To follow along with the example described here, type the information as shown in Figure 10-7.

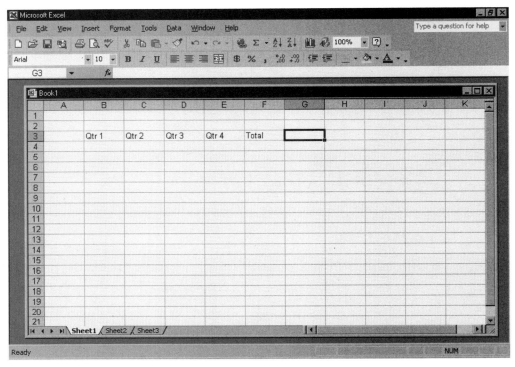

Figure 10-7 Typing the labels as shown.

9. Tell the Macro Recorder to stop recording.

From the Stop Recording toolbar or Visual Basic toolbar, click Stop Recording so that the Macro Recorder stops recording. Figure 10-8 displays the macro recorded with relative cell references (Macro2).

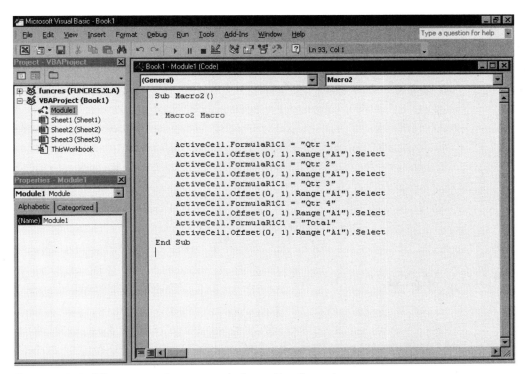

Figure 10-8 The macro that uses relative cell referencing.

NOTE *Each macro uses the same number of lines of code, but Macro1 uses ActiveCell.FormulaR1C1 while Macro2 uses ActiveCell.Offset. If you need labels in the same range every time, use Macro1; otherwise, use Macro2 for greater flexibility.*

Copying Macro Code

You can use existing macro code to create new macros using the Visual Basic Editor. To do so, open the workbook that contains the code you want to reuse. Then open the workbook that you want to contain the code. In the Visual Basic Editor, open the modules you want to copy from and to. In the Code window, simply select the code you want to copy, click the Edit menu, and then click Copy, in a manner similar to any Microsoft Windows select and copy operation. Then select the Code window that contains the macro you want to paste to, click the Edit menu, and click Paste. The code is ready for your use.

TIP   *Use one of the Tile commands or the Cascade command from the Visual Basic Editor's Window menu to arrange the Code windows to help you quickly copy and paste macro code.*

Typing Macro Code

As your macros become more advanced you'll need to type your code directly into the Code window. For example, to use a looping procedure, such as a FOR-NEXT loop, you'll need to type the code from the keyboard or copy it from another source, because the Macro Recorder is unable to duplicate this process.

Running Macros

To run macros, you can use the following options:

- Excel's Tools menu
- A shortcut key combination
- A toolbar tool
- An object on a worksheet
- Automatically each time you open a workbook

The method you choose depends on the purpose of the macro and your personal preference, or what is appropriate for your audience if you are developing a macro for others' use. Keep in mind that you are not limited to one method but rather you can use any combination of options from those listed above, depending on how you created the macro initially. For example, you can run macros from the Tools menu, by using a shortcut key combination, and by clicking a toolbar tool. The following sections help you decide which methods are best for your situation.

Running a Macro from the Tools Menu

You can run macros from Excel's Tools menu. Because the Macro dialog box displays the names of all currently available macros, use this method to select the macro you want to run. To run a macro this way, follow these steps:

1. Open the Macro dialog box, as shown in Figure 10-9.

Click the Tools menu, click Macro, and then click Macros.

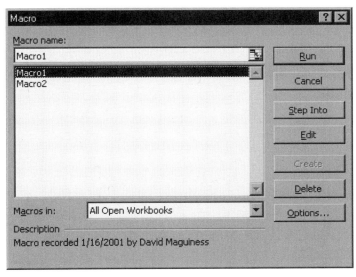

Figure 10-9 The Macro dialog box.

2. Select the macro you want to run.

Click the macro name to select it in the Macro Name list.

3. Click Run.

The Macro dialog box closes, and the selected macro runs.

TIP   *Click the Run tool on the Visual Basic toolbar to quickly display the Macro dialog box.*

Using Shortcut Keys

You can run a macro using its shortcut key if you assigned one to it when you created the macro. Simply press and hold down one of the Ctrl keys as you press the letter of the key of the macro. If you have forgotten the shortcut key combination, open the Macro dialog box, select the name of a macro from the list of macros, and then click Options to display the shortcut key. Using the shortcut key method to run macros is most appropriate for macros you create for your own use.

TIP   *Keep a list of the names of your macros and their corresponding shortcut keys in a separate worksheet in the workbook.*

Using Toolbar Tools

Using a tool on a toolbar is probably the most convenient method for running a macro. Running a macro in this manner enables you to avoid using Excel's menus and having to remember shortcut keys. If the toolbar that contains the tool is visible, all you need to do is click the tool to run your macro. You can assign a macro to the tools that are included with Excel toolbars or to tools you create yourself.

Assigning a Macro to a Toolbar Tool

To assign a macro to a toolbar tool, follow these steps:

1. **Make sure the macro you want to assign to a tool is available.**

   Review the list of macros in the Macro dialog box to determine whether the macro is currently available. If not, open the workbook that contains the macro.

2. **Display the toolbar that will include the new tool.**

   If the toolbar isn't displayed, right-click one of the toolbars that is displayed. When Excel displays the Toolbars menu—this is just a list of the toolbars available—click the toolbar.

3. **Open the Customize dialog box, as shown in Figure 10-10.**

   Click the Tools menu, and click Customize.

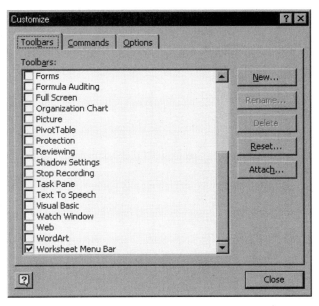

Figure 10-10 The Customize dialog box.

4. Indicate you want to add a toolbar command.

Click the Commands tab, and select Macros from the Categories list. Then click the Custom button.

5. Add a tool to the toolbar.

To add a tool, click it to select it and then drag it to the toolbar.

6. Assign the macro to the tool.

Right-click the tool, and choose Assign Macro from the shortcut menu, as shown in Figure 10-11.

Figure 10-11 The tool shortcut menu.

When Excel displays the Assign Macro dialog box, as shown in Figure 10-12, select the macro and click OK. The macro is assigned to the toolbar tool.

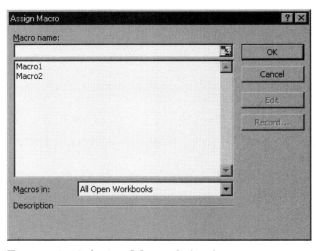

Figure 10-12 Assign Macro dialog box.

Once you've assigned the macro to a toolbar tool, you can run the macro by clicking the toolbar tool.

TIP   *The tool shortcut menu enables you to select another image or create your own by using the Change Button Image and Edit Button Image commands, respectively.*

Running a Macro from a Worksheet Object

Using a worksheet object is a convenient way to run a macro, and it is most useful if you create worksheets for others. To assign a macro to a worksheet object, follow these steps:

1. **Make sure the macro you want to assign to a tool is available.**

   Review the list of macros in the Macro dialog box to determine whether the macro is currently available. If not, open the workbook that contains the macro.

2. **Add an object if necessary.**

   If your worksheet does not contain an object, use the Drawing toolbar to create one.

3. **Right-click the object.**

   A shortcut menu appears, as shown in Figure 10-13.

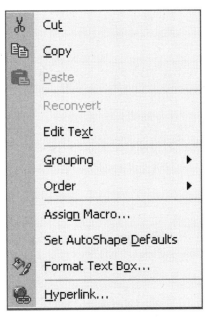

Figure 10-13 The object shortcut menu.

4. **Open the Assign Macro dialog box, as shown in Figure 10-14.**

Click Assign Macro on the shortcut menu.

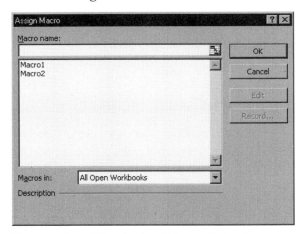

Figure 10-14 The Assign Macro dialog box.

5. **Select the macro you want to run.**

Click the macro to select it in the Macro Name list.

6. **Click OK.**

The macro is assigned to the object.

The mouse pointer appears as a pointing finger when the pointer passes over the object. Clicking once runs your macro. If you need to assign a different macro to the object, repeat steps 3 through 6.

Running a Macro Automatically

You can have a macro run each time a workbook is opened by creating a macro named Auto_Open. If you want the macro to run each time Excel starts, place the workbook with the Auto_Open macro in your XLStart directory.

Editing Macros

You can edit the macros you or someone else has created. To do so, you use the Visual Basic Editor. You begin editing a macro by displaying it in the Code window.

To display a macro, click the Tools menu, click Macro, and then click Macros. When Excel displays the Macros dialog box, select the macro you want to edit from the Macro Name list. Then click Edit. The macro appears in the Code window.

You edit the code in the same way that you would in any Windows text or word-processing program. You select, delete, or add code by using the keyboard, mouse, and pasting from the Clipboard. For example, if you accepted the information in the Description box of the Record Macro dialog box, you can delete it from your macro by selecting this information in the Code window and then pressing the Delete key.

Sharing Macros

You can share macros that you or others have created. You can use the macros created by another user by making a copy of his or her PERSONAL.XLS workbook and using it as your own workbook. You can also open a copy of the workbook that contains macros that you want to use and copy one or more. Then you activate the workbook in which you want to store the macros. You paste the copied macro into a new or existing macro in the Code window.

Macro Examples

The macro examples in this section can easily be created using the Macro Recorder. They are presented here to demonstrate the Macro Recorder's capability and to give you a feel for an Excel task and its VBA equivalent.

- Erase a range.

```
Sub Macro1()
    Selection.Clear
End Sub
```

- Erase only the formatting of a selected range.

```
Sub Macro2()
    Selection.ClearFormats
End Sub
```

- Format a range with the currency symbol and comma.

```
Sub Macro3()
    Selection.NumberFormat = "$#,##0.00"
End Sub
```

- Delete the current row.

```
Sub Macro4()
    Selection.EntireRow.Delete
End Sub
```

- Delete the current column.

```
Sub Macro5()
    Selection.EntireColumn.Delete
End Sub
```

- Paste values.

```
Sub Macro6()
    Selection.PasteSpecial Paste:=xlValues, Operation:=xlNone, SkipBlanks:= _
    False, Transpose:=False
End Sub
```

- Paste values.

```
Sub Macro7()
With ActiveSheet.PageSetup
    .PrintTitleRows = ""
    .PrintTitleColumns = ""
End With
ActiveSheet.PageSetup.PrintArea = ""
With ActiveSheet.PageSetup
    .LeftHeader = ""
    .CenterHeader = ""
    .RightHeader = ""
    .LeftFooter = ""
    .CenterFooter = ""
    .RightFooter = ""
    .LeftMargin = Application.InchesToPoints(0.75)
    .RightMargin = Application.InchesToPoints(0.75)
    .TopMargin = Application.InchesToPoints(1)
    .BottomMargin = Application.InchesToPoints(1)
    .HeaderMargin = Application.InchesToPoints(0.5)
    .FooterMargin = Application.InchesToPoints(0.5)
    .PrintHeadings = False
    .PrintGridlines = True
    .PrintComments = xlPrintNoComments
    .PrintQuality = 600
    .CenterHorizontally = False
    .CenterVertically = False
```

```
.Orientation = xlPortrait
.Draft = False
.PaperSize = xlPaperLetter
.FirstPageNumber = xlAutomatic
.Order = xlDownThenOver
.BlackAndWhite = False
.Zoom = 100
End With
End Sub
```

Summary

New and casual Office users sometimes fear macros, but that's too bad. As this chapter shows, macros don't have to be that difficult to understand, create, or use. Simple macros can easily be created using the Macro Recorder. So anytime you have a repetitive, multiple-step task that you perform in Excel or one of the other Office programs, consider writing and then using a macro.

Chapter 11

CREATING CHART OBJECTS

Featuring:

- Understanding Excel's Charting Terms
- Presenting Data with Charts
- Customizing Your Charts

As an Office user, you have two tools you can use to create chart objects for your documents: the Microsoft Graph applet and Excel's Chart Wizard. Because the Chart Wizard is the more powerful and more flexible tool, this book assumes you will use the Chart Wizard. And in this chapter we explain how you can quickly and easily create professional, presentation-quality charts based on worksheet data. We walk you through the steps you take to work with the Chart Wizard, paying particular attention to how you can use charts as powerful tools for better communicating complex information.

Understanding Excel's Charting Terms

In order to easily work with Excel's Chart Wizard, you'll want to learn both how Excel views to-be-plotted data and the terminology that Excel uses to refer to the parts of a chart.

How Excel Sees Chart Data

To easily use Excel for charting, you need to learn three key terms: *data points*, *data series*, and *data categories*.

The individual values you plot in a chart are called *data points*. Because a chart visually represents one or more numeric values, data points are always values. Note, however, that most formula results are also numeric, which means that you can also plot formulas. (Actually, in this case, you're really plotting the values that the formula calculates.)

The term *data series* refers to a collection of values that are all related—that are all part of the same set. That might sound complicated, but it's really not. If you want to chart monthly interest rates over the last 10 years, that collection of interest-rate percentages is a data series. If you want to plot advertising expenditures over the last 12 months, that collection of expense values is a data series.

Most charts you create will use more than one data series. For example, if you wanted to compare sales revenues of three competitors, each competitor's sales revenues would probably constitute its own data series. In the worksheet shown in Figure 11-1, you can see the annual sales revenues for three fictitious companies: Anderson Company, Baker Incorporated, and Carson Corporation. The data points that show Anderson's revenue represent a data series. The data points that show Baker's revenue represent another data series. And the data points that represent Carson's revenue represent still a third and final data series.

	A	B	C	D	E	F	G
1		Year 1	Year 2	Year 3	Year 4	Year 5	
2	Anderson Company	1000000	1100000	1210000	1331000	1464100	
3	Baker Incorporated	3000000	2940000	2881200	2823576	2767104	
4	Carson Corporation	2000000	2050000	2100000	2150000	2200000	
5							

Figure 11-1 A simple worksheet with sales revenue data.

The term *data categories* refers to the secondary view, or perspective, on to-be-charted data. If you look at Figure 11-1 again, you can also see Year 1 data points, Year 2 data points, Year 3 data points, and so on. Each year's collection of data points represents a data category. The collection of Year 1 data points represents the Year 1 data category. Similarly, the Year 2 data points represent the Year 2 data category. The same thing is true of the Year 3, Year 4, and Year 5 data points.

People commonly get confused about the differences between data series and data categories (in part because Microsoft's product documentation typically hasn't done a very good job of defining and distinguishing these two terms). You can use the following tips to help distinguish between data series and data categories in your own charts:

- In general, if you look at a chart and ask "What does this chart show?" every concise answer identifies a data series. Figure 11-2 shows a simple line chart that plots the fictitious sales revenue from the worksheet shown in Figure 11-1. If someone asks you to describe what this chart shows, you'll probably say something like, "Well, it shows Anderson's revenue, Baker's revenue, and Carson's revenue." Which is not a coincidence; charts show data series. Anderson's revenue is a data series. And so is Baker's revenue, and so is Carson's revenue.

- Any chart that shows how some value changes over time is a *time-series chart*. In any time-series chart, the data categories will be some time interval, such as months or quarters or years. In Figure 11-2, for example, the chart plots sales revenue over a five-year period of time. Therefore, the chart is a time-series chart and uses time-interval data categories. In the case of Figure 11-2, the data categories are years.

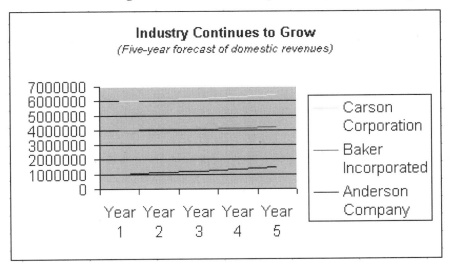

Figure 11-2   A line chart of the sales revenue data shown in Figure 11-1.

Now that you understand the three terms *data points*, *data series*, and *data categories*, you need to know just two final details about the to-be-charted Excel data. First, and as Figure 11-1 shows, you want not only to provide the actual data point values but you also want to enter labels that name the data series and the data categories. In Figure 11-1, for example, you can see that cells A2, A3, and A4 hold labels that describe the names of the companies. In cells B1, C1, D1, E1, and F1, you see labels that identify the time intervals used as the data categories. Including data category and data series names in your worksheet is important. If you include this information in your worksheet, it's easily added later to your chart.

Second, note that Excel limits the number of data points and data series you can plot in a chart. A data series may hold no more than 4,000 data points, for example. A chart may show no more than 255 data series. These constraints mean that you may sometimes need to arrange large data series or big sets of data series vertically by putting data series into worksheet columns rather than rows. Note that for smaller data series or small numbers of data series, a horizontal arrangement like that shown in Figure 11-1 works well.

Components of Excel Charts

Excel's Chart Wizard and documentation use several charting terms: *data markers, data-marker descriptions, legend, chart text, plot area,* and *chart area.* You'll find it useful to understand just what these words and phrases mean, so the bulleted list that follows provides definitions.

- *Data markers* are the graphical elements used to represent individual data point values in a chart. Figure 11-2, for example, uses symbols, or points, on a line to show data point values. Other types of charts in Excel use other data markers. A chart that uses columns or bars, for example, has column or bar data markers. A pie chart has pie-slice data markers, as shown in Figure 11-3, and so on.

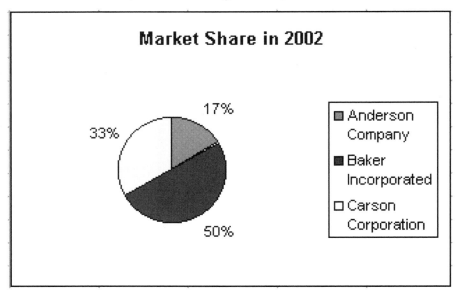

Figure 11-3 A simple pie chart.

- Excel typically describes and qualifies data markers using the *data-marker descriptions* such as axis scales and data labels. Different types of charts use different data-marker descriptions. Bar, column, and line charts use axis scales. (This is what Figure 11-2 shows, of course.) Pie and doughnut charts use data labels (see Figure 11-3).

- A *legend* names and identifies the data series you've plotted. In Figure 11-3, the legend names the data series and then shows which colors are used for which pie slices.

- *Chart text* describes a chart or some part of a chart. Figure 11-2, for example, shows a chart title (Industry Continues to Grow) and subtitle (Five-year forecast of domestic revenues). Figure 11-3 shows an example of a text box such as you might use to provide free-form annotation of a chart.

- The *plot area* of a chart is the area that includes the data markers and data-marker descriptions. In Figure 11-2, the rectangle that shows the lines and scales represents the plot area. In the chart shown in Figure 11-3, the circle that shows the slices of pie and the data labels that identify the slices of pie comprise the plot area.

- The *chart area* includes plot area, any chart text, and a legend.

Presenting Data with Charts

Once you understand the terms that Excel uses to describe to-be-charted data and the parts of a chart, you can easily create charts. In essence, you need to simply select the worksheet data you want to chart, indicate where Excel should place the chart, and then tell the Chart Wizard to create the chart.

Using the Chart Wizard

To use the Chart Wizard, first enter your to-be-charted data in an Excel worksheet. As mentioned earlier, you want to include not only the data series data points but also the labels that identify the data series and the data categories. Figure 11-4 shows an example of how you might do this.

	A	B	C	D	E	F	G	H
1		January	February	March	April	May	June	
2	Revenues	1000000	750000	1200000	1300000	1100000	800000	
3	Expenses	550000	475000	610000	640000	580000	490000	
4								
5								

Figure 11-4 A simple worksheet with data you might plot in a chart.

Once you have the data in a worksheet, follow these steps to create a chart that visually depicts the data:

1. Select the data you want to plot in the chart.

To select the data, select the worksheet range that includes the data series and any data series names and data categories names. In Figure 11-4, you would select the worksheet range A1:G3.

NOTE   *If you arrange your data series in the way shown in Figure 11-4, Excel can usually correctly guess what the data series are, what labels show data series names, and what labels show the data categories' names.*

2. Start the Chart Wizard.

You can do this by clicking the Chart Wizard button on the toolbar. Or you can click the Insert menu and click Chart. Excel displays the first Chart Wizard dialog box, as shown in Figure 11-5.

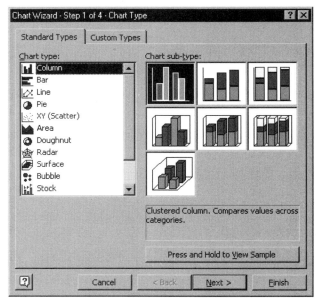

Figure 11-5   The first Chart Wizard dialog box.

3. Select the type of chart you want.

Select one of Excel's chart types from the Chart Type list box. Excel provides 14 different types of charts: Column, Bar, Line, Pie, XY (Scatter), Area, Doughnut, Radar, Surface, Bubble, Stock, Cylinder, Cone, and Pyramid.

TIP   *The "Choosing the Right Chart Type" section summarizes some of the rules of thumb that people often use to choose a particular chart type.*

4. Select the Chart sub-type.

After you select the Chart type, Excel displays the different versions available for the chart type as clickable buttons in the Chart Sub-Type box. Excel displays a short description of the selected chart sub-type in the area below the Chart Sub-Type box. To select a chart, click the button that looks like the chart you want. After making your selection, click Next.

NOTE *You can tell Excel to display a rough-draft version of the chart you're creating by clicking the Press And Hold To View Sample button.*

5. Verify that Excel has correctly interpreted the to-be-charted data.

When Excel displays the second Chart Wizard dialog box, as shown in Figure 11-6, use it to verify that Excel is retrieving the correct data from the worksheet (this should be the case if you select the data correctly in step 1) and that it has correctly identified the data series. If Excel hasn't correctly interpreted the to-be-plotted data, click the worksheet button at the right end of the Data Range text box. When Excel minimizes the Chart Wizard dialog box, reselect the correct range. To restore the Chart Wizard dialog box, click the worksheet button a second time. If Excel has misinterpreted how you've organized your worksheet data—Excel assumes the chart has fewer data series than data categories—click the other Series In option button. Click Next when you're finished.

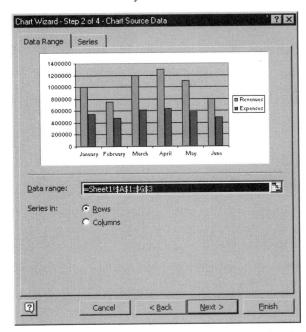

Figure 11-6 The second Chart Wizard dialog box.

NOTE *You can return to a previous Chart Wizard dialog box by clicking the Back button.*

6. Add chart text as needed.

When Excel displays the third Chart Wizard dialog box, as shown in Figure 11-7, you use its Titles tab to add a chart title and axis titles. To add such chart text, just click the appropriate text box and type the text you want. Click Next when you're finished.

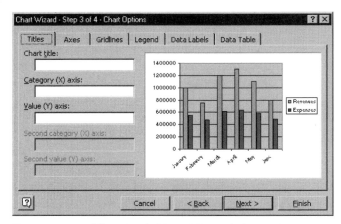

Figure 11-7   The third Chart Wizard dialog box.

NOTE *Excel updates the chart picture shown on the third Chart Wizard dialog box for any text you add.*

TIP *The other tabs of the third Chart Wizard dialog box provide options for changing and customizing the chart's appearance. The "Customizing Your Charts" section of this chapter describes how to use these tools to tailor Excel's charts to your requirements.*

7. Choose a location for the new chart.

Excel lets you place charts either as free-floating graphical objects in a worksheet or on their own individual chart sheets. You use the fourth Chart Wizard dialog box, as shown in Figure 11-8, to choose which location you want for your chart. To add a new sheet to the chart, click the As New Sheet option button and then enter a name for the new chart sheet. To add the chart as a free-floating object to an existing worksheet, click the As Object In option button and then select the worksheet from the As Object In drop-down list box. When you complete this step, you've finished creating the chart. Click Finish.

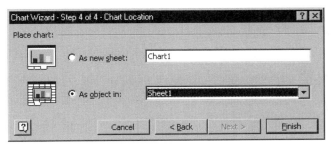

Figure 11-8 The fourth Chart Wizard dialog box.

Figure 11-9 shows how the worksheet data from Figure 11-4 looks in a column chart that resides on its own chart sheet. To view the chart, click its sheet tab. To print the chart in the selected sheet, simply click the Print toolbar button or click the File menu and click Print.

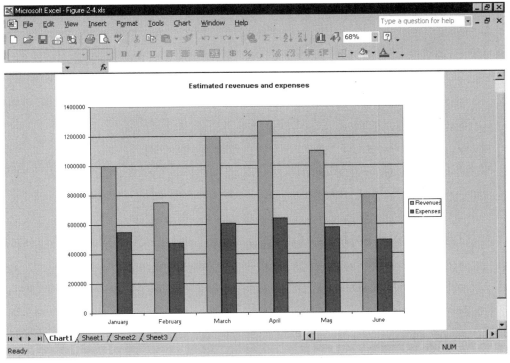

Figure 11-9 A column chart on a chart sheet.

Figure 11-10 shows the same worksheet data as that shown in Figure 11-9, except this time the worksheet data is depicted in an area chart that's free-floating as an object in a worksheet. You can resize any worksheet object, including a chart, by clicking the object and then dragging the square selection handles that appear on the sides and corners of the object.

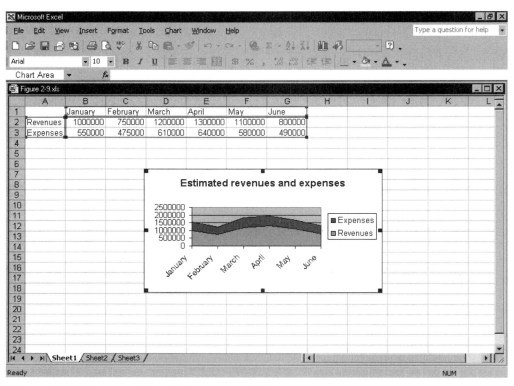

Figure 11-10 An area chart object in a worksheet.

To print a free-floating chart object, click it and then click the Print toolbar button or click the File menu and click Print. You can also print the chart object by printing the worksheet over which it floats.

Using Excel Chart Objects in Other Office Programs

You can easily use Excel chart objects in Word documents, PowerPoint presentations, and other Office programs' documents, too. To do this, you simply copy the chart object and then paste it into the other document. To copy a chart object, click the chart, click the Edit menu, and click Copy. To paste the chart object into another document, make that document active (for example, by clicking its button on the taskbar), click the Edit menu, and then click Paste.

NOTE   *Some Office programs provide a Paste Special command that you can use to specify how the chart object should be pasted.*

Choosing the Right Chart Type

Choosing the appropriate chart type is at least as much art as science. Nevertheless, it's still worthwhile to briefly discuss the three issues that you'll commonly want to consider as you choose a chart type: the basic data comparison that you want a chart to make, the principal message that you want a chart to communicate, and the relative strengths and weaknesses of the various chart types. All three factors greatly affect your choice of a chart type.

The Five Data Comparisons That Charts Make

Charts allow you to visually compare data in five ways, which means that your first step in determining the appropriate chart type is often simply to consider what data comparison you want to make. Suppose, for example, that you've collected detailed product sales revenue data for a golf equipment manufacturer. Using a chart, you might decide to look at this data in any of the ways summarized in Table 11-1.

COMPARISON	DESCRIPTION
Part-to-whole	Compares an individual data point value to the sum of a data series. Comparing sales of a particular golf club set to total sales, for example, is a part-to-whole comparison.
Whole-to-whole	Compares individual data point values to each other or data series to each other. Comparing sales of a starter men's golf club set to a starter women's golf club set, for example, is a whole-to-whole comparison.
Time-series	Compares data point values from different time periods to show how values change over time. Showing monthly sales over the last year, for example, is a time-series comparison.
Correlation	Compares different data series to explore correlation between the data series. Comparing industrywide sales to the average age of the population, for example, is a correlation comparison.
Geographic	Compares data values using a geographic map. Comparing sales by country, for example, is a geographic comparison.

Table 11-1   Summary of the five data comparisons made in charts.

Once you decide what data comparison you want to make, it's generally quite straightforward to identify the appropriate Excel chart types and sometimes even to identify appropriate chart sub-types.

- To make a *part-to-whole* comparison when working with just a single data series, you might choose a pie chart. (Pie charts plot only a single data series.) You might choose a doughnut chart or area chart if you're working with more than one data series.

- To make a *whole-to-whole* comparison, you might choose a chart that uses horizontal data markers, such as a bar chart or one of the cylinder, cone, or pyramid chart sub-types that uses a vertical data category axis and data markers. You might also choose a doughnut chart or radar chart.

- To make a *time-series* comparison, you would typically choose a chart that uses vertical data markers, such as a column chart, a line chart, or one of the cylinder, cone, or pyramid chart sub-types that uses a horizontal data category axis and data markers. You might also choose the stock chart if you're performing technical analysis of security prices. (Time-series charts typically use a horizontal data category axis because of the Western convention of using a horizontal axis to denote the passage of time.)

- To make a *correlation* comparison, you might choose the XY (scatter) chart if you're working with two data series or the bubble chart if you're working with three data series. You might also choose the surface chart if you want to explore trends in two dimensions.

- To make a *geographic* comparison, you would probably use the surface chart.

Importance of the Chart's Essential Message

A second important factor to consider is exactly what message you want to visually communicate with your chart. Typically, you can use the message as the chart title. But beyond this, you may want to experiment with different chart types and sub-types to see which best support your message.

NOTE   *Of course, a chart can and should also be used to visually explore data. Oftentimes, information that's hidden in raw, tabular presentations of data suddenly becomes visible once you depict the data in a chart. This point is worth mentioning because when you are exploring data—something you might do by viewing data in different chart types—there probably shouldn't be any rules. Quite literally, thinking "outside the box" might often mean that you want to examine your data in unusual ways.*

Strengths and Weaknesses of Different Chart Types

A third factor you'll want to consider as you choose the best chart type is the relative strengths and weaknesses of each chart type. Someone could, of course, write an entire book on this subject. But you might find it useful to consider the strengths and weaknesses that people generally ascribe to the basic chart types as you choose a chart.

NOTE   *In fact, someone has written a book—actually several books—about visually representing quantitative data. Edward Tufte has self-published several excellent books about the visual representation of data, including the bestseller The Visual Display of Quantitative Information. These books, available from online bookstores, will be of real interest and outstanding value to Excel users who frequently present data using charts. Note that one of Tufte's most elegantly argued points is that your charts shouldn't use more dimensions than your data—which essentially means that three-dimensional charts (with the exception of well-crafted surface charts) are usually just plain wrong.*

Area charts plot data point values using lines. Optimally, they stack the lines so they show cumulative data point values and color the areas between the lines. Accordingly, area charts have two noteworthy strengths: They can show both the trend in the first data series and also the total of all the data series, and they can often create implicit total data series. Figure 11-11, for example, plots two data series: one for total expenses and one for profits. However, the total of these data series implicitly creates a third data series for total revenues.

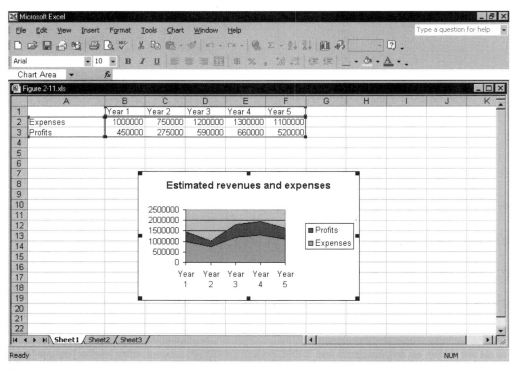

Figure 11-11 Area charts, which plot data series as stacked areas, also show the total data series.

NOTE   *You have the option of not stacking the areas of an area chart, and sometimes you'll want to do this, too. If an area chart plots revenues and expenses but doesn't stack the areas, the chart also createds an implied, third data series because the visible portion of the revenue area shows profits.*

Area charts also suffer from several noteworthy weaknesses, however. They make it difficult to see the individual data point values (although this is a two-edged sword because the reduced emphasis on individual data point values also makes it possible to plot data series with large numbers of data point values). They make it next to impossible to compare data point values of the second and subsequent data series. (You can usually get a pretty good idea about the first data series data point values, though.)

NOTE   *Area charts, as with any time-series graph, tend to suggest that time explains the apparent trends. This can be misleading, first, because there may not really be any trends and, second, because even if there are trends, the simple passage of time may likely not be the cause.*

Bar charts plot data point values in individual bars but arrange the bars so you calibrate them using a horizontal values axis. Accordingly, bar charts work really well when you want to compare data point values in a whole-item to whole-item data comparison and when the data categories are *not* time periods. Another feature of a bar chart is that the horizontal orientation of the chart makes it possible to comfortably use more lengthy data series names, as shown in Figure 11-12. Bar charts suffer from one weakness in particular: because they show each data point value with its own data marker, as you increase the number of data points you're plotting, the bars themselves become more narrow and less legible.

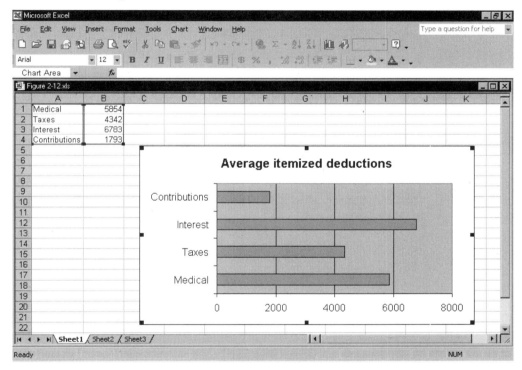

Figure 11-12 A simple bar chart that plots average tax deductions.

TIP   *Cylinder, cone, and pyramid chart types possess the same general strengths and suffer from the same general weaknesses as do the bar and column charts. In addition, cylinder, cone, and pyramid chart types, because of their three-dimensionality, also suffer from an additional weakness. The added dimension, while admittedly interesting, often makes it more difficult to precisely compare data point values.*

Bubble charts let you visually explore the relationships between data series by treating the horizontal axis as a second values axis. To accomplish this, bubble charts plot pairs of data points. In Figure 11-13, for example, the chart shows income and contribution and suggests, perhaps surprisingly, that as people make more money, they only modestly increase their charitable giving. Bubble charts differ from XY charts, which also show this same information, in that Excel sizes the bubbles using the values of a third data point. While initially confusing, a bubble chart lets you explore the relationships between two data series. (The only other Excel chart type that lets you do this is the XY [scatter] chart.) If the bubble chart suffers from a weakness, it is that the chart may suggest correlations or relationships that don't exist.

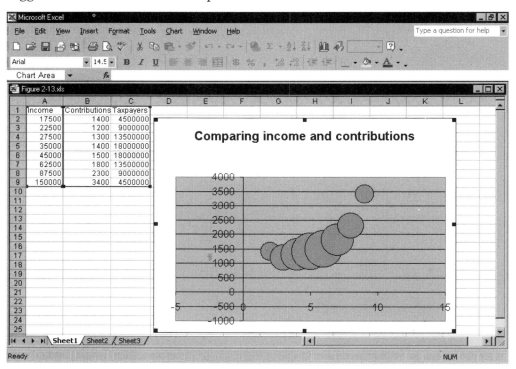

Figure 11-13 A simple bubble chart that shows U.S. Internal Revenue Service data on the relationship between income and charitable contributions.

NOTE   You *can statistically examine correlations and relationships using Excel's regression analysis tool.*

TIP   *Compare the bubble chart shown in Figure 11-13 with the XY chart shown in Figure 11-21 to see the other way you might choose to visually show a relationship between two data series.*

Column charts plot data point values in individual bars but arrange the bars so you calibrate them using a vertical values axis. Accordingly, column charts work really well when you want to view data point values in a whole-item to whole-item data comparison and when the data categories *are* time periods. Figure 11-14 shows a column chart that plots the future value of a retirement savings account based on $2,000-a-year contributions and a 9% annual return.

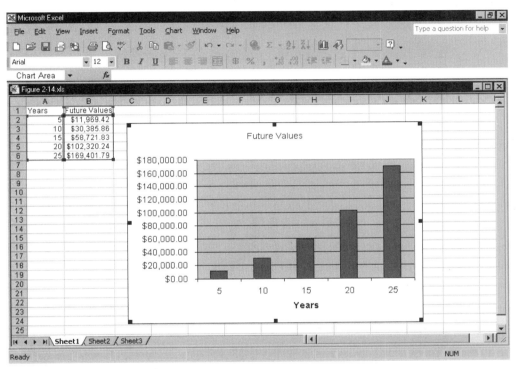

Figure 11-14 A simple column chart that plots future values of a retirement account at various points in the future.

Doughnut charts work similar to pie charts, plotting data series in concentric rings and showing each data point value as a segment, or bite, of the ring. Compared to pie charts, doughnut charts possess an advantage: they allow you to plot more than one data series. As a practical matter, they suffer from the same weaknesses as pie charts: they don't let you compare data point values between series (even though they paradoxically show multiple data series). They also limit you to small data sets. Almost always, something that appears in a doughnut chart should instead be shown with some other chart type.

Figure 11-15, for example, compares the average deduction of taxpayers with $15,000 to $20,000 of adjusted gross income (shown with the inner doughnut) with those taxpayers with $100,000 to $200,000 of adjusted gross income (shown with the outer doughnut).

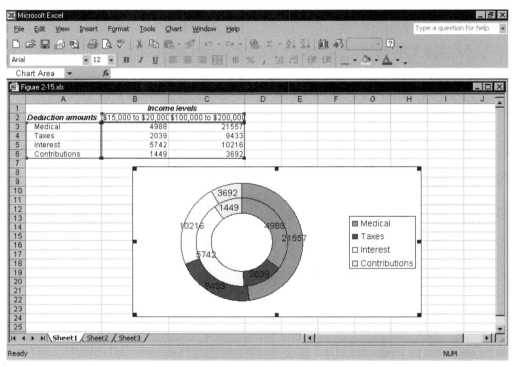

Figure 11-15 Doughnut charts let you plot data series in concentric rings.

Line charts generally plot individual data points in a line, using either different data marker symbols or different colored lines to distinguish the data series, and using a horizontal data category axis. Because line charts de-emphasize individual data point values, they work well for large data sets. With a line chart, you can literally plot thousands of data points. What's more, of all the Excel chart types, line charts tend to emphasize changes and trends in the data point values, which can be useful. Figure 11-16, for example, uses a logarithmic values axis, which means that it lets the viewer compare the rates of growth of a large company growing at 5% annually with a small company growing at 50% annually. Predictably, however, line charts suffer from some weaknesses: a de-emphasis of individual data point values, which can camouflage inappropriately small data sets and make it impossible to compare individual data points; a tendency to show time-based trends that don't exist; and a tendency to show relationships between data series that don't exist.

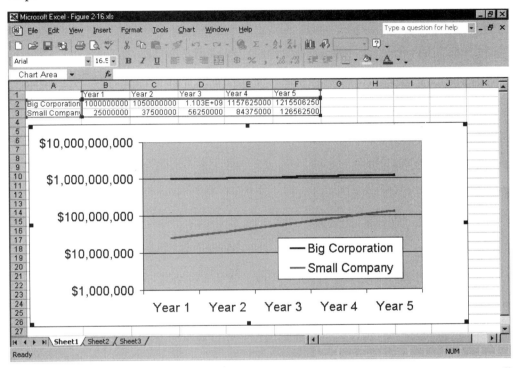

Figure 11-16 A line chart with a logarithmic values axis lets you visually compare a small company's 50% growth rate with a large company's 5% growth rate.

NOTE   *In Figure 11-16, the small company's higher growth rate shows up in its sales line's greater slope. With regular arithmetic scaling, however, the difference in growth rates is hidden.*

Pie charts, as almost everybody knows, show a single data series and depict individual data points as segments of the circle, or slices of the pie. While this means that they allow people to compare individual data point values to the total of all the data point values—and one might argue this is a strength—in general, pie charts are without merit because they can show only a single small data series. Almost always, something that appears in a pie chart should instead be shown in a table. Figure 11-17, for example, uses both a table and a pie chart to show the same data set: populations of major English-speaking countries. You'll probably agree that the table shown in the worksheet range A1:B6 works much better as a communication tool than the pie chart.

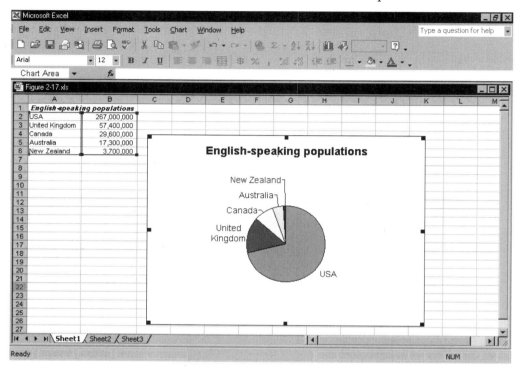

Figure 11-17 Although pie charts let you compare individual data point values to the total data point values in a data series, a table almost always presents the information more clearly.

Radar charts plot each data category's data point values on separate value axes and connect the data point values of each data series with a line, as shown in Figure 11-18. The strength of a radar chart is that it may make it possible to precisely compare individual data point values within a data category. The weakness of a radar chart is that it may make it difficult for you to compare data point values in different categories (although this isn't always a problem). You're also practically limited to a small set of data categories because the chart uses a separate value axis for each. (You obviously can't, for example, plot a set of data with 200 categories.)

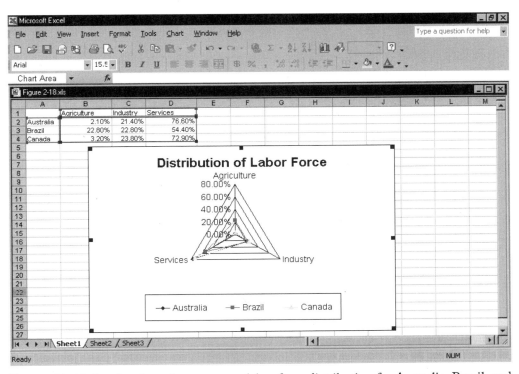

Figure 11-18 A radar chart that compares labor force distribution for Australia, Brazil, and Canada.

Stock charts plot security prices in a common open-high-low-close format, as shown in Figure 11-19. Note that if you do choose to create a stock chart, Excel expects you to organize your data series in this order: volume, opening price, high price, low price, and closing price, as shown in Figure 11-19.

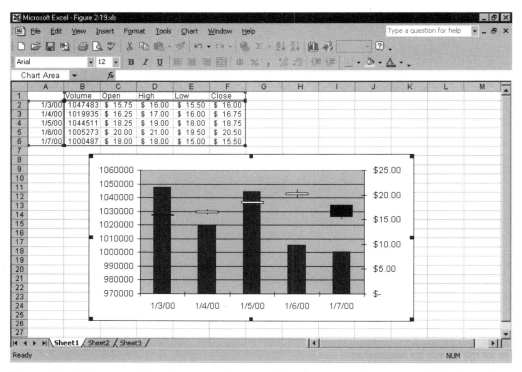

Figure 11-19 A stock chart lets you plot up to five data series in an open-high-low-close format.

NOTE *While this chart type comes from technical security analysis, the chart type can be useful even to people who don't chart security prices. You might use such a chart, for example, to plot daily temperatures.*

Surface charts plot data series in a three-dimensional grid, generally using color not to identify data series but rather to indicate value axis ranges. The principal strength of a surface chart is that it lets you show with equal emphasis both relationships within a data series and within a data category. A surface chart, however, also suffers from two weaknesses: One, because the chart does show a three-dimensional surface, it's easy for the topography of the plot area to hide data—for peaks to hide valleys. Two, although the surface uses color in its value calibrations, there isn't any agreed-upon order to colors. Is the color red "greater" than blue, for example? Is yellow "less than" green? Figure 11-20 shows a surface chart that plots labor force distribution data for Australia, Brazil, and Canada.

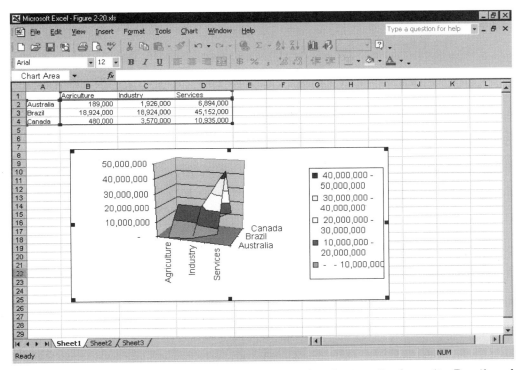

Figure 11-20 A surface chart that shows labor force distributions for Australia, Brazil, and Canada.

XY (Scatter) charts let you visually explore the relationships between data series by treating the horizontal axis as a second values axis. To accomplish this, XY charts actually plot pairs of data points. In Figure 11-21, for example, the chart shows years of education and monthly income and suggests, not surprisingly, that more educated people make more money. The huge strength of an XY chart is that it lets you explore the relationships—perhaps causation or simply correlation—between two data series. The XY chart is the only Excel chart type that lets you do this. If the XY chart suffers from a weakness, it is that the chart may suggest correlations or relationships that don't exist. (You can use Excel's regression analysis tools, discussed in Chapter 4, to examine whether two data series are correlated.)

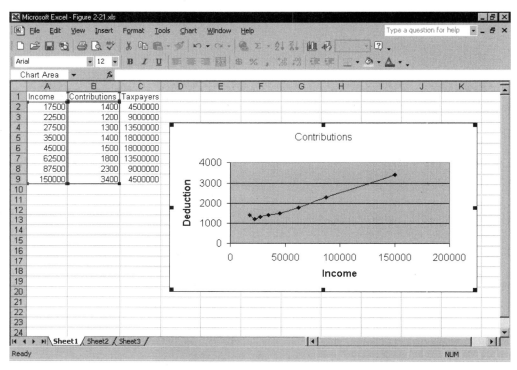

Figure 11-21 A simple XY chart that compares U.S. Internal Revenue Service data on the relationship between education and income.

NOTE   *You aren't limited to showing a single data series in an XY chart. Each data series, however, must use the same pair of data point values.*

Customizing Your Charts

You can easily customize your charts so they better fit your needs. You can, for example, rerun the Chart Wizard. This approach is usually simplest. But you can also use Chart menu commands to change specific elements of a chart. The paragraphs that follow discuss each of the two approaches, because you'll find occasion to use both.

Using the Chart Wizard to Customize a Chart

To use the Chart Wizard to customize a chart, select the chart and then click the Chart Wizard toolbar button. Excel restarts the Chart Wizard, and you can step through the four dialog boxes (described earlier in this chapter) to make your changes.

Note that you can make changes not described in the earlier discussion of the Chart Wizard, too. Figure 11-22, for example, shows the Custom Types tab of the first Chart Wizard dialog box. The Custom Types tab displays a variety of hybrid charts in which different data series use different data markers and also charts that use unusual color schemes. To use one of these custom chart types, select it from the Chart Type list.

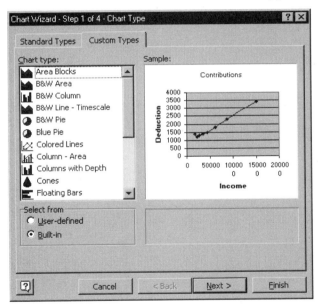

Figure 11-22 The Custom Types tab of the first Chart Wizard dialog box.

NOTE   *You can also change the chart type by clicking a chart, clicking the Chart menu, and clicking Chart Type. When you do this, Excel displays a dialog box that closely resembles the dialog box shown in Figure 11-22.*

You can add to or change the data series plotted in a chart using the Series tab of the second Chart Wizard dialog box, which is shown in Figure 11-23. To change a data series, select its name in the Series list box and then change the values in the Name and

Values boxes. To add a data series to the chart, click Add, and then after Excel adds the new series, use the Name and Values boxes to name the data series and identify the worksheet range holding the data series. To remove a data series, click the data series and then click Remove. Note, too, that the Series tab also provides a box you use to specify which worksheet range holds the data category names.

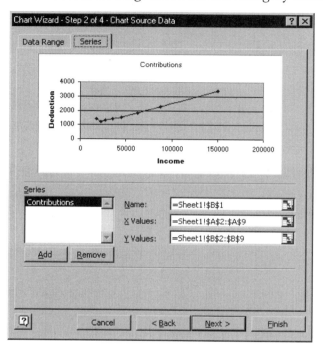

Figure 11-23 The Series tab of the second Chart Wizard dialog box.

TIP   *If you click the worksheet button shown at the right end of the Name and Values boxes, Excel minimizes the dialog box. You can then select the cell or worksheet range holding the name, to-be-plotted data, or data category names.*

NOTE   *You can also change the chart type by clicking a chart, clicking the Chart menu, and clicking Source Data. When you do this, Excel displays a dialog box, which closely resembles the dialog box shown in Figure 11-23.*

You can use the third Chart Wizard dialog box, shown in Figure 11-24, to change the text you've used to annotate the change, the appearance of the chart's axes, the gridlines used within the plot area, the location of a legend (and whether you even want one of these), whether data labels appear next to data markers, and whether a table of the plotted data also appears in the chart. Figure 11-24, for example, shows the Axes tab. You use its check boxes to indicate whether you want a Value (X) axis and a Value (Y) axis and, for the Value (X) axis, what formatting you want. Rather than reading about what each of these options does, experiment with them yourself. If your experimentation still leaves you with questions, click the Help button in the dialog box's upper right corner and then click the option you have a question about.

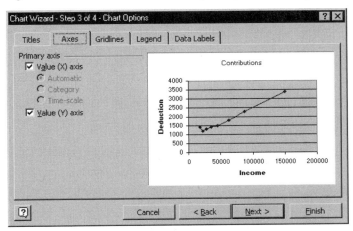

Figure 11-24 The Axes tab of the third Chart Wizard dialog box.

TIP   *Typically you do want to apply common sense to your axes scaling, and especially the scaling of your Value (Y) axis. Using inappropriately small scaling factors, for example, can exaggerate differences in data point values and changes in values—as illustrated almost every night on the news report of the major stock market indexes. Similarly, using inappropriately large scaling factors can hide important differences in values and changes in values.*

NOTE   *If you want to show the relative changes in values, you typically want to use logarithmic scaling of the values axis. To use the logarithmic scaling, right-click the axis you want to logarithmically scale, choose the shortcut menu's Format Axis command, click the Scale tab, and click the Logarithmic Scale check box.*

This book doesn't show pictures of the other tabs. You can easily see them yourself by clicking the appropriate tab. Note, however, what each of the other tabs allows you to do. The Gridlines tab displays check boxes you can select to add horizontal and vertical gridlines to plot the area of your chart. The Legend tab displays a Show Legend check box you can click to add a legend to the chart and then Placement option buttons—Bottom, Corner, Top, Right, or Left—which you can use to indicate where you want the legend placed. The Data Labels tab displays a set of option buttons you can use to indicate whether you want the actual data point values or equivalent percentages written next to their data markers. Finally, the Data Table tab (if it appears) provides two check boxes you can click to add a table and, optionally, a legend of the data point values to the bottom of the chart area.

NOTE   *You can also change the chart text, axes, gridlines, legend, data labels, or data table by clicking a chart, clicking the Chart menu, and clicking Chart Options. When you do this, Excel displays a dialog box that closely resembles the dialog box shown in Figure 11-24.*

You can use the fourth Chart Wizard dialog box, shown in Figure 11-25, to relocate a chart. To do this, simply select the other option when you see this dialog box. For example, if the dialog box initially shows the As New Sheet option button selected, click the As Object In option button—or vice versa.

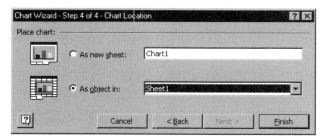

Figure 11-25 The fourth Chart Wizard dialog box.

NOTE   *You can also change the chart location by clicking a chart, clicking the Chart menu, and clicking Location. When you do this, Excel displays a dialog box that closely resembles the dialog box shown in Figure 11-25.*

Using the Shortcut Menu's Format Command

While you can use the Chart Wizard or some of the equivalent Chart menu commands to customize a chart, Excel doesn't allow you to make every change using just these methods. If you can't use the Chart Wizard or an equivalent command to change some element of a chart, you can right-click the part of the chart that you want to change and then choose the shortcut menu's Format command. For example, if you want to change the scaling of the values axis, you can right-click the values axis and then choose the Format Axis command. (Obviously, if you right-click other parts of a chart, Excel displays a different Format command which, in turn, displays a different dialog box.)

Some books on Excel spend pages describing the myriad changes you can make to each specific part of a chart. But you probably don't really need that level of instruction. In a nutshell, you make only a handful of changes to each part of a chart:

- Patterns. Many of the Format dialog boxes display a Patterns tab that you can use to select the colors and lines you want Excel to use to draw the chart object.

- Fonts. Any Format dialog box for an element that includes text provides a Font tab that you can use to choose font, font style, font point size, and special text effects.

- Number. Any Format dialog box for an element that includes numbers provides a Number tab that you can use to choose a numeric formatting style.

- Alignment. Any Format dialog box for an element that includes text provides an Alignment tab that you can use to align text.

- Scale. The Format dialog box for both the axes and the gridlines provides a Scale tab that you can use to specify how Excel should calibrate and draw the axis or grid.

TIP   *Remember that if you have a question about how to work with some dialog box option, you can click the Help button and then click the option to get a brief but usually very helpful description. The Help button appears in the upper right corner of the dialog box and is marked with a question mark.*

Summary

The familiar saying, "A picture is worth a thousand words," has dubious origins. The phrase actually comes from nineteenth-century advertising. Nevertheless, the saying has become part of our conventional wisdom because it really is true. Often, conveying information with a picture makes all the difference for people's understanding. And with Excel's Chart Wizard—the subject of this chapter—you have a powerful tool for turning numbers into pictures.

Chapter 12

USING THE OFFICE APPLETS

Featuring:

- Creating Text Graphics with WordArt
- Designing Graphic Objects with Microsoft Draw
- Inserting Art
- Creating an Organization Chart
- Creating Diagrams

Almost any business document can be enhanced with graphics and art. A newsletter practically cries out for some graphics, and even a long annual report containing financial information can benefit from some colorful charts.

Several of the Office programs contain small programs, known as *applets,* that you can use to add graphical interest. This chapter will explore how to add art, diagrams, and graphics in Word, Excel, PowerPoint, and FrontPage. Although you can't create graphics in Access, you can copy graphics into a report or form once you've created them in one of the other applications.

Creating Text Graphics with WordArt

WordArt is available in Word, PowerPoint, Excel, and FrontPage, and you can use it to create a letterhead, the title page of a document, text logos for use on a slide, some jazzy text for a Web page, or even to emphasize the column titles in a worksheet. A restaurant-owner friend of ours uses WordArt quite successfully to spruce up his daily menus. Figure 12-1 shows a simple letterhead created with WordArt.

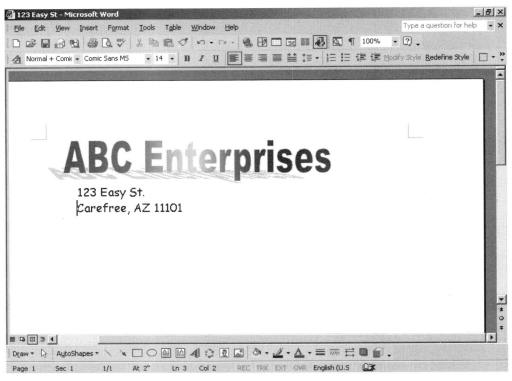

Figure 12-1 Letterhead created with WordArt.

Inserting a WordArt Object

The easiest way to access WordArt is to display the Drawing toolbar, which is shown at the bottom of the screen in Figure 12-1. Click the View menu, click Toolbars, and then click Drawing to display the Drawing toolbar. (The Drawing toolbar is displayed by default in PowerPoint.) To create a text graphic with WordArt, display the Drawing toolbar and then follow these steps:

1. **Open the WordArt Gallery, as shown in Figure 12-2.**

   Click the Insert WordArt button on the Drawing toolbar.

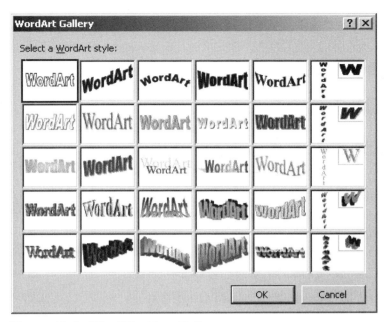

Figure 12-2 The WordArt Gallery.

2. Select a style for your text graphic.

The WordArt Gallery contains a variety of styles that you can use to create your text graphic. To select one, click it and then click OK. You'll see the Edit WordArt Text dialog box, as shown in Figure 12-3.

Figure 12-3 The Edit WordArt Text dialog box.

3. **Enter the text for your WordArt graphic.**

Replace the words *Your Text Here* by typing the text you want.

4. **Select a font for your text.**

Click the Font drop-down list to display a list of available fonts. The Text box shows you how your text will look in the selected font.

5. **Select a point size.**

Click the Size drop-down arrow to display a list of the available sizes in points. One point equals 1/72 inch. Therefore, if you want your WordArt graphic to measure 1 inch tall, set the size at 72. If you want your graphic to measure ½ inch tall, set the size at 36.

TIP   *Some styles look good in some fonts and at some sizes, but not in others. You can experiment to see the effects.*

6. **Add boldface or italic emphasis if you like.**

Click the Bold or Italic button to boldface or italicize the text. Again, adding this emphasis works well with some styles and not others, so experiment to get exactly the effect you want. If you will be using your text graphic on a printed page, you'll also want to test how boldfacing or italicizing a style looks when printed.

7. **Add the text graphic to your document.**

Click OK. The text graphic is added to your document, and the WordArt toolbar is displayed, as shown in Figure 12-4.

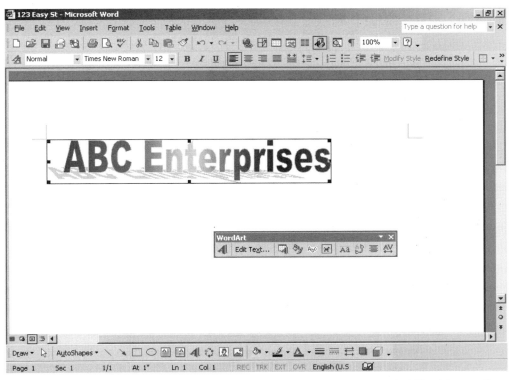

Figure 12-4 Inserting a WordArt object in a document also displays the WordArt toolbar.

Editing a WordArt Object

After you insert a text graphic into your document, you can move and resize it by clicking and dragging. To reposition it, click inside it and drag it to a new location. To change the size, click a selection handle (selection handles are the small black squares) and drag it. You can shrink or expand the text graphic horizontally by clicking and dragging the colored square.

Using the WordArt Toolbar

You can use the buttons on the WordArt toolbar, which is shown in Figure 12-4, to make additional changes to your text graphic. Point to a button to display a ScreenTip that identifies the button. The following sections describe these buttons in order from left to right. (The buttons you see on the WordArt toolbar depend on the style of the text graphic and the Office program you are using to create it.)

Insert WordArt

Clicking this button displays the WordArt Gallery, which you can use to add another text graphic to your document.

Edit Text

Clicking this button displays the Edit WordArt Text dialog box. You can use this dialog box to change the font, font size, emphasis, or the actual text of your graphic.

WordArt Gallery

If you want to change the style for an existing text graphic, click this button to display the WordArt Gallery. Select another style, and click OK. You'll see that the style of your text graphic has changed in the document.

Format WordArt

Clicking this button opens the Format WordArt dialog box. Figure 12-5 shows this dialog box open in Word after we inserted the text graphic shown in Figure 12-1. The tabs displayed in this dialog box depend on the style you selected and the Office program you are using.

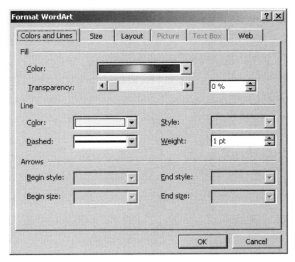

Figure 12-5   The Format WordArt dialog box in Word.

You can use the various tabs to change the following:

- Click the Colors And Lines tab to change the fill color, line color and style, and arrow style, if the graphic contains them.

- Click the Size tab to change the dimensions of the graphic.

- Click the Layout tab to specify how text will wrap around the graphic.

- Click the Web tab to specify alternative text for the graphic if you will be using it on a Web page.

- Click the Position tab (you'll see it in PowerPoint) to adjust how the WordArt is arranged in relationship to other objects.

WordArt Shape

Click this button on the WordArt toolbar to display the palette of shapes shown in Figure 12-6. Simply click a shape to impose it on your text graphic.

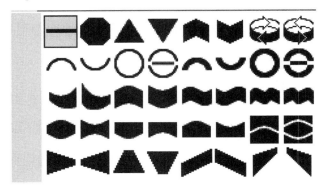

Figure 12-6   The palette of WordArt shapes.

Text Wrapping

Clicking this button displays a list of ways that you can wrap text around your graphic.

WordArt Same Letter Heights

Click this button to make all the letters, whether upper- or lowercase, exactly the same height. To return to the original size of the letters, click this button again.

WordArt Vertical Text

Click this button to display your text graphic vertically rather than horizontally. To return to the original horizontal formation, click the WordArt Vertical Text button again.

WordArt Alignment

Clicking this button displays a menu of alignment choices. Select an item to change the alignment of your text graphic.

WordArt Character Spacing

Click this button to specify the type of spacing between letters in your text graphic. Simply select an item from the menu to apply that type of spacing.

TIP   *When you no longer need to use the WordArt toolbar, click outside your text graphic to hide the toolbar.*

Designing Graphic Objects with Microsoft Draw

Creating an attractive text graphic with WordArt is within the abilities of those of us who were not gifted with artistic talent. Creating a graphic object with the Drawing tools, however, is another matter. You really do need some drawing skills, and you need the time to become familiar with the Drawing tools and how to use them. We doubt that most business managers and professionals have the inclination or care to devote the time.

Nevertheless, in this section we'll introduce you to these tools, which are available in Word, PowerPoint, Excel, and FrontPage. Figure 12-7 shows the Drawing toolbar. As you know, you can point to a button to display a ScreenTip that describes it.

Figure 12-7 The Drawing toolbar.

Drawing an Object

To draw any object, you first select the tool and then you drag the mouse. For example, to draw an arrow, click the arrow button, and then drag the mouse across an empty space in your document. You'll draw a straight line in the direction you are dragging, and when you release the mouse button, an arrowhead will appear at the right end of the line.

To draw a rectangle, click the Rectangle tool and then drag the mouse to create the rectangle. If you want a square instead, hold down the Shift key as you drag the mouse. To draw an oval, click the Oval tool and then drag the mouse. To draw a circle instead, hold down the Shift key while you drag the Oval tool.

Clicking the AutoShapes button displays a menu of a number of categories, each containing a variety of shapes you can select and insert in a document. If you click the More AutoShapes item, you display the Insert Clip Art task pane. Place the insertion point where you want to insert clip art, and then click the item to insert it. Figure 12-8 shows an item inserted into a PowerPoint slide from the Insert Clip Art task pane.

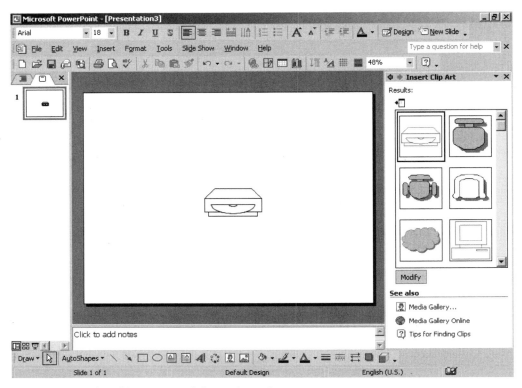

Figure 12-8 An object inserted from the task pane.

Editing an Object

Once you create an object, you can change it in the following ways:

- To move an object, select it and then drag it.

- To change an object's shape, click a selection handle and then drag the handle.

- To delete an object, select it, and then press the Delete key.

- To copy an object, right-click it, choose Copy from the shortcut menu, move the insertion point to the location where you want the copied object, right-click, and then choose Paste from the shortcut menu.

Inserting a Text Box

You can use tools on the Drawing toolbar to insert either a vertical or a horizontal text box in a document. You can then type inside the box to enter text. Click the Text Box button or the Vertical Text Box button, drag to draw a box in your document, and then release the mouse button. You can now enter text at the blinking insertion point. Figure 12-9 shows a horizontal text box inserted on a PowerPoint slide, ready for text to be entered.

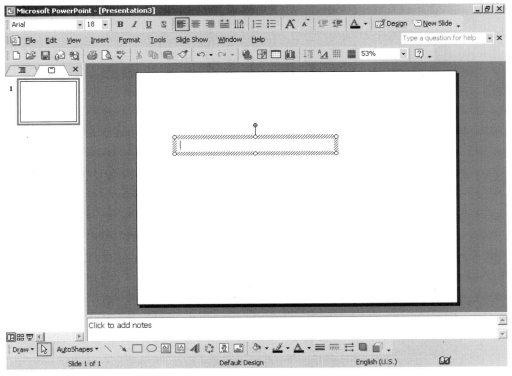

Figure 12-9   A text box ready for text to be entered.

TIP   *To place existing text in a text box, select the text and then click the Text Box button.*

Formatting Drawn Objects

If you intend to use the Drawing toolbar for serious design purposes, you'll want to become familiar with how to use the items on the Draw menu. To display it, click the Draw button at the far left of the Drawing toolbar. Figure 12-10 shows the Draw menu.

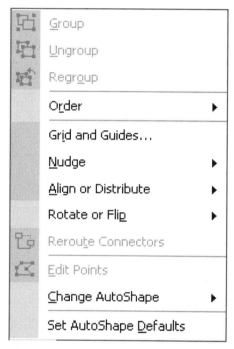

Figure 12-10 The Draw menu.

Using the items on the Draw men is not for the faint of heart, and it will take some practice. For details, open Help in any of the Office programs that use the Drawing toolbar, and search on "draw."

Inserting Art

If you have art of any kind stored on your computer, you can insert it in a Word, PowerPoint, Excel, or FrontPage document. You can insert clip art (images that are included with Office) and digital pictures that are stored as files, and, if you have the equipment, you can insert a photo directly from a scanner or a camera. You can also use some tools that come with Office to size a picture, change it from color to black and white or grayscale, and adjust the brightness.

Inserting Clip Art

To insert clip art, place the insertion point in the document where you want to place the art and then follow these steps:

1. Open the Object dialog box, as shown in Figure 12-11.

Click the Insert menu, and then click Object.

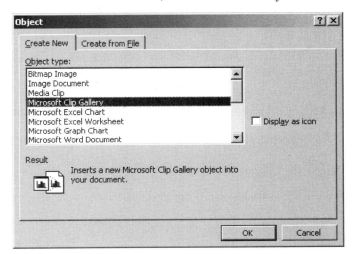

Figure 12-11 The Object dialog box.

2. Open the Microsoft Clip Gallery, as shown in Figure 12-12.

In the Object Type list box, select Microsoft Clip Gallery, and then click OK.

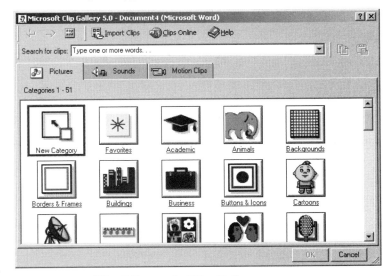

Figure 12-12 The Microsoft Clip Gallery.

3. Insert a picture.

On the Pictures tab, click a category to see the images in it. When you find one you like, click it, and then click the Insert Clip button on the button menu that appears.

The image now appears in your document at the insertion point, and the Picture toolbar is displayed on your screen, as shown in Figure 12-13.

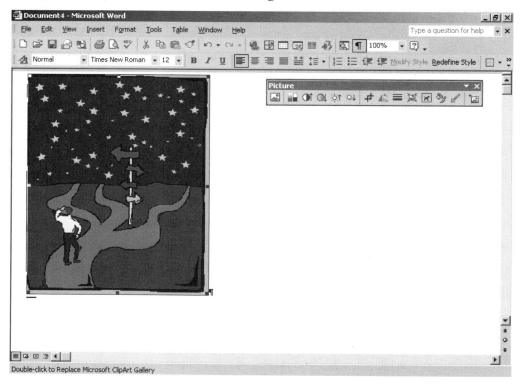

Figure 12-13 Inserting clip art in a document.

You can use the Picture toolbar to manipulate the picture (clip art or other pictures) in various ways:

- Click the image to select it, and then simply drag it to move it to a new location in the document.

- To make the image larger or smaller, click one of the selection handles (the little squares on the edges of the image) and drag it.

- To crop the image (cut part of it away), click the Crop button on the Picture toolbar and drag across the area you want to cut. When you're finished, click outside the image. The original image remains uncropped; only the copy that's in your document is trimmed.

- To change the color of the image, select the image, click the Color button on the Picture toolbar, and then select Grayscale, Black & White, or Washout.

- To increase or decrease the contrast, select the image and then click the More Contrast or Less Contrast button on the Picture toolbar.

- To vary the brightness, select the image and then click the More Brightness or Less Brightness button on the Picture toolbar.

- To rotate the image, select it and click the Rotate Left button.

Inserting a Picture from a File

If you have a photo or any other image stored as a file, you can insert it in your document. Follow these steps:

1. Open the Insert Picture dialog box, as shown in Figure 12-14.

Click the Insert menu, click Picture, and then click From File.

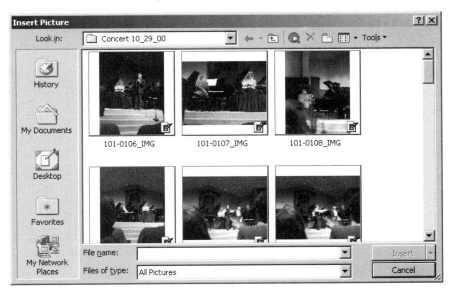

Figure 12-14 The Insert Picture dialog box.

2. Locate the file you want to insert.

Find the file, and click the Insert button.

Click the picture to select it and to display the Picture toolbar. You can now manipulate this picture in all the ways discussed in the previous section.

NOTE *For information about how to insert a picture directly from a scanner or a camera, check Help in an Office program.*

Wrapping Text Around a Picture

Using the text-wrapping feature, you can create some professional effects and vary the layout of your document. To see the options, select your picture and then click the Text Wrapping button on the Picture toolbar. The little illustrations show how text will align when you select an option. Click an option, and then start typing at the paragraph mark (¶).

Creating an Organization Chart

Word, PowerPoint, and Excel include some diagramming tools that often come in handy when you're composing a business document. You can insert and customize a cycle diagram, a radial diagram, a pyramid diagram, a Venn diagram, a target diagram, and an organization chart. The techniques for manipulating, adding text, and shaping all the diagrams are similar. This section walks through the steps for creating an organization chart, an indispensable visual communication tool in an office environment. Place the insertion point in your document where you want the chart, and then follow these steps:

1. Open the Diagram Gallery dialog box, as shown in Figure 12-15.

Click Insert, and then click Diagram.

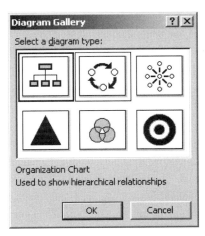

Figure 12-15 The Diagram Gallery dialog box.

2. Place an outline of the diagram in your document.

Click the Organization Chart, which is the first item in the first row, and then click OK. Word places the beginnings of a chart in your document and displays the Organization Chart toolbar, as shown in Figure 12-16.

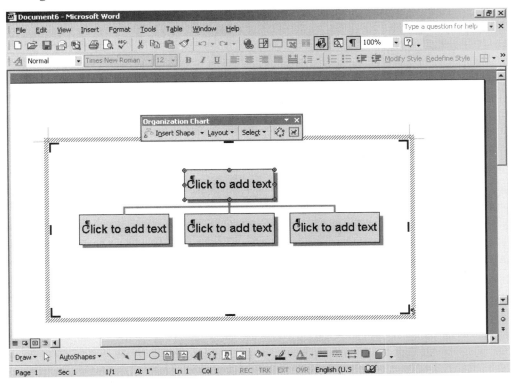

Figure 12-16 The beginnings of an organization chart.

3. **Add names, positions, boxes, and lines that reflect your organization or your proposed organization.**

To add text in a box, click in a box and start typing. To add levels of organization to your chart, select a box, click the Insert Shape button on the Organization Chart toolbar, and then select Subordinate, Coworker, or Assistant. To modify the style of your chart, click the AutoFormat button on the toolbar to open the Organization Chart Style Gallery dialog box, select a style from the list, and then click Apply. To modify the colors, size, and layout of the chart, right-click outside the chart but within the gridlines and choose Format Organization Chart from the shortcut menu to open the Format Organization Chart dialog box.

Clicking outside the gridlines closes the Organization Chart toolbar and hides the gridlines. When the chart is to your liking, save the file.

Customizing an Organization Chart

You can further change an organization chart either before or after you save it:

- To change the font inside a position box, select the text, click the Font drop-down list on the Formatting toolbar, and select a font.

- To change the font size inside a position box, select the text, click the Font Size drop-down list on the Formatting toolbar, and select a font.

- To add emphasis to text inside a position box, select the text and then click the Bold, Italic, or Underline button on the Formatting toolbar.

- To change the alignment of text inside a position box, select the text and then click one of the alignment buttons on the Formatting toolbar.

Creating Diagrams

In Word, PowerPoint, and Excel you can create several types of diagrams, as we mentioned at the beginning of the previous section. Using the Diagram Gallery dialog box, you can insert the following types of diagrams:

- A cycle diagram, which shows a process with a continuous cycle.

- A radial diagram, which shows the relationships of a core element.

- A pyramid diagram, which shows foundation-based relationships.

- A Venn diagram, which shows areas of overlap between elements.

- A target diagram, which shows steps toward a goal.

To create any of these, you use the same basic steps as those for creating an organization chart. When you click a diagram type in the Diagram Gallery dialog box and then click OK, the Office program inserts that type of diagram in your document. Figure 4-17 shows a target diagram inserted in an Excel worksheet.

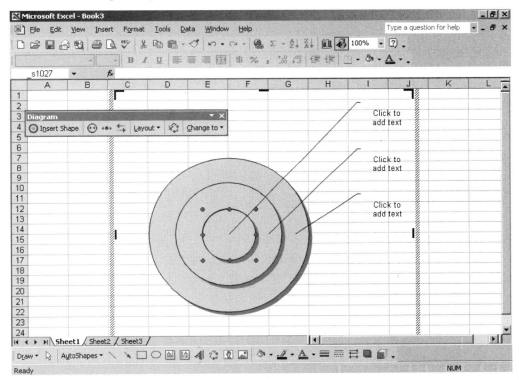

Figure 4-17 A target diagram inserted in an Excel worksheet.

To add text, click in the Click To Add Text areas. Use the buttons on the Diagram toolbar to format the diagram. For example, to add another ring to the target diagram, click the Insert Shape button. To change the style of the diagram, click the AutoFormat button to open the Diagram Style Gallery, select a style, and click Apply. You can even change to another diagram altogether by clicking the Change To button and selecting one of the other diagrams from the drop-down list.

Summary

Whether your are creating a Word document, a PowerPoint presentation, an Excel worksheet, or a FrontPage Web site, you can increase the visual communication with graphics. This chapter has introduced the Office tools you can use to create graphics and insert them in your documents. A well-placed piece of art can significantly enhance the value of almost any document. If you're ever having difficulty explaining something in words or numbers, consider whether a chart or a diagram might be more effective.

Chapter 13

MAIL MERGE USING WORD

Featuring:

- Creating a Form Letter
- Sending Personalized E-Mail Messages to a Group
- Printing Labels
- Creating a Directory

If your office is in sync with the current trend, you probably have far less paper to deal with than you did five years ago. Many businesses have converted many processes to a totally electronic system. Nevertheless, we still need to address envelopes, prepare name badges for a convention or a seminar, do periodic paper mailings, print business cards, and the like.

Mail merge is a Word tool that you can use to send personalized holiday greetings to several hundred of your closest friends, create mass enrollment instructions for participants in your company's health plan, print out labels from a directory of entries, even print out fancy awards to a number of different people, as well as a number of other tasks that involve merging a list with another document.

As I do, you probably receive several form letters each week that were created using a mail merge program. Your name is in the salutation and, sometimes, in the body of the letter as well.

You can use the mail merge feature when working with letters, e-mail messages, enve-lopes, labels, and a directory. (A *directory* is a single document that contains a catalog or a list of addresses.) Word provides two ways to perform a mail merge: the Mail Merge toolbar and the Mail Merge Wizard. After you become familiar with the steps involved, you may find it faster to use the toolbar, but in the beginning, using the wizard is much easier, and this chapter will use the wizard.

Creating a Form Letter

First, let's create a form letter. Open a new, blank document window and enter the basic text of your letter, or if you have an existing letter, open the file. Now, click the Tools menu, click Letters And Mailings, and then click Mail Merge Wizard to open Mail Merge in the task pane, as shown in Figure 13-1.

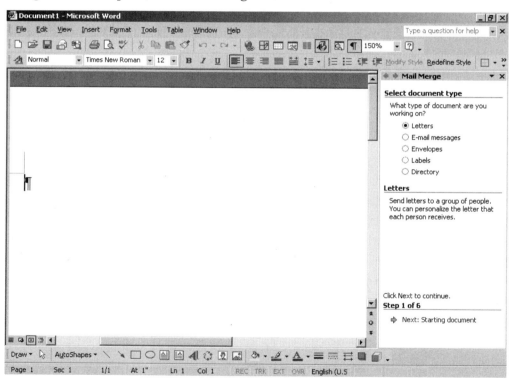

Figure 13-1 The first step of the Mail Merge Wizard.

In the Select Document Type section, click the Letters option button, and then click Next. In step 2 of the wizard, which is shown in Figure 13-2, indicate how you want to set up your letter. If, as suggested, your letter is the current document, click the Use The Current Document option button, and then click Next.

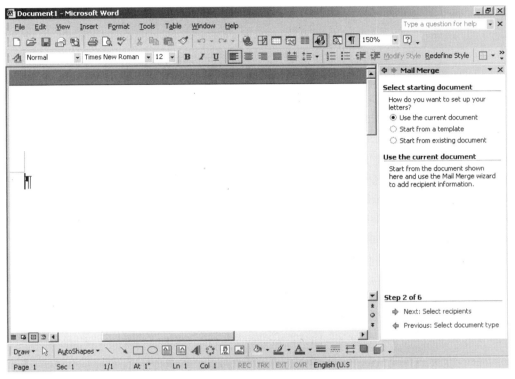

Figure 13-2 The second step of the Mail Merge Wizard.

Now you need to select the recipients of your form letter. If you have an existing list or a list of contacts in Outlook, you can use that list. To create a new list, click the Type A New List option button, and then click Create to open the New Address List dialog box, as shown in Figure 13-3.

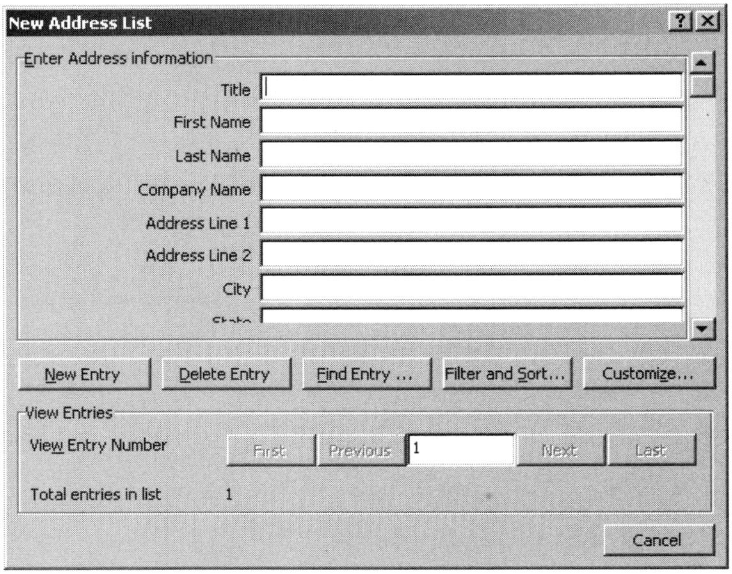

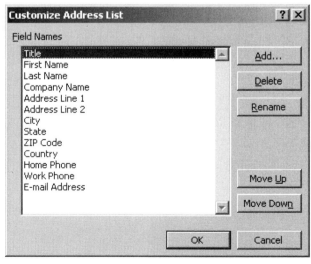

Figure 13-3 The New Address List dialog box.

For a form letter, you will probably want only the Title, First Name, Last Name, Company Name, Address Line 1, City, State, and Zip Code information, so you'll need to delete the other boxes from the form. Click the Customize button to open the Customize Address List dialog box, as shown in Figure 13-4. Select the fields you don't need, and click the Delete button. When you are finished, click OK.

Figure 13-4 The Customize Address List dialog box.

Type the information in the boxes, pressing the Tab key to move from box to box. When you've finished one entry, click the New Entry button to display clean boxes and enter the information for the next recipient. When you've entered all the names and addresses, close the dialog box. Word displays the Save Address List dialog box, as shown in Figure 13-5. In the File Name box, enter a name for your list, and click the Save button. By default, Word stores your lists in the My Data Sources folder.

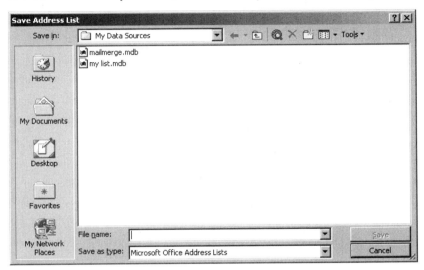

Figure 13-5 The Save Address List dialog box.

Word now displays the Mail Merge Recipients dialog box, as shown in Figure 13-6. You can use the options in this dialog box to sort the list, select recipients, and add and remove recipients. When you're finished, click OK to return to step 3 of the wizard. Click Next to open step 4, in which you'll add recipient information to your letter. Figure 13-7 shows your choices in step 4.

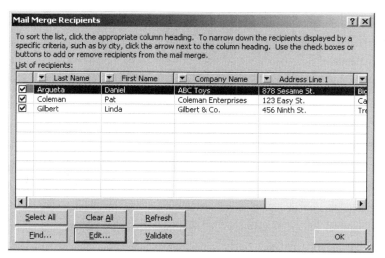

Figure 13-6 The Mail Merge Recipients dialog box.

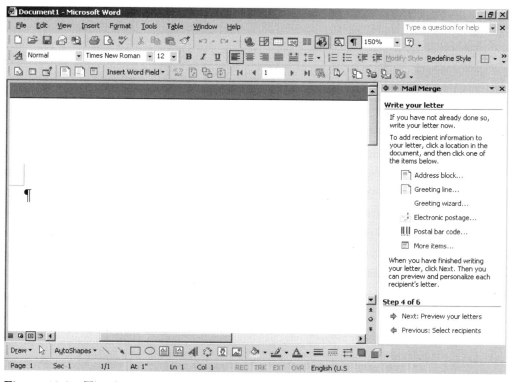

Figure 13-7 The fourth step of the Mail Merge Wizard.

To add address information, click Address Block to open the Insert Address Block dialog box, as shown in Figure 13-8. Specify the format for the recipients' names, whether to insert the company name, and how to format the postal address. To change the information associated with a field, click the Match Fields button to open the Match Fields dialog box. Follow the instructions on the screen.

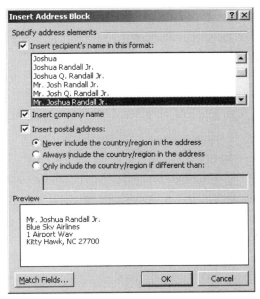

Figure 13-8 The Insert Address Block dialog box.

Back in the Insert Address Block dialog box, click OK to insert the Address Block field in your document. Now, in step 4 of the wizard, click Greeting Line to open the Greeting Line dialog box, as shown in Figure 13-9. Use the drop-down lists to specify the greeting line format, and then click OK to insert the greeting line field in your document. Back in step 4 of the wizard, click Next.

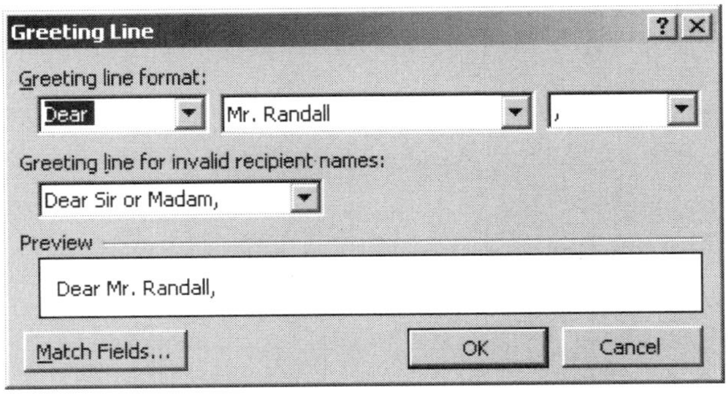

Figure 13-9 The Greeting Line dialog box.

In step 5 you are given the opportunity to review your merged letters. To move to the next or previous letter, click the Back or Forward buttons. To check a specific letter, click Find A Recipient to open the Find Entry dialog box. Enter a name in the Find box, and click the Find Next button. When you've completed your review, click Next to move to step 6, as shown in Figure 13-10. Click Print to open the Merge To Printer dialog box, specify what you want to print, and click OK to start the printing.

Figure 13-10 The Merge To Printer dialog box.

Seven Tips for Creating Professional Form Letters

1. Be absolutely sure that your letter doesn't contain any typographical errors before you print the merged documents. Run the spelling checker, read through the document on the screen and on paper, and then ask a coworker to check the document. In most organizations, someone is designated as the final authority to sign off on a document that will be sent to hundreds or even thousands of recipients. I recently heard of a company about to stuff several hundred envelopes with form letters containing information about open enrollment for the company's health plan. A major typo was discovered—it wasn't a pretty picture.

2. If you want your recipients to actually read your letter, be sure that it contains only the information necessary to the topic at hand. If you go on for pages and pages, your letter will go straight into the wastebasket or even the shredder.

3. The recipient's address on the form letter may include a courtesy title, such as Dr., Professor, Mrs., or Ms., but most of the time the first and last name is sufficient. In the salutation, the word *Dear* is usually followed by a courtesy title and the last name, although these days simply the first and last names are often used, and the courtesy title is omitted. For example, if you write *Dear Pat Coleman,* you avoid the issue of gender and marital status altogether.

4. Although a block style is often used for a business letter, other styles are also acceptable. For some examples, check out the letter templates that come with Word. Click the File menu, and then click New to open the New Document task pane. In the New From Template section, click General Templates to open the Templates dialog box, and then click the Letters & Faxes tab.

5. The body of your letter should reflect good business-style writing. Be concise, but fluent and conversational. Avoid jargon and pretentious-sounding words and phrases.

6. When you're composing your letter, insert the date and then leave space for the address block.

7. Some companies create a mythical employee whose name appears in the signature line of a form letter. This protects a real employee from receiving unwanted letters, e-mail messages, and phone calls and ensures that any communication directed to the mythical person gets routed to one person or several people who have assumed responsibility for the feedback. It's something to consider.

Printing Envelopes for Your Form Letters

If your printer supports doing so, you can place a stack of envelopes in the paper tray and print envelopes from the list you created for your form letters. (Check the manual that came with your printer for details.) Once again, you use the Mail Merge Wizard.

Click the Tools menu, click Letters And Mailings, and then click Mail Merge Wizard to open the wizard in the task pane. Click the Envelopes option button, and then click Next. In step 2, click the Use The Current Document option button, and then click Envelope Options to open the Envelope Options dialog box and select the envelope size and format. When you've made your selections, click OK. Back in the wizard, click Next.

In step 3, click the Use An Existing List option button, and then click Next. In the document window, click the Style drop-down list, and select Envelope Return. The insertion point moves to the appropriate location on the envelope, where you can type your return address. Click the Style drop-down list again, and select Envelope Address. Word displays a box in which you can insert the address block. Back in step 4 of the wizard, click Address Block to open the Insert Address Block dialog box. Select the format for the address, and click OK to insert the address field on the envelope.

If you have electronic postage software, click Electronic Postage to add the stamp. To add the postal bar code, click Postal Bar Code to open the Insert Postal Bar Code dialog box. Select the appropriate address fields, and click OK. Click Next to open step 5, in which you can preview your envelopes. When you're assured that they're satisfactory, click Next to open step 6. Verify that your envelopes are correctly inserted in your printer, and click Print.

Electronic Postage

Trips to the post office can become a thing of the past if you use electronic postage. If you don't have electronic postage software installed on your system, click the E-Postage Properties button in the Envelopes And Labels dialog box. You'll see a message asking if you want to visit the Office Update Web site to find out more about electronic postage. Click Yes to go to the site.

You can then check out both E-Stamp Internet Postage and Stamps.com. When you purchase E-Stamp Internet Postage, you get the software and a little device, called an electronic vault, that plugs in to the back of your computer. You then connect to e-stamp.com, buy postage using your credit card or electronic funds transfer from your bank account, and then download your postage into the electronic vault. Now when you want to use electronic postage, you don't need to be connected to the Internet. In the Envelopes And Labels dialog box, you simply click the Add Electronic Postage check box.

To use the electronic system at Stamps.com, you download the software from the stamps.com site for free and then connect to the site to print postage, envelopes, labels, and so on. Various pricing plans are available depending on the size of your business and your usage.

Using an Excel List as a Data Source

Many businesses store lists of contact information in applications other than Word. It's quite common to store lists as a worksheet in Excel. And if this is the case in your organization, you can easily use such a list as the *data source* for a mail merge in Word.

First, verify that the Excel worksheet contains a top row that identifies the field name for each column, as shown in Figure 13-11.

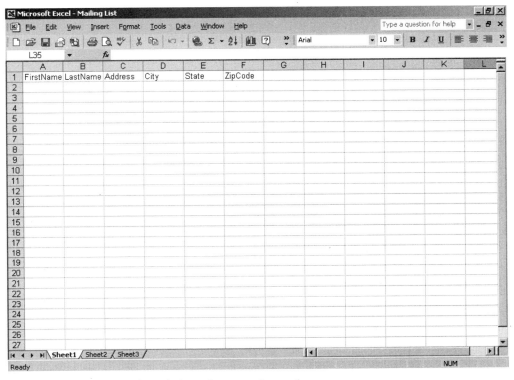

Figure 13-11 An Excel worksheet formatted as a data source.

Then save the worksheet as a data source. In Excel, follow these steps:

1. **Open the Save As dialog box, as shown in Figure 13-12.**

   Click the Save menu, and then click Save As.

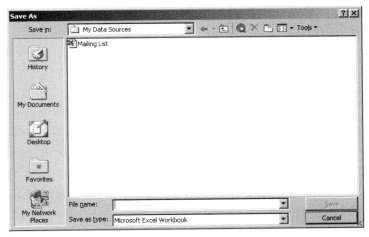

Figure 13-12 The Save As dialog box in Excel.

2. Save the file in the My Data Sources folder.

Double-click the My Data Sources folder to select it, type a name for the list in the File Name box, and then click the Save button.

Now, back in Word, start the Mail Merge Wizard, and go to step 3. Click Select A Different List to open the Select Data Source dialog box, as shown in Figure 13-13. Select the Excel file, and click Open. In the Select Table dialog box, click OK to open the Mail Merge Recipients dialog box. You'll see that it contains the list you saved in Excel as a data source. You can use this list just as you'd use a list you created in Word.

Figure 13-13 The Select Data Source dialog box.

TIP   *If you're interested in learning more about how to use Excel in your business, check out* Effective Executive's Guide to Excel 2002, *by David B. Maguiness and Stephen L. Nelson, published by Redmond Technology Press.*

Using an Access Database as a Data Source

If your organization maintains contact lists in Access, you can also use an Access table or query as a data source for a mail merge. In Access, simply save the table or query as a data source, and then open it and use it following the procedure outlined previously for an Excel worksheet.

TIP   *If you're interested in learning more about how to use Access in your business, check out* Effective Executive's Guide to Access 2002, *by Scott H. A. Clark and Doug Kleiber, published by Redmond Technology Press.*

Editing Your Data Source

Regardless of which program you used to create your data source, you can use the Mail Merge Recipients dialog box to edit contact information, to add new contacts, to delete contacts, and so on. In the Mail Merge Wizard, click Edit Recipient List to open the Mail Merge Recipients dialog box, as shown earlier in this chapter in Figure 13-6. Then click the Edit button to open the following dialog box:

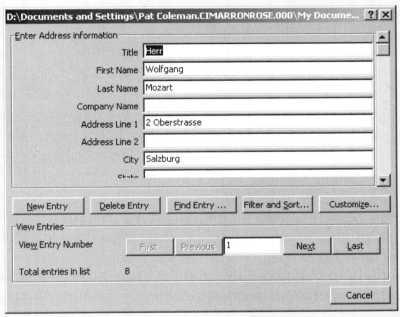

To move from entry to entry, click the Next or Previous button. To edit an entry, simply select it and change it; to add new information, type it in the appropriate field. To delete an entry, select it and then click the Delete Entry button. To add a new entry, click the New Entry button and then enter the information in the fields.

To add or delete fields or to change the name of a field in your data source, click the Customize button to open the Customize Address List dialog box:

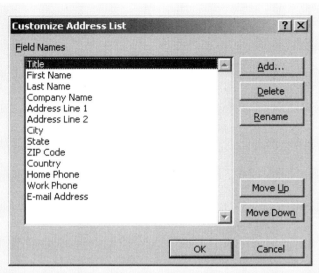

Select an item, and then click the corresponding button to add, delete, or rename a field. To rearrange the order of fields, select a field and then click the Move Up or Move Down button until the field is where you want it. When you're finished, click OK.

Sending Personalized E-Mail Messages to a Group

If you also have Outlook installed on your computer system, you can use the Mail Merge Wizard in Word to send a personalized e-mail message to a group of people. First, be sure that your data source includes the e-mail addresses of all your recipients, and then start the wizard. (Click the Tools menu, click Letters And Mailings, and then click Mail Merge Wizard.) Now follow these steps:

1. **Tell the wizard which type of document you'll create.**

   In step 1, select E-Mail Messages in the Select Document Type section, and then click Next.

2. **Tell the wizard the source of your document.**

   In step 2 of the wizard, select whether to use the current document as the basis for your message, to use a template, or to use an existing document, and then click Next.

3. **Tell the wizard which data source to use.**

   In step 3, you can choose to use an existing list, to use your Outlook contacts, or to create a new list, just as you did when using Mail Merge with a form letter. Make a selection, and then click Next. After you choose the data source, you'll see the Mail Recipients dialog box. If you don't want to change anything in your data source, simply click OK.

4. **Compose your message.**

Unless you are using an existing document, type your message in the document window, using the fields in the task pane to incorporate recipient information, as we did earlier in this chapter when creating a form letter. When your message is complete, click Next.

5. **Preview your message.**

In step 5, which is shown in Figure 13-14, you'll see a preview of the message you composed, and you can make any changes or select and include individual recipients. Click the buttons in the Preview Your E-Mail Messages section to move forward and backward through the messages that are now addressed to the recipients in your data source. When you're finished, click Next.

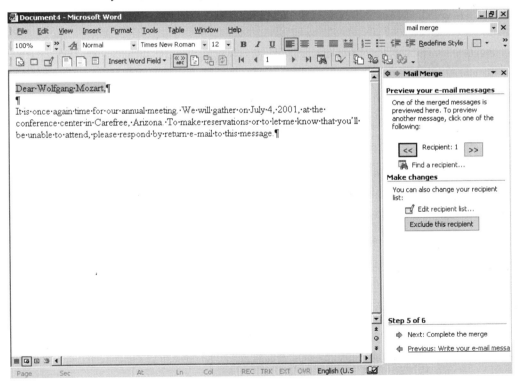

Figure 13-14 Previewing the messages to be merged.

6. Complete the merge.

In step 6, click the Electronic Mail link to open the Merge To E-Mail dialog box, as shown in Figure 13-15. In the To box, Email_Address is selected by default; type a subject in the Subject Line box. Select a format for your message in the Mail Format drop-down list, and then click OK. If you are connected to the Internet, all your messages are sent to those recipients in your data source.

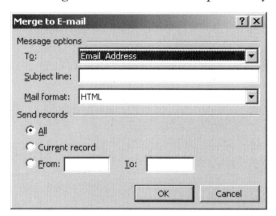

Figure 13-15 The Merge To E-Mail dialog box.

TIP   *You can use the steps outlined in this section to distribute an e-mail newsletter. Chapter 15 discusses how to publish an e-mail newsletter and distribute it using Outlook, but you can easily distribute it using the Mail Merge Wizard as described here. Be sure to take a look at Chapter 15, though, for the steps involved in creating and producing a newsletter. You can then decide for yourself whether you prefer to distribute it using Outlook or the Mail Merge Wizard in Word.*

Printing Labels

When you use the Mail Merge Wizard to print labels, you are not limited to address labels. You can also use this wizard to print file folder labels, stickers, note cards, postcards, business cards, name badges, and so on. The only caveat is that the information you merge is in an appropriate data source form, as we mentioned earlier in this chapter.

To print "labels," start the Mail Merge Wizard, and then follow these steps:

1. **Tell the wizard you want to print labels.**

   In step 1, click Labels in the Select Document Type section, and then click Next.

2. **Tell the wizard what kind of label you want to print.**

   In step 2, click Label Options to open the Label Options dialog box, as shown in Figure 13-16. Specify information for your printer, and then click the Label Products drop-down list to select the manufacturer of the labels you will use. In the Product Number list box, select the number that corresponds to the number on your box of labels. Select whether to print the labels horizontally or vertically. If you don't see a listing for your particular type of label, click the New Label button to open the New Custom Laser dialog box and specify your label's dimensions. Click OK after you've specified the kind of label you'll be printing. You'll see something similar to the screen in Figure 13-17. Click Next.

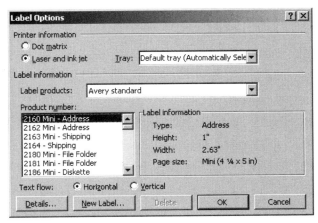

Figure 13-16 The Label Options dialog box.

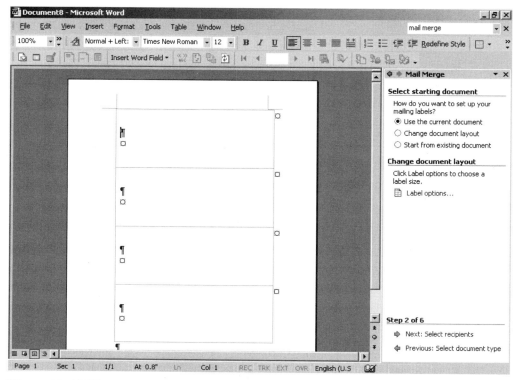

Figure 13-17 The screen layout for address labels.

3. Tell the wizard which data source to use.

As you did in the earlier section of this chapter, specify the list you will use to create the labels, and then click Next.

4. Tell the wizard how to lay out your labels.

In step 4, add information to the first record by clicking items in the Arrange Your Labels section, and then click the Update All Labels button to tell the wizard that you want the same types of information in all the labels. When you're finished, you'll see something similar to Figure 13-18. Click Next.

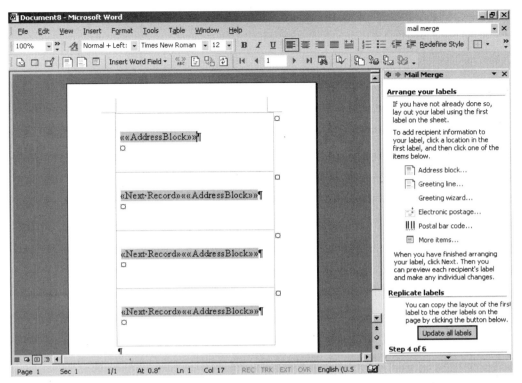

Figure 13-18 Arranging your labels.

5. Preview your labels.

Step 5 shows you what your labels will look like when printed. Click the buttons in the Preview Your Labels section to move forward or backward and view all your labels. If you want to change the information on any of them, click Edit Recipient List to open the Mail Merge Recipients dialog box. When you're satisfied with your labels, click Next.

6. Print your labels.

In step 6, click Print.

Creating a Directory

In addition to producing form letters, printing envelopes and labels, and sending group e-mail messages, you can use the Mail Merge Wizard to create a directory of a data source. Sometimes known as a *catalog*, this directory can include contact information, product information, or anything else you keep in a data source in Excel, Access, or Outlook or a list you've created with the Mail Merge Wizard.

When you create a directory, you merge all the information in your data source into a single document, thereby creating a list that you can distribute or print. To create a directory of contact information, start the Mail Merge Wizard, and then follow these steps:

1. **Tell the wizard you want to create a directory.**

   In step 1, click Directory in the Select Document Type section, and then click Next.

2. **Tell the wizard what kind of document to create.**

   In step 2, specify the current document, a template, or an existing document, and then click Next.

3. **Tell the wizard which data source to use.**

   In step 3, select your data source, and then click Next.

4. **Tell the wizard which fields to include in your directory.**

   In step 4, click More Items to open the Insert Merge Field dialog box, as shown in Figure 13-19. To insert a field, select it in the Fields list, click the Insert button, and then click Close. To continue inserting fields, place the insertion point where you want the next field, click More Items again to open the Insert Merge Field dialog box, select the field, click the Insert button, and then click Close. When you have added all the fields you want in your directory, click Next to preview your directory.

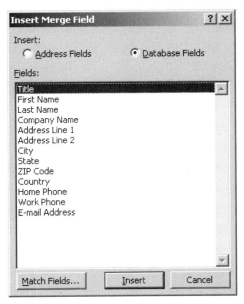

Figure 13-19 The Insert Merge Field dialog box.

5. Complete the merge.

Click Next, and then in step 6, click To New Document to open the Merge To New Document dialog box, as shown in Figure 13-20. Select the records you want to include in the merge, and then click OK.

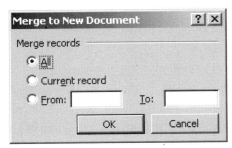

Figure 13-20 The Merge To New Document dialog box.

Summary

This chapter discusses a Word feature that any size business can use to automate several tedious, time-intensive tasks. Once you have a complete data source, you can use it to produce all sorts of mass mailings (both electronic and printed), to print many kinds of "labels," and to create directories that contain contact information, catalog lists, or any other information that you maintain in a data source.

Part 3

OFFICE BUSINESS PROJECTS

Chapter 14

CREATING A CONTACTS DATABASE WITH OUTLOOK

Featuring:

- Creating a Contact
- Viewing Contact Information
- Sorting Contact Information
- Using Contact Information
- Searching the Contacts Folder
- Printing Contact Information

The Contacts module in Outlook is the repository for all the information you collect about your contacts. It can contain both business and personal information and is referred to as a contact management system. The Contacts folder, however, is much more than an address book because it is integrated with the other Outlook modules. You can even use it as a data source when you're doing a mail merge in Word.

Creating a Contact

You, no doubt, already have a contacts database. In fact, you probably have more than one. You may have a personal address book on your computer, you may have a Rolodex on your physical desktop that contains information for business and professional contacts, you may have a small address book that you carry in your pocket or briefcase, and you might even have a tabbed address section in your DayRunner or Franklin Planner.

We know a retired New York businessman who keeps a contacts database of restaurants in a little black notebook that he always carries with him. This guy is never at a loss for where to "do lunch."

If you are creating an Outlook Contacts database from scratch, you'll probably want to start by entering the information you have in these other paper and electronic databases. Of course, you'll have to enter all the information that's currently stored on paper, but you can import some electronic address books.

Importing an Address Book

To import an address book into your Contacts folder, follow these steps:

1. Start the Import And Address Wizard, as shown in Figure 14-1.

Click the File menu, and then click Import And Export.

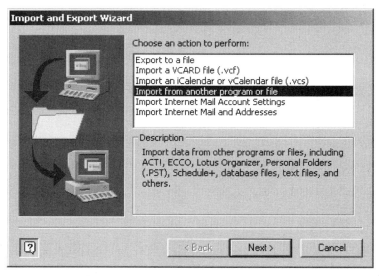

Figure 14-1   The Import And Export Wizard.

2. Tell Outlook what you want to import.

In the Choose An Action To Perform list, select Import From Another Program Or File, and then click Next to open the Import A File screen, as shown in Figure 14-2.

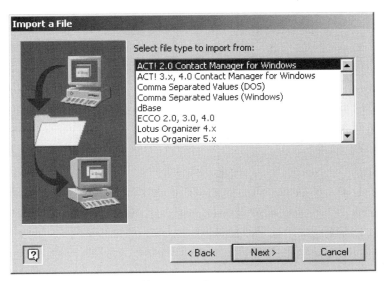

Figure 14-2 Select a file type to import.

3. **Tell Outlook the file type of the address book you want to import.**

   In the Select File Type To Import From list, select a type, and then click Next.

4. **Tell Outlook where to send the file.**

   In the Select Destination Folder list, click Contacts, and then click Next. Now follow the wizard's onscreen instructions to complete the import.

NOTE *You cannot import a Windows Address Book into the Contacts folder.*

Entering Your First Contact

You enter information about a contact on the Contact form, which you can open in the following ways:

- If you have a totally empty Contacts folder, click the Contacts icon in the Outlook bar, and then double-click Double-Click Here To Create A New Contact.

- Click the New drop-down list on the toolbar, and then click Contact.

- Press Ctrl+N.

- Click the Actions menu, and then click New Contact.

Whichever method you use, you'll see a blank Contact form, as shown in Figure 14-3.

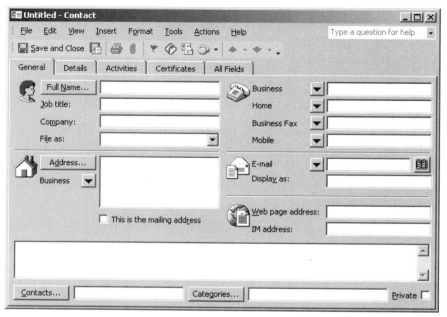

Figure 14-3 A blank Contact form open at the General tab.

Entering Name and Company Information

To enter name and company information for a new contact, follow these steps:

1. Enter the person's name.

You can simply type the person's name in the Full Name field, but to be sure that you are including all the information you'll want later, click the Full Name button to open the Check Full Name dialog box, as shown in Figure 14-4, and enter the information there. Press the Tab key to move from one field to the next, and when you are finished, click OK. If you enter the information in the Full Name field and Outlook considers it incomplete, the Check Full Name dialog box also opens so that you can verify that the name will be stored correctly.

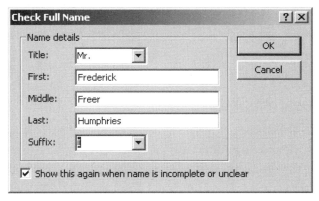

Figure 14-4 The Check Full Name dialog box.

2. Enter the person's job title and company.

In the Job Title field, type the person's job title, and then enter the name of the organization for which the person works in the Company field.

3. Tell Outlook how to file this person's name.

You can file a person's name in any number of ways, and how you do so doesn't affect your ability to sort your contact information. Click the File As drop-down list to specify how to file this person's name. If you normally look up the person under the company name, select the company name, for example. If you want to file the name in a way that's not listed, select some text in the File As list and type what you want. For example, if your contact's name is Frederick Freer Humphries, but you usually refer to him as Freer, you might file his name as Freer Humphries.

Entering Phone Number Information

These days we all tend to have multiple phone numbers. For example, even in a small home office, you might have a couple of voice lines, a modem line, a fax line, and a mobile phone number. Outlook allows you to enter as many as 19 phone numbers for any one contact, and you display four of them on the General tab of the Contact form. To enter phone numbers, you can simply type a number in one of the fields, or you can click a drop-down list to choose a type of phone number for which a field is not present.

When you enter a phone number, type only the digits. After you move to another field, Outlook will display the number with the appropriate parentheses, dashes, and spaces. If you enter a seven-digit number, Outlook assumes the number is in your area code and supplies that area code number in the display.

When you enter a number for a field that is not currently displayed in the Contact form, Outlook places a check mark by its type in the drop-down list. To display numbers for a contact when you have entered more than four numbers, click the drop-down list and then click the number type.

Entering Address Information

You can enter three types of addresses—business, home, and other—and you designate one of these addresses as the mailing address. By default, Outlook considers the first address you enter as the mailing address, so if you want a different address as the mailing address, display it in the Address field, and then click the This Is The Mailing Address check box. The mailing address is the address that is displayed in most views of your Contacts folder, and it is the address that is used when you use your Contacts list as the data source for a mail merge in Word.

To enter address information, you can simply type the address in the Address field, or you can click the Address button to open the Check Address dialog box, as shown in Figure 14-5, and fill in the fields. As is the case with the Check Full Name dialog box, if you enter address information in the Address field that Outlook considers incomplete, the Check Address dialog box will open.

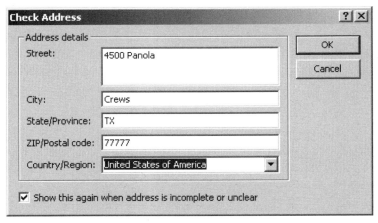

Figure 14-5 The Check Address dialog box.

To enter other types of addresses, click the Business, Home, or Other button, and type the information.

Entering E-Mail and Web Addresses

You can enter as many as three e-mail addresses for a contact. To add the first address, simply type it in the E-Mail field. To add other e-mail addresses, click the down arrow, select E-Mail 2 or E-Mail 3, and type the address.

In the Display As field, Outlook displays the person's full name as you entered it. If you prefer to display a different name, for example, a nickname or an informal name for the person, select the name that Outlook displays and then type the name you want.

If this contact has a Web page, enter the URL in the Web Page Address field. You can enter something like *www.br.com*, and Outlook will add the *http://* prefix. If the Web page uses another protocol, such as FTP, for example, you'll need to enter the entire URL.

Adding Notes About This Contact

In the blank text box at the bottom of the General tab on the Contact form, you can enter additional information about the contact. For example, you might want to make a note about where and when you met, special projects that might interest this person, and the like.

Categorizing This Contact

As Chapter 6 pointed out, you can assign any item in Outlook to a category. Categories are useful for grouping items so that you can retrieve and review everything about a category, whether the item is a contact, an e-mail message, a task, or an appointment. You can use any of the preexisting categories that Outlook provides, or you can create new categories. For example, you might want to create categories for each of the projects your department or organization is working on, and then assign all the items that relate to that project to that category.

To assign a contact to a category that you create, simply type the category in the text box next to the Categories button. To assign a contact to an existing category, click the Categories button to open the Categories dialog box, as shown in Figure 14-6. Click the check box next to a category, and click the Add To List button. You can add the person's name to as many categories as you like. When you're finished, click OK. The categories you selected will be displayed in the text box next to the Categories button.

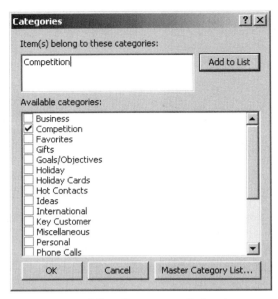

Figure 14-6 The Categories dialog box.

Making a Contact Private

If you work on a corporate network, you may share your Contacts folder with other users, or you might use a public folder to store your Contacts list. If you don't want others to see the information for a contact you are adding, click the Private check box in the lower right of the screen in the General tab.

NOTE *After you enter multiple contacts, you can relate them by clicking the Contacts button in the lower left portion of the General tab. We'll look at how to do this later in this chapter after we discuss how you use the other tabs in the Contact form to continue collecting information about a contact.*

Adding Details About a Contact

You can store additional information about a contact on the Details tab in the Contact form, as shown in Figure 14-7. You can sort and filter on these fields, so inasmuch as possible, you'll want to use identical entry forms. For example, if you wanted to see a list of all your contacts who are CPAs, you can easily be sure that you have the entire list if you've entered CPA in the Profession field. You won't be able to find all of them if you enter CPA for one contact, Certified Professional Account for others, and Cert. Prof. Acct. for still others. It really doesn't matter which you use, as long as you always enter the same thing for the same entity.

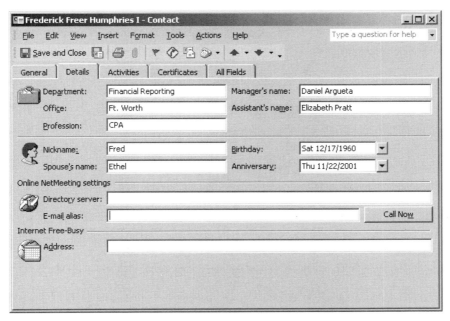

Figure 14-7   The Contact form open at the Details tab.

In the Birthday and Anniversary fields, you can click the drop-down list to display a calendar from which you can select the date, but if you aren't entering a date from the current, a recent, or the next year, it's faster to simply type the date. You can enter the date in just about any format, and Outlook will convert it to the correct style.

NetMeeting is a conferencing application that is included with Windows, and you can use the fields on the Details tab to enter NetMeeting information about the current contact:

- In the Directory Server field, enter the address of the Internet Locator Server (ILS) that you will use for meetings with this contact, for example, ils4.microsoft.com.

- In the E-Mail Alias field, enter the contact's e-mail alias, which is usually his or her e-mail address.

NOTE   *Before you can use NetMeeting the first time, you need to set it up. When you first open the application, a wizard will walk you through the steps.*

If you are working on a corporate network, you may be able to share your schedule with coworkers so that they can see when you are free, busy, out of the office, and so on, and others can share such information with you. If a contact has told the location of his or her schedule file, enter this information in the Address field in the Internet Free-Busy section of the Details tab.

Tracking Activities Related to a Contact

After you enter information about a contact and save the Contact form, Outlook automatically tracks all activities that relate to you and that contact on the Activities tab in the Contact form, as shown in Figure 14-8.

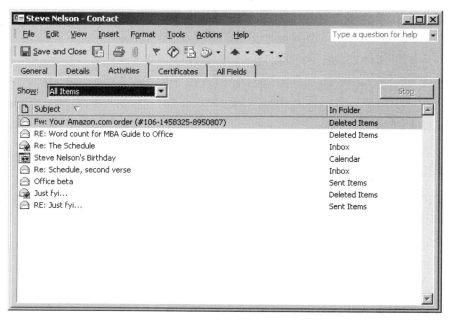

Figure 14-8   The Contact form open at the Activities tab.

Adding and Viewing Digital Certificates

A *digital certificate,* or digital ID, is an electronic credential that verifies that people are who they say they are when connected to the Internet. You can get the digital certificate for a contact when he or she sends you digitally signed mail, and it is then listed in the Certificates section of the Certificates tab of the Contact form, which is shown in Figure 14-9. If you know the location of a certificate file for a contact, you can get it by clicking the Import button to open the Locate Certificate dialog box and opening the certificate.

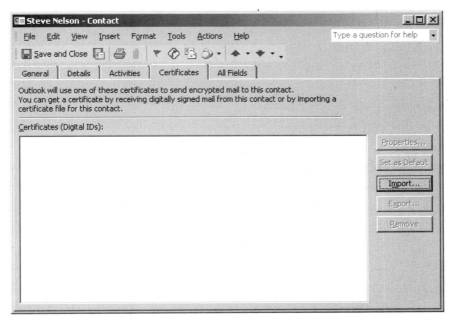

Figure 14-9 The Contact form open at the Certificates tab.

Viewing Fields for a Contact

The All Fields tab in the Contact form displays, in tabular form, groups of fields that have been identified for the current contact. When you first click this tab, you probably won't see any fields listed because by default user-defined fields are displayed. That is, if someone has customized your Outlook forms and added fields, they will be displayed. But even if you don't have user-defined fields, you can use this tab to display useful information.

For example, if you want to see a list of all the phone numbers for the current contact, click the Select From drop-down list, and choose Phone Number Fields. You'll see something similar to Figure 14-10. To display a table of all the information you've collected for a contact, select All Contact Fields in the Select From drop-down list.

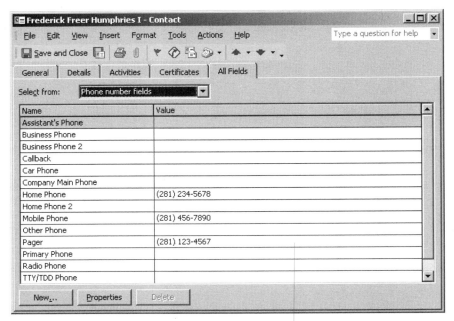

Figure 14-10 The Contact form open at the All Fields tab.

Saving Contact Information

After you enter all the information for a contact, click the Save And Close button to save the information. You'll see this information in the default Address Card view for your Contacts folder. If you will be entering information for more contacts, you can instead click the Save And New button, which opens a blank Contact form at the General tab.

If you will be entering information for a contact at the same company as the current contact, click the Actions menu, and then click New Contact From Same Company. A Contact form opens that contains all the information you already entered for the company, including phone numbers, addresses, and Web addresses.

Relating Contacts

Earlier in this chapter, we mentioned that once you have multiple contacts in your Contacts folder you can relate them. For example, if you have contact information on several members of the same family or you want to connect clients and referrals, it would be helpful to store these names along with a contact.

To relate one contact with another, follow these steps:

1. **Open the Contact form for the contact.**

   In the current view of your Contacts folder, double-click the contact's name.

2. **Open the Select Contacts dialog box, as shown in Figure 14-11.**

   Click the Contacts button on the General tab of the Contact form.

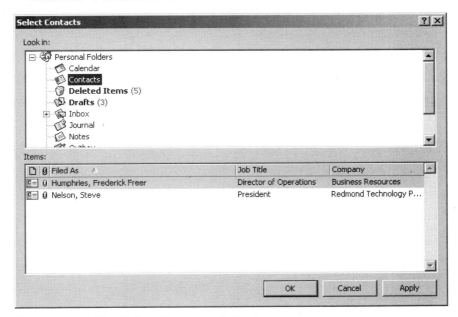

Figure 14-11 The Select Contacts dialog box.

3. **Tell Outlook which contact to relate to the current contact.**

   Select the name of the contact you want to relate, and then click OK. You'll now see that contact's name listed in the text box next to the Contacts button in the General tab. Click Save And Close to save the relationship.

Deleting a Contact

You can delete a contact and all his or her associated information in the following ways in the current view of your Contacts folder:

- Right-click the contact, and then choose Delete from the shortcut menu.

- Select the contact, and then press the Delete key.

- Select the contact, and then click the Delete button on the toolbar.

- Select the contact, click the Edit menu, and then click Delete.

- Select the contact, and press Ctrl+D.

WARNING *You will not be prompted to confirm the deletion, so if you delete a contact in error, immediately click the Edit menu and then click Undo Delete.*

Viewing Contact Information

As this chapter mentioned earlier, the default view for the information stored in your Contacts folder is Address Card, as shown in Figure 14-12. As you can see, the names are listed in alphabetic order, regardless of the order in which you entered them.

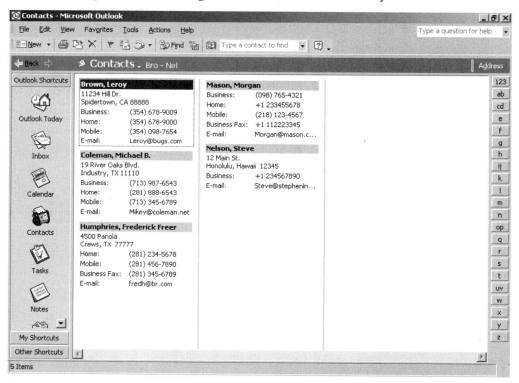

Figure 14-12 The Contacts folder in Address Card view.

You can also display your Contacts folder in the following views by clicking the View menu, clicking Current View, and then choosing a view from the submenu:

- Detailed Address Cards

- Phone List

- By Category

- By Company

- By Location

- By Follow-Up Flag

In addition, you can create your own views and add and remove fields from the current view. Select Customize Current View or Define Views from the Current View submenu to open a dialog box from which you can make selections.

Sorting Contact Information

In any list view, you can rearrange the order in which contact information is displayed. For example, in Phone List view, as shown in Figure 14-13, you can sort by any column heading. To do so, simply click the heading.

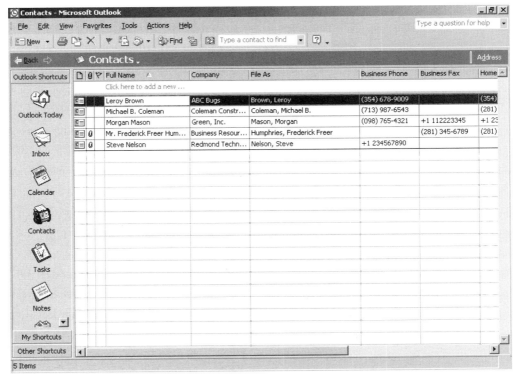

Figure 14-13 The Contacts folder in Phone List view.

TIP   *To see the headings that don't appear in the display, drag the horizontal scroll bar to the right.*

To see how a list will sort, point to the icon in the heading or to the title in the heading.

Using Contact Information

The importance of creating and maintaining a Contacts list lies in how you can use it to streamline your Outlook business activities, some of which are not even possible until you have a Contacts list.

Sending E-Mail to a Contact

You can send an e-mail message to a contact in the following ways:

- In any view of your Contacts folder, right-click a contact's name, and choose New Message To Contact to open the Message window. Your contact's name will appear in the To field. Add a subject line, type your message, and then click the Send button.

- In the Contact form for a contact, click the New Message To Contact button to open the Message window. Your contact's name will appear in the To field. Add a subject line, type your message, and the click the Send button.

- In your Inbox folder, click the New Mail Message button on the toolbar to open the Message window. Click the icon next to the To field to open the Select Names dialog box. Double-click a name in the Name list, and click OK. Add a subject line, type your message, and click the Send button.

Composing a Letter to a Contact

To compose a letter (the printed, paper type) to a contact, select the contact's name in any view, click the Actions menu, and then click New Letter To Contact. Word will open and start the Letter Wizard, as shown in Figure 14-14. Follow the wizard's instructions to format the letter, insert recipient information, add elements such as mailing instructions, and include information about yourself. When you've entered the information, click the Finish button, and you'll see the basics of your letter displayed as a Word document. You can now compose the body of the letter, save it, print it, print an envelope for it, and so on. (For more information about the basics of working with Word, see Chapter 3.)

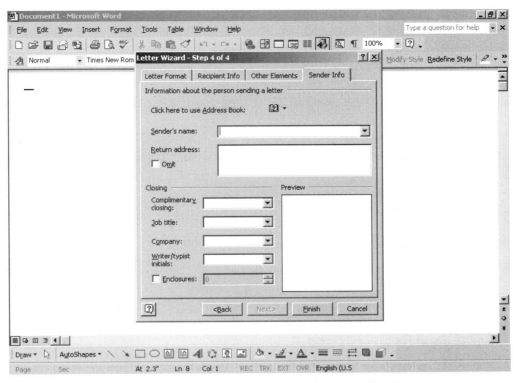

Figure 14-14 Using the Letter Wizard to compose a letter in Word.

Setting Up a Meeting or an Appointment

From within your Contacts folder, you can set up a meeting or schedule an appointment with a contact. To set up a meeting, right-click the contact, click the Actions menu, and then choose New Meeting Request To Contact from the shortcut menu to open the Meeting form. (See Chapter 6 for details on using the Meeting form.)

To set up an appointment, right-click the contact, and then choose New Appointment With Contact from the shortcut menu to open the Appointment form. (See Chapter 6 for details on using the Appointment form.)

NOTE   *To assign a task to a contact, right-click the contact, and then choose New Task For Contact from the shortcut menu to open the Task form.*

Telephoning a Contact

If you bought your computer recently, you may have all the equipment you need to place a telephone call using Outlook. Basically, you need speakers, a microphone, and a modem connection to your phone line. Even if your computer didn't include a microphone, you can get a perfectly good one for about $15.00.

You place a phone call using the Contacts folder. In any view, follow these steps:

1. Open the New Call dialog box, as shown in Figure 14-15.

Right-click the contact, and choose Call Contact from the shortcut menu.

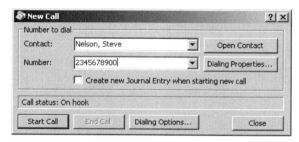

Figure 14-15 The New Call dialog box.

2. Tell Outlook to dial the number.

If the number you want to dial appears in the Number box, click the Start Call button. If you want to choose another number, click the drop-down arrow to select it, or simply type another number in the Contact box.

3. Complete the call.

When you're finished with your conversation, click the End Call button to hang up.

Creating a Mail Merge with a Word Document

In Chapter 13, you saw how to create a mail merge using Word, and we mentioned that you can use an Outlook Contacts list as your data source. You can also initiate a mail merge from within Outlook using your Contacts list. Open your Contacts folder, and then follow these steps:

1. Create a Contacts view that includes the fields you want to use.

Click the View menu, click Current View, and then click Customize Current View to open the View Summary dialog box, as shown in Figure 14-16.

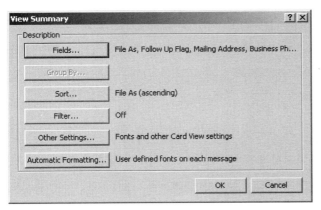

Figure 14-16 The View Summary dialog box.

2. Select the fields you want to include.

Click the Fields button to open the Show Fields dialog box, as shown in Figure 14-17. In the Select Available Fields From drop-down list box, select the type of fields you want to use. Then from the Available Fields list, select the fields, and click the Add button to place them in the Show These Fields In This Order list. To remove fields from either list, select them and click the Remove button. When the fields you want to use for the merge are selected, click OK. Click OK again in the View Summary dialog box.

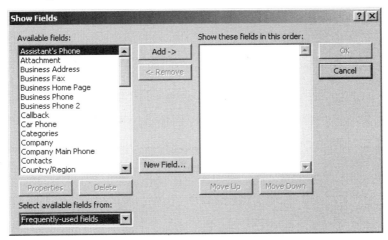

Figure 14-17 The Show Fields dialog box.

3. Open the Mail Merge Contacts dialog box, as shown in Figure 14-18.

Click the Tools menu, and then click Mail Merge.

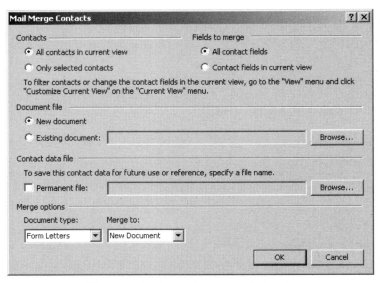

Figure 14-18 The Mail Merge Contacts dialog box.

4. Specify your merge options.

In the Mail Merge Contacts dialog box, you have the following options:

- In the Contacts section, specify whether to merge all contacts in the current view or only selected contacts.

- In the Fields To Merge section, specify whether to merge all contact fields or only those in the current view.

- In the Document File section, specify whether to create a new mail merge document or use an existing document. Click the Browse button to locate any existing files.

- In the Contact Data File section, you can specify that a permanent file be created for the contact information you are using in the current merge.

- In the Merge Options section, specify the document type you want to merge to and where you want to merge to—a new document, the printer, or e-mail.

When you've specified your options, click OK to open Word and your main document. Now follow the steps for completing the merge as outlined in Chapter 13.

Searching the Contacts Folder

Once your Contacts list grows to a substantial size, and this is likely in a business setting, you need a way to find specific information quickly and easily. To search your Contacts folder, open the folder, and then click the Find button on the Standard toolbar to display boxes in which you can enter your search term, as shown in Figure 14-19.

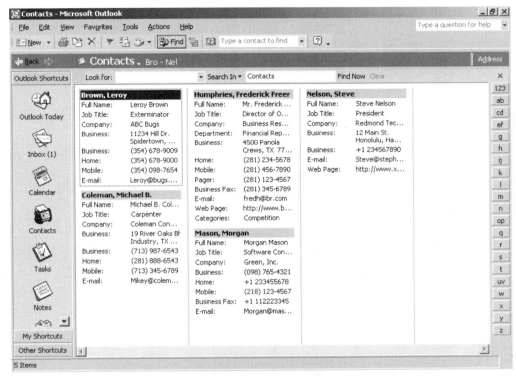

Figure 14-19 Searching the Contacts list.

In the Look For box, you can enter any information you've collected in your Contacts list. For example, if you want to find a contact and you know only his last name, enter that. Or perhaps you remember the location of a business but can't remember the name of the vice-president of the organization, you can enter the city or town.

After you enter your search term, click the Search In drop-down list box, and select Contacts if it doesn't already appear in the Search In box, and then click Find Now. Outlook will display information for all contacts that meet the search criteria in the current view. To return to the previous view, click the Clear button.

TIP   *To move quickly to a particular section of the alphabet in your Contacts list, click a tabbed letter along the right side of the Contacts window.*

Printing Contact Information

You can print your entire Contacts list, or you can print selected contacts. And you can print in several styles:

- Card, which prints address cards in two columns, with six blank cards at the end. Letter tabs and headings precede each alphabetic section.

- Small Booklet, which prints all address cards on both sides of the paper, with eight cards per page, in landscape orientation. You can then fold and staple the printed pages to create a booklet.

- Medium Booklet, which prints all address cards on both sides of the paper, with four cards per page, in portrait orientation. You can then fold and staple the printed page to create a booklet.

- Memo, which prints selected cards one to a page.

- Phone Directory, which prints names and phone numbers in a two-column format with letter tabs and headings preceding each alphabetic section.

To print your contacts, click the File menu, click Page Setup, and then click a print style to open the Page Setup dialog box for that style. Figure 14-20 shows the Page Setup dialog box for the Small Booklet style open at the Format tab.

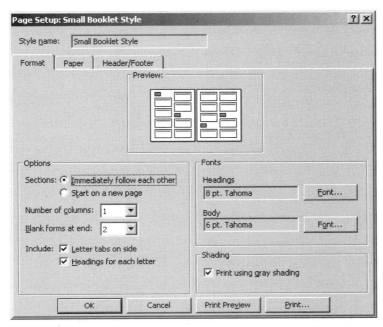

Figure 14-20 The Page Setup: Small Booklet Style dialog box open at the Format tab.

On the Format tab, you can see a preview of how your pages will look when printed. You can specify the following options:

- In the Options section, specify how sections will be printed, the number of columns, how many blank cards you want at the end, and whether you want to include letter tabs and headings for each alphabetic section.

- In the Fonts section, you can select a heading font and a body font for your printed document. Click the Font button to open the Font dialog box and make a selection.

- In the Shading section, clear the Print Using Gray Shading check box if you don't want to waste cartridge ink (and time, in some cases) printing the shading on individual entries.

Click the Paper tab, which is shown in Figure 14-21, to specify the settings for the paper you will use.

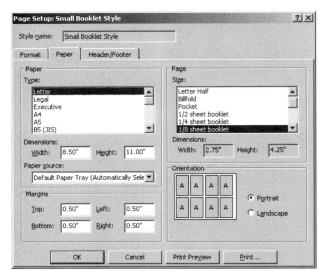

Figure 14-21 The Page Setup: Small Booklet Style dialog box open at the Paper tab.

TIP   *From Outlook, you can print pages for your DayRunner or your Day-Timer if you have the appropriate Avery paper. In the Type list, click the Avery listing that corresponds to the product number on the Avery box.*

Click the Paper tab, as shown in Figure 14-22, to add headers and footers to your printed document. Simply click in a box and type to enter information, or click a button on the toolbar at the bottom of the tab to automatically insert items. From left to right, these buttons do the following:

- Click the Page # button to insert page numbers.

- Click the Total Pages button to a reference to the total number of pages. If you click the Page # button and then click the Total Pages button, you'll insert something like Page 2 of 20 on each page.

- Click the Date Printed button to insert the date you printed the document.

- Click the Time Printed button to insert the time you printed the document.

- Click the User Name button to insert your name in the header or footer.

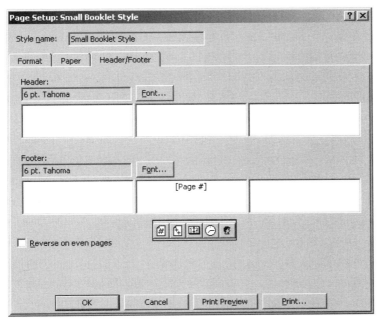

Figure 14-22 The Page Setup dialog box, open at the Header/Footer tab.

If you insert something in the header or footer and then change your mind, just click the item, and press the Delete button.

When you've selected all your options, click the Print button to open the Print dialog box, as shown in Figure 14-23. Tell Outlook how many pages to print, copies, and so on, and then click the OK button to print your document.

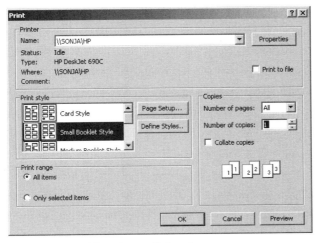

Figure 14-23 The Print dialog box.

TIP   *If your printer doesn't do two-sided printing, insert your pages, open the Print dialog box, and in the Number Of Pages drop-down list box, select Odd, and then print those pages. Take them out of the printer, turn the pages over, and reinsert them. Now open the Print dialog box again, and this time select Even in the Number Of Pages drop-down list box. Print those pages. You can now fold and staple them into a booklet.*

Summary

Taking the time to create a Contacts list in Outlook can save you time when you need to take care of several business tasks, including doing a mail merge, sending letters to clients and prospects, communicating via e-mail, and finding all your contacts that might be interested in a certain product or service. Once your contact information is stored, you can print it in a variety of useful ways using the print styles that are included with Outlook.

Chapter 15

PUBLISHING AN E-MAIL NEWSLETTER USING OUTLOOK

Featuring:

- Will a Newsletter Help Your Business?
- Getting Started
- Publishing with Outlook
- Guidelines for Producing an Award-Winning Newsletter

In the next chapter, we'll show you how to set up a Web site for a business, and publishing on a Web site certainly gets the lion's share of attention in the marketplace these days. But we think businesses should also consider publishing an e-mail newsletter.

An e-mail newsletter is much like its paper counterpart, but it has three major advantages:

- It costs less to produce and distribute.
- It's delivered faster.
- It can support a firm's Web site and build traffic (since it's easy to include hyperlinks in the newsletter text).

In some ways, an e-mail newsletter is a more efficient way to reach your intended audience. For example, if you put information on your Web site about new services or new products, people will find out only when and if they visit your Web site. If you put such information into a regularly delivered e-mail newsletter, you place that information into the hands of people who have already said they want to receive it and in a timely fashion.

NOTE   *An e-mail newsletter is sometimes called an ezine, short for electronic magazine, and technically an ezine can be a newsletter or a magazine that is distributed by e-mail, on a Web site, or both.*

Will a Newsletter Help Your Business?

One way to find out is to subscribe to some business newsletters for a while, see what they are like, and see how they work. At many commercial Web sites, you'll see a box to check to indicate that you'd like to receive the company's newsletter. You'll also find a list of business newsletters at *http://www.topica.com*. On the home page, click the More link, and then click the Business link in the List Directory to display a list of business newsletters, as shown in Figure 15-1.

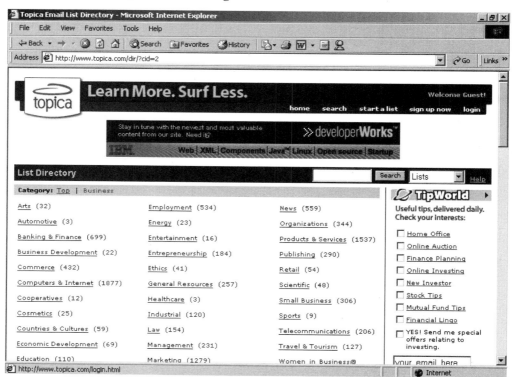

Figure 15-1   Finding business newsletters at the Topica site.

A lot of e-mail newsletters start out as small, perhaps in-house communications tools, such as an employee newsletter or a newsletter that's distributed to the sales force. Those targeted at potential or current customers or clients can grow large quickly, and if you are thinking about using an e-mail newsletter as a marketing tool, you will need to be willing to invest some time and make a commitment to the project.

Some marketing experts think an e-mail newsletter is a great marketing tool in a time when most of us are opting out of databases that mean telemarketing calls at the most inappropriate hour of the day and tons of junk e-mail. An e-mail newsletter epitomizes the concept of permission marketing. Everyone who subscribes to your newsletter has done so on purpose and expects to read about your ideas, products, and services. In addition, e-mail newsletters are a great way to create brand awareness for your company, product, or service.

From the consumer's point of view, e-mail newsletters are advantageous for a couple of reasons:

- They get information they want without having to search for it.
- They get only the information they want, and the information is current.

An e-mail newsletter can also serve as a general forum that a community of professionals can use to share information. We participate both as readers and writers in several newsletters that discuss the business of writing and technology publishing, for example.

Getting Started

If all this interests you and you are on the verge of opening your word-processing program to compose number 1 of volume 1, hang on a minute. As with all business projects, you need to do some planning first. Here are some questions to ask and answer before you get started:

- Who is your target audience?
- What is the specific topic of your newsletter?
- How often will you distribute it?
- Who will write it?
- Who will edit it?
- Who will respond to e-mail messages you receive as a result of your newsletter?

- Will you attempt to publish it yourself or will you outsource this task?

- If you work in a corporation, have resources of time and money been allocated that you can access for this project?

As we mentioned earlier, publishing an e-mail newsletter involves a commitment to the project. Distributing a great first edition and then not following up with regular publications will just about totally defeat your purpose. And, speaking of purpose, define it at the outset. To be successful, a newsletter needs to meet its audience's expectations. For example, if you commit to keeping your existing customer base updated on the latest products and services with a newsletter, your rating on their confidence meter will plummet if they see a TV commercial about the product before they get your newsletter.

Before you distribute your first newsletter, be sure that the answers to the above questions are feasible in your organization. If you intend to write the newsletter yourself, be sure that you really, really have the time or will make the time. In fact, put together a written plan, distribute it to anybody who will be involved, and get their commitment to the project.

When you distribute your newsletter using Outlook, you can produce your newsletter in *plain text* or *HyperText Markup Language (HTML)*. Without question, a newsletter composed as a Web page is the most attractive. Figure 15-2 shows a plain-text newsletter, and Figure 15-3 shows a newsletter created in HTML. Not all e-mail programs can read a message composed in HTML, but when that is the case, most e-mail programs automatically display a plain-text version.

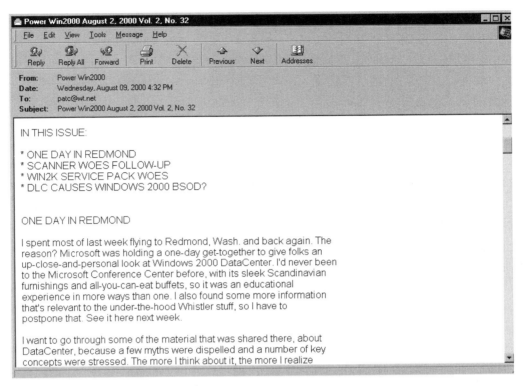

Figure 15-2 A plain-text newsletter.

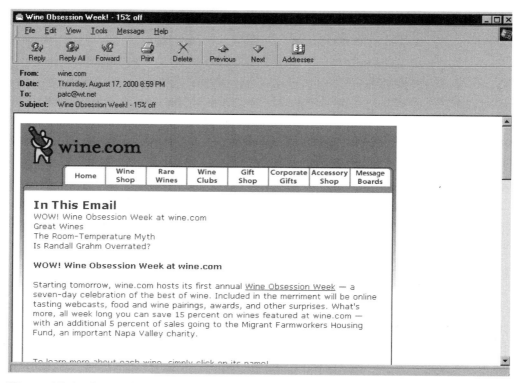

Figure 15-3 A newsletter that looks like a Web page.

If your organization has a Web site, check with the Webmaster about placing a link to your newsletter on the home page, as well as the means for subscribing to it. You'll also want to link from your newsletter to your company's Web site.

Publishing with Outlook

The easiest, most straightforward way to publish an e-mail newsletter if you have no more than, say, 100 subscribers is to use Outlook. You can certainly use Outlook if you have more than 100 subscribers, but remember that you'll need to manually add and remove subscribers from your distribution list. A distribution list simply contains e-mail addresses. When you tell Outlook to send an e-mail message (like your newsletter) to the distribution list, Outlook sends the e-mail message to all the e-mail addresses on the list.

To set up a new distribution list, open Outlook and follow these steps:

1. **Open the Distribution List window, as shown in Figure 15-4.**

   Click the drop-down arrow next to the New button on the toolbar, and then click Distribution List.

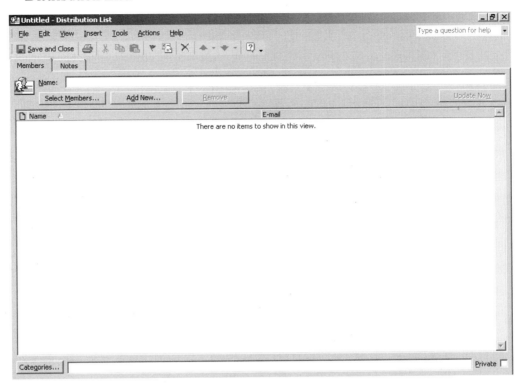

Figure 15-4 The Distribution List window.

2. **Give your list a name.**

   In the Name box, enter a name for your distribution list.

3. **Add e-mail addresses to your list.**

   If you already have an e-mail address in your Contacts folder, click the Select Members button to open the Select Members dialog box. Select a name from the list on the left, and click the Members button to place it in the distribution list on the right. When you're finished selecting, click OK. The names will be added to the list in the Distribution List window.

   To add an e-mail address that is not in your Contacts folder, click the Add New button to open the Add New Member dialog box, as shown in Figure 15-5. Enter the person's name in the Display Name box, enter the person's e-mail address in the E-Mail Address box, and click OK. If you also want to add this person to your

Contacts folder, click the Add To Contacts check box. Click the Save And Close button to close the Distribution List window and save your new list.

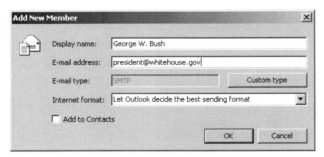

Figure 15-5 The Add New Member dialog box.

To compose your newsletter, click the New button to open the Untitled Message – Microsoft Word window. When you're ready to send your newsletter out, click the To button to open the Select Names dialog box, as shown in Figure 15-6. Select the name of your list, click the To button, and then click OK. The name you gave your distribution list will appear in the To line.

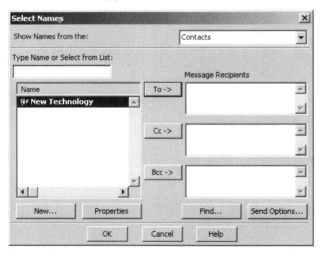

Figure 15-6 The Select Names dialog box.

When your newsletter arrives in your recipients' mailbox, they will see the name of your distribution list in the From line of the message, but they can also find out the addresses of everyone on the list. If they are using Outlook, for example, they can right-click the distribution list name, click Properties on the shortcut menu, and then display the list of names. If you want to keep the identities of your subscribers secret, enter the distribution list name in the Bcc box of the message window. To do so, click the Cc button to open the Select Names dialog box, select the distribution list name, click the Bcc button, and click OK. Outlook will display the address to you but not to the people receiving your newsletter.

TIP   *You might also want to set up a special e-mail account for sending your newsletter and for receiving e-mail from your subscribers. For example, if we set up an account as newsletter@coleman.com, all subscribers know right away the source of the material. In addition, we'd know that all e-mail sent to this account concerned the newsletter.*

Guidelines for Producing an Award-Winning Newsletter

Determining whether an e-mail newsletter is a good idea for your business and then learning how to distribute it are both critical path items when you're thinking about publishing a newsletter. But neither task is as important as the editorial process and the content of your newsletter. As we were exploring Web directories of business newsletters, we came across the following blurb:

"Tightly written and edited. A 3-minute read each week."

In our opinion, this tag line describes the perfect business newsletter—no words are wasted in the writing; the newsletter has been edited for spelling, grammar, punctuation, word choice, organization, and format; and you can glean its valuable information in about the same amount of time it takes to read the column on the business page of your daily newspaper. In our collective experience as writers, editors, managers, and publishers, the best advice we can give you is to establish an editorial process that complies with publishing standards and stick to it.

TIP   *A good e-mail newsletter should probably be a maximum of 1,000 words.*

Adhering to the Editorial Process

The first step in the editorial process is to determine the focus of your newsletter and then give it a title. If you're creating a newsletter for your sales force, your audience determines the focus and the content. If you're creating a newsletter for your employees, the audience still determines the focus although it broadens. The title of your newsletter should be appropriate for its audience, which may well be influenced by the corporate culture. In any case, the title should be descriptive of the content.

Create an Outline

The next step is to think about content, not just for the first publication but perhaps for the quarter or even the year, especially if you expect to publish monthly. We suggest creating an outline with the major points being the focus for each publication and the minor points being the two or three headings in each issue. Yes, what Ms. Cooper made you do before you began writing a term paper still applies. All good publications start with an outline.

Here's the beginning of an outline for a newsletter to the sales force that will be published monthly. Roman numerals identify the major subject matter for each issue, and the capital letters identify the sections for the issue.

I. Welcome to the ABC E-Letter

    A. Our purpose

    B. Our schedule

    C. How you can contribute

II. Understanding Quotas and Bonuses

    A. How quotas work—who sets them, who monitors them, how to achieve them

    B. How bonuses are determined

    C. Salesperson of the month

    D. Answering your questions

III. New Products and Services

    A. Products and services to introduce this quarter

    B. Sales retreat scheduled

    C. Salesperson of the month

    D. Answering your questions

And so on. As you can see, continuity is established by running some sections in every issue, and interest is maintained by creating one or two special sections for each issue. Obviously, if a major corporate event occurs, such as a reorganization or the purchase of a subsidiary, for example, you can adjust your outline and cover that topic instead. But creating and maintaining an outline gives you the following advantages:

- Your newsletter is focused and flows logically.

- Because you know ahead of time, you can begin to gather any needed information well in advance.

- You avoid last-minute sleepless nights wondering what you're going to put in the newsletter tomorrow.

- You can ensure that in the course of the newsletter's regular publication schedule you're covering all the pertinent information.

Do the Writing

All the rules for writing well apply, and in this section we'll review some of them.

- Use active voice. Why? Because it's more direct and alive. Passive voice is used by those who don't want to take responsibility for what they're writing, and, indeed, the first part of this sentence is in passive voice. Here's another example: The selection of the new CFO was made public. This sentence raises some questions: Who did the selecting? Who made it public and how? A more alive and more informative sentence: The board of directors selected the new CFO and then announced their choice during this morning's news conference.

- The paragraph is the basic unit of composition. It begins with a topic sentence and then proceeds to elaborate on that. Especially, when you're writing for the computer screen, keep paragraphs short, and format chunks of text that are manageable when the reader is scrolling through your newsletter.

- Don't use complicated words when simple ones will do nicely. Example: The widget has fallen into desuetude. *Desuetude* is a perfectly good word, and you'll find it in the *Merriam Webster's Collegiate Dictionary*, but chances are just about zero that your readers are going to know that it means "disuse."

- Use only as many words as necessary. A particularly annoying example is the use of the phrase "the fact of the matter is." You never need to include this phrase; the "fact" stands on its own and is the reason you are writing the sentence in the first place. Choose words that are specific to your subject matter and that will attract your audience. If you are writing about a technical topic for a nontechnical audience, always explain a technical term in context.

- Never begin a sentence with "There is" or "There are" if you can find a noun or a pronoun and a strong verb to do the job. For example, which is the stronger sentence: "There are a number of people who agree with you" or "A number of people agree with you"?

These are only some of the handy devices you can use to maintain the dynamic nature of your e-mail newsletter. They aren't difficult to remember, and using them will make you a better communicator of the written word. You'll find variations on them as well as many more in a tiny book that has become a classic since it was first published in 1935—*The Elements of Style,* by William Strunk, Jr., and E. B. White. The most recent edition was published in 1995 and is available at bookstores on- and offline. The 85 pages that compose this book constitute what should be the daily companion of anyone who writes.

Send Your Newsletter to an Editor

Everybody needs an editor, and the more you write and the longer you write, the more you will find this to be a necessity. You can, and should, spell-check your document, and if the program in which you are creating your newsletter has one, run its grammar checker. Neither one, however, takes the place of an editor.

For example, if you type "for" when you mean "four," the spell checker won't see it as a mistake. And if you begin three sentences in a row with "There are," a grammar checker might or might not call your attention to this. You might also want to give your newsletter a read-through before passing it on to an editor.

Here are the editor's tasks:

- Correcting spelling.

- Correcting grammatical mistakes.

- Fixing punctuation.

- Querying you if he or she can't understand a sentence or a paragraph.

- Pointing out any statement that could be factually incorrect.

- Tightening your words and making suggestions about better word choices.

- Suggesting something that you might want to include.

- Noting any useless repetition.

- Applying any house style rules if your organization has a style guide.

NOTE   *A house style guide is a list of rules that specify the distinctive treatment of words, how organizational entities are to be treated in print, trademarks, and so on.*

If you can't find a person in your organization with these skills, you can obtain the services of a professional. Many editors work on a freelance, per-hour, or per-assignment basis, and you can find them through an editorial agency or even on the Internet.

The most efficient way to work with an editor is to work online. Whether someone within your organization will do the editing or you contract for the services of a freelancer, you can send your newsletter file to the editor as an attachment to e-mail. He or she can then open it in a program such as Word and turn on the Track Changes feature, which keeps your original but displays all the editorial changes and queries in a different color and indicates insertions and deletions. When you get the file back, it's easy to see who did what when. You can then accept or reject the changes, finalize your document, and distribute it.

Final Formatting

Whether you distribute your newsletter as a straight-text file or as a Web page, you need to ensure that what your subscribers see on the screen is readable and attractive. Here are some suggestions for formatting a good-looking straight-text newsletter:

- Visibly separate the sections using characters, symbols, or blank lines.
- Use a monospaced font so that readers with older e-mail programs can read your newsletter easily.
- Set off URLs by enclosing them in angle brackets (< >) and include a link to the home page of your Web site if you have one.

Here are some tips for formatting a newsletter in HTML:

- Don't add animation and sound to the page, which will detract from your message rather than enhancing it.
- Use colors and different fonts sparingly, and don't use a black background against which text must contrast. Light text on a dark screen background is very difficult to read, and a bunch of different-colored objects detract from the content.
- Separate sections by placing the heading in a larger size font and perhaps in bold-face. Keep all body text in the same size and type of font.
- Keep your newsletter all on one page, and include a link to the home page of your Web site, if you have one.

NOTE *For information about how to create Web pages with FrontPage, see Chapter 8.*

Creating a Publishing Schedule

Whether you decide to publish weekly, monthly, quarterly, or on some other schedule, establish the publication date—the day and the time of day that your newsletter is sent out to subscribers—and work backward to determine how much time you need to allot to each stage of the process. After you do the first couple of issues, you'll be able to reasonably estimate how long the writing takes. In general, build in a day for the editing, and build in a day for the final formatting. Neither task will take that long, but you need to allow for the unexpected.

Allow some time in your personal schedule for the manual adding and deleting of subscribers, or assign that task to someone who can handle this task for you. If you're creating a newsletter that will be distributed internally to only a finite number of employees, this will not be a Herculean task. But if your list grows, managing subscribers manually can become a time sink that you want to be prepared for.

Summary

In this chapter, we've looked at a rather simple way to stay in touch with departmental employees, customers, potential customers, and professional colleagues—an e-mail newsletter. You can use it to enhance the effectiveness of your Web site, and you can use your Web site to publicize your newsletter. This chapter gives you the information you need to get started and includes some nontechnical guidelines that you can use to publish a newsletter that not only contains valuable information for your subscribers but also sends a professional, attractive message about you and your business.

Chapter 16

SETTING UP A WEB SITE USING FRONTPAGE

Featuring:

- Developing a Web Strategy
- Setting Up Your Domain
- Collecting and Creating Digital Content
- Creating Your Web Pages
- Testing Your Web Site
- Publishing Your Web Site
- Publicizing Your Web Site

No business discussion of Office is complete without coverage of Web publishing. Accordingly, this chapter provides a fast-paced discussion of the seven steps required to Web publish successfully.

NOTE   *Two other books published by Redmond Technology Press describe these steps in more detail and in the context of specific Web-authoring tools:* New Webmaster's Guide to FrontPage *and* New Webmaster's Guide to Dreamweaver.

Developing a Web Strategy

Developing a good Web strategy involves thoughtfully answering the following three questions:

- Why does it make sense to have a Web site?
- What makes for good Web content?
- How should a Web site be developed?

Fortunately, none of these questions needs to be particularly difficult to answer, as the paragraphs below explain.

Why Does It Make Sense to Have a Web Site?

Although a great deal of exuberance surrounds the Internet and especially the Web, it's fairly easy to identify and describe the handful of reasons why it makes good business sense for an organization to have a Web site: the reasons include advertising, publishing, information collection, and transaction processing.

Advertising

The Web lets you create powerful advertisements and publicity for a very modest cost. The quickest way to visualize this is to think of your Web site and its Web pages as substitutes for enhanced versions of any telephone directory advertising you do now.

It's not an exaggeration to say that anything you can do in a directory listing or advertisement you can do better and more cheaply using a Web page. You can also change and update your information more frequently as well.

TIP   *The Web really levels the playing field for small businesses and nonprofit organizations. A small business or nonprofit organization can create a Web site as good or better in many ways than a larger company's Web site, without a large amount of expense or time, giving it an unprecedented ability to compete and communicate.*

Publishing

Many organizations are de facto publishers. For example, if your business creates and distributes brochures, newsletters, product or service literature, or similar items, you are actually publishing. The Web provides a convenient way to complement or even replace this paper-based publishing.

Developing material for publication on the Web doesn't cost any more than developing equivalent material for paper publishing. But with the Web, you don't have the costs of printing or mailing. Furthermore, with the Web, you can more quickly update your information.

Information Collection

In addition to the advertising and publishing advantages that the Web offers to organizations, the Web also offers the ability to collect information from the people for whom you advertise and publish. You can put forms right on a Web page to collect information from the visitors to your site. For example, you might gather names for a mailing list, get feedback from customers, or take in sales orders.

Transaction Processing

One further advantage of the Web that is of great value is the opportunity for transaction processing. As an extension of the Web's information collection ability, transaction processing lets you use the Web as a virtual store, salesperson, or distribution facility.

NOTE   *Chapter 17 discusses in more detail the work involved in setting up a Web site that includes transaction processing.*

Using the Web for transaction processing is considerably trickier than using it for advertising or publishing. Obviously, your Web pages need to list and describe the products you sell. But practically speaking, you need to do more than simply list products or services. Good Web stores have the following features:

- Information about product availability and about the lead times for ordering items that aren't immediately available.

- A variety of ways to track down your products and services so that they are easy to find and buy.

- A shopping cart feature that lets customers build a list of the items they want.

- A checkout feature that lets customers easily order all the items in their shopping cart. (It's during this checkout process, of course, that customers provide their credit card numbers and shipping instructions.)

- A non-Web way for resolving problems the Web store can't handle, such as lost or damaged goods.

NOTE *Regardless of what you think about Amazon.com, you should visit their site (http://www.amazon.com)—even if you compete with them (perhaps especially if you compete with them). They've done an impressive job of providing numerous paths to find their products and different ways to search through their inventory. For example, they have several different bestseller lists for Microsoft Excel books, each listing books in a different order for a different group of Excel readers. We strongly suspect their several bestseller lists of Excel books, each really an alternative path to the same products, boost their sales of Excel books because they make it more likely someone will find one of them.*

What Makes for Good Web Content?

No matter what you choose to use your Web site for—advertising, publishing, information collection, or transaction processing—three main features differentiate effective sites: useful content, easy navigation, and aesthetic appeal.

Useful Content

More than anything else, useful content is the single most important feature of an effective Web site. Useful content brings visitors back repeatedly. If your site is the only place, or the best place, or the first place where someone can get needed information, you are providing useful content.

Easy Navigation

Although good content is the most important feature of an effective Web site, good content needs to be supported and enhanced by good site layout. Not only should visitors be able to easily find what they're looking for but the organization of Web pages and hyperlinks should also give visitors a clear idea of the site's contents at a glance from the home page.

Visual Appeal

Aesthetics is very important for Web sites, but it is also the part of Web site creation that is most overemphasized by many businesses. Professional artists and programmers are hired to create custom interfaces using trendy technologies, and altogether too much time, money, and resources are spent making sites look sophisticated instead of filling them with good content.

A flashy site may grab the attention of visitors, but a clean and simple site can be just as effective (or more so), and much less expensive to create and maintain. Complex effects and graphics can also make a site slow to download and confusing to use. Not to mention that sophisticated Web page programming can be incompatible with older browsers, along with some handheld devices and standalone Internet appliances.

How Should a Web Site Be Developed?

As you might imagine, more than one organization has stalled trying to decide how to develop a Web site. For this reason, we recommend that you consider employing a bulletin-board methodology for developing your Web content. By this, we mean that you could develop the content for your Web site in much the way that the content for the bulletin board in your coffee room or at your local market is developed.

NOTE   *Spend a small amount of time planning your site's structure, even if you use a bulletin-board approach. Your site structure doesn't have to be perfect, but taking a few hours or so to plan how you want to structure content on your site can help keep your site from degenerating into chaos.*

Following a bulletin-board methodology, as you find or create some appropriate Web content, you simply pin the content to the bulletin board—or post the content to your site. When content needs to change, you update the content or replace it. If content needs to be removed, you remove, or "unpin," it from the bulletin board.

Setting Up Your Domain

Before you can begin constructing a Web site, you need to lay a foundation by acquiring a *domain name* and choosing a company to host your site.

Picking a Domain Name

Picking a domain name is a small step in the creation of a Web site, but in many cases your domain name is at least as important as the name of your business. Your domain name identifies your site, and by extension, your business or organization. You actually have two choices to make in picking a domain name: You need to pick a host name, and you need to pick a top-level domain.

Picking a Host Name

Several points should be considered when picking a domain name. First of all, you want your domain name to be descriptive of your business or organization. Your first choice is your business's name, but in some instances you might choose a domain name that's based on your business's purpose instead. For example, it might be much better for a business named Vladimir Berkowitz Faucets, Inc. to select the *www.greatfaucets.com* domain name instead of *www.vladamirberkowitzfaucets.com*.

Second, your domain name should be easy to remember and spell. While a name like *www.rhythm.com* may be short and easy to remember, some people will have trouble spelling *rhythm*, potentially eliminating a large number of visitors. Perhaps something like *www.beat.com* would be a better choice.

Third, short domain names are far preferable to long ones, although not if the name is difficult to remember. This is particularly important since most of the desirable short domain names have already been taken. It may be tempting to abbreviate your domain name to shorten it, but do this only if the abbreviation doesn't make the name harder to remember.

Picking a Top-Level Domain

Besides the domain name itself, you also need to choose which top-level domain to use, such as *.com* or *.net* or *.org*. By far the most popular top-level domain to use is *.com*. Since this is the top-level domain most people will look under first, we recommend that businesses look for a *.com* domain name. The *.net* domain is more appropriate for ISPs, Web hosting companies, and other Internet technologies companies. Nonprofit organizations should probably use the *.org* top-level domain, although depending on the nature of the organization you might also consider registering your domain name with a *.com* top-level domain.

Once you've come up with some ideas for domain names, it's time to check for their availability. Because a large number of domain names are registered every day, make a list of alternative domain names in case the domain name you want is already taken. Then either go to any registrar's Web site (Network Solutions is the original, and most expensive, registrar at *http://www.networksolutions.com*) or go to *http://www.betterwhois.com* and enter your domain name idea in the box provided, as shown in Figure 16-1.

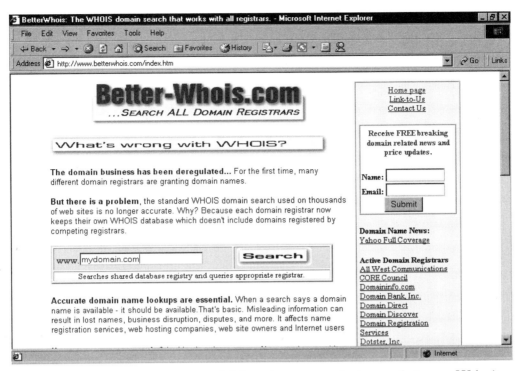

Figure 16-1 Checking out a potential domain name at the betterwhois.com Web site.

TIP   *Although most companies will naturally choose a valid domain name, there are a few restrictions on domain names to keep in mind. Domain names are case insensitive; so don't spend time thinking about what letters to capitalize. Also, you can use only letters and the hyphen character; but a hyphen can't start or finish a domain name. Lastly, the domain name can be a maximum of 67 characters long, not including the www. and the top-level domain (.com, .net or .org).*

Choosing a Web Hosting Service

Choosing a company to host your Web site can be a bewildering experience. With thousands of Web hosting companies, each usually offering several different hosting plans, it takes knowledge and a certain amount of patience to choose a Web hosting company.

In general, however, you want to look at which features the company offers for its price and the reliability and quality of the company's service. The following list provides summary descriptions of the features that are often available, along with information you can use to determine which ones are relevant for your business.

- Virtual domains/Domain hosting. The Web hosting company you choose must support virtual domains or domain hosting if you want to be able to use your own domain name (which you do).

- FrontPage Server Extensions. Because you'll want to use FrontPage to create and manage your site, you want your Web hosting company to support FrontPage Server Extensions. FrontPage Server Extensions allow you to easily publish your site without using cumbersome tools such as FTP or the Microsoft Web Publishing Wizard. They also provide server-based tools that can be indispensable when creating a Web site for an organization, such as the support for forms, discussion groups, and Web site search capability.

- Disk space allotment. Most businesses have small sites, and generally don't have trouble fitting comfortably in the 25MB of Web space provided by even the most barebones Web hosting plans you might look at. If you plan on having a large number of images, audio, or video files on your site, however, disk space allotment becomes an important issue. You may want to opt for a hosting plan that offers 100MB, 200MB, or unlimited disk space.

- Database support and Active Server Pages. If you want to use a database on your Web site and dynamically create pages based on data from the database (this is what Active Server Pages are), your Web hosting company needs to support both databases and Active Server Pages. (Setting up a database on your site is a difficult task, although it is something you could hire a consultant to do, after which your business or organization could then maintain it in-house.)

- Subdomains. Some Web hosting companies allow you to create subdomains for your Web site, such as *support.yourcompany.com* or *events.yourcompany.com*. If your company has separate divisions that want their own sites, subdomains are a cost-effective solution, since you don't have to pay additional registration fees for them.

- Mailing lists, list servers, and Majordomo. Depending on your business or organization, you may want to start an e-mail mailing list. A number of methods exist for creating mailing lists, so if you think this might be a capability you need, consider finding a Web hosting company that includes some sort of mailing list capability at little or no extra cost.

- Data transfer limitations. Some Web hosting companies have a limit on how much data can be transferred per month. Every time someone views a page on your site or downloads a file, that visitor is transferring data from your site. Similarly, when you upload new pages or files to your site, you're also transferring data. If your site goes above its limit (because of lots of visitors or large file downloads), you're charged extra.

- Security. Secure Sockets Layer (SSL) is a way of encrypting data that is transferred to and from a Web site, and it is typically used for Web stores that process credit card transactions. As such, it is an important feature if you plan to set up an online store.

- Technical support. All Web hosting companies provide technical support for any problems with publishing your Web site, Web site availability, e-mail, and so forth. However, the type, quality, and availability of this support will vary. Not all companies provide toll-free technical support phone numbers; not all companies provide 24-hour, 7-day-a-week (24/7) technical support.

- Web server speed. The speed of a Web server is fairly difficult to ascertain from reading promotional material on a company's Web site. Nevertheless, to be thorough, you probably want to ask some questions: How much bandwidth is available? How many sites does the Web server host? How fast is the server? You might also ask for the URLs of other Web sites stored on the same server and then visit those sites.

- Web server reliability. Even more important than Web server speed is the reliability of the server. To assess Web server reliability, most people rely on the uptime percentage, which is something that can be easily measured. Most organizations aim for 99.9 percent uptime (roughly 9 hours of downtime a year).

Where to Find a Web Hosting Company

With the thousands of Web hosting companies that you can choose from, narrowing your list of candidates to a reasonable number can be a time-consuming and difficult process. Several useful resources exist, however, to point you in the right direction.

TIP   *Choosing a Web hosting company isn't a permanent decision. You can easily switch companies at almost any time (although you might choose to sign up for a one-year contract to avoid setup fees). So don't waste too much time trying to find "the one." If you later locate a better one, switch when your contract is up.*

Microsoft's Locate A Web Presence Provider Web Site

Located at *http://www.microsoftwpp.com*, the Microsoft Locate A Web Presence Provider Web site shown in Figure 16-2 allows you to perform a search for a Web hosting company that is a Microsoft registered host for FrontPage Web sites. This is probably the best place to search for a Web hosting company if you plan on using FrontPage 2000 to build your site.

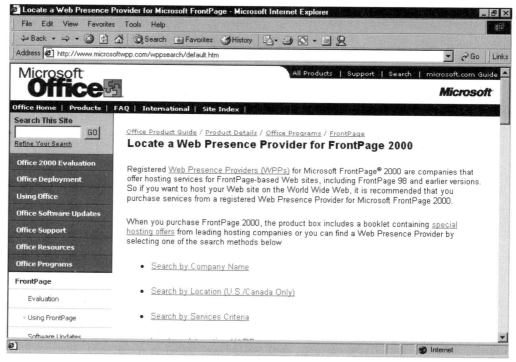

Figure 16-2 Microsoft's Locate A Web Presence Provider Web site.

DN Resources

The DN Resources site at *http://www.dnresources.com* has a special hosting section that lists sites that provide a list of Web hosting companies. It's a little confusing, since each site shows a different list of Web hosting companies. Once you sort it out, however, it can be a good place to find a company to host your site.

Local Computer Papers

If you're looking for a local Web hosting company, check out any local computer papers or the technology section of your newspaper for ads from local companies. You can also check the Yellow Pages under "Internet."

Signing Up for Service

After deciding on a domain name, locating a Web hosting company, and selecting the appropriate hosting plan, you need to sign up for the actual service. The details of the sign-up process are different for every company, so you'll need to ask the Web hosting company for instructions and help.

Collecting and Creating Digital Content

Once you pick a domain name and sign up for Web hosting, you're ready to collect and create your digital content. In any business or organization already using computers, this work is easier than you might suspect.

Collecting Existing Digital Content

Your business may already have a large amount of digital content that can be used on a site with only a minimal amount of work. When we say digital content, we mean any content that can be opened using a computer application such as a word processor or an image-editing program. This includes data on hard drives, your local network, the Internet (though be careful about copyrights), floppy and Zip disks, CD-ROMS, and so forth.

To use existing digital content (which comes in many types), you first need to locate it and, if necessary, convert the content to an appropriate format for later importing into your Web-authoring tool. (This tool might be FrontPage, for example.)

Just about any kind of digital content you have can be adapted for use on the Web:

- Word processor documents (.doc, .txt, .wpf) such as project reports, manuals, company objectives, newsletters, and notices to customers created with a word processing program, such as Microsoft Word, AppleWorks, or WordPerfect, can be a big reservoir of content.

- PowerPoint presentations (.ppt), lecture slides, or demos might be great additions to your site.

- Spreadsheet documents (.xls) might also be good content for your site, provided the data relates to your site's purpose and target audience. This could include financial information, analyzed data from technical companies, or statistical data from tests.

- Digital images (.jpg, .gif, .png, .fpx) are a staple of any Web site. This includes logos or graphics.

- Flyers, brochures, or other computer-created content stored in some sort of computer format (perhaps created using Microsoft Publisher or Adobe PageMaker) are also excellent sources of content for a site.

- E-mails can often be a rich source of content for a Web site, although you must use special care when using e-mail conversations. Special messages sent out to customers can be placed in a Web page for users who didn't receive the e-mail, customer questions and answers can be integrated into a Frequently Asked Questions page, or visitor comments can be placed on a Feedback page (usually with names removed).

- Existing Web pages might seem an obvious source, but if your business or organization already has Web pages it has created for one reason or another, you should probably evaluate how useful they would be on your new site.

- Sound files and/or video files (.wav, .au, .mp3, .mpg, .avi, .mov) are usually very large and should generally be avoided, but you might find audio and/or video files that would be perfect for your site. Use discretion with these files because of their large size and the slow speed of most visitors' Internet connections.

Creating New Digital Content

Not all content for your Web site is going to be available in digital format. Some of it will exist in print form and yet more will need to be created from scratch.

In general, the new content falls into two categories: images and documents. Images are usually created by using a digital camera, a scanner, or an art program of some sort. Documents are generally created from scratch by using a word processor or spreadsheet program, although some companies will give in to the urge to scan printed documents that aren't already available in digital format.

Digital Images

There are several ways to create new digital images for use on a Web site. Photographs can be scanned into the computer using a scanner or imported using a Photo CD picture disk or online image processing service, or they can be taken using a digital camera and imported directly into the computer. Digital images can also be created in the computer using an art program.

Documents

Documents are the other half of the new content equation, and, unfortunately, not every document that belongs on your site is going to already exist, or at least not in digital form. If you can't find a digital version of content that you want for your site, retyping the document may become a necessity. However, in special circumstances you may also be able to scan the document and use an optical character recognition (OCR) program.

Although OCR programs have greatly improved and are now quite useful, unless you have a long document that needs to be placed in its entirety on your site, it's usually faster to retype a document than it is to scan it, run it through the OCR program, and then correct the mistakes.

TIP   *OCR programs are standalone programs that convert a scanned document into text that can be used in a word-processing program or Web page editor. They can provide an easy way to digitize existing, typewritten content, but these programs do produce errors in the scanned documents. Therefore, we recommend that you carefully evaluate the amount of time involved in correcting scanned documents before relying heavily on OCR programs.*

Creating New Documents

When creating new content for use on a Web site, you can take specific steps to make the content import into your Web-authoring tool more easily and more elegantly:

- Create any large amounts of text you want to use on your site using Microsoft Word or another word-processing program, and then either save the document in appropriate format for importing into your Web-authoring tool or save it directly as a HyperText Markup Language (HTML) document that the Web-authoring tool can then edit. It's much easier and more efficient to create and edit content of any substantial length in a dedicated word processor.

- Avoid using complex formatting or graphics in documents. These generally don't import accurately into a Web-authoring tool. An exception to this rule is when the program used to create the content has special HTML output capabilities that enable it to handle complex formatting or documents. However, these exported pages may prove difficult to edit, so test out this capability before you rely on it extensively.

- Before creating a large amount of content with a particular application, test out how well the content can be imported by your Web-authoring tool or exported to HTML from the application. Knowing the limitations of the process beforehand can save a lot of time and money in the long run.

- Save new documents in a central content folder with a useful filename that allows everyone working on the site to easily identify the document.

Creating Your Web Pages

The precise steps you take to create your Web pages depend on the Web creation or Web-authoring tool that you've selected. In general, you use a wizard to create a set of blank Web pages and then add the text and images that you've already collected.

Most of the popular programs provide wizards that step you through the process of creating blank Web pages. FrontPage works this way, for example. Using FrontPage's Web wizards is an efficient way to rapidly create a Web site, and they are especially useful if you don't have a clear idea of how your site should be structured.

When you use a FrontPage wizard, FrontPage creates many of the essential pages for your Web, based on the information you type into the various screens.

NOTE   *Chapter 8 talks about how to create a simple local FrontPage Web site using the FrontPage wizards. If you're not already familiar with FrontPage, refer to that chapter for more information.*

The FrontPage wizard also provides other dialog boxes that you use to enter your business's name and address, telephone numbers, and e-mail addresses. Typically, a wizard also lets you choose a design or coordinated look for your site.

Although these Web pages will need some modifications and you'll still need to insert your own content, they can streamline the process of creating your initial pages.

Testing Your Web Site

You probably won't need to perform the exhaustive testing that large e-commerce sites must go through when rolling out a new site, but testing your Web site before publishing it can result in a more effective site, as well as fewer complaints from visitors. Testing generally looks at three areas: hyperlinks, Web browser compatibility, and usability.

Verifying Hyperlinks

Your Web-authoring tool may provide a command for checking external hyperlinks for validity. FrontPage, for example, provides a Verify Hyperlinks button on its Reporting toolbar. If your program has such a feature, we recommend that you use it before you publish your pages to the Internet.

Testing Your Site in Different Browsers

The easiest way to test your site in several browsers is to open each Web browser and enter the local address of your site in the Address or Location box, as shown in Figures 16-3, 16-4, and 16-5. For example, if your FrontPage Web site is named *mycompany* and is stored on a Web server on your local network named *WKS1*, you would enter *http://wks1/mycompany* to open the site.

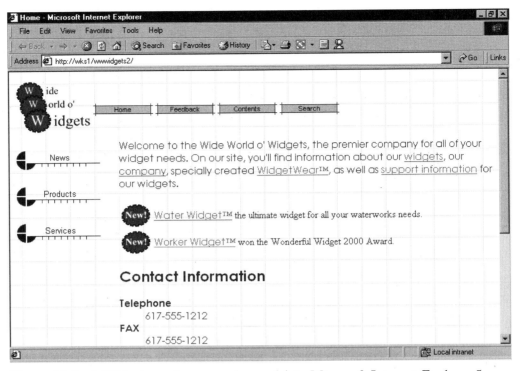

Figure 16-3 A Web site as it appears (properly) in Microsoft Internet Explorer 5.

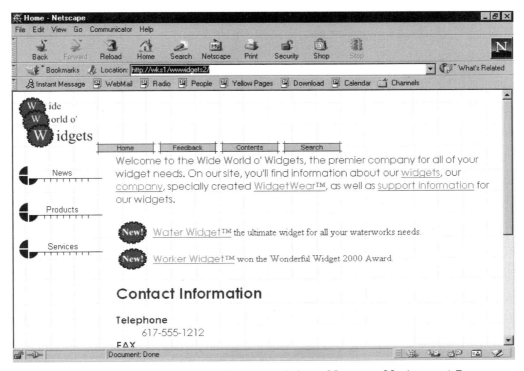

Figure 16-4 The same Web site, differing slightly in Netscape Navigator 4.7.

NOTE *Test your site with the latest versions of Internet Explorer and Netscape Navigator. If you have access to computers running older versions of the browsers or a different browser, such as Opera, test your site in these browsers, too. Testing on Macintosh and information appliances (such as WebTV) is usually easiest to do after your site has been published to the Internet.*

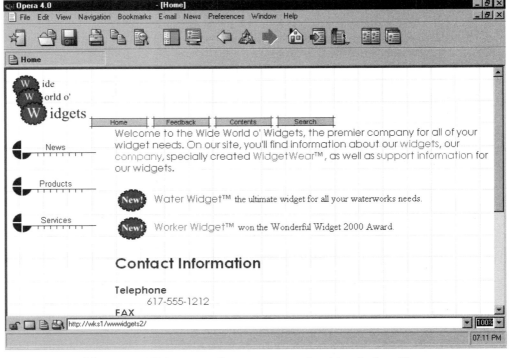

Figure 16-5 The same Web site in Opera 4, appearing identical to Netscape.

After opening your site in a couple of browsers, spend a few minutes testing all the links and examining each page. Is the layout consistent on all the browsers? Does the browser display the fonts properly? Do all the features work as expected? Make notes on which pages have problems, and then go back into FrontPage and see whether you can fix them. (To change the compatibility options for FrontPage; click the Tools menu, click Page Options, and then modify any elements that don't display properly.)

Usability Testing

In addition to testing for broken links and browser incompatibilities, you will find it informative to perform some degree of usability testing. Here are some recommendations for simple usability tests:

- Recruit people who aren't involved in the Web site project to test your site. The feedback of your customers or other people in your target audience can be invaluable in evaluating the effectiveness of your site. For very small businesses, even recruiting family and friends to test your site can generate important feedback.

- Develop some purposeful tasks for your testers to perform, and then watch how they accomplish them. You might use tasks such as "Find the company contact information" or "Find the product information for product x." If you need to interject and help the testers, your site might need more work.

- Pay special attention to the navigational structure of your Web site. How well can users locate information using your site?

- Test your Web site at a variety of resolutions. We recommend that you test your site at 640x480 (a low resolution) and at 1024x768 (a typical high resolution).

- If you decide to publish your site immediately, perform the testing after it is published. A short user survey on your Web site can also be a valuable way of gathering feedback on the effectiveness of your site.

NOTE   *If your site contains online ordering capabilities, it is very important to thoroughly test your system no matter what the size of your business or Web site.*

Publishing Your Web Site

When you're ready to make your Web site available to the general public on the World Wide Web, you need to publish it to the Internet. Typically, publishing your Web to your Web hosting company's Web server is an easy step. All that really needs to happen is that the HTML documents and any another necessary files (such as images) need to be copied to the Web server.

Many Web-authoring tools, including FrontPage, provide built-in support for publishing to Web servers. For example, in FrontPage, all you need to do is click the Publish Web toolbar button and then fill out the Publish Destination dialog box, as shown in Figure 16-6.

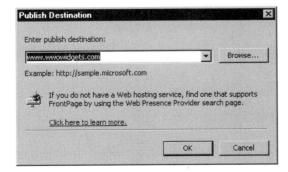

Figure 16-6 The Publish Destination dialog box.

NOTE To use the Publish Destination dialog box shown in Figure 16-6, enter the location where you want to publish your Web site (most likely your domain name, www.mycompany.com or perhaps ftp://www.mycompany.com) and click OK. When the Name And Password Required dialog box appears, enter the name and password you use to administer your Web site (on your Web hosting company's Web server, not on your local Web server) and then click OK.

Publicizing Your Web Site

In order for your Web site to succeed, you need to publicize it. There are a number of ways to publicize your site, both on and off the Internet. The online methods include search engines, online advertising, newsgroups, and mailing lists. Offline methods include placing links on all print material your business or organization creates, Yellow Pages ads, and newspaper ads.

Submitting Your Site to Search Engines and Directories

Since most people locate a Web site using a search engine or a directory, the most important step you can take to publicize your site is to submit it to the top search engines and directories. Although this process takes some time, it is very important.

Although you might be tempted, avoid using a search engine submission service. These services usually offer to submit your site to hundreds of search engines for a sum of money—sometimes with recurring fees. Since the vast majority of searches are conducted on only a handful of search engines, this level of submission is superfluous. In addition, submission firms usually don't submit your site to directories, or if they do, they do an inadequate job of it. Take the time to submit to search engines and directories yourself—it's worth it.

Search engines automatically crawl (explore) the Web, examining Web sites and adding the relevant information from each site into their search databases. Directories such as Yahoo! take descriptions submitted by Web site authors and use human editors to review the submissions. The editors then create a hierarchical, topic-based directory out of the Web sites submitted that visitors can either browse by topic or perform a search on. Hybrid search engines are usually search engines that also contain a human-created directory. Editors create the directory by looking at the search engine's results, the actual Web sites, and sometimes sites that are submitted by site authors to the hybrid directory.

The type of search engine or directory determines how you'll submit your site. Crawler-based search engines generally request only your Web site's URL, as shown in Figure 16-7. The search engine then automatically visits your site, determines the content of your site, and adds it to the search engine's database.

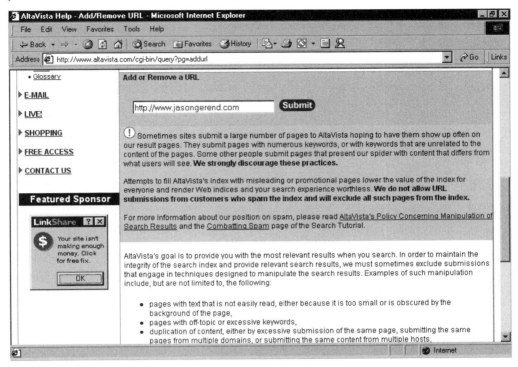

Figure 16-7 Submitting to a crawler-based search engine.

TIP   *Although search engines generally look into your Web site for what content is contained on pages other than your home page, this isn't always reliable, and it's prudent to submit your two or three most important pages separately to each search engine. But limit yourself to two or three pages; submitting too many pages to the same search engine can actually cause a search engine to exclude your site.*

You'll need to do a bit of work to submit your site to a directory. First, visit the directory (such as Yahoo!) and perform some searches for content similar to your Web site. Second, take note of the kinds of sites that are returned in the search results and the categories under which they're listed. It's very important with directories to find the most specific and appropriate category for your Web site, so do some exploring. (Your site may belong in multiple categories. If this is the case, make a note of each one.) Third, read the directory's Site Submission Tips or the equivalent page. This will tell you exactly the procedure the directory wants you to follow when submitting your Web site. Most require that you navigate to the category under which you want to list your site, and then click the Suggest A Site link. Fourth, in the actual submission form, as shown in Figure 16-8, submit the title of your Web site (generally your official business or company name), your site's URL, and a 25-word-or-less description of your site.

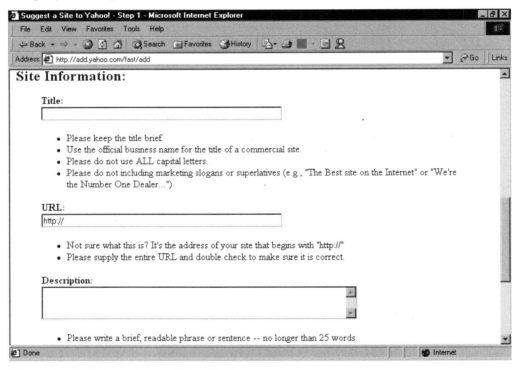

Figure 16-8 Submitting to Yahoo!'s directory.

TIP   *Make your site description more than just a series of keywords. It should be a succinct, well-written summary of what visitors will find on your site.*

Table 16-1 lists search engines and directories that we recommend you submit your site to, their URLs, and their type.

SEARCH ENGINE	URL	SEARCH ENGINE TYPE
AltaVista	http://www.altavista.com	Hybrid using Open Directory and LookSmart
AOL Search	http://www.search.aol.com	Hybrid using Open Directory
Direct Hit	http://www.directhit.com	Crawler-based, modified by popularity
Excite	http://www.excite.com	Crawler-based
Go (Infoseek)	http://www.go.com	Hybrid
Google	http://www.google.com	Crawler-based, modified by popularity
HotBot	http://www.hotbot.com	Hybrid, with results from Direct Hit and Open Directory
LookSmart	http://www.looksmart.com	Directory
Lycos	http://www.lycos.com	Hybrid, using Open Directory
MSN Search	http://www.search.msn.com	Hybrid, using LookSmart
Netscape Search	http://www.search.netscape.com	Hybrid, using Open Directory
Northern Light	http://www.northernlight.com	Crawler-based
Open Directory	http://www.dmoz.org	Directory
WebCrawler	http://www.webcrawler.com	Crawler-based
Yahoo!	http://www.yahoo.com	Directory

Table 16-1 The major search engines and directories.

Online Advertising

In addition to submitting your Web site to search engines and directories, a number of other methods are available for advertising on the Web. Some of these are fairly effective in increasing the number of visitors to your site, and some are probably a waste of time and money. In the following sections we offer some recommendations on which methods to consider and which to ignore.

Purchasing Banner Ads

The most obvious method of online advertising is the banner ad. Banner ads are the ubiquitous (and often disregarded) rectangular ad boxes that adorn most Web sites. In general, we recommend that you avoid paying for banner ads. They require too much time and effort to create, cost money, and are limited in their ability to draw visitors to your site.

Link Exchanges

One of the best methods of advertising online is to get other sites to link to your site, creating what's known as a link exchange. This method is cost-effective (free) and can also increase your ranking in search engines that pay attention to the number of links to a particular Web site.

You can establish links to your site in the following three ways:

- Use a Link Exchange service that allows you to exchange links with other random sites.

- Join a Web ring of sites that are similar to your own

- Contact sites personally and inquire about exchanging links.

Using a Link Exchange service usually doesn't work well for most businesses and organizations. This is because the site that ends up linking to yours inevitably has nothing in common with your site's purpose, so it is unlikely to generate visitors who are interested in viewing your site.

Web rings devoted to a topic covered by your site are an effective means of generating traffic to your site. The way a Web ring works is that sites with a common topic contact each other, decide to set up a Web ring, and then pay to place a banner ad for the Web ring on their home pages, as shown in Figure 16-9. This banner ad is usually configured with automatically updated links to other sites in the Web ring. By joining the Web ring, your site becomes accessible through these links and is also listed in the Web ring's directory. The site at *http://www.webring.com* is a good place to look if you are interested in joining a Web ring.

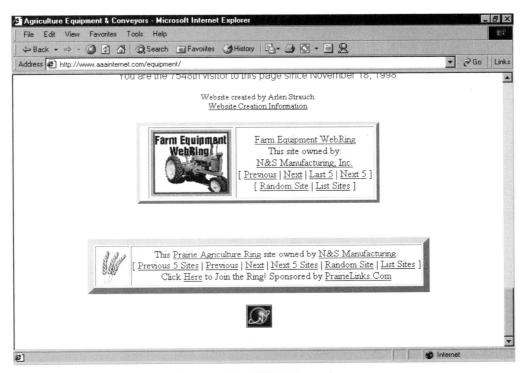

Figure 16-9 A Web site with a couple of Web ring ads.

Another method of establishing links to your site is to manually identify Web sites useful to your visitors with which you can exchange links. Once you've identified sites that cover similar or related topics, contact the sites' Webmasters about setting up a link exchange. Predictably, one way to convince a site to exchange links is to place a link to their site on your site, send them an e-mail informing them of this, and then suggest that they link to your site as well.

Using Newsgroups to Gain Exposure

Newsgroups in general aren't the best place to publicize a Web site. Newsgroup participants usually react negatively to ads placed on newsgroups, and the dynamic nature of newsgroups ensures that anything you post will stay up for only a couple of weeks before getting archived or deleted.

Creating a Mailing List

Mailing lists are a voluntary form of bulk e-mailing that allow you to easily send out mail, such as a newsletter or an update, to a large number of people. Sending regular e-mails about your Web site or business to visitors who have joined your mailing list is an effective way of reminding visitors about your business and also featuring new or changed parts of your site. This increases the chances that they will visit your site again.

Make sure that what you send via your mailing list is valuable content to subscribers. Otherwise, your subscribers will delete the message or unsubscribe from your list. This content can include tips, how-to sections, product specials, and new additions to your site. Always include instructions for unsubscribing to the list with every message you send.

TIP   *If you are interested in creating a mailing list yourself, you can find out about the process at* http://www.lsoft.com/manuals/1.8d/owner/owner.html. *This page at the L-Soft site provides a manual for creating a mailing list with Listserv. If you want to add your mailing list to the Liszt site, go to* http://www.liszt.com/submit.html.

Mailing lists can be developed using three different types of programs: a standard mail program, a standalone bulk mail program, or a Web server-based mailing list program. Most businesses will find that Web-based mailing list providers such as eGroups.com and Listbot (*http://www.listbot.com*) are a better solution than the traditional Listserv and Majordomo programs. Additionally, many of these Web-based list servers can be used for free, provided you don't mind having ads inserted in your messages.

Offline Publicizing

You can get so caught up in publicizing your Web site online that you forget about the more traditional channels of publicity, such as business and industry publications, phone books, and newspaper ads, and traditional marketing methods, such as speaking engagements.

Any time that you draw attention to your business or organization, you'll increase the number of visitors to your site—provided that you make it clear to your audience how to find your site. Generally, you publicize your Web site in the same way that you would publicize your business, but in addition to (or possibly instead of) providing a phone number as a contact method, list your URL. Many people consider the Web their preferred source of information, so any time you want to provide people with a way of obtaining additional information about your business, list your URL.

Summary

Web publishing isn't as complicated as you might think. In many cases, the Web simply becomes another tool your business can use for sharing information. To make the process as efficient and fast as possible, it helps to break down the work into seven discrete steps: developing a Web strategy, setting up your domain and server, collecting and creating digital content, creating your Web pages, testing your site, publishing your site, and then publicizing your finished Web site.

Chapter 17

SETTING UP A WEB STORE

Featuring:

- What Is a Web Store?
- Setting Up a Non-interactive Web Store
- Setting Up a Simple Interactive Web Store
- Reviewing Other Web Store Options

In a short chapter like this, we can't describe everything you need to know to set up a large, successful Web store. Some parts of the Web store development process go way beyond the skills of even the most sophisticated business professional. But even so, we can describe how you or a coworker can add a simple Web store to your Web site.

NOTE *This chapter assumes you've already set up a Web site. If you want information about how that project works, refer to Chapter 16.*

What Is a Web Store?

Regardless of whether we are talking about the local corner market or a large Web store, a store and its staff perform only four basic activities:

- Display the items for sale.
- Show which items are available for immediate purchase and which must be ordered.
- Answer questions from customers about items.
- Arrange for customers to purchase or, if necessary, backorder items.

Very small stores and large stores are required to do these four tasks. (Obviously, large stores do more of all four things and with far greater sophistication.)

A Web store and its staff perform the same four tasks—except using a Web site rather than a physical, brick-and-mortar location. A Web store displays items for sale, shows which items are in inventory and which must be backordered, answers (or should answer) questions from customers, and arranges for customers to purchase or backorder items.

Web stores like amazon.com, for example, usually do a good job of displaying items for sale. All they need to do is create a Web page for each product they sell, as shown in Figure 17-1, and then provide an easy-to-use search engine so that shoppers can find products.

Figure 17-1 The amazon.com Web page for another book from Redmond Technology Press, *MBA's Guide to Excel 2000*.

NOTE   *The Web-buying experience is in many ways inferior to the brick-and-mortar experience because the shopper can't physically examine the product. A buyer can't thumb through a novel, try on a pair of shoes, or test-drive a car, for example.*

Web stores also make it easy for people comfortable with computers to use the Web to order an item. Figure 17-2 shows an amazon.com order form. Essentially, a shopper completes this form and clicks a button to place his or her order.

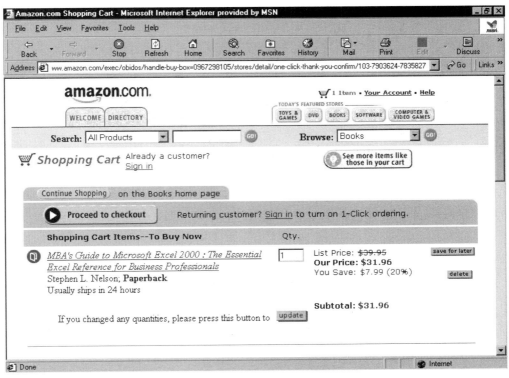

Figure 17-2 The amazon.com order form.

Web stores don't do everything that a regular brick-and-mortar store does, and sometimes they don't do things as well as a brick-and-mortar store. In a brick-and-mortar store, you know whether a product is in stock simply by looking at the shelf; if you have questions about a product, you can ask a salesperson.

Using an Inventory Database

An inventory database allows a Web store's pages to access this database to report on stock availability. Most of the sophisticated and all of the large Web stores use inventory databases.

We suggest that, at least at first, you consider doing without this enhancement. Adding an inventory database feature to a Web store requires the help of a professional Web store developer, which is expensive. And the feature often doesn't deliver the benefits that it promises.

What we know about bookselling, for example, is that the large Web bookstores (see Figure 17-1) only hint at stock availability. If amazon.com provides the availability description, "Usually ships in 24 hours," that reportedly means the book is stocked at amazon.com. But the availability description, "Usually ships in 1–2 days," actually means that amazon.com's principal distributor had inventory yesterday. The bottom line is that the often unreliable nature of inventory reports coupled with the large up-front cost involved makes Web stores with integrated inventory systems impractical for most businesses.

Setting Up a Non-Interactive Web Store

The easiest Web store to set up is a simple non-interactive site. This site needs only to describe the items you'll be selling and tell customers how to contact you to place their orders.

To describe the items you sell, set up a Web page for each item. Chapter 13 shows how to set up Web pages. (That chapter also explains preparation necessary to begin posting Web pages to a Web server, including registering for a domain name and signing up for Web hosting.) Figure 17-3 shows a page from the Redmond Technology Press Web site that describes an item for sale.

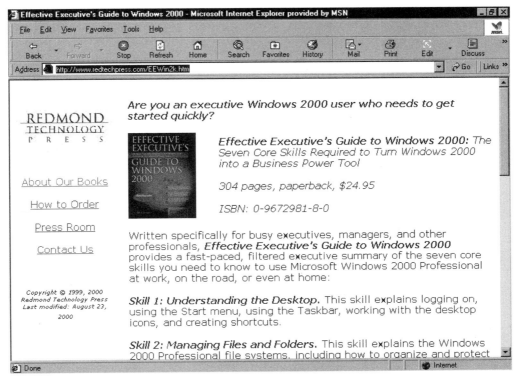

Figure 17-3 A page from the Redmond Technology Press Web site.

To tell customers how to contact you, all you really need to do is provide contact information: a telephone number, a fax number, or even a mailing address. Figure 17-4 shows an order information page from the Redmond Technology Press Web site.

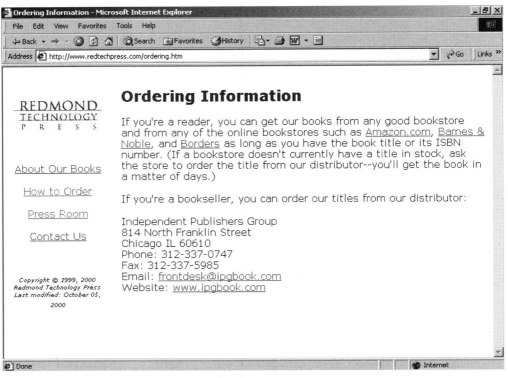

Figure 17-4 A page of ordering information at the Redmond Technology Press Web site.

A non-interactive Web store only does our first task of retailing, that is, showing which items are for sale. But especially for small-volume Web stores, this approach might be the best.

TIP   *A non-interactive Web store or a simple interactive Web store (described in the next section) might work well for retailers who already operate a brick-and-mortar location. Such a Web store operates as a virtual kiosk, generating easy, extra sales each year.*

Setting Up a Simple Interactive Web Store

If you don't require a shopping cart feature, an interactive Web store doesn't have to be complicated. All you need to do is create a Web form that collects order information from customers and then have the Web store send this information to a person who will fill and process the orders.

NOTE   *A shopping cart aggregates orders from a shopper, allowing the person who needs several items to grab everything they need and then "check out" just once. Adding a shopping cart to a Web store requires the services of a professional developer or an e-commerce provider.*

Creating an Order Form

Creating a Web page order form isn't difficult—especially if you're familiar with how Web forms work because you've used with them at other Web sites.

To build a Web order form with FrontPage, for example, start FrontPage and follow these steps:

1. **Start the Form Page Wizard.**

   Click the File menu, and then click New. When FrontPage displays the New Page Or Web task pane, click Page Templates to open the Page Templates dialog box, as shown in Figure 17-5. Click the Form Page Wizard icon to start the wizard, and then click Next to move past the first introductory dialog box.

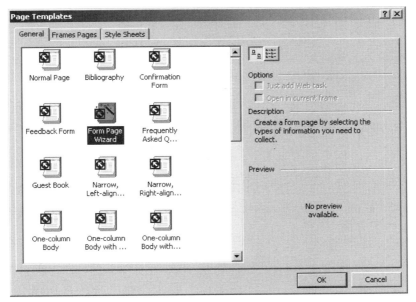

Figure 17-5 The Page Templates dialog box.

2. Specify the categories of information you want to collect with the form.

When the Form Page Wizard asks what type of information you want to collect with the form, click the Add button. The Form Page Wizard opens dialog boxes that ask what kind of information you want to collect using the form. Indicate that you want to collect a category of information such as account information or ordering information using the dialog box shown in Figure 17-6.

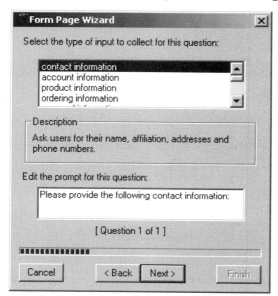

Figure 17-6 The Form Page Wizard dialog box that asks what categories of information you want to collect.

3. Describe the specific information you want to collect.

The Form Page Wizard opens a dialog box, as shown in Figure 17-7, that provides option buttons and check boxes that you use to indicate which boxes and buttons you want added to the form.

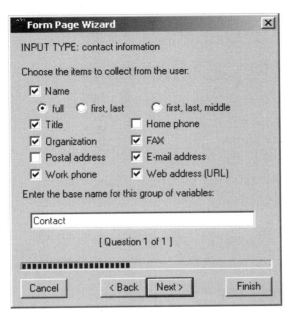

Figure 17-7 The Form Page Wizard dialog box that asks you to identify the specific information you want to collect.

If you want to collect more than one category of information, repeat steps 2 and 3 as needed. For example, if you want to collect product and ordering information, you would repeat steps 2 and 3 one time to describe the product information you want to collect and another time to describe the ordering information you want to collect.

4. **Review the list of information types you want to collect.**

Once you finish with steps 2 and 3 and indicate as much to the Form Page Wizard, FrontPage displays a list of the information types you want to collect, as shown in Figure 17-8. Review this list, and, if it's complete, click Next. If the list isn't complete, click Back and then repeat steps 2 and 3 as needed.

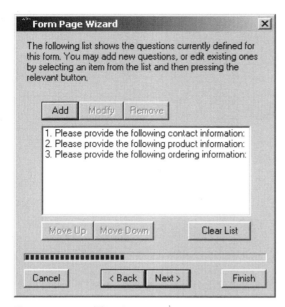

Figure 17-8 The Form Page Wizard dialog box that asks you to review the types of information you've said you want to collect.

5. Specify how the wizard should create a draft form.

The Form Page Wizard opens a dialog box that asks how you want the list of questions presented, as shown in Figure 17-9. Use this dialog box's buttons to make your choices, and click Next.

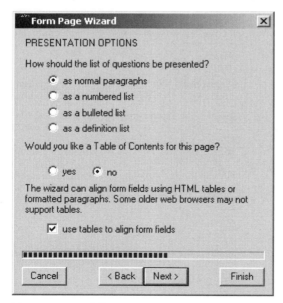

Figure 17-9 The Form Page Wizard dialog box that asks how you want your form to look.

6. **Specify how form results should be saved.**

   The Form Page Wizard opens a dialog box that asks how you want the form results—the information that people enter into your form—saved, as shown in Figure 17-10. Typically, you choose to save the form results on the Web server in a file or have the form results sent to you in an e-mail message. (You can also choose to use a custom CGI script—especially a simple program—to specify how form results are saved, but that option is more complicated and beyond the scope of this book.) To make your choices, use this dialog box's buttons. Optionally, use this dialog box's box to specify what name should be used for the file. In order to save form results to a file or e-mail form results, your Web site must reside on a Web server that supports FrontPage Server Extensions.

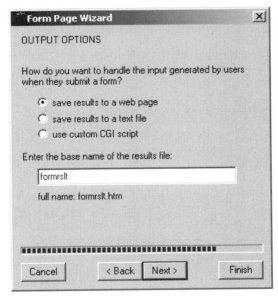

Figure 17-10 The Form Page Wizard dialog box that asks how you want form results saved.

NOTE   *Your credit card processing agreement may specify how you must process credit card orders. You might, for example, be required to transmit credit card information using encryption. In this case, you can't use e-mail messages to send order information. You'll have to store order information on the Web server. You'll also have to store at least the order form on a secure Web server so that order information gets encrypted before it's sent. For more information about how this works, ask your ISP.*

7. Create the draft form.

Click Finish to create a draft version of the form, as shown in Figure 17-11.

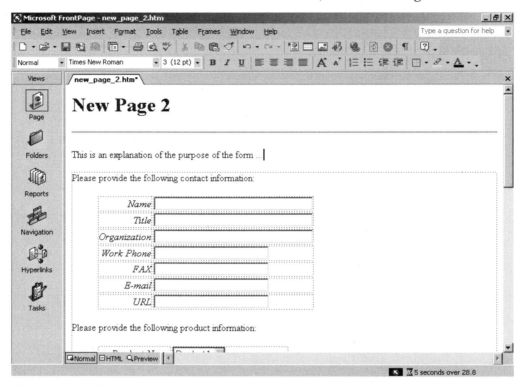

Figure 17-11 The draft order form.

8. Add ordering instructions and other needed information to the form.

Add ordering instructions to the form by typing them into the area above the ordering information boxes. You can add any other needed information in the same way.

NOTE *At the very bottom of the Web order form, FrontPage includes some boilerplate text that's supposed to name the author of the form and the organization publishing the form. You will need to edit this information.*

9. Optionally, fine-tune the way orders are transmitted.

Right-click the form, and choose Form Properties from the shortcut menu to open the Form Properties dialog box, as shown in Figure 17-12.

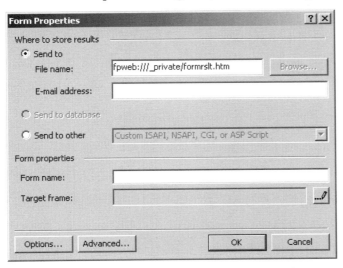

Figure 17-12 The Form Properties dialog box.

The Send To button and boxes will indicate how the Web server should transmit order information (choices you already made as part of running the Form Page Wizard), so you shouldn't need to make changes to this dialog box's settings (although you can).

Click the Options button in the Form Properties dialog box to open the Saving Results dialog box, as shown in Figure 17-13. You can use the File Results tab to control how the information is stored in a file—for example, what directory and filename should be used for the file.

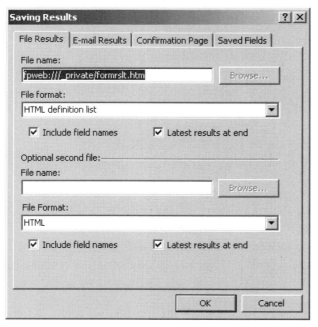

Figure 17-13 The Saving Results dialog box open at the File Results tab.

You can use the E-Mail Results tab, as shown in Figure 17-14, to control how information is e-mailed. For example, you can specify that all e-mail orders use the subject "Web Store Order."

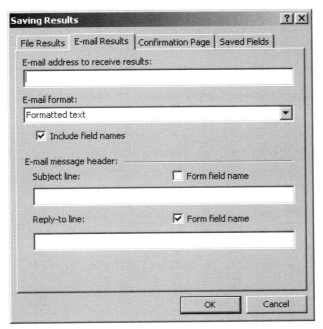

Figure 17-14 The Saving Results dialog box open at the E-Mail Results tab.

10. Add the order form to the Web site.

Save the Web page to your Web server (click the File menu and then click Save), and then add hyperlinks to your existing Web pages so that customers can reach the order form.

Filling Out the Order Form

When a customer decides to order an item, he or she clicks the order form hyperlink that leads to the Web order form page, as shown in Figure 17-15. To order an item, the shopper fills in the blanks and then clicks the Send button.

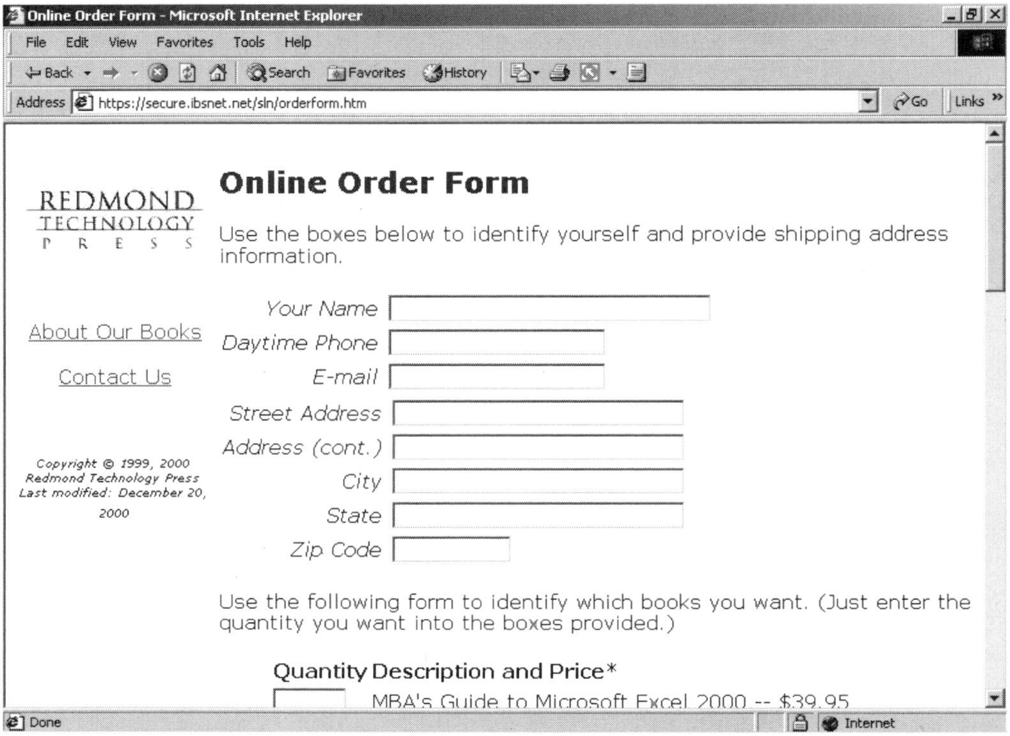

Figure 17-15 The example Web order form.

When the customer sends the order information to the Web store, depending on how you've told the Web store to process the form results, one of two things happens:

- The Web store sends an e-mail to the Web store e-mail Inbox with the order, shipping, and billing information.

- The Web store creates a text file on your Web server with the order, shipping, and billing information.

Processing an Order Form

Mechanically, an e-mail-based system would simply require someone to perform the duties of a shipping clerk. These duties would include the following:

- Checking the e-mail Inbox or the Web server order file for orders.

- Printing e-mail order messages or the contents of an order file to use as pick lists.

- Fulfilling orders using the pick lists.

- Forwarding a copy of the pick list to the person performing the billing duties.

The simple system described here doesn't aggregate orders automatically the way a shopping cart does. But with low order volumes—a few orders a day—these deficiencies might not matter. A reasonably alert shipping clerk would be able to combine items being shipped to the same address.

Reviewing Other Web Store Options

The two Web store options described in this chapter are easy to implement. But as we've noted several times, you can become considerably more sophisticated in the way you set up a Web store by tying it to an inventory database that provides stock availability information and by setting up a shopping cart system so customers can easily purchase multiple items.

If you want to implement a more complex Web store—one that uses these sorts of features—you have two other choices:

- Contract with an e-commerce provider such as BigStep.com, FreeMerchant.com, Store.Yahoo.com, or JumboStore.com. You can visit these e-commerce providers' Web sites for more information, but these companies will help you create Web stores that include a shopping cart system.

- Build your own Web store from scratch by hiring developers. This approach can get you exactly what you want, but it comes at a price. We've heard people say you can do this for as little as $10,000. We think the minimum is probably several times this amount if you want something that's more unique than what an e-commerce provider will sell.

Summary

The work required to build a Web store goes beyond the skills of many business professionals. But simple Web stores can be surprisingly easy to set up and can often provide better service than the big Web retailers. For this reason, we think simple Web stores are something that many businesses should consider. They can be profitable—especially if they're developed and run by retailers who already understand their customers.

Chapter 18

CREATING A BUSINESS PLAN WITH EXCEL

Featuring:

- Using the Business Planning Workbook
- Understanding the Business Planning Workbook's Calculations
- Customizing the Business Planning Workbook

Pro forma financial statements—income statements, balance sheets, and cash flow statements—usually constitute an integral part of business planning and the overall budgeting process. But that only makes sense. Any planning for a firm's future must take into account likely profits, cash flows, and financial condition. The business planning workbook (BIZPLAN.XLS) for use with Excel, which is described in this chapter and is available from the Redmond Technology Press Web site (*www.redtechpress.com*), provides a framework to use in constructing pro forma income statements, balance sheets, and cash flow statements and for then performing ratio analysis on these statements.

NOTE *To retrieve the BIZPLAN.XLS workbook, visit the* www.redtechpress.com_*Web site, click the hyperlink to the* MBA's Guide to Office XP, *and then follow the instructions for downloading the BIZPLAN.XLS workbook.*

Financial Statements and Ratios

Financial statements describe either the past or the future financial condition and performance of a business. The term *financial statement* can refer to one of several types of schedules and summaries of economic information. Typically, however, the term describes a set of documents that include an income statement (also called a statement of operations), a balance sheet (also called a statement of financial condition), and a cash flow statement.

An *income statement* details the profits and losses of a business for a specific period. For example, you might want to know the profits or losses of your business over the past month. Therefore, you would prepare an income statement that lists your revenues and expenses and calculates the profits or losses for the month.

A *balance sheet* identifies and lists the assets and liabilities of a business as of a specific time. It paints a clear picture of what the business owns, what the business owes, and the difference between the two (often called the net worth or owner equity). Typically, you prepare a balance sheet as of the end of the period for which an income statement is prepared. For example, if you prepare an income statement for a month, you might also want to prepare a balance sheet as of the last day of the month.

A *cash flow statement* outlines the cash inflows and outflows of a business for a specific period. Generally, you prepare a cash flow statement for the same period for which you prepare an income statement.

Financial ratios express relationships among the amounts reported in the financial statements. The ratios can offer insights into the economic health of a business. The ratios can also indicate the reasonableness of the assumptions implicit in a forecast. For example, by comparing the ratios of your business with the ratios of similar businesses, you can compare the financial characteristics of your business with those of other businesses. By comparing the ratios in your pro forma model with industry averages and standards, you also test your modeling assumptions for reasonableness.

Two general categories of financial ratios exist: common size ratios and intrastatement or interstatement ratios. *Common size ratios* convert a financial statement—usually a balance sheet or an income statement—from dollars to percentages. Common size ratios allow for comparisons of the assets, liabilities, revenues, owner equity, and expenses of businesses of various sizes. The comparison can be either at a point in time or as a trend over time. *Intrastatement* or *interstatement ratios* quantify relationships among amounts from different financial statements or from different parts of the same financial statement. Intrastatement and interstatement ratios are an attempt to account for the fact that amounts usually cannot be interpreted alone, but must be viewed in the context of other key financial factors and events. In general, both categories of ratios are most valuable when compared with industry averages and trends.

Using the Business Planning Workbook

You can use the business planning workbook to construct pro forma financial statements that let you forecast profits and losses, financial condition, and cash flows for a business or organization. To use the workbook, you develop and then enter information on the assets; the creditor and owner equities at the start of the forecasting horizon; the expected changes in the assets and equities over the forecasting horizon; and the revenues and expenses for each period on the forecasting horizon.

Given data that includes your starting assets, liabilities, owner equity balances, and expected changes in these amounts for the forecasting horizon, this workbook constructs a balance sheet. Given data that includes sales and costs of sales, operating expenses, interest income and expenses, and marginal income tax rates, this workbook constructs an income statement. From the balance sheet and income statement, this workbook constructs a cash flow statement.

To enter your own data in the business planning workbook, use the following steps. Enter positive balances or increases as positive amounts, and enter negative balances or decreases as negative amounts.

1. **Retrieve the business planning workbook, BIZPLAN.XLS, from the Redmond Technology Press Web site.**

   You can retrieve the workbook by visiting the Redmond Technology Press Web site at *www.redtechpress.com*, clicking the hyperlink for the *MBA's Guide to Office XP*, and then following the onscreen instructions for downloading this and any of the other workbooks. The workbook initially contains the default inputs shown in Figure 18-1.

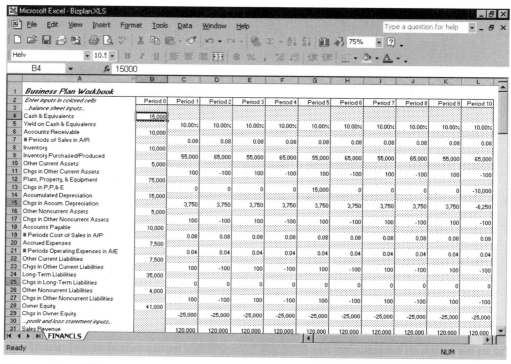

Figure 18-1 The inputs area of the business planning workbook.

2. Enter the Cash & Equivalents balance for the start of the forecasting horizon.

The value you enter for Cash & Equivalents is the starting cash and cash equivalents (marketable securities), the dollar total of all the cash held at the beginning of the forecasting period.

3. Enter the forecasted period yield that you expect the cash and equivalents to deliver.

The model estimates the period interest income by multiplying the cash and equivalents balance by the yield on cash and equivalents.

4. Enter the accounts receivable balance for the start of the forecasting horizon.

The value you enter for Accounts Receivable (A/R) is the starting accounts receivable balance, the balance at the beginning of the forecasting horizon, excluding any allowance for uncollectible amounts.

5. **Enter the number of periods of sales in accounts receivable.**

   The value you enter for # of Periods of Sales in A/R, or number of periods of sales in accounts receivable, is the number of periods or the fraction of a period for which sales are held in accounts receivable. If accounts receivable typically amount to about 30 days of sales and you use months as your forecasting periods, you hold one period of sales in accounts receivable. Alternatively, if accounts receivable typically amount to about 30 days of sales and you use years as your forecasting periods, you hold one-twelfth of a period of sales in accounts receivable.

6. **Enter the dollar amount of the inventory held at the start of the forecasting horizon.**

   The Inventory value is the starting inventory balance, the total dollar amount of the inventory purchased for resale or manufactured for resale and held at the beginning of the forecasting horizon.

7. **Enter the forecasted dollar amount of inventory purchased or produced for each period of the forecasting horizon.**

   The Inventory Purchased/Produced value is the dollar total of items purchased or produced over the period.

8. **Enter the amount of the other current assets held at the start of the forecasting horizon.**

   The Other Current Assets starting balance is the dollar total of any other current assets with which you begin the forecasting horizon. These other current assets might include prepaid expenses, short-term investments, and deposits made with vendors.

9. **Enter the amount of the change in the other current assets for each period in the forecasting horizon.**

   The value for Chgs in Other Current Assets, or changes in other current assets for the period, is the dollar total of increases or decreases in the accounts included in the starting other Current Assets balance.

10. **Enter the amount of the plant, property, and equipment at the start of the forecasting horizon.**

    The starting Plant, Property, & Equipment balance is the dollar total of the fixed assets. This amount includes such items as realty, manufacturing equipment, and furniture.

11. **Enter the amount of the change in the plant, property, and equipment (P, P, & E) for each period of the forecasting horizon.**

The Chgs in P, P, & E value is the dollar total of decreases or increases in the plant, property, and equipment accounts for the period. Increases in these accounts probably stem from purchases of additional fixed assets. Decreases in these accounts probably stem from disposal of assets.

12. **Enter the amount of the accumulated depreciation on the plant, property, and equipment at the start of the forecasting horizon.**

The starting Accumulated Depreciation balance represents the depreciation expenses charged to date on the assets identified in the starting Plant, Property, & Equipment balance.

13. **Enter the amount of the change in the accumulated depreciation for each period of the forecasting horizon.**

The Chgs in Accum. Depreciation value is the dollar total of increases and decreases in the accumulated depreciation account for the period. Increases in the accumulated depreciation balance probably stem from the current period depreciation expense. Decreases in the accumulated depreciation balance probably stem from removing the accumulated depreciation attributed to a fixed asset that you disposed of.

14. **Enter the amount of the other noncurrent assets at the start of the period.**

The starting Other Noncurrent Assets balance is the dollar total of all other noncurrent assets held at the start of the forecasting period. Other noncurrent assets might include copyrights, patents, and goodwill.

15. **Enter the amount of the change in the other noncurrent assets for each period of the forecasting horizon.**

The Chgs in Other Noncurrent Assets value is the dollar total increase or decrease for the period in the accounts included in the starting Other Noncurrent Assets balance.

16. **Enter the amount of the accounts payable balance at the start of the forecasting horizon.**

The starting Accounts Payable (A/P) balance is the dollar total of amounts owed vendors for inventory at the start of the forecasting horizon. This workbook calculates future Accounts Payable balances, based on the cost of sales volumes. To add precision to the forecasts of accounts payable, the model assumes that accounts payable represent debt incurred for the cost of sales.

17. **Enter the number of periods of the cost of sales in accounts payable.**

The # Periods Cost of Sales in A/P is the number of periods or the fraction of a period for which the cost of sales is held in accounts payable. If accounts payable typically amount to about 30 days of cost of sales and you use months as your forecasting periods, you hold one period of cost of sales in accounts payable. Alternatively, if accounts payable typically amount to about 30 days of cost of sales and you use years as your forecasting periods, you hold one-twelfth of a period of cost of sales in accounts payable.

18. **Enter the amount of the accrued expenses balance at the start of the forecasting horizon.**

The starting Accrued Expenses (A/E) balance is the dollar total of amounts owed vendors for operating expenses at the start of the forecast horizon. This workbook calculates future Accrued Expenses balances, based on the operating expenses levels. To add precision to the forecasts of accrued expenses, the model assumes that accrued expenses represent debt incurred for operating expenses.

19. **Enter the number of periods of operating expenses in accrued expenses.**

The # Periods Operating Expenses in A/E value is the number of periods or the fraction of a period for which operating expenses are held in accrued expenses. If accrued expenses typically amount to 30 days of operating expenses and you use months as your forecasting periods, you hold one period of operating expenses in accrued expenses. Alternatively, if accrued expenses typically amount to about 30 days of operating expenses and you use years as your forecasting periods, you hold one-twelfth of a period of operating expense in accrued expenses.

20. **Enter the amount of the other current liabilities at the start of the forecasting period.**

The Other Current Liabilities starting balance is the dollar total of all other current liabilities held at the start of the forecasting period. Other current liabilities might include income tax payable, product warranty liability, and the current portion of a long-term liability.

21. **Enter the amount of the change in the other current liabilities for each period of the forecasting horizon.**

The Chgs in Other Current Liabilities value is the dollar total of increases or decreases for the period in the accounts included in the starting Other Current Liabilities balance.

22. **Enter the amount of the long-term liabilities balance at the start of the forecasting horizon.**

   The starting Long-Term Liabilities balance is the dollar total of debt that will be paid back sometime after the next year.

23. **Enter the amount of the change in the long-term liabilities for each period of the forecasting horizon.**

   The Chgs in Long-Term Liabilities value is the increase or decrease for the period in the outstanding long-term debt. These changes might include decreases stemming from the amortization of principal through debt service payments and increases stemming from additional funds provided by creditors. You need to include the principal component of debt service payments as negative amounts because they decrease the amount of long-term liability.

24. **Enter the amount of the other noncurrent liabilities at the start of the forecasting horizon.**

   The Other Noncurrent Liabilities starting balance is the dollar total of all other noncurrent liabilities held at the start of the forecasting period. These might include deferred income tax, employee pension plan liabilities, and capitalized lease obligations.

25. **Enter the amount of the change in the other noncurrent liabilities for each period of the forecasting horizon.**

   The Chgs in Other Noncurrent Liabilities value is the dollar total of increases or decreases for the period in the accounts included in the starting Other Noncurrent Liabilities balance. These changes might include decreases stemming from the amortization of principal through debt service payments and increases stemming from additional funds provided by creditors.

26. **Enter the amount of the owner equity balance at the start of the forecasting horizon.**

   The Owner Equity starting balance is the dollar total of the capital originally contributed by owners and the earnings retained by the business at the start of the forecasting horizon.

27. **Enter the amount of the change in the owner equity balance for each period of the forecasting horizon stemming from additional capital contributions, dividends, and other special distributions to owners.**

   The Chgs in Owner Equity value is the dollar total of increases for the period in owner equity, other than those stemming from the profits of a business and all decreases in owner equity. For example, increases in the Owner Equity balance might result from additional offerings of common or preferred stock and treasury stock transactions; decreases in the Owner Equity balance might result from dividends and other distributions to stockholders.

NOTE *Changes to owner equity balance resulting from the profit or loss for the period are calculated in the income statement; they are not entered.*

28. **Enter the sales revenue forecasted for each period of the forecasting horizon.**

    The Sales Revenue values represent the forecasted sales revenues generated by the business over each period of the forecasting horizon.

29. **Enter the cost of sales forecasted for each period of the forecasting horizon.**

    The Cost of Sales values represent the forecasted costs of the inventory sold for the forecasting horizon.

30. **Enter those costs that fall into the first, second, and third operating expense classification or category for each period of the forecasting horizon.**

    The operating expenses for Cost Centers 1, 2, and 3 represent the operating expenses for the forecasting horizon. These figures might be three expense classifications related to operating the business, or they might be the total expenses for three groups of expenses.

31. **Enter the interest expense of carrying any debt used to fund operations or asset purchases.**

    The Interest Expense values represent the period interest expenses of carrying any debt related to the business.

32. **Enter the marginal income tax rate that, when multiplied against the profit or loss for the period, calculates the income tax expense (or savings).**

    The Marginal Income Tax Rate value is the percentage that, when multiplied by the operating profit (or loss), calculates the income tax expense (or savings). If you are interested only in calculating pretax profits and losses, enter this amount as zero.

After you enter the required inputs, the business planning workbook makes the calculations necessary to construct pro forma financial statements and calculate a set of standard financial ratios.

Understanding the Business Planning Workbook's Calculations

The business planning workbook has seven parts: the inputs forecast, Balance Sheet, Common Size Balance Sheet, Income Statement, Common Size Income Statement, Cash Flow Statement, and Financial Ratios Table. We want to briefly describe the calculations that occur within each of these parts in case you have questions or in case you want to modify the workbook so it works for your situation.

Forecasting Inputs

The inputs area of the business planning workbook has one set of formulas. The second row identifies the period for which the results are calculated. The *period identifier* numbers the periods for which values are entered. The start of the first period is stored in cell B2 as the integer 0. Periods that follow are stored as the previous period plus 1.

The period identifiers in the Balance Sheet, Common Size Balance Sheet, Income Statement, Cash Flow Statement, and Financial Ratios Table schedules use similar formulas.

NOTE   *The cells that hold the period identifiers use a custom number format that precedes each period with identification with the word* Period. *To remove this, reformat the cells using another number format.*

Balance Sheet

The Balance Sheet schedule has 20 rows with calculated data, but the first row contains only the text label Period, as shown in Figure 18-2. (As in the inputs area of the business planning workbook, the period identifier numbers the periods for which values are forecasted.) The rest of the Balance Sheet's values are described in the paragraphs that follow.

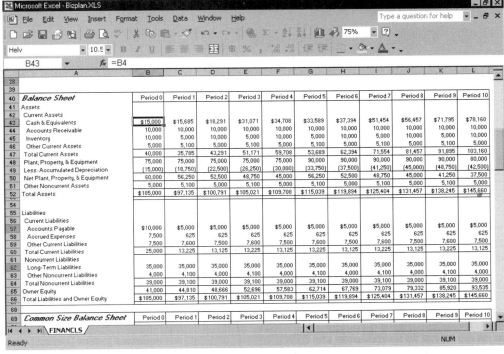

Figure 18-2 The Balance Sheet portion of the business planning workbook.

Cash & Equivalents

The Cash & Equivalents figures show the projected cash on hand at the end of each of the forecasting periods. The starting balance is the value you enter in the inputs area of the business planning workbook. The balance for the first and subsequent periods is pulled from the Cash Flow Statement schedule, where it is calculated.

Accounts Receivable

The Accounts Receivable (A/R) figures show the net receivables held as of the end of each forecasting period. The starting balance is the value you enter in the inputs area of the business planning worksheet. The balance for the first and subsequent periods is based on the Sales Revenue and the # Periods of Sales in A/R values you enter in the inputs area of the business planning workbook. For example, the formula for the first period is:

```
=C7*C31
```

The formula for the second period is:

```
=D7*D31
```

and so on.

Inventory

The Inventory values show the dollar total of the inventory held at the end of each forecasting period. The starting balance is the value you enter in the inputs area of the business planning workbook. The balance for the first and subsequent periods is the previous period balance plus any inventory purchases or production costs minus any cost of sales. For example, the formula for the first period is:

```
=B45+C9-C32
```

The formula for the second period is:

```
=C45+D9-D32
```

and so on.

Other Current Assets

The Other Current Assets figures show the dollar total of the other current assets held at the end of each forecasting period. The starting balance for Other Current Assets is the value you enter in the inputs area of the business planning workbook. The balance for the first and subsequent periods is the previous balance plus the change in the balance. For example, the formula for the first period is:

```
=B46+C11
```

The formula for the second period is:

```
=C46+D11
```

and so on.

Total Current Assets

The Total Current Assets figures show the dollar total of the current assets at the end of each of the forecasting horizons. The balance at any time is the sum of Cash & Equivalents, Accounts Receivable, Inventory, and Other Current Assets. For example, the formula for the starting Total Current Assets balance is:

```
=SUM(B43:B46)
```

The formula for the first period is:

```
=SUM(C43:C46)
```

and so on.

Plant, Property, & Equipment

The Plant, Property, & Equipment figures show the original dollar cost of the plant, property, and equipment at the end of each forecasting horizon. The starting Plant, Property, & Equipment balance is the value you enter in the inputs area of the business planning workbook. The balance for the first and subsequent periods is the previous balance plus any additions to the plant, property, and equipment accounts. For example, the formula for the first period is:

```
=B48+C13
```

The formula for the second period is:

```
=C48+D13
```

and so on.

Less: Accumulated Depreciation

The Accumulated Depreciation figures show the cumulative depreciation expenses charged through the current period for the plant, property, and equipment. The starting balance is the value you enter in the inputs area of the business planning workbook. The balance for the first and subsequent periods is the previous balance minus the current period's changes in accumulated depreciation. For example, the formula for the first period is:

```
=B49-C15
```

The formula for the second period is:

```
=C49-D15
```

and so on. Because the accumulated depreciation is shown as a negative amount, you need to subtract the positive number pulled from the forecasting inputs.

Net Plant, Property, & Equipment

The Net Plant, Property, & Equipment figures show the difference between Plant, Property, & Equipment and Accumulated Depreciation at the end of each of the forecasting horizons. For example, the formula for the starting balance is:

```
=B48+B49
```

The formula for the first period is:

```
=C48+C49
```

and so on. Because the Accumulated Depreciation balance is shown as a negative amount, you simply add these two amounts in the formula for the Net Plant, Property, & Equipment amount.

Other Noncurrent Assets

The Other Noncurrent Assets figures show the dollar total of any other noncurrent assets held at the end of each of the forecasting periods. The starting balance is the value you enter in the inputs area of the business planning workbook. The balance for the first and subsequent periods is the previous period balance plus the change in the account in the current period. For example, the formula for the first period is:

```
=B51+C17
```

The formula for the second period is:

```
=C51+D17
```

and so on.

Total Assets

The Total Assets figures show the dollar total of all the assets held at the end of the forecasting periods. The balance at any time is the sum of Current Assets; Net Plant, Property, & Equipment; and Other Noncurrent Assets. For example, the formula for the starting balance is:

```
=B47+B50+B51
```

The formula for the first period is:

```
=C47+C50+C51
```

and so on.

Accounts Payable

The Accounts Payable figures show the debt that is related to the cost of sales outstanding at the end of each forecasting period. The starting balance is the value you enter in the inputs area of the business planning workbook. The balance for the first and subsequent periods is Cost of Sales for the period times # of Periods of Cost of Sales in A/P. For example, the formula for the first period is:

```
=C19*C32
```

The formula for the second period is:

```
=D19*D32
```

and so on.

Accrued Expenses

The Accrued Expenses figures show the debt that is related to the operating expenses outstanding at the end of each forecasting period. The starting balance is the value you enter in the inputs area of the business planning workbook. The balance for the first and subsequent periods is the operating expenses times # of Periods Operating Expenses in A/E. For example, the formula for the first period is:

```
=C21*SUM(C33:C35)
```

The formula for the second period is:

```
=D21*SUM(D33:D35)
```

and so on.

Other Current Liabilities

The Other Current Liabilities figures show the dollar total of other debts outstanding at the end of the forecasting periods that will be paid within the current year or business cycle. The starting balance is the value you enter in the inputs area of the business planning workbook. The balance for the first and subsequent periods is the previous balance plus the change in the current period. For example, the formula for the first period is:

```
=B59+C23
```

The formula for the second period is:

```
=C59+D23
```

and so on.

Total Current Liabilities

The Total Current Liabilities figures show the dollar total of all the current liabilities at the end of each of the forecasting periods. The balance at any time is the sum of Accounts Payable, Accrued Expenses, and Other Current Liabilities. For example, the formula for the starting balance is:

```
=SUM(B57:B59)
```

The formula for the first period is:

```
=SUM(C57:C59)
```

and so on.

Long-Term Liabilities

The Long-Term Liabilities figures show the dollar total of the long-term outstanding debt at the end of each forecasting period. The starting balance is the value you enter in the inputs area of the business planning workbook. The balance for the first and subsequent periods is the previous balance plus any changes in the Long-Term Liabilities balance in the current period. For example, the formula for the first period is:

```
=B62+C25
```

The formula for the second period is:

```
=C62+D25
```

and so on.

Other Noncurrent Liabilities

The Other Noncurrent Liabilities figures show the dollar total of any other noncurrent outstanding debt at the end of each forecasting period. The starting balance is the value you enter in the inputs area of the business planning workbook. The balance for the first and subsequent periods is the previous period balance plus the change in the current period. For example, the formula for the first period is:

```
=B63+C27
```

The formula for the second period is:

```
=C63+D27
```

and so on.

Total Noncurrent Liabilities

The Total Noncurrent Liabilities figures show the dollar totals of the long-term debt and the other noncurrent outstanding debt at the end of each of the forecasting periods. The balance at any time is the sum of Long-Term Liabilities and Other Noncurrent Liabilities. For example, the formula for the starting balance is:

```
=B62+B63
```

The formula for the first period is:

```
=C62+C63
```

and so on.

Owner Equity

The Owner Equity figures show the dollar totals of the owner equity accounts at the end of each forecasting period. The starting balance is the value you enter in the inputs area of the business planning workbook. The balance for the first and subsequent periods is the previous period balance plus Net Income After Taxes for the period plus other adjustments, such as additional capital contributions and dividends. For example, the formula for the first period is:

```
=B65+C29+C116
```

The formula for the second period is:

```
=C65+D29+D116
```

and so on.

Total Liabilities and Owner Equity

The Total Liabilities and Owner Equity figures show the dollar totals of Current Liabilities, Noncurrent Liabilities, and Owner Equity at the end of each forecasting period. For example, the formula for the starting balance is:

```
=B60+B64+B65
```

The formula for the first period is:

```
=C60+C64+C65
```

and so on.

TIP   *The Total Assets value should equal the Total Liabilities and Owner Equity value. If they differ, your model contains an error.*

Common Size Balance Sheet

The Common Size Balance Sheet schedule lists, in the balance sheet format, what percentage of the total assets each individual asset represents and what percentage of the total liabilities and owner equity each individual liability and the owner equity represents, as shown in Figure 18-3. When you compare these percentages with those of business peers, you can see the relative financial strength or weakness of your business. Trends in the percentages over time can indicate improvement or deterioration in the overall financial condition of your business.

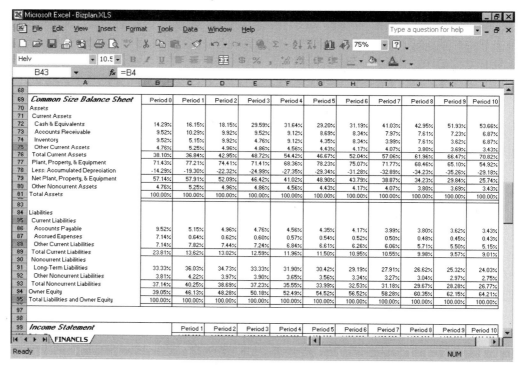

Figure 18-3 The Common Size Balance Sheet portion of the business planning workbook.

The Common Size Balance Sheet schedule has 19 rows with calculated data that express line-item amounts as percentages of the total. For the asset side of the Balance Sheet, assets are expressed as a percentage of the total assets. For the creditor and owner equity side of the Balance Sheet, equities are expressed as a percentage of the total liabilities and owner equity. The formulas for all rows except Total Assets and Total Liabilities and Owner Equity simply convert the Balance Sheet values to percentages. For example, the Cash & Equivalents formula for the first period is:

```
=B43/B$52
```

The formula for the second period is:

```
=C43/C$52
```

and so on. All asset percentages are derived from dividing by total assets, which explains why the absolute reference to row $52 is used in all asset formulas. Similarly, the absolute reference to row $66 appears in all formulas in the liabilities and equity formulas.

The formula for the Total Assets percentage at any time is the sum of the Current Assets; the Net Plant, Property, & Equipment; and the Other Noncurrent Assets percentages. The result always equals 100 percent.

Similarly, the formula for the Total Liabilities and Owner Equity percentage at any time is the sum of the Current Liabilities, the Noncurrent Liabilities, and Owner Equity percentages. The result is always 100 percent.

Income Statement

The Income Statement schedule has 14 rows of calculated data, as shown in Figure 18-4. As in other schedules, the period identifier simply numbers the periods for which values are calculated. The first period is stored in cell C99 as the integer 1, and periods that follow are stored as the previous period plus 1. The other values in the Income Statement are calculated as described in the following paragraphs.

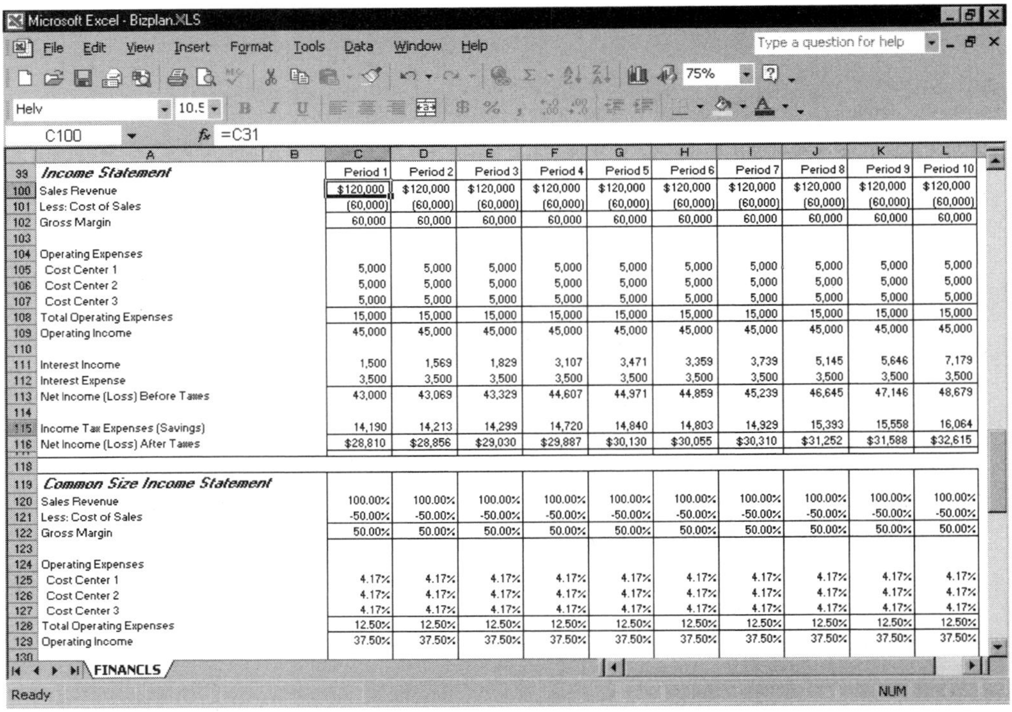

	A	C	D	E	F	G	H	I	J	K	L
99	*Income Statement*	Period 1	Period 2	Period 3	Period 4	Period 5	Period 6	Period 7	Period 8	Period 9	Period 10
100	Sales Revenue	$120,000	$120,000	$120,000	$120,000	$120,000	$120,000	$120,000	$120,000	$120,000	$120,000
101	Less: Cost of Sales	(60,000)	(60,000)	(60,000)	(60,000)	(60,000)	(60,000)	(60,000)	(60,000)	(60,000)	(60,000)
102	Gross Margin	60,000	60,000	60,000	60,000	60,000	60,000	60,000	60,000	60,000	60,000
103											
104	Operating Expenses										
105	Cost Center 1	5,000	5,000	5,000	5,000	5,000	5,000	5,000	5,000	5,000	5,000
106	Cost Center 2	5,000	5,000	5,000	5,000	5,000	5,000	5,000	5,000	5,000	5,000
107	Cost Center 3	5,000	5,000	5,000	5,000	5,000	5,000	5,000	5,000	5,000	5,000
108	Total Operating Expenses	15,000	15,000	15,000	15,000	15,000	15,000	15,000	15,000	15,000	15,000
109	Operating Income	45,000	45,000	45,000	45,000	45,000	45,000	45,000	45,000	45,000	45,000
110											
111	Interest Income	1,500	1,569	1,829	3,107	3,471	3,359	3,739	5,145	5,646	7,179
112	Interest Expense	3,500	3,500	3,500	3,500	3,500	3,500	3,500	3,500	3,500	3,500
113	Net Income (Loss) Before Taxes	43,000	43,069	43,329	44,607	44,971	44,859	45,239	46,645	47,146	48,679
114											
115	Income Tax Expenses (Savings)	14,190	14,213	14,299	14,720	14,840	14,803	14,929	15,393	15,558	16,064
116	Net Income (Loss) After Taxes	$28,810	$28,856	$29,030	$29,887	$30,130	$30,055	$30,310	$31,252	$31,588	$32,615
118											
119	*Common Size Income Statement*										
120	Sales Revenue	100.00%	100.00%	100.00%	100.00%	100.00%	100.00%	100.00%	100.00%	100.00%	100.00%
121	Less: Cost of Sales	-50.00%	-50.00%	-50.00%	-50.00%	-50.00%	-50.00%	-50.00%	-50.00%	-50.00%	-50.00%
122	Gross Margin	50.00%	50.00%	50.00%	50.00%	50.00%	50.00%	50.00%	50.00%	50.00%	50.00%
123											
124	Operating Expenses										
125	Cost Center 1	4.17%	4.17%	4.17%	4.17%	4.17%	4.17%	4.17%	4.17%	4.17%	4.17%
126	Cost Center 2	4.17%	4.17%	4.17%	4.17%	4.17%	4.17%	4.17%	4.17%	4.17%	4.17%
127	Cost Center 3	4.17%	4.17%	4.17%	4.17%	4.17%	4.17%	4.17%	4.17%	4.17%	4.17%
128	Total Operating Expenses	12.50%	12.50%	12.50%	12.50%	12.50%	12.50%	12.50%	12.50%	12.50%	12.50%
129	Operating Income	37.50%	37.50%	37.50%	37.50%	37.50%	37.50%	37.50%	37.50%	37.50%	37.50%

Figure 18-4 The Income Statement and Common Size Income Statement areas of the business planning workbook.

Sales Revenue

The Sales Revenue figures are the estimates you enter in the inputs area of the business planning workbook. The amount for the period is the value you enter in the inputs area of the business planning workbook.

Less: Cost of Sales

The Cost Of Sales figures are the Cost of Sales estimates you enter in the inputs area of the business planning workbook.

Gross Margin

The Gross Margin figures show the amounts left over from the sales proceeds after subtracting Cost of Sales. Subtracting your other expenses from the Gross Margin amount gives you your profit figure. The Gross Margin formula is Sales Revenue for the period minus Cost of Sales. For example, the formula for the first period is:

```
=C100+C101
```

The formula for the second period is:

```
=D100+D101
```

and so on. Notice that because the Cost of Sales figures are pulled into the Income Statement schedule as negative amounts, the Gross Margin formula simply adds the Sales Revenue figure to the negative Cost of Sales figure.

Operating Expenses – Cost Centers 1, 2, and 3

The Operating Expenses figures for Cost Centers 1, 2, and 3 show the amount for each operating expense classification or category that you enter in the inputs area of the business planning workbook.

Total Operating Expenses

The Total Operating Expenses figures show the sums of the operating expenses you enter in the inputs area of the business planning workbook for these three operating expense categories or classifications. The total for each period is the sum of the operating expenses for Cost Centers 1, 2, and 3. For example, the formula for the first period is:

```
=SUM(C105:C107)
```

The formula for the second period is:

```
=SUM(D105:D107)
```

and so on.

Operating Income

The Operating Income figures show the sales dollar amounts left after paying the Cost of Sales and the Operating Expenses. The Operating Income figures represent the amounts that go toward paying your financing expenses and income tax, and the amount that constitutes your profits. The amount for each period is the Gross Margin figure for the period minus the Total Operating Expenses figure. For example, the formula for the first period is:

```
=C102-C108
```

The formula for the second period is:

```
=D102-D108
```

and so on.

Interest Income

The Interest Income figures show the earnings from investing the cash of the business. The amount for each period is the beginning Cash & Equivalents balance from the inputs area of the business planning workbook times the period yield on Cash & Equivalents. For example, the formula for the first period is:

```
=B43*C5
```

The formula for the second period is:

```
=C43*D5
```

and so on.

Interest Expense

The Interest Expense figures show the costs of using borrowed funds for operations and asset purchases. The amount for each period is the value you enter in the inputs area of the business planning workbook.

Net Income (Loss) Before Taxes

The Net Income (Loss) Before Taxes figures show the amount of operating income left after receiving any interest income and paying any interest expense. The amount for each period is the Operating Income figure for the period plus the Interest Income figure for the period minus the Interest Expense figure for the period. For example, the formula for the first period is:

```
=C109+C111-C112
```

The formula for the second period is:

```
=D109+D111-D112
```

and so on.

Income Tax Expenses (Savings)

The Income Tax Expenses (Savings) figures show the income tax expenses (or savings) that use the calculated Net Income (Loss) Before Taxes figures and the Marginal Income Tax Rate figures you forecasted in the inputs area of the business planning workbook. Notice that the model calculates a current period savings in income taxes when there is a net loss before taxes. This might be the case when a current period loss is carried back to a prior period or when the current period loss is consolidated with the current period income of related businesses. Basically, then, the model assumes that a net loss before income taxes results in a current period tax refund—that is, an overall tax savings—because you can deduct a loss in one business from the profits of another business. However, if a current period loss does not result in a current period income tax savings, you need to modify the formula, as described in the section "Customizing the Business Planning Workbook."

The amount for each period is the Net Income (Loss) Before Taxes times the Marginal Income Tax Rate figure. For example, the formula for the first period is:

```
=C37*C113
```

The formula for the second period is:

```
=D37*D113
```

and so on.

Net Income (Loss) After Taxes

The Net Income (Loss) After Taxes figures calculate the after-tax profits of operating the business. The amount for each period is the Net Income (Loss) Before Taxes figure minus the Income Tax Expenses (Savings) figure. For example, the formula for the first period is:

```
=C113-C115
```

The formula for the second period is:

```
=D113-D115
```

and so on.

Common Size Income Statement

The Common Size Income Statement schedule lists, in income statement format, what percentage of the total sales revenue each income statement line item represents, as shown in Figure 18-4. When you compare these percentages against those of business peers, you can see the relative financial performance of your business. Trends in the percentages over the forecasting horizon can indicate improvement or deterioration in the financial performance of your business.

The Common Size Income Statement schedule has 13 rows of calculated data that express the component line-item amount for each period as a percentage of the sales revenue figure for the period. The formulas for all rows except Sales Revenue simply convert the Income Statement values to percentages.

The Sales Revenue figures add the Cost of Sales, Total Operating Expenses, Interest Income, Interest Expense, Income Tax Expenses (Savings), and Net Income (Loss) After Taxes percentages. The results always equal 100 percent.

NOTE   *The Sales Revenue percentage calculations adds the expense and profit percentages. Those expenses shown as negative amounts, therefore, are subtracted.*

Cash Flow Statement

The Cash Flow Statement schedule has 18 rows of calculated data, as shown in Figure 18-5. As in other schedules, a period identifier numbers the periods for which values are calculated. The first period is stored in cell C141 as integer 1. Periods that follow are stored as the previous period plus 1. Other Cash Flow Statement values are calculated as described in the paragraphs that follow.

		Period 1	Period 2	Period 3	Period 4	Period 5	Period 6	Period 7	Period 8	Period 9	Period 10
141	*Cash Flow Statement*	Period 1	Period 2	Period 3	Period 4	Period 5	Period 6	Period 7	Period 8	Period 9	Period 10
142	Beginning Cash Balance	$15,000	$15,685	$18,291	$31,071	$34,708	$33,589	$37,394	$51,454	$56,457	$71,795
143											
144	Sources of Cash										
145	Net Income After Taxes	$28,810	$28,856	$29,030	$29,887	$30,130	$30,055	$30,310	$31,252	$31,588	$32,615
146	Addback of Depreciation	3,750	3,750	3,750	3,750	3,750	3,750	3,750	3,750	3,750	(6,250)
147	Accounts Payable Financing	(5,000)	0	0	0	0	0	0	0	0	0
148	Accrued Expenses Financing	(6,875)	0	0	0	0	0	0	0	0	0
149	Other Current Liabilities Financing	100	(100)	100	(100)	100	(100)	100	(100)	100	(100)
150	Long-Term Liabilities Financing	0	0	0	0	0	0	0	0	0	0
151	Other Noncurrent Liabilities Financing	100	(100)	100	(100)	100	(100)	100	(100)	100	(100)
152											
153	Uses of Cash										
154	Accounts Receivable Investments	0	0	0	0	0	0	0	0	0	0
155	Inventory Investments	(5,000)	5,000	(5,000)	5,000	(5,000)	5,000	(5,000)	5,000	(5,000)	5,000
156	Other Current Assets Investments	100	(100)	100	(100)	100	(100)	100	(100)	100	(100)
157	Plant, Property, & Equip Investments	0	0	0	0	15,000	0	0	0	0	(10,000)
158	Other Noncurrent Assets Investments	100	(100)	100	(100)	100	(100)	100	(100)	100	(100)
159	Other Owner Equity Changes	25,000	25,000	25,000	25,000	25,000	25,000	25,000	25,000	25,000	25,000
160	Net Cash Generated (Used)	685	2,606	12,780	3,637	(1,120)	3,805	14,060	5,002	15,338	6,365
161	Ending Cash Balance	$15,685	$18,291	$31,071	$34,708	$33,589	$37,394	$51,454	$56,457	$71,795	$78,160
163											
164											
165	*Financial Ratios Table*	Period 1	Period 2	Period 3	Period 4	Period 5	Period 6	Period 7	Period 8	Period 9	Period 10
166	Working Capital Ratios:										
167	Current Ratio	2.71	3.30	3.87	4.55	4.06	4.75	5.41	6.21	6.95	7.86
168	Quick Ratio	1.94	2.16	3.11	3.41	3.30	3.61	4.65	5.06	6.18	6.72
169	Working Capital to Total Assets	0.23	0.30	0.36	0.42	0.35	0.41	0.47	0.52	0.57	0.62
170	Receivables Turnover	12.00	12.00	12.00	12.00	12.00	12.00	12.00	12.00	12.00	12.00
171	Inventory Turnover	12.00	6.00	12.00	6.00	12.00	6.00	12.00	6.00	12.00	6.00
172	Operating Ratios:										

Figure 18-5   The Cash Flow Statement and Financial Ratios Table areas of the business planning workbook.

Beginning Cash Balance

The Beginning Cash Balance figures show the forecasted cash and equivalents balance at the start of each forecasting period. The starting balance is the value you enter in the inputs area of the business planning workbook. For subsequent periods, the Beginning Cash Balance is the previous period's Ending Cash Balance.

Net Income After Taxes

The Net Income After Taxes figures show the amounts calculated in the Income Statement schedule as the business profits for each forecasting period.

Addback of Depreciation

The Addback of Depreciation figures show the change in the accumulated depreciation balance for each forecasting period. Normally, this change stems from the period depreciation expense; it must be added back into the Net Income After Taxes figure because the depreciation expense uses no cash. The depreciation added back for each period is the value you enter in the inputs area of the business planning workbook as the change in accumulated depreciation.

Accounts Payable Financing

The Accounts Payable Financing figures show the change in the Accounts Payable balance for the period. Increases in this balance result when the cost of sales expense paid during the period is lower than the expense incurred. Decreases in this balance result when the cost of sales expense paid is higher than the expense incurred. By recognizing the changes in this account balance, the model adjusts for differences between the Income Statement's accrual-based accounting of cost of sales expenses and the actual cash disbursements for cost of sales expenses.

The Accounts Payable Financing figure for each period is the difference between the Accounts Payable balance at the end of the previous period and the balance at the end of the current period. For example, the formula for the first period is:

```
=C57-B57
```

The formula for the second period is:

```
=D57-C57
```

and so on.

Accrued Expenses Financing

The Accrued Expenses Financing figures show the change in the accrued expenses balance for the period. Increases in this balance result when the operating expense paid during the period is lower than the expense incurred. Decreases in this balance result when the operating expense paid during the period is higher than the expense incurred. By recognizing the changes in this account balance, the model adjusts for differences between the Income Statement's accrual-based accounting expenses and the actual cash disbursements for operating expenses.

The Accrued Expenses Financing figure for each period is the difference between the Accrued Expenses balance at the end of the previous period and the balance at the end of the current period. For example, the formula for the first period is:

```
=C58-B58
```

The formula for the second period is:

```
=D58-C58
```

and so on.

Other Current Liabilities Financing

The Other Current Liabilities Financing figures show the change in the Other Current Liabilities balance for the period. This amount increases when, either directly or indirectly, cash is generated by borrowing. This amount decreases when, either directly or indirectly, cash is used to pay off short-term borrowing.

The Other Current Liabilities Financing figure for each period is the difference between the Other Current Liabilities balance at the end of the previous period and the balance at the end of the current period. For example, the formula for the first period is:

```
=C59-B59
```

The formula for the second period is:

```
=D59-C59
```

and so on.

Long-Term Liabilities Financing

The Long-Term Liabilities Financing figures show the changes in the long-term liabilities amount for the period. This balance increases when, either directly or indirectly, cash is generated by long-term borrowing. This amount decreases when, either directly or indirectly, cash is used to pay off long-term borrowing.

The Long-Term Liabilities Financing figure for each period is the difference between the Long-Term Liabilities balance at the end of the previous period and the balance at the end of the current period. For example, the formula for the first period is:

```
=C62-B62
```

The formula for the second period is:

```
=D62-C62
```

and so on.

Other Noncurrent Liabilities Financing

The Other Noncurrent Liabilities Financing figures show the changes in the Other Noncurrent Liabilities balance for the period. This amount increases when, either directly or indirectly, cash is generated by other long-term borrowing. This amount decreases when, either directly or indirectly, cash is used to pay off other long-term borrowing.

The Other Noncurrent Liabilities Financing figure for each period is the difference between the Other Noncurrent Liabilities balance at the end of the previous period and the balance at the end of the current period. For example, the formula for the first period is:

```
=C63-B63
```

The formula for the second period is:

```
=D63-C63
```

and so on.

Accounts Receivable Investments

The Accounts Receivable Investments figures show the change in the Accounts Receivable balance for each forecasting period. This amount increases when the sales revenue collected during the period is less than the revenue recorded. This amount decreases when the sales revenue collected during the period is more than recorded. By recognizing the changes in the account balance, the model adjusts for differences between the income statement's accrual-based accounting of sales revenues and the actual cash collections for sales.

The Accounts Receivable Investments figure for each period is the difference between the Accounts Receivable balance at the end of the previous period and the balance at the end of the current period. For example, the formula for the first period is:

```
=C44-B44
```

The formula for the second period is:

```
=D44-C44
```

and so on.

Inventory Investments

The Inventory Investments figures show the change in the inventory balance for each forecasting period. This amount increases when the inventory sold is less than the inventory acquired. This amount decreases when the inventory sold is more than the inventory acquired. By recognizing the changes in this account balance, the model recognizes the cash effects of changing inventory balances.

The Inventory Investments figure for each period is the difference between the Inventory balance at the end of the previous period and the balance at the end of the current period. For example, the formula for the first period is:

```
=C45-B45
```

The formula for the second period is:

```
=D45-C45
```

and so on.

Other Current Assets Investments

The Other Current Assets Investments figures show the changes in the Other Current Assets balance for the period. This amount increases when, either directly or indirectly, cash is used to acquire current assets. This amount decreases when indirectly or directly cash is generated by converting current assets to cash.

The Other Current Assets Investments figure for each period is the difference between the Other Current Assets balance at the end of the previous period and the balance at the end of the current period. For example, the formula for the first period is:

```
=C46-B46
```

The formula for the second period is:

```
=D46-C46
```

and so on.

Plant, Property, & Equip Investments

The Plant, Property, & Equip Investments figures show the change in the Plant, Property, & Equipment balance for the period. This amount increases when, either directly or indirectly, cash is used to acquire plants, property, and equipment. This amount decreases when, either directly or indirectly, cash is generated by converting plants, property, and equipment to cash.

The Plant, Property, & Equip Investments figure for each period is the difference between the Plant, Property, & Equipment balance at the end of the previous period and the balance at the end of the current period. For example, the formula for the first period is:

```
=C48-B48
```

The formula for the second period is:

```
=D48-C48
```

and so on.

Other Noncurrent Assets Investments

The Other Noncurrent Assets Investments figures show the changes in the Other Noncurrent Assets balance for the period. This amount increases when, either directly or indirectly, cash is used to acquire other noncurrent assets. This amount decreases when, either directly or indirectly, cash is generated by converting other noncurrent assets to cash.

The Other Noncurrent Assets Investments figure for each period is the difference between the Other Noncurrent Assets balance at the end of the previous period and the balance at the end of the current period. For example, the formula for the first period is:

```
=C51-B51
```

The formula for the second period is:

```
=D51-C51
```

and so on.

Other Owner Equity Changes

The Other Owner Equity Changes figures show the cash flows stemming from any additional capital contributions made by the owners to the business or from dividends and other distributions made by the business to the owners. The Other Owner Equity Changes figure is the value you enter in the inputs area of the business planning workbook. The Other Owner Equity Changes figures are pulled into the Uses of Cash section as negative values because a positive change in the owner equity, such as an additional capital contribution, such as from a stock offering, doesn't use cash but provides cash; and a negative change in the owner equity, such as a dividend, does use cash.

Net Cash Generated (Used)

The Net Cash Generated (Used) figures show the total cash flow for each period of the forecasting horizon, based on the listed sources and uses of cash. The amount for each period is the sources of cash for the period less the uses of cash for the period. For example, the formula for the first period is:

```
=SUM(C145:C151)-SUM(C154:C159)
```

The formula for the second period is:

```
=SUM(D145:D151)-SUM(D154:D159)
```

and so on.

Ending Cash Balance

The Ending Cash Balance figures show the forecasted cash and equivalents balance at the end of each period. The balance is the Beginning Cash Balance figure for the period plus the Net Cash Generated (Used) figure for the period. For example, the formula for the first period is:

```
=C142+C160
```

The formula for the second period is:

```
=D142+D160
```

and so on.

Financial Ratios Table

The Financial Ratios Table has 12 rows of calculated data (see Figure 18-5). As in other schedules, the period identifier numbers the periods for which values are calculated. The first period is stored in cell C165 as the integer 1, and periods that follow are stored as the previous period plus 1. The other values in the Financial Ratios Table are calculated as described in the following paragraphs.

Current Ratio

The Current Ratio figures show the ratio of current assets to current liabilities. The current ratio provides one measure of a business's ability to meet its short-term obligations. The Current Ratio figure for each period is the Total Current Assets figure from the Balance Sheet schedule divided by the Total Current Liabilities figure. For example, the formula for the first period is:

```
=C47/C60
```

The formula for the second period is:

```
=D47/D60
```

and so on.

Quick Ratio

The Quick Ratio figures show the ratio of the sum of the cash and equivalents plus the accounts receivable to the current liabilities. The quick ratio provides a more stringent measure of a business's ability to meet its short-term financial obligations than other ratios. The Quick Ratio figure for each period is the sum of the Cash & Equivalents figure and the Accounts Receivable figure divided by the Total Current Liabilities figure. For example, the formula for the first period is:

```
=(C43+C44)/C60
```

The formula for the second period is:

```
=(D43+D44)/D60
```

and so on.

Working Capital to Total Assets

The Working Capital to Total Assets figures show the ratio of working capital (the current assets minus the current liabilities) to the total assets. The Working Capital to Total Assets ratio is another measure of a firm's ability to meet its financial obligations and gives an indication as to the distribution of a business's assets into liquid and nonliquid resources. The Working Capital to Total Assets ratio for each period is calculated by dividing the difference between the Current Assets and Current Liabilities figures by the Total Assets figure. For example, the formula for the first period is:

```
=(C47-C60)/C52
```

The formula for the second period is:

```
=(D47-D60)/D52
```

and so on.

Receivables Turnover

The Receivables Turnover figures show the ratio of sales to the accounts receivable balance. The Receivables Turnover ratio indicates the efficiency of sales collections. One problem with the measure as it's usually applied is that both credit and cash sales might be included in the ratio denominator. Two potential shortcomings exist with this approach. First, the presence of the cash sales might make the receivables collections appear more efficient than is the case. Also, mere changes in the mix of credit and cash sales might affect the ratio, even though the efficiency of the receivables-collections process has not changed.

The Receivables Turnover figure for each period is calculated by dividing the Sales Revenue figure for the period by the Accounts Receivable balance outstanding at the end of the period. For example, the formula for the first period is:

```
=C100/C44
```

The formula for the second period is:

```
=D100/D44
```

and so on.

Inventory Turnover

The Inventory Turnover row shows the ratio of the cost of sales to the inventory balance. The Inventory Turnover ratio calculates how long inventory is held. It can indicate depleted or excessive inventory balances. The Inventory Turnover ratio for each period is calculated by dividing the Cost of Sales figure for the period by the inventory held at the end of the period. For example, the formula for the first period is:

```
=-C101/C45
```

The formula for the second period is:

```
=-D101/D45
```

and so on.

Times Interest Earned

The Times Interest Earned row shows the ratio of the sum of the net income after taxes plus the interest income to the interest expense. The ratio indicates the relative ease with which the business is paying its financing costs. The Times Interest Earned ratio for each period is calculated by dividing the sum of the Operating Income and Interest Income figures from the Income Statement schedule by the Interest Expense figure. For example, the formula for the first period is:

```
=(C109+C111)/C112
```

The formula for the second period is:

```
=(D109+D111)/D112
```

and so on.

Sales to Operational Assets

The Sales to Operational Assets row shows the ratio of sales revenue to net plant, property, and equipment. The ratio indicates the efficiency with which a business uses its operational assets to generate sales revenue. The Sales to Operational Assets ratio for each period is the Sales Revenue figure you enter in the inputs area of the business planning workbook divided by the Net Plant, Property, & Equipment figure from the Balance Sheet schedule. For example, the formula for the first period is:

```
=C100/C50
```

The formula for the second period is:

```
=D100/D50
```

and so on.

Return on Total Assets

The Return on Total Assets row shows the ratio of the sum of the net income after taxes plus the interest expense to the total assets for each period. The ratio indicates the overall operating profitability of the business, expressed as a rate of return on the business assets. The formula for the first period is:

```
=(C16+C112)/C52
```

The formula for the second period is:

```
=(D116+D112)/D52
```

and so on.

Return on Equity

The Return on Equity row shows the ratio of the net income after taxes to the owner equity for each period. The ratio indicates the profitability of the business as an investment of the owners. The Return on Equity ratio for each period is the Net Income (Loss) After Taxes figure from the Income Statement schedule divided by the Owner Equity figure from the Balance Sheet schedule. For example, the formula for the first period is:

```
=C116/C65
```

The formula for the second period is:

```
=D116/D65
```

and so on.

Investment Turnover

The Investment Turnover row shows the ratio of the sales revenue to the total assets. The ratio, like the Sales to Operational Assets ratio, indicates the efficiency with which a business uses its assets (in this case, its total assets) to generate sales. The Investment

Turnover ratio for each period is the Sales Revenue figure you enter in the inputs area of the business planning workbook divided by the Total Assets figure from the Balance Sheet schedule. For example, the formula for the first period is:

=C100/C52

The formula for the second period is:

=D100/D52

and so on.

Financial Leverage

The Financial Leverage row shows the difference between the return on the owner equity and the return on the total assets. The ratio indicates the increase or decrease in an equity return as a result of borrowing. A positive value indicates an improvement in the return on owner equity by using financial leverage; a negative value indicates deterioration in the return on owner equity. The Financial Leverage figure for each period is the Return on Total Assets figure minus the Return on Equity figure. For example, the formula for the first period is:

=C176-C175

The formula for the second period is:

=D176-D175

and so on.

Customizing the Business Planning Workbook

You can use the business planning workbook for many business projections. However, you might want to change the workbook so that it more closely matches your requirements. For example, you can add text that describes the business and the forecasting horizon. You can also increase or decrease the number of periods. For example, you can increase the number of periods to 12 if your periods are months and you want to forecast an entire year. Before you change anything on the workbook other than the forecasting inputs, unprotect the document.

NOTE   *Unless you turn off cell protection, input cells in the inputs area of the business planning workbook are the only cells into which you can enter data.*

Changing the Number of Periods

You can easily increase or decrease the number of forecasting periods. To increase the number of periods, remove the borders from the last column and then copy the current last column to the right as needed. To decrease the number of periods, simply delete any unneeded column from the right side of the schedule. When you finish these steps, you can replace the borders on the right and reinstate cell protection as needed.

Ratio Analysis on Existing Financial Statements

If you want to perform financial ratio analysis on a set of existing financial statements, copy the contents of column C, from the row in the inputs area of the business planning workbook that contains the sales revenue forecast (row 31) through the last row of the ratios table, into column B. Then remove the columns for periods 1 through 10 (columns C through L), following the steps described in the preceding section, "Changing the Number of Periods." Optionally, you can delete the Cash Flow Statement and add appropriate column headings as needed.

To use the modified workbook, enter the necessary Balance Sheet and Income Statement data in each of the unshaded cells in column B of the inputs area of the business planning workbook. (Typically, the "as of" date of the Balance Sheet and the ending date of the Income Statement period are the same.)

Calculating Taxes for a Current Net Loss Before Taxes

To calculate the income tax expense as zero when there is a current period net loss before income taxes, you need to edit the formula in the cell that calculates the income tax expense (or savings) for the first period (cell C115) so that it takes the maximum of the calculated expense amount or zero by using the MAX function:

```
=MAX(C37*C113,0)
```

After you've done this, you can copy the formula into the rest of the cells in the forecasting horizon that calculate the income tax expense (or savings).

Summary

Forecasting a firm's profits, cash flows, and financial condition will always require much thought and work. But by using Excel and the business planning workbook described in this chapter, the process will be quicker and smoother.

Chapter 19

CREATING A SALES PRESENTATION USING POWERPOINT

Featuring:

- What Is a Sales Presentation?
- Developing an Outline for Your Presentation
- Is PowerPoint Your Best Tool for a Sales Presentation?
- Creating Your Presentation
- Creating Speaker's Notes
- Preparing Handouts
- Rehearsing Your Presentation

Many studies have shown that using visual aids is a powerful persuasion tool, and in the past, teachers, sales professionals, motivational speakers, and many others have made effective use of whiteboards, easels, 35mm slides, and overhead projectors. Today, however, PowerPoint is rapidly becoming an industry standard for creating business and technical presentations. In this chapter, we'll look at how to use PowerPoint to enhance one of the oldest and most important business skills—making a sales presentation.

What Is a Sales Presentation?

Basically, a sales presentation is the approach you take when you have something to sell and you want to persuade someone else to buy it. A more sophisticated definition is that a sales presentation is a complete sales package that you give to prospects for the purpose of getting them to commit to purchase a product or a service. In addition, the basis for your presentation is your prospects' needs and how you intend to meet them.

Thus, many sales professionals consider preparation the starting point for a successful sales presentation, and step one in this phase is getting organized. Make a list of the materials you need and what you need to know. Step two then is acquiring these materials and this information. Your information-gathering process will concentrate on the following categories:

- What you are selling. It is said that successful sales professionals are as familiar with their product or service as they are with their own bodies. They know their product or service inside out and are constantly trying to learn more.

- The competition. Find out how they advertise their product or service, the strengths and weaknesses of their company and their product or service, and how they work their territories or regions and when. Compare what you are selling with what your competition is selling.

- Your prospect. Become familiar with all aspects of your prospect's business—how long they have been in business, their main product or service, their clients, whether they're currently doing business with your competition, and so on.

Developing an Outline for Your Presentation

Once you've done your homework, the next step is to develop an outline for your sales presentation. In this section, we'll suggest several approaches to outlining, but before we do that we want to emphasize how important this step is to a successful presentation.

Over the years, we've heard all sorts of excuses for not creating an outline before starting to write a business plan, prepare a brochure, compile an annual report, or create a sales presentation. But the reason that most people don't want to do it is that it's just plain hard work—plain hard work that is absolutely necessary. The purpose of outlining is simple: you want to put all the material on the same subject in the same place. If you don't, your ideas will be physically disorganized, and your prospects won't be able to follow your train of thought.

When you're tempted to skip the outlining step, think about the following consequences:

- Your argument, which should be persuasive, becomes hard to follow.

- Your prospect doesn't know where you are going next.

- You don't know where you are going next.

- You don't emphasize the main features of your product or service clearly enough.

- You wander off the subject.

- You spend too much time on one feature of your product or service and not enough on another.

- You leave out important facts about your product or service.

- You repeat yourself and get wordy.

- Your presentation is so hard to follow that your prospect misunderstands it or loses interest or, worst of all, sees no value whatsoever in what you're trying to sell.

You can create your outline on a paper napkin, in Word, or in PowerPoint, but whichever you use, every strong sales presentation consists of four key components:

I. The introduction.

Identify yourself and your firm and state your purpose and what you intend to present.

II. The body.

Provide a clear, concise, convincing description of what you can do for your prospects.

III. The conclusion.

Summarize the main points of your presentation.

IV. The Q&A.

Provide an opportunity to answer questions and to clarify any of your points.

Now, let's look in detail at how to outline the content of your presentation. In a later section, we'll look at how to put your outline into PowerPoint.

A Simple, Four-Point Outline

As we pointed out earlier, a sales presentation is a tool with which you seek to persuade others to purchase your product or service. You could use the following format for anything from a 6-minute presentation to a 30-minute presentation to a several-hour session if discussion is involved. The goal is to create a desire for your product or service.

I. So that...

List the advantages your prospects will have when they buy your product or service. Or warn them about the negative consequences they will avoid by buying your product or service. Begin with benefits, and then follow with advice, requests, or features. Promise your prospects what they will gain before you tell them what to buy.

II. Do this...

Tell your prospects exactly what you want them to do. This should be an action that can be recorded with a video camera.

III. Instead of...

Clarify what you want your prospect to do by telling them what not to do. Sometimes, you may want to reverse steps II and III here. For example, you might say, "Instead of buying your office supplies from individual vendors, place all your orders with us."

IV. Because...

State the logical, rational, factual, legal, or legitimate reasons the person should take the action you suggest. For example, the reason to buy all their office supplies from you might be that they could get a bulk discount.

A Seven-Step Format

If the product or service you provide is more complicated or the needs of your prospects more involved, you'll probably want to use an outline that lets you develop all your points more thoroughly. After you collect all the information we mentioned earlier, you can use the following outline to define the prospect's need, discuss your approach to that need, describe the benefits of that approach, and calculate the cost associated with the product or the service.

I. Introduction

Discuss the nature of your prospect's need, indicate how your presentation is organized, and state the qualifications of your company and yourself that make you a credible provider.

II. Objectives and Scope

Describe what you will do and give your prospect an accurate time-frame for the delivery of the product or the completion of the service.

III. Fill in the Details

Include the result or deliverables associated with key steps.

IV. Benefits

Describe the benefits the prospect can expect. List what you can do to help make your prospect successful. Don't skimp on details. Present any possible upside that your product or service will provide.

V. Cost

Estimate the charge for your goods or services as accurately as possible. If you're quoting for a large project, break the costs into stages. Notice that this is step 5 in your outline. If you include the costs earlier in your presentation, your prospect may not understand what you're proposing and its benefits and may reject the sale before realizing the full impact.

VI. Reiterate Your Qualifications

Remind your prospects why you and your company are qualified to meet their needs. Include a brief history of your company and background of the principals, and describe your facilities. Tell your prospect when you can begin supplying the product or service.

VII. Conclusion

Outline again the benefits of your product or service, and provide an opportunity for questions and answers.

A Plan for Preparation and Outlining

Sales professionals know that a well-prepared presentation turns a prospect into a client. The following approach to preparation and outlining takes this statement quite literally. You begin by writing out the following:

- Your audience context. Describe who your audience is, why they are present, the speaking situation, who you are, who you represent and in what capacity. Then describe the attitudes and beliefs of your audience toward your product or service.

- Your purpose. In a complete sentence or sentences, describe the purpose of your presentation.

Now compose your outline, using the following format:

I. Introduction

    A. Attention-getter. Write out your opening remarks, the object of which is to gain your prospects' immediate interest.

    B. Preview your presentation. Describe your presentation, detailing the specific steps that you will take to persuade your prospects to buy your product or service.

    C. Present your credentials. State your qualifications, background, experiences, education, and so on, and give the reason that your prospects should buy the service or product that you are selling. Also establish the credibility of your company.

II. Body

    A. Establish your prospects' need for the product or service. Describe vividly how your product or service meets that need.

    B. Describe the purpose of the product or service and its advantages and special features.

    C. Acknowledge any objections to your product or service.

III. Conclusion

    A. Tell your prospects how, where, and when they can buy your product or service.

    B. Summarize your main ideas and the major selling points of your product or service.

    C. In your closing remarks, leave your prospects something to think about.

As you can see, you can take various approaches to a sales presentation outline. When you use the PowerPoint templates, you'll find an approach that in some ways combines the ideas incorporated in the outlining formats in this section.

Is PowerPoint Your Best Tool for a Sales Presentation?

In our opinion, a PowerPoint presentation is an ideal medium for a sales presentation if you can answer yes to all the following questions:

- Can you use PowerPoint in the place where you'll be making the presentation? You'll need a laptop, a projector, screen, and cables.

- Can the seating and viewing be arranged so that everyone can see your presentation?

- Is your audience positively inclined to a PowerPoint presentation?

- Do you have the time to prepare a backup presentation if, for example, the power goes out, the equipment malfunctions, or some other disaster occurs?

In addition to answering these questions, we also would include this caveat: PowerPoint slides can enhance the impact of your presentation but only if they are attractive, if they increase the value of your message, and if you have carefully planned and rehearsed your presentation so that it is smooth and professional. Some black text thrown on a white screen is not enticing, and a presenter who merely reads what is on the screen might as well have sent the handouts and not bothered to show up him- or herself.

That said, let's now look at how to create a PowerPoint sales presentation that's guaranteed to make a positive impression on prospects.

Creating Your Presentation

As you know from Chapter 5, you can create a PowerPoint presentation in three ways:

- Using the AutoContent Wizard

- Using an outline

- Creating individual slides

In this chapter, we'll use an outline because we want to focus on the content of the presentation, and we'll look at how to do so using a presentation template and a blank presentation.

Using a Presentation Template

PowerPoint includes a template that is ideal to use as a starting point for a sales presentation, especially if you are new to PowerPoint. Follow these steps to select it:

1. Start PowerPoint.

Click the Start button, click Programs, and then click Microsoft PowerPoint. You'll see something similar to the screen shown in Figure 19-1.

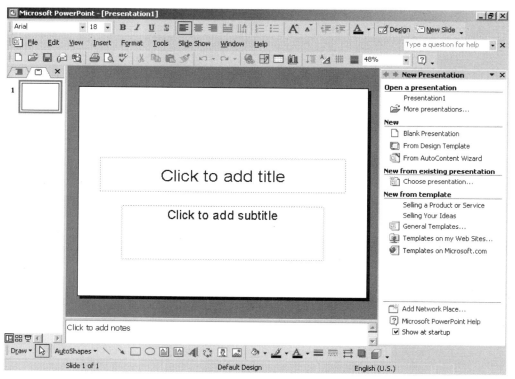

Figure 19-1   Starting PowerPoint.

2. Open the Templates dialog box at the Presentations tab, as shown in Figure 19-2.

In the task pane, click the General Templates link in the New From Template section, and then click the Presentations tab.

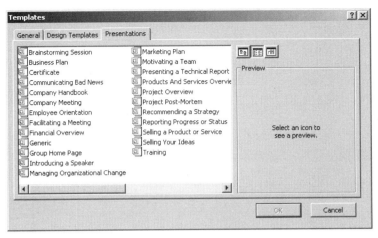

Figure 19-2   The Templates dialog box open at the Presentations tab.

3. Open the Selling A Product Or Service template, as shown in Figure 19-3.

Click Selling A Product Or Service on the Presentations tab, and then click OK.

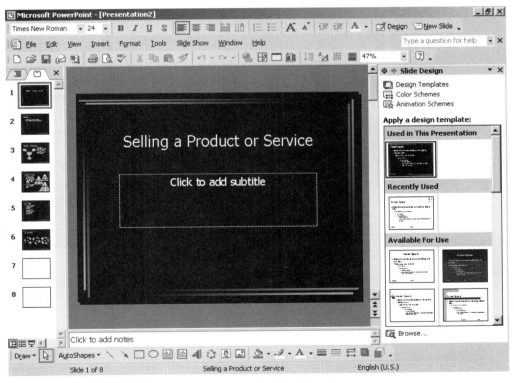

Figure 19-3   A presentation template open in Outline view.

Selecting a Design for Your Presentation

By selecting the Selling A Product Or Service presentation template, we now have a basic set of slides and an outline for our presentation. You can keep the default design, but if you want another design, follow these steps:

1. Open the Slide Design task pane, as shown in Figure 19-4.

Click the Format menu, and then click Slide Design.

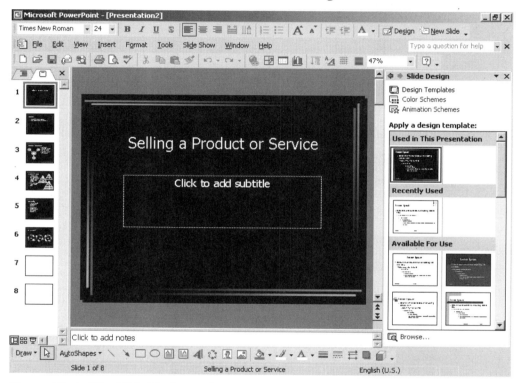

Figure 19-4 The Slide Design task pane open in PowerPoint.

2. Select a design template.

Scroll down the Apply A Design Template list to see the available designs. Click a design to display it on the slide. To apply it to the presentation, simply close the task pane.

Now is a good time to name and save your presentation.

Selecting a Color Scheme

Although you can change the color schemes associated with a design template or the background of a template, we suggest that you use the design templates and color schemes that are included with PowerPoint or those that you can download by clicking the Templates on Microsoft.com link in the New Presentation task pane. All these were created by professional artists who took into consideration aspects such as contrast, readability, font style and size, and the judicious use of white space.

When selecting a color scheme or a design template, you also want to keep in mind where you will be making your presentation. To be easy to read, words and pictures on slides need to be bright and clear and contrast strongly with the color of the background, and the ambient light in the room must be subdued enough for the slides to appear bright. You can achieve brightness with a powerful projector or by having sufficient darkness in the room or in the end of the room where the slides are being projected. Generally, the darker the background color and the lighter the lettering or line color on a slide, the greater the contrast and readability.

Creating Your Outline

To begin creating your outline, you simply replace the placeholder text with text of your own. Figure 19-5 shows the first slide in a presentation template in which we've done exactly that.

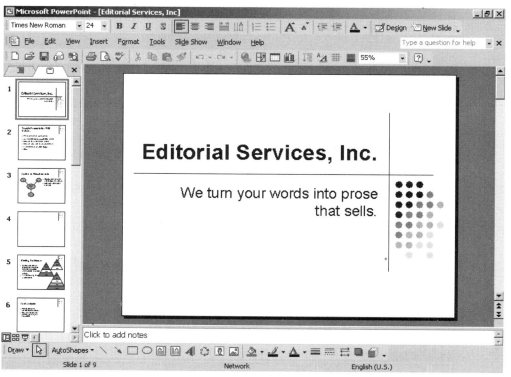

Figure 19-5 Creating an outline with a presentation template.

To continue working with this template, you can enter your text on the slide or on the outline. To enter text on the slide, click an area and then type in the box. To enter text on the outline, select the placeholder text and then type to replace it. You may need to include more slides in your presentation than the template shows. For example, slide 4 in the Selling A Product Or Service template is formatted so that you can enter the needs of your prospect. If you want to list more needs than will fit attractively on that slide, you can insert a duplicate. Click in the slide, click the Insert menu, and then click Duplicate Slide.

TIP   *As you learned in Chapter 5, you can also import an outline that you create in Word into a PowerPoint presentation.*

Using a Blank Presentation

Another way to create a sales presentation is to use a blank presentation. In the New Presentation task pane, click Blank Presentation to open the Slide Layout task pane, as shown in Figure 19-6. The Slide Layout task pane contains three categories of layouts: Text, Content, and Other. These layouts are simply blank slides that include placeholders for text and other objects.

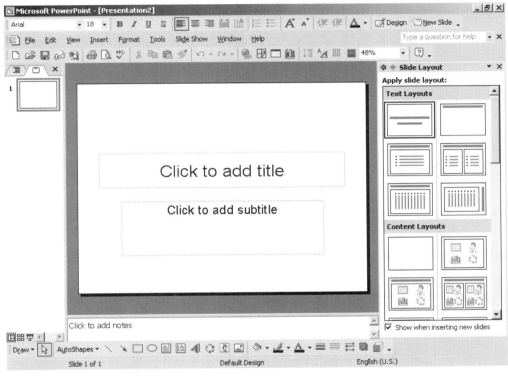

Figure 19-6 Selecting a blank presentation.

To use these layouts to create a sales presentation, follow these steps:

1. Name your presentation.

By default, the first text layout slide is selected, as you can see in Figure 19-6. Click the Click To Add Title text box, and type the title of your presentation. If you want a subtitle, enter that. Figure 19-7 shows how this slide appears after you enter your text.

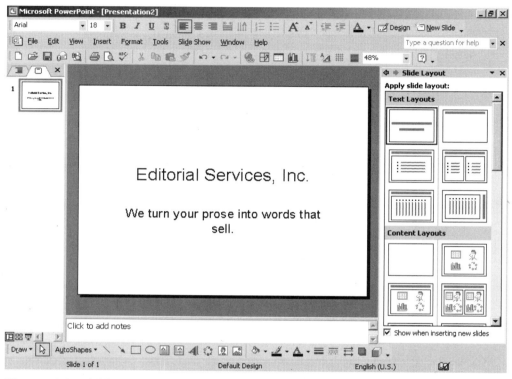

Figure 19-7   Adding title information to the first slide.

2. Create the next slide.

To slide 2, select a layout, click the down arrow, and then click Insert New Slide. If you're following one of the outlines presented earlier in this chapter, your second slide might preview your presentation. A bulleted list is a good way to present this kind of information, and so we've used the third text layout to create the slide shown in Figure 19-8.

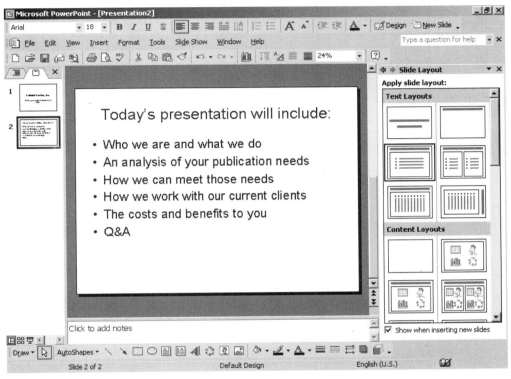

Figure 19-8 Presenting information in a bulleted list.

3. Create the remainder of your slides.

Repeat step 2 until you have entered the main points in your outline and as much of the text as you want.

4. Save your presentation.

Click the File menu, click Save, name your file and select a folder in which to store it, and then click Save.

As you select slides for your sales presentation, consider the type of content and which format might best be used to present it. Here are some ideas:

- Use the Diagram Or Organization Chart layout in the Other Layouts category to describe the management in your company or the people who would be involved in the product or service you are selling.

- Use the Large Content layout in the Content Layouts category to insert a picture of your product.

- Use the Table layout or the Chart layout to present financial projections.

After you enter your outline, you'll want to apply a design or a color scheme to your sales presentation. Follow the steps given earlier in the section "Selecting a Design for Your Presentation."

NOTE   *You can also add charts, diagrams, and other graphic effects to your sales presentation using the instructions we presented in Chapter 5.*

Creating Speaker's Notes

Speaker's notes are written notes that you can refer to while making your presentation. Many sales professionals write out everything they plan to say and adhere religiously to these written notes. Others make brief notations to remind themselves and then use these notes as a guide to a more extemporaneous presentation. If you are an experienced public speaker, you might want to do the latter. If you're just starting out, you'll do well to begin by creating a script and sticking to it.

To create speaker's notes for a PowerPoint sales presentation, follow these steps:

1. Open your presentation.

Open PowerPoint, and then in the task pane, click the title of your presentation. You'll see a window similar to that in Figure 19-9.

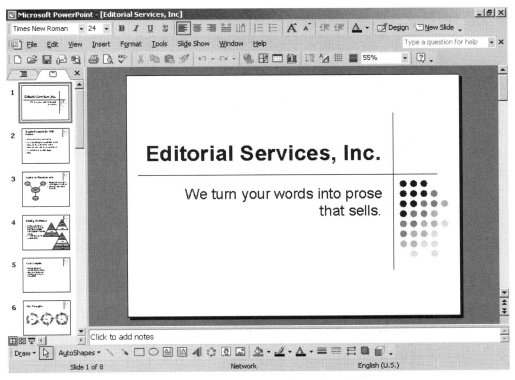

Figure 19-9 The Speaker's Notes pane is just below the slide.

2. Enter notes for your first slide.

In the pane that contains the words *Click to add notes*, click and start typing what you want to say when you display the first slide.

3. Create speaker's notes for the other slides in your presentation.

Click the subsequent slides in your presentation. In the Speaker's Notes pane, type what you plan to say when each slide is displayed.

After you create your speaker's notes, you'll probably want to print them to make reading them easier. The onscreen pane is small, even if you resize it. It's also easier to rehearse your script if you have a printed copy to follow. To print your notes, follow these steps:

1. Open the Print dialog box, as shown in Figure 19-10.

Click the File menu, and then click Print.

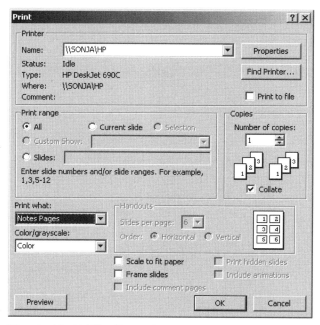

Figure 19-10 The Print dialog box in PowerPoint.

2. Tell PowerPoint what you want to print.

In the Print What drop-down list box, select Notes Pages, and then click OK to print your notes.

TIP   *At this point, there's no reason to waste ink or time, so also select Grayscale or Pure Black And White in the Color/Grayscale drop-down list box.*

PowerPoint prints each slide and each slide's speaker's notes on a single piece of paper.

Preparing Handouts

Handouts are black-and-white printed copies of your slides that you can distribute to your prospects. If you give them out before your presentation, your prospects can use them to take notes. You might also distribute them at the close of your presentation as a way to remind your prospects of what you've said.

WARNING   *Don't forget our earlier caveat about reading your presentation from slides that are simply black text on a white background. Your prospects will be doubly bored if they are also staring at a handout that duplicates what they are seeing on the screen.*

To print handouts of your slides, follow these steps:

1. **Open the Print dialog box.**

   Click the File menu, and then click Print.

2. **Tell PowerPoint what you want to print.**

   In the Print What drop-down list box, select Handouts, as shown in Figure 19-11. In the Color/Grayscale drop-down list box, select whether you want to print in color, black and white, or grayscale.

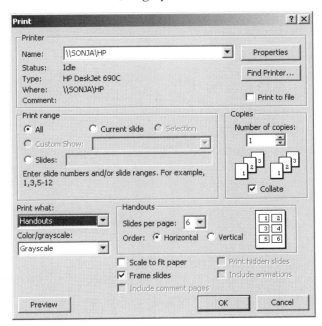

Figure 19-11 Selecting to print handouts.

3. **Tell PowerPoint how to print your handouts.**

   In the Handouts section of the Print dialog box, click the Slides Per Page drop-down list box, and select the number of slides you want to print on each page. If you print three slides per page, PowerPoint includes lines that your prospects can use to take notes. Click an Order option button, either Horizontal or Vertical, to indicate how you want the slides arranged on the page. You can see the effect of your choice in the little preview box.

4. **Tell PowerPoint how many copies of your handouts to print.**

   In the Number Of Copies spin box, select the number of copies. If you will be making your presentation to a large audience and will thus need lots of copies, you might want to print only one copy and then duplicate it on a photocopy machine. When you've selected all your options, click OK to print your handouts.

Rehearsing Your Presentation

Many sales professionals recommend that you script your presentation, memorize it, and then practice delivering it in front of a friend or another sales person, asking them to play the role of your prospect(s). PowerPoint includes a handy tool that you can use to rehearse your script and to time your sales presentation.

To begin rehearsing a PowerPoint sales presentation, follow these steps:

1. **Open your presentation.**

   In the New Presentation task pane, select the presentation from the Open A Presentation section.

2. **Start the rehearsal.**

   Click the Slide Show menu, and then click Rehearse Timings. Figure 19-12 shows how your screen looks.

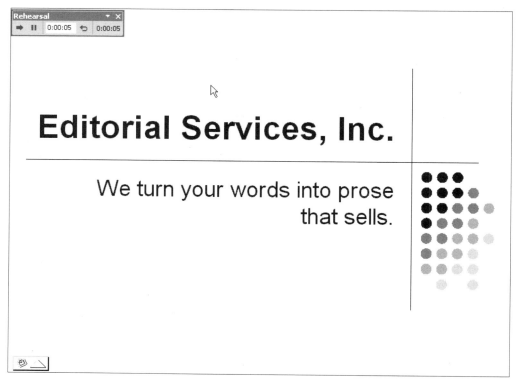

Figure 19-12 Rehearsing a presentation.

The main part of the screen displays the first slide from your presentation. In the upper left corner of the screen is the Rehearsal dialog box, which you use as follows in order from left to right:

- Click the Next button to display the next slide.
- Click the Pause button to temporarily halt the rehearsal.
- The Slide Time box displays the time you've been showing the current slide.
- Click the Repeat button to restart the rehearsal timing.
- The time display at the far right of the dialog box shows the total time for the presentation.
- Click the Close button to stop the rehearsal.

TIP   *Point to a button in the Rehearsal dialog box to display a ScreenTip that describes its function.*

To rehearse your presentation, simply say whatever you want to say about a slide using your speaker's notes, and then click the Next button to display the next slide. As you continue through your slides, PowerPoint tracks your time.

TIP   *Strive to attain a delivery rate of 160 words a minute. This is the current average for business and technical presentations.*

After you complete your rehearsal, PowerPoint displays a message box like the one shown in Figure 19-13. It shows the total time you spent for the slide show. If you want to record the time you spent on each slide and store this information with the slide, click Yes.

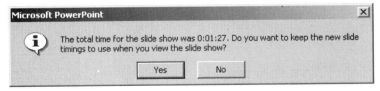

Figure 19-13 PowerPoint reports rehearsal timing information.

Evaluating Your Presentation

Some sales professionals recommend that you evaluate your performance after every presentation. Take note of what went well and what didn't, and then think about what you might want to do differently during the next presentation. Here are some questions to ask yourself:

- Did you know what must be said before you spoke?
- Did you think about your prospects—who they are and their level of understanding and interest?
- Did you identify your prospects' problems and provide solutions?
- Were you prepared? Had you rehearsed sufficiently?
- Did you use the right words for these particular prospects, avoiding slang and jargon if appropriate—on your slides and in your spoken presentation?
- Did you begin the presentation with an attention-getting statement of purpose?
- Did you speak with confidence and authority?
- Were you aware of the physical environment and its impact?
- Did you solicit feedback from your prospects?
- Were you patient and did you listen carefully when others were speaking?
- Were your remarks targeted to the task at hand or did you wander off topic?
- Did the slides in your presentation enhance the value of your spoken presentation?
- Could your prospects easily read the text and see the graphics on your slides?

Summary

A PowerPoint presentation may not be possible in every sales situation, but it can be a powerful enhancement in a great many cases. This chapter has given you guidelines for how to prepare for a sales presentation and how to outline a presentation. It also includes the steps for creating a sales presentation using a PowerPoint presentation template or a blank presentation. In addition, it walks you through the process of creating speaker's notes and handouts and rehearsing and evaluating your sales presentation.

Chapter 20

PERFORMING PROFIT-VOLUME-COST ANALYSIS WITH EXCEL

Featuring:

- Using the Profit-Volume-Cost and Break-Even Analysis Workbook
- Understanding the Workbook's Calculations
- Customizing the Workbook
- Charting Profit-Volume-Cost Analysis Data

Profit-volume-cost analysis lets you look at the revenues, costs, and profits of a business for a range of business volumes, or revenues. By using profit-volume-cost analysis, you can see how sensitive profits are to changes in business volume and where break-even points occur.

The profit-volume-cost and break-even analysis workbook (PROFTVOL.XLS), which is described in this chapter and is available from the Redmond Technology Press Web site (*www.redtechpress.com*), provides a framework to use in performing profit-volume-cost analysis and in calculating break-even points. This chapter shows how to use the workbook and modify it. In addition, this chapter includes two charts useful in portraying profit-volume-cost and break-even analysis data.

NOTE   *To retrieve the PROFTVOL.XLS workbook, visit the* www.redtechpress.com *Web site, click the hyperlink to the* MBA's Guide to Office XP, *and then follow the instructions for downloading the PROFTVOL.XLS workbook.*

Profit-Volume-Cost and Break-Even Analysis

Profit–volume–cost analysis calculates the profits of a business at different volumes, or revenue levels. *Break-even analysis,* a component of profit-volume-cost analysis, calculates the revenue level at which a business shows neither a profit nor a loss.

Generally, profit-volume-cost analysis involves five steps. First, set a range of business volumes for which you examine *costs* and *profits*. This step is probably one of the most critical because all the information you input—unit sales price, variable costs, fixed costs, and costs varying with profits—is usually valid only over a limited range of volumes. By carefully considering the relationships between costs and changes in volume over a specific range, you can increase the accuracy of your analysis.

Second, calculate the *unit sales price,* the amount for which you sell your product or service. For example, if you build and sell single-family homes and your average sales price is $100,000, your unit sales price is $100,000.

Third, identify the costs that vary with revenue, the *variable costs.* Typically, it's easiest to express and calculate these variable costs either as an amount determined per unit or as an amount determined as a percentage of revenues. For example, if you build houses, many of your costs are best described as an amount per house. For example, your land costs might average $15,000 per house and your material costs and your labor costs each might average $40,000. Other costs, however, are better described as a percentage of revenues. For example, you might calculate sales commissions as 7% of the sales price and a state sales tax as 1½% of the sales price. The key assumption for the purpose of profit-volume-cost analysis, however, is that within the range of business volumes you define, the variable costs change proportionally, based on revenue.

Fourth, determine your *fixed costs.* Fixed costs are those that stay constant, within the range of business volumes you define. You label these costs "fixed," not because you cannot change them but because small to moderate changes in revenue don't change them. Examples of fixed costs are salaries of administrative personnel, office rent, and business insurance.

Fifth, calculate your profits and any *costs varying with profits.* Examples of these costs are income taxes and profit-sharing plans. Obviously, the precise determination of income taxes and similar costs requires detailed tax accounting. But you might be able to estimate these income taxes and costs by applying an appropriate percentage to the profits before income taxes and other costs that vary with profits.

You can calculate the *contribution margin* (the revenues minus the variable costs) and profit at any volume within the range for which your inputs are valid. Although the analysis is only as good as your assumptions and is subject to the inevitable inaccuracies that creep into any projection of the future, profit-volume-cost analysis allows you to see roughly what happens to your profits over the likely range of business volumes.

One common profit-volume-cost analysis calculation is estimating the revenue level that provides exactly enough contribution margin to cover fixed costs. In this calculation, because no profits exist, none of the costs that vary with profits exist. At the break-even point, revenues leave exactly enough contribution margin to cover fixed costs. The general formula used to calculate the break-even point is as follows:

```
Break-even point in units=Fixed costs/Contribution margin per unit
```

If you use more than one of the Vary-with-Profit Costs categories presented in the profit-volume-cost and break-even analysis workbook, you need to recognize the correct relationships between variables as you input them. Basically, three types of relationships exist: independent-independent, independent-dependent, and dependent-dependent. Independent-independent is easiest to calculate because all of the costs that vary with profits are calculated independent of the other. The other two types of relationships can be more difficult. With the independent-dependent relationship, you need to calculate one cost so that you can calculate the next. As an example of this relationship and how you might recognize it in your inputs, suppose that the state income tax rate is 10% and is deducted from the Profit Before Vary-with-Profits Costs (PBVPC) and that after deducting the state income tax from the PBVPC, the federal income tax rate of 20% is applied to the PBVPC. The correct input percentage for the state income tax rate is 10%, because 10% of the PBVPC calculates the correct state income tax cost, as follows:

```
State Income Tax=10%*PBVPC
```

However, the federal income tax percentage must recognize the state income tax costs:

```
Federal Income Tax=20%*(PBVPC-(10%*PBVPC))
```

This formula can be further modified as follows to express the federal income tax rate as a percentage of the PBVPC and, therefore, your input to the profit-volume-cost and break-even analysis workbook:

```
Federal Income Tax=18%*PBVPC
```

A third type of relationship that might exist between the costs that vary with profits is a dependent-dependent, or circular, relationship. For example, suppose that you have an employee bonus cost equal to 10% of the after-tax profits. You need to know the amount of the bonus before you can calculate the federal income taxes because it's a tax-deductible expense, and you need to know the federal income tax because it determines the after-tax profits, upon which the bonus is calculated, before you can calculate the bonus. Assuming that your only tax is a federal income tax rate of 20%, you calculate your federal income tax as follows:

```
Federal Income Tax=20%*(PBVPC-bonus)
```

Assuming that the employee bonus is 10% of the after-tax profits, your employee bonus cost equals:

```
Bonus=10%*(PBVPC-Federal Income Tax)
```

Given these definitions, you can define the federal income tax percentage by substituting the formula for the bonus in the federal income tax formula, as follows:

```
Federal Income Tax=20%*(PBVPC-(10%*(PBVPC-Federal Income Tax)))
```

You could state this formula algebraically as:

```
Federal Income Tax=20%*(PBVPC-(10%*PBVPC)+(10%*Federal Income Tax))
```

or:

```
Federal Income Tax=20%*((90%*PBVPC)+(10%*Federal Income Tax))
```

or:

```
Federal Income Tax=(18%*PBVPC)+(2%*Federal Income Tax)
```

or:

```
98%*Federal Income Tax=18%*PBVPC
```

or to show the federal income tax as a percentage of the PBVPC:

```
Federal Income Tax=18.3673%*PBVPC
```

Given this number, it's easy to define the bonus as a percentage of the PBVPC by substituting the following formula for federal income tax in the bonus formula:

```
Bonus=10%*(PBVPC-(18.3673%*PBVPC))
```

or to show the bonus as a percentage of the PBVPC:

```
Bonus=10%*(81.6327%*PBVPC)
```

or to show the bonus as a percentage of the PBVPC in another way:

```
Bonus=8.16372%*PBVPC
```

Using the Profit-Volume-Cost and Break-Even Analysis Workbook

You can use the profit-volume-cost and break-even analysis workbook (PROFTVOL) to test the effect of changing revenues on business profits. To complete the schedule, you define the following:

- Revenue variables, including the unit sales price, the low revenue in unit volume tested, and the high revenue in unit volume tested.

- Variable costs best expressed as an amount per unit, including the direct labor, the direct materials, and the factory overhead.

- Variable costs best expressed as a percentage of revenue, including sales commissions and sales tax.

- Any costs commonly calculated as a percentage of profits, including state income tax and federal income tax.

The workbook shown in Figure 20-1 calculates the break-even point in units; shows the revenues, costs, and profits for the break-even point; and calculates the revenues, costs, and profits for the low units volume, the high units volume, and four intervals between the low and high volumes.

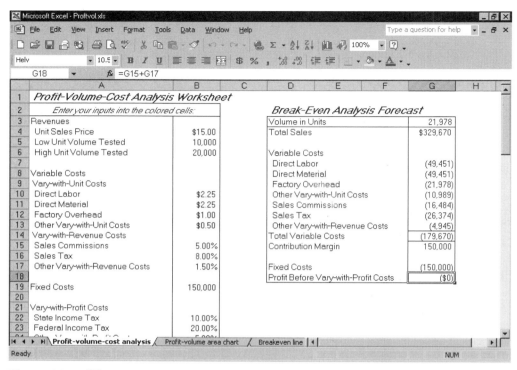

Figure 20-1 The inputs area and Break-Even Analysis Forecast of the profit-volume-cost and break-even analysis workbook.

Two charts included with the workbook let you look at the results of your profit-volume-cost analysis graphically. The first chart shows the revenues, costs, and profits at various revenue levels. The second chart shows the revenues plotted against the total fixed and variable costs; the point at which the revenue line intersects the total fixed and variable costs identifies the break-even point.

To enter your own data in the profit-volume-cost and break-even analysis workbook, follow these steps:

1. **Retrieve the profit-volume-cost and break-even analysis workbook, PROFTVOL.XLS, from the** *www.redtechpress.com* **Web site.**

   To retrieve the workbook, use your Web browser to display the *www.redtechpress.com* home page, click the hyperlink that points to the *MBA's Guide to Office XP* Web page, and then follow the onscreen instructions for downloading the PROFTVOL.XLS workbook. The workbook initially contains the default inputs shown in Figure 20-1.

2. **Estimate the unit sales price of the product or service you sell.**

   In cell B4, enter the Unit Sales Price value as the amount per unit you will receive from the sales of the product or service for which you are performing profit-volume-cost and break-even analysis.

3. **Estimate the lowest business volume in units for which you want to calculate total sales, costs, and profits.**

   You enter this value in cell B5. Low Unit Volume Tested is the minimum revenue level (in units) for which you will calculate revenues, costs, and profits.

4. **Estimate the highest business volume in units for which you want to calculate total sales, costs, and profits.**

   You enter this value in cell B6. High Unit Volume Tested is the maximum revenue level (in units) for which you will calculate revenues, costs, and profits.

5. **Estimate any direct labor costs that vary with the units sold and that are calculated as an amount per unit.**

   Enter this value in cell B10. Direct Labor is the dollar amount of labor per unit.

6. **Estimate any direct material costs that vary with the units sold and that are calculated as an amount per unit.**

   Enter this value in cell B11. Direct Material is the dollar amount of materials per unit.

7. **Estimate any factory overhead costs that vary with the units sold and that are calculated as an amount per unit.**

   Enter this value in cell B12. Factory Overhead is the dollar amount of factory overhead per unit.

8. **Estimate any other costs that vary with the units sold and that are calculated as an amount per unit.**

   If you have other costs that you want to express as a dollar amount per unit, enter the dollar amount of these other costs as the Other Vary-with-Unit Costs amount in cell B13.

9. **Estimate any sales commissions as a percentage of the price or the total sales.**

   Enter this value as a percentage in cell B15.

10. **Estimate any sales tax as a percentage of the unit sales price or the total sales.**

    Enter this value as a percentage in cell B16.

11. **Estimate any other costs that vary with revenues as a percentage of the unit sales price or the total sales.**

If you have other costs that you want to express as a percentage of revenues, enter that percentage as the Other Vary-with-Revenue Costs amount in cell B17.

12. **Estimate the total fixed costs.**

Enter the Fixed Costs value in cell B19. Fixed costs are those costs that will not change, given the range of revenue levels for which you are testing.

13. **Estimate the state income tax as a percentage of profits before federal income tax and other costs that vary with profits.**

Enter this value in cell B22. The workbook assumes that state income taxes are a percentage of your profits before federal income taxes and any other costs that vary with profits (such as profit-sharing plans).

14. **Estimate the federal income tax as a percentage of profits before state income tax and other costs that vary with profits.**

Enter this value in cell B23. The workbook assumes that federal income taxes are a percentage of your profits before state income taxes and other costs that vary with profits (such as profit-sharing plans).

15. **Estimate as a percentage any other costs that vary with the profits before taxes.**

If you have other costs that you want to express as a percentage of profits, enter that percentage as the Other Vary-with-Profit Costs amount in cell B24.

Understanding the Workbook's Calculations

The profit-volume-cost and break-even analysis workbook has six parts: the Profit-Volume Inputs box and the Break-Even Analysis Forecast (see Figure 20-1), the Profit Volume Forecast, the Common Size Profit Volume Forecast, and the Profit Volume Area and the Break-Even Analysis Line Chart Data.

For convenience and good documentation within the model, cell B4 contains the Unit Sales Price amount and is named Unit_Sales_Price, cell B5 contains the Low Unit Volume Tested amount and is named Low_Unit_Volume_Tested, cell B6 contains the High Unit Volume Tested amount and is named High_Unit_Volume_Tested, cell B10 contains the Direct Labor amount and is named Direct_Labor, cell B11 contains the Direct Material amount and is named Direct_Material, cell B12 contains the Factory Overhead amount and is named Factory_Overhead, cell B13 contains the Other Vary-with-Unit Costs amount and is named Other_Vary_Unit_Costs, cell B15 contains the

Sales Commissions percentage and is named Sales_Commissions, cell B16 contains the Sales Tax percentage and is named Sales_Tax, cell B17 contains the Other Vary-with-Revenue Costs percentage and is named Other_Vary_Revenue_Costs, cell B19 contains the Fixed Costs amount and is named Fixed_Costs, cell B22 contains the State Income Tax percentage and is named State_Income_Tax, cell B23 contains the Federal Income Tax percentage and is named Federal_Income_Tax, and cell B24 contains the Other Vary-with-Profit Costs percentage and is named Other_Vary_Profit_Costs. The formulas within the workbook use these cell names rather than the cell addresses.

NOTE   *To confirm these variables in the PROFTVOL.XLS workbook, click one of these cells. In a toolbar near the upper left corner of the spreadsheet, you will see a drop-down box with all the variable names listed.*

Break-Even Analysis Forecast

The Break-Even Analysis Forecast calculates the volume level in units at which you break even and displays the revenues, variable costs, and fixed costs forecasted at this volume level (see Figure 20-1). The schedule has only one column containing calculated data. Within it, revenues appear as positive amounts, and expenses appear as negative amounts.

Volume in Units

The Volume in Units amount is the number of units at which the break-even point occurs. The amount is rounded to the nearest whole unit, because selling partial units usually is impossible. This Volume in Units amount is calculated by dividing the Fixed Costs amount by the contribution margin per unit. The contribution margin per unit is calculated by subtracting each of the variable costs (expressed as an amount per unit) from the Unit Sales Price value. Those variable costs, which you enter as a percentage of the Unit Sales Price amount, are converted to an amount per unit. Because the calculated revenue level is the level at which no profits are generated, no costs based on profits are included in the formula or are shown in the forecast of revenues and costs and the break-even point. The formula for the break-even point in units (in cell G3) is:

```
=ROUND(Fixed_Costs/(Unit_Sales_Price-
(Direct_Labor+Direct_Material+Factory_Overhead+Other_Vary_Unit_Costs)-
(Unit_Sales_Price*(Sales_Commissions_+Sales_Taxes+Other_Vary_Revenue_Costs))),0)
```

which is essentially the break-even point equation from the "Profit-Volume-Cost and Break-Even Analysis" section, where:

```
Break-even point in units=Fixed costs/Contribution margin per unit
```

Total Sales

The Total Sales amount shows the revenue in dollars for the break-even point. The Total Sales amount is the break-even Volume in Units times the Unit Sales Price value. The Total Sales formula (in cell G4) is:

```
=G3*Unit_Sales_Price
```

Direct Labor

The Direct Labor figure shows the direct labor costs for the break-even volume. The amount is the break-even Volume in Units amount times the Direct Labor cost per unit. The Direct Labor formula (in cell G7) is:

```
=-G3*Direct_Labor
```

Direct Material

The Direct Material figure shows the direct material costs for the break-even volume. The amount is the break-even Volume in Units amount times the Direct Material cost per unit. The Direct Material formula (in cell G8) is:

```
=-G3*Direct_Material
```

Factory Overhead

The Factory Overhead figure shows the factory overhead costs for the break-even volume. The amount is the break-even Volume in Units amount times the Factory Overhead cost per unit. The Factory Overhead formula (in cell G9) is:

```
=-G3*Factory_Overhead
```

Other Vary-with-Unit Costs

The Other Vary-with-Unit Costs figure shows any other costs you have expressed as an amount per unit for the break-even volume. The amount is the break-even Volume in Units amount times the Other Vary-with-Unit Costs per unit. The Other Vary-with-Unit Costs formula (in cell G10) is:

```
=-G3*Other_Vary_Unit_Costs
```

Sales Commissions

The Sales Commissions figure shows the sales commissions costs for the break-even volume. The amount is the break-even revenue level times the Sales Commissions percentage. The Sales Commissions formula (in cell G11) is:

```
=-G4*Sales_Commissions
```

Sales Tax

The Sales Tax figure shows the sales tax costs for the break-even volume. The amount is the break-even revenue level times the Sales Tax percentage. The Sales Tax formula (in cell G12) is:

```
=-G4*Sales_Tax
```

Other Vary-with-Revenue Costs

The Other Vary-with-Revenue Costs figure shows any other costs you have expressed as a percentage of revenues for the break-even volume. The amount is the break-even revenue level times the Other Vary-with-Revenue Costs percentage. The Other Vary-with-Revenue Costs formula (in cell G13) is:

```
=-G4*Other_Vary_Revenue_Costs
```

Total Variable Costs

The Total Variable Costs figure shows the total variable costs for the break-even volume. The Total Variable Costs formula (in cell G14) is:

```
=SUM(G7:G13)
```

Contribution Margin

The Contribution Margin figure shows the difference between the total sales and the total variable costs. For break-even analysis, this amount must equal the fixed costs. However, because the break-even point in unit volume is rounded to an integer, this amount might differ. The formula (in cell G15) is:

```
=G4+G14
```

Fixed Costs

The Fixed Costs figure shows the fixed costs at the break-even volume. The formula (in cell G17) is:

```
=-Fixed_Costs
```

Profit Before Vary-with-Profit Costs

The Profit Before Vary-with-Profit Costs figure shows the amount of profit for the break-even volume and is the Contribution Margin amount minus the Fixed Costs figure. None of the costs that vary with profits are included, because profits must equal 0. In some situations, the profit will equal some amount other than zero, even though, by definition, the true break-even point is the revenue volume at which profits equal zero. Typically, however, firms cannot sell fractional units of products or services. Accordingly, the break-even Volume in Units is rounded to an integer, and the workbook assumes that this is the closest to a break-even volume that you can actually operate. The Profit Before Vary-with-Profit Costs formula (in cell G18) is:

```
=G15+G17
```

Profit Volume Forecast

The Profit Volume Forecast shown in Figure 20-2 calculates the revenue, costs, and profits at the low unit volume you specify, the high unit volume you specify, and four intermediate volumes between these two boundaries. In the forecast, revenues appear as positive amounts and expenses appear as negative amounts.

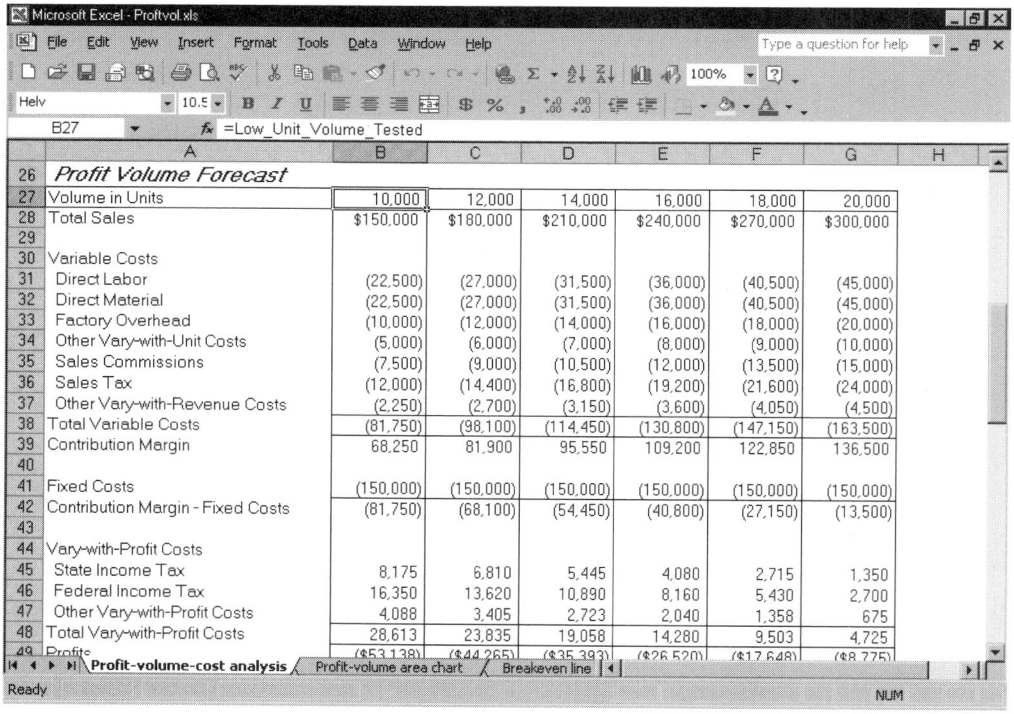

	A	B	C	D	E	F	G
26	*Profit Volume Forecast*						
27	Volume in Units	10,000	12,000	14,000	16,000	18,000	20,000
28	Total Sales	$150,000	$180,000	$210,000	$240,000	$270,000	$300,000
29							
30	Variable Costs						
31	Direct Labor	(22,500)	(27,000)	(31,500)	(36,000)	(40,500)	(45,000)
32	Direct Material	(22,500)	(27,000)	(31,500)	(36,000)	(40,500)	(45,000)
33	Factory Overhead	(10,000)	(12,000)	(14,000)	(16,000)	(18,000)	(20,000)
34	Other Vary-with-Unit Costs	(5,000)	(6,000)	(7,000)	(8,000)	(9,000)	(10,000)
35	Sales Commissions	(7,500)	(9,000)	(10,500)	(12,000)	(13,500)	(15,000)
36	Sales Tax	(12,000)	(14,400)	(16,800)	(19,200)	(21,600)	(24,000)
37	Other Vary-with-Revenue Costs	(2,250)	(2,700)	(3,150)	(3,600)	(4,050)	(4,500)
38	Total Variable Costs	(81,750)	(98,100)	(114,450)	(130,800)	(147,150)	(163,500)
39	Contribution Margin	68,250	81,900	95,550	109,200	122,850	136,500
40							
41	Fixed Costs	(150,000)	(150,000)	(150,000)	(150,000)	(150,000)	(150,000)
42	Contribution Margin - Fixed Costs	(81,750)	(68,100)	(54,450)	(40,800)	(27,150)	(13,500)
43							
44	Vary-with-Profit Costs						
45	State Income Tax	8,175	6,810	5,445	4,080	2,715	1,350
46	Federal Income Tax	16,350	13,620	10,890	8,160	5,430	2,700
47	Other Vary-with-Profit Costs	4,088	3,405	2,723	2,040	1,358	675
48	Total Vary-with-Profit Costs	28,613	23,835	19,058	14,280	9,503	4,725
49	Profits	($53,138)	($44,265)	($35,393)	($26,520)	($17,648)	($8,775)

Figure 20-2 The Profit Volume Forecast of the profit-volume-cost and break-even analysis workbook.

Volume in Units

The Volume in Units figure shows the business volume in units for each of the six volume levels for which revenues, costs, and profits are calculated. The first Volume in Units amount is pulled into the Profit Volume Forecast as the Low Unit Volume Tested amount you enter in the Profit Volume inputs box. The second through the sixth Volume in Units amounts, however, are calculated as the previous Volume in Units amounts plus an increase equal to the range of volumes tested, divided by the number of volumes tested. The range of volumes tested is the High Unit Volume Tested figure minus the Low Unit Volume Tested figure. The number of volumes tested is set at 5 and is defined with the reference name Increments within the workbook. The formula for the second Volume in Units figure (in cell C27) is:

```
=B27+((High_Unit_Volume_Tested-Low_Unit_Volume_Tested)/Increments)
```

The formula for the third volume is:

```
=C27+((High_Unit_Volume_Tested-Low_Unit_Volume_Tested)/Increments)
```

and so on.

Total Sales

The Total Sales amount shows the revenue in dollars for each volume tested. The Total Sales figure is the Volume in Units figure times the Unit Sales Price figure. For example, the Total Sales formula for the first volume tested (in cell B28) is:

```
=B27*Unit_Sales_Price
```

The formula for the second volume tested is:

```
=C27*Unit_Sales_Price
```

and so on.

Direct Labor

The Direct Labor figure shows the direct labor costs for each of the volumes tested. The amount is the Volume in Units figure times the Direct Labor cost per unit. The Direct Labor formula for the first volume (in cell B31) is:

```
=-B27*Direct_Labor
```

The formula for the second volume is:

```
=-C27*Direct_Labor
```

and so on.

Direct Material

The Direct Material figure shows the direct material costs for each of the volumes. The amount is the Volume in Units figure times the Direct Material cost per unit. The Direct Material formula for the first volume (in cell B32) is:

```
=-B27*Direct_Material
```

The formula for the second volume is:

```
=-C27*Direct_Material
```

and so on.

Factory Overhead

The Factory Overhead figure shows the factory overhead costs for each of the volumes. The amount is the Volume in Units figure times the Factory Overhead cost per unit. The Factory Overhead formula for the first volume (in cell B33) is:

```
=-B27*Factory_Overhead
```

The formula for the second volume is:

```
=-C27*Factory_Overhead
```

and so on.

Other Vary-with-Unit Costs

The Other Vary-with-Unit Costs figure shows any other costs you have expressed as an amount per unit for each volume tested. The amount is the Volume in Units figure times the Other Vary-with-Unit Costs per unit. The other Vary-with-Unit Costs formula (in cell B34) is:

```
=-B27*Other_Vary_Unit_Costs
```

The formula for the second volume is:

```
=-C27*Other_Vary_Unit_Costs
```

and so on.

Sales Commissions

The Sales Commissions figure shows the sales commissions costs for each of the volumes tested. The amount is the Total Sales figure times the Sales Commissions percentage. The Sales Commissions formula for the first volume (in cell B35) is:

```
=-B28*Sales_Commissions
```

The formula for the second volume is:

```
=-C28*Sales_Commissions
```

and so on.

Sales Tax

The Sales Tax figure shows the sales tax costs for each of the volumes tested. The amount is the Total Sales figure times the Sales Tax percentage. The Sales Tax formula for the first volume (in cell B36) is:

```
=-B28*Sales_Tax
```

The formula for the second volume is:

```
=-C28*Sales_Tax
```

and so on.

Other Vary-with-Revenue Costs

The Other Vary-with-Revenue Costs figure shows any other costs you have expressed as a percentage of revenues for each of the volumes tested. The amount is the Total Sales figure times the Other Vary-with-Revenue Costs percentage. The Other Vary-with-Revenue Costs formula for the first volume (in cell B37) is:

```
=-B28*Other_Vary_Revenue_Costs
```

The formula for the second volume is:

```
=-C28*Other_Vary_Revenue_Costs
```

and so on.

Total Variable Costs

The Total Variable Costs figure shows the total variable costs for each of the volumes tested. The Total Variable Costs formula for the first volume (in cell B38) is:

```
=SUM(B31:B37)
```

The formula for the second volume is:

```
=SUM(C31:C37)
```

and so on.

Contribution Margin

The Contribution Margin figure shows the difference between the Total Sales figure and the Total Variable Costs figure. The Contribution Margin formula for the first volume (in cell B39) is:

```
=B28+B38
```

The formula for the second volume is:

```
=C28+C38
```

and so on.

Fixed Costs

The Fixed Costs figure shows the fixed costs you enter for the range of volumes tested. The formula is simply a named cell reference and is the same for each of the volumes tested. The formula for the first volume (in cell B41) is:

```
=-Fixed_Costs
```

Contribution Margin – Fixed Costs

This figure is the Contribution Margin figure minus the Fixed Costs figure. It is the amount used to calculate any costs that vary with profits. The Contribution Margin – Fixed Costs formula for the first volume (in cell B42) is:

```
=B39+B41
```

The formula for the second volume is:

```
=C39+C41
```

and so on.

State Income Tax

The State Income Tax figure shows the state income tax costs for each of the volumes tested. The amount is the Contribution Margin – Fixed Costs figure times the State Income Tax percentage. The State Income Tax formula for the first volume (in cell B45) is:

```
=-B42*State_Income_Tax
```

The formula for the second volume is:

```
=-C42*State_Income_Tax
```

and so on.

Federal Income Tax

The Federal Income Tax figure shows the federal income tax costs for each of the volumes tested. The amount is the Contribution Margin – Fixed Costs figure times the Federal Income Tax percentage. The Federal Income Tax formula for the first volume (in cell B46) is:

```
=-B42*Federal_Income_Tax
```

The formula for the second volume is:

```
=-C42*Federal_Income_Tax
```

and so on.

Other Vary-with-Profit Costs

The Other Vary-with-Profit Costs figure shows any other costs that are calculated as a percentage of profits for each of the volumes tested. The amount is the Contribution Margin – Fixed Costs figure times the Other Vary-with-Profit Costs percentage. The Other Vary-with-Profit Costs formula for the first volume (in cell B47) is:

```
=-B42*Other_Vary_Profit_Costs
```

The formula for the second volume is:

```
=-C42*Other_Vary_Profit_Costs
```

and so on.

Total Vary-with-Profit Costs

The Total Vary-with-Profit Costs figure shows the total of the costs that vary with profits for each of the volumes tested. The formula for the first volume (in cell B48) is:

```
=SUM(B45:B47)
```

The formula for the second volume is:

```
=SUM(C45:C47)
```

and so on.

Profits

The Profits figure shows the profits for each of the volumes tested and is the Contribution Margin – Fixed Costs amount minus the Total Vary-with-Profit Costs amount. The Profits formula for the first volume (in cell B49) is:

```
=B42+B48
```

The formula for profits for the second volume is:

```
=C42+C48
```

and so on.

Common Size Profit Volume Forecast

The Common Size Profit Volume Forecast shown in Figure 20-3 simply converts the costs and profits in the Profit Volume Forecast to percentages of the total sales for each of the volumes for which revenue, costs, and profits are calculated.

	A	B	C	D	E	F	G
53	*Common Size Profit Volume Forecast*						
54	Volume in Units	10,000	12,000	14,000	16,000	18,000	20,000
55	Total Sales	100.00%	100.00%	100.00%	100.00%	100.00%	100.00%
56							
57	Variable Costs						
58	Direct Labor	-15.00%	-15.00%	-15.00%	-15.00%	-15.00%	-15.00%
59	Direct Material	-15.00%	-15.00%	-15.00%	-15.00%	-15.00%	-15.00%
60	Factory Overhead	-6.67%	-6.67%	-6.67%	-6.67%	-6.67%	-6.67%
61	Other Vary-with-Unit Costs	-3.33%	-3.33%	-3.33%	-3.33%	-3.33%	-3.33%
62	Sales Commissions	-5.00%	-5.00%	-5.00%	-5.00%	-5.00%	-5.00%
63	Sales Tax	-8.00%	-8.00%	-8.00%	-8.00%	-8.00%	-8.00%
64	Other Vary-with-Revenue Costs	-1.50%	-1.50%	-1.50%	-1.50%	-1.50%	-1.50%
65	Total Variable Costs	-54.50%	-54.50%	-54.50%	-54.50%	-54.50%	-54.50%
66	Contribution Margin	45.50%	45.50%	45.50%	45.50%	45.50%	45.50%
67							
68	Fixed Costs	-100.00%	-83.33%	-71.43%	-62.50%	-55.56%	-50.00%
69	Contribution Margin - Fixed Costs	-54.50%	-37.83%	-25.93%	-17.00%	-10.06%	-4.50%
70							
71	Vary-with-Profit Costs						
72	State Income Tax	5.45%	3.78%	2.59%	1.70%	1.01%	0.45%
73	Federal Income Tax	10.90%	7.57%	5.19%	3.40%	2.01%	0.90%
74	Other Vary-with-Profit Costs	2.73%	1.89%	1.30%	0.85%	0.50%	0.23%
75	Total Vary-with-Profit Costs	19.08%	13.24%	9.08%	5.95%	3.52%	1.58%
76	Profits	-35.43%	-24.59%	-16.85%	-11.05%	-6.54%	-2.92%

Figure 20-3 The Common Size Profit Volume Forecast of the profit-volume-cost and break-even analysis workbook.

Predictably, the formulas used in this forecast are all very simple. For example, the formula for the Total Sales percentage for the first volume shown (in cell B55) is:

```
=B28/B$28
```

The volume in Units formulas are simply cell references to the Volume in Units figures calculated in the Break-Even Analysis Forecast. For example, the Volume in Units formula for the first volume shown (in cell B54) is:

```
=B27
```

Interpreting the Profit Volume Charts and Chart Data

The Profit Volume Area Chart Data shown in Figure 20-4 provides the data graphed in the profit-volume area chart discussed later in the chapter.

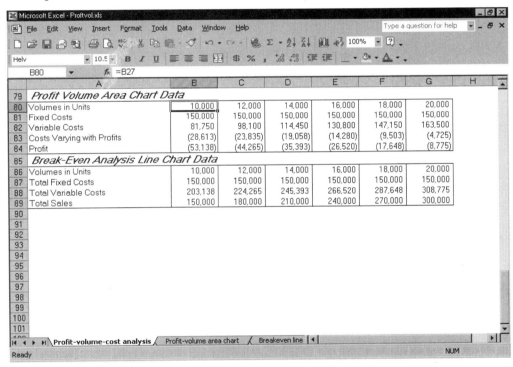

Figure 20-4   The Profit Volume Area Chart Data portion of the profit-volume-cost and break-even analysis workbook.

All the figures are simply pulled from the Profit Volume Forecast by cell references. For example, the Volume in Units figure for the first volume is pulled from the Profit Volume Forecast by the following formula:

```
=B27
```

The Fixed Costs, Variable Costs, and Costs Varying with Profits figures are pulled as positive numbers from the Profit Volume Forecast, in which they appear as negative numbers. For example, the formula for the first volume of the Fixed Costs row is:

```
=-B41
```

The Break-Even Analysis Line Chart Data (see Figure 20-4) provides the data to the line chart discussed later in the chapter, which identifies the break-even point by showing the intersection of the total sales line with total costs line. The Volume in Units, Total Fixed Costs, and Total Sales figures are pulled from the Profit Volume Forecast by cell references. For example, the formula for the first volume of the Volume in Units row is:

```
=B27
```

The Fixed Costs figure is pulled as a positive number from the Profit Volume Forecast, in which it appears as a negative number. For example, the formula for the first volume is:

```
=-B41
```

The Total Variable Costs figure includes those costs that vary with profits. The figure is the sum of the Fixed Costs, the Total Variable Costs, and the Total Vary-with-Profit Costs figures calculated in the Profit Volume Forecast. Fixed costs are included because the line chart plots total cost data against fixed cost data. You see the difference between the two lines, or the total variable costs. The formula for the first volume is:

```
=-B38-B41-B48
```

Customizing the Workbook

You can use the profit-volume-cost and break-even analysis workbook for testing the sensitivity of your costs and profits to changes in revenues and for calculating your break-even point. However, you probably want to change the workbook so that it more closely matches your requirements. For example, if you want to test more than six volumes at one time, you can increase or decrease the number of volumes for which revenue, costs, and profits are calculated. You can change the text describing the revenue, costs, and profits, or you can remove those cost categories unnecessary to your profit-volume-cost and break-even analysis. You can define minimums and maximums for specific costs and then include these minimums and maximums in your profit-volume-cost analysis. Before you change anything on the schedule other than the inputs, unprotect the document.

Changing the Number of Volumes Tested

You can easily increase or decrease the number of volumes tested in the profit-volume-cost analysis workbook. For example, to increase the number of volumes for which you test revenue, costs, and profits, follow these steps:

1. **Make room for more columns.**

   Remove the right border from the last column of the Profit Volume Forecast.

2. **Create columns for the increased number of volumes.**

   Copy the current last column to the right into as many additional columns as there are additional volumes for which you want to test revenue, costs, and profits.

3. **Redefine the Increment reference.**

   Change the Increment reference so that it equals one number less than the number of different unit volumes you show in your new Profit Volume Forecast. For example, with six unit volumes in the Profit Volume Forecast, Increment is set to 5.

To decrease the number of volumes in the Profit Volume Forecast, follow these steps:

1. **Clear any unneeded columns from the right side of the forecast.**

2. **Redefine the Increment reference.**

   Change the Increment reference so that it equals the one number less than the number of different unit volumes you now show in your new Profit Volume Forecast. For example, with six unit volumes in the schedule, Increment is set to 5.

NOTE   *After you add or subtract volumes from the workbook, replace the right border and reinstate cell protection as needed.*

Removing Forecasts from the Workbook

You can remove the Break-Even Analysis Forecast, the Common Size Profit Volume Forecast, or both the Profit Volume Forecast and the Common Size Profit Volume Forecast. (The Common Size Profit Volume Forecast uses information in the Profit Volume Forecast, so if you remove the Profit Volume Forecast, also remove the Common Size Profit Volume Forecast.) To remove any of these forecasts from the workbook, simply clear the forecast you want to remove.

Adding Minimums and Maximums to the Profit Volume Forecast

In your business, you might need to keep certain expenses below or above certain amounts. If so, you can, for example, specify that those costs the workbook calculates as a percentage of profits not become positive if the expenses should be expressed as negatives. To set a minimum expense as zero, edit the formula in the first volume column in the Profit Volume Forecast so that it checks for a minimum, as follows:

```
=MIN("old formula", "minimum amount")
```

in which the old formula is the formula currently in the cell and the minimum amount is the dollar amount shown as zero, or a negative value, which you don't want the calculated result to fall below. For example, you could set the State Income Tax formula to never fall below zero by editing the formula currently in cell B45 to read:

```
=MIN(-B42*State_Income_Tax,0)
```

Notice that to keep an expense amount from falling below a certain floor value you use a MIN function because the workbook calculated expenses as negative amounts. To set a maximum amount, use a MAX function, with the maximum amount specified as zero, or a negative value in the formula:

```
=MAX("old formula","maximum amount")
```

NOTE   *Because expenses are expressed as negative amounts, setting an amount above which an expense should not rise uses a MAX function with one of the arguments set as zero or a negative "ceiling" value. Setting an amount below which an expense should never fall uses a MIN function, with one of the arguments set as zero or a negative "floor" value.*

Charting Profit-Volume-Cost Analysis Data

Two charts included with the PROFTVOL workbook let you look at the results of your profit-volume-cost analysis graphically. The first chart shows the revenues, costs, and profits at various revenue levels. The second shows the revenues plotted against the total fixed and variable costs; the point at which the revenue line intersects the total fixed and variable costs identifies the break-even point.

Using the Profit-Volume Area Chart

Figure 20-5 shows an area chart of the variable costs, fixed costs, costs varying with profits, and profits forecasted for volumes modeled in a profit-volume-cost analysis. To use the area chart for your own profit-volume-cost analysis, simply follow the instructions in the earlier section "Using the Profit-Volume-Cost and Break-Even Analysis Workbook" to enter inputs for the profit-volume-cost and break-even analysis workbook.

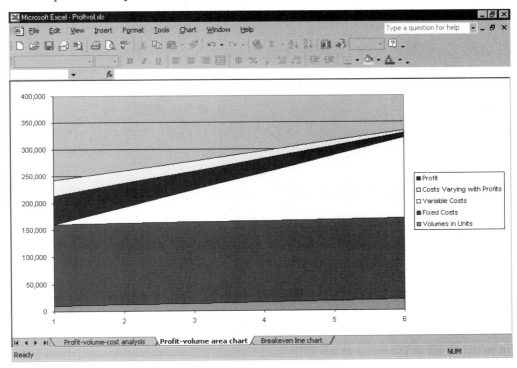

Figure 20-5 The profit-volume area chart.

The profit-volume area chart resides on the Profit-Volume Area Chart tab of the workbook. Click the Profit-Volume Area Chart sheet tab to view the chart once you've collected and entered the workbook's input data.

Notice that although the total sales are not explicitly included in the chart, they are implicitly included because the sum of the variable costs, fixed costs, costs varying with profits, and profits add up to the total sales.

Using the Breakeven Line Chart

Figure 20-6 shows a line chart of total sales plotted against total costs, including variable costs, fixed costs, and costs varying with profits. To use the line chart for your own break-even analysis, first follow the instructions in the section "Using the Profit-Volume-Cost and Break-Even Analysis Workbook" to enter inputs for the profit-volume-cost and break-even analysis workbook.

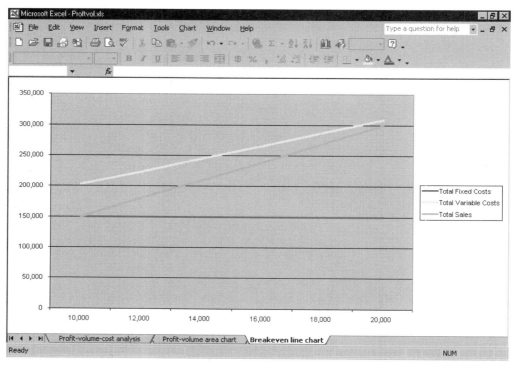

Figure 20-6 The breakeven line chart.

The breakeven line chart resides on the Breakeven Line Chart tab of the workbook. Click the Breakeven Line Chart sheet tab to view the chart once you've collected and entered the workbook's input data.

Because area and line charts emphasize the differences in a variable or variables over time, the scaling for the values axis greatly affects the perceived differences. By using small scaling units, you increase the perceived change in the variable or variables. By using large scaling units, you decrease the perceived change. In general, common sense suggests that the scaling units for charts of financial information be determined by the materiality of the changes. This means that you might need to override the automatic scaling provided by Excel because it scales the data based on the minimum and maximum values, not on your subjective definition of materiality.

Summary

One of the simplest yet most useful forms of business planning is profit-volume-cost analysis. By roughly estimating a firm's profits at various sales volumes, you can often gain valuable insights into the financial health and future prospects for a firm. You can usually learn a firm's break-even point, for example. And you also sometimes learn that small changes in sales make large changes in profits. The workbook described in this chapter and available from the *www.redtechpress.com* Web site will help you perform the tasks that reveal the data you can then use to make important decisions about your business.

Chapter 21

ANALYZING A CAPITAL INVESTMENT WITH EXCEL

Featuring:

- Using the Cash Flow Forecast and Analysis Workbook
- Understanding the Workbook's Calculations
- Customizing the Workbook

Capital budgeting and investment analysis require that you forecast pretax and after-tax cash flows based on both holding and disposing of each asset or investment. Financial measures of profitability and liquidity are applied to these cash flows. The cash flow forecast and analysis workbook (CASHFLOW.XLS), which is described in this chapter and is available at the Redmond Technology Press Web site (*www.redtechpress.com*), provides a framework for forecasting pretax and after-tax cash flows, internal rates of return, internal rates of return adjusted for reinvestment of interim cash flows, net present values, and payback periods. You should find this workbook useful for cash flow forecasts for both capital assets and financial investments.

NOTE *To retrieve the CASHFLOW.XLS workbook, visit the* www.redtechpress.com *Web site, click the hyperlink to the* MBA's Guide to Office XP, *and then follow the instructions for downloading the CASHFLOW.XLS workbook.*

Cash Flow Forecasting and Analysis

Cash flow forecasting and analysis, a basic component of capital budgeting and investment analysis, requires that you forecast each of the variables that might affect cash flows on the forecasting horizon. These variables include the initial outlay to acquire an asset or investment, the cash inflows and the cash outflows from holding an asset or investment, and any cash flows from disposing of an asset or investment. Using these variables, you can forecast the initial cash investment, the operating cash flows, and any liquidation cash flows.

To these cash flows, you apply profitability and liquidity measures. Because all the profitability measures use discounting, it's important to understand what discounting means. *Discounting* is the technique of reducing future cash to its equivalent in current cash, thereby providing a basis for an "apples-to-apples" comparison. To convert future cash amounts to current cash amounts, you first need to determine the time value of money, commonly called the *interest rate,* or the *discount rate.* The discount rate applied one period at a time is the *period discount rate.* To discount future cash into equivalent current cash, you divide the cash flow by the sum of one plus the period discount rate as many times as there are periods. For example, if the period discount rate equals 10% and you want to convert a $2,300 cash flow two years from now into equivalent current cash, you make the following calculation:

```
2300/(1+10%)/(1+10%)
```

or:

```
2300/ (1+10%)²
```

Similarly, if you have a cash flow of $5,000 occurring five years from now, you make the following calculation:

```
5000/(1+10%)/(1+10%)/(1+10%)/(1+10%)/(1+10%)
```

or:

```
5000/(1+10%)⁵
```

In any of the discounted cash flow profitability measures, this is the basic calculation: discounting future cash into its equivalent in current cash by using the time value of money expressed as an interest rate. With this background, you will be better able to understand the definitions of the profitability measures employed in the cash flow forecast and analysis workbook.

The *internal rate of return,* another term used in the workbook, is the discount rate that equates all the future cash flows to the initial cash investment. In other words, given a stated initial cash investment and a set of stated cash flows, the internal rate of return calculates the assumed interest rate delivered by the investment.

The internal rate of return adjusted for reinvestment of the interim cash flows, sometimes called the *adjusted rate of return,* is like the internal rate of return measure except that it assumes cash flows occurring between the beginning and the end of the forecasting horizon are reinvested until the end of the forecasting horizon at some stated reinvestment rate and then are paid at the end of the forecasting horizon with the final cash flow.

Although the internal rate of return and adjusted rate of return measures calculate the assumed interest rate based on the stated initial investment and the stated future cash flows, the *net present value* measure calculates an assumed initial investment based on the stated future cash flows and a stated interest rate. By comparing the actual investment with the assumed investment, you discover whether the investment is falling short of, meeting, or exceeding your stated interest rate. When the assumed initial investment falls short of the actual initial investment, the internal rate of return that the asset delivers falls short of the discount rate. When the assumed initial investment equals the actual initial investment, the internal rate of return that the asset delivers equals the discount rate. When the assumed initial investment exceeds the actual investment, the internal rate of return delivered by the asset exceeds the discount rate.

The workbook also incorporates a common liquidity, or closeness to cash, measure: the *payback period.* The payback period measure indicates how many periods are required to pay back or return the initial cash investment. Although liquidity is generally less important than profitability, in some situations businesses prefer more-liquid investments to less-liquid investments.

Using the Cash Flow Forecast and Analysis Workbook

You can use the cash flow forecast and analysis workbook to construct cash flow forecasts and analysis summaries for assets or investments for which you want to measure profitability and liquidity. To complete it for an asset or investment, develop and then enter information on the initial cash outlay needed to acquire the asset or investment, information on the cash inflows and outflows resulting from holding the asset or investment, and information on any residual cash flows from disposing of the asset or investment.

Given a set of data that includes your initial cash investment, sales and cost of sales, operating expenses, interest expenses, marginal income tax rates, depreciation and other noncash expenses, and debt principal payments and other cash nonexpenses, this workbook calculates the operating profit (or loss) and cash flows stemming from holding an investment. (Noncash expenses are those expenses, such as depreciation, that do not require any cash outflow. Other noncash expenses include the depletion expense of using up an intangible asset. Cash nonexpenses are those cash payments, such as debt principal payments, that represent a cash outflow but that are not considered an expense when calculating profit.) Given a set of data that includes gross residuals, transaction/disposal costs, outstanding debt, nontaxable portions of the residual, and marginal capital gains tax rates, this workbook calculates the capital gain (or loss) and cash flows stemming from disposing of an asset or investment. (The gross residual is the amount you can sell the asset or investment for. The marginal capital gains tax rate is the percentage that, when multiplied by the capital gains, correctly calculates the capital gains tax.) Given all of this data and your reinvestment and discount rates, the workbook calculates pretax and after-tax internal rates of return, pretax and after-tax adjusted rates of return, pretax and after-tax net present values, and the asset or investment payback period. You need some or all of this information to evaluate the economics of alternative investments and assets and to calculate overall profits (or losses), overall capital gains (or losses), and overall cash flows.

To enter your own data in the cash flow forecast and analysis workbook, follow these steps:

1. **Open the cash flow forecast and analysis workbook, CASHFLOW.XLS, from the** *www.redtechpress.com* **Web site.**

   To open the CASHFLOW.XLS workbook, visit the Redmond Technology Press Web site at *www.redtechpress.com*, click the hyperlink that points to the *MBA's Guide to Office XP* Web page, and then follow the instructions for downloading the CASHFLOW.XLS workbook. The workbook initially contains the default inputs shown in Figure 21-1.

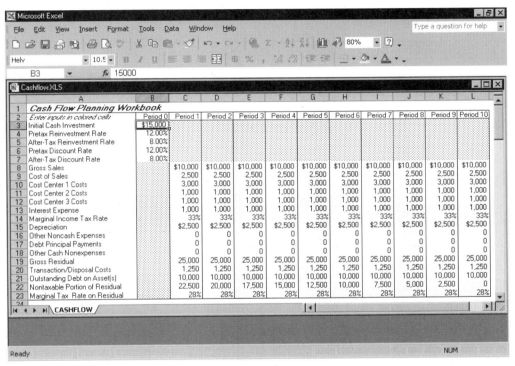

Figure 21-1 The inputs area of the cash flow forecast and analysis workbook.

2. **Enter the Initial Cash Investment value.**

   The initial cash investment is the amount required to acquire the investment. Enter a cash outflow as a positive amount and a cash inflow as a negative amount. If you use debt to fund a portion of the purchase, the initial cash investment is probably the gross sales price of the asset less the amount of the debt.

3. Enter the Pretax and After-Tax Reinvestment Rates.

The Pretax and After-Tax Reinvestment Rate figures apply to the adjusted rate of return calculations. The rates represent the forecasted returns at which interim cash flows will be reinvested over the holding period. Generally, pretax rates approximate the yields delivered by intermediate-term taxable bonds, and the after-tax rates approximate the yields delivered by intermediate-term tax-exempt bonds. You don't want to commingle returns with different tax treatment. Both the pretax return and the interest income from a taxable bond are taxable. Both the after-tax return and the interest income from a tax-exempt bond are nontaxable. You pick bonds with intermediate maturities because the maturity of the asset or investment is typically intermediate.

NOTE   *You use the Pretax Reinvestment Rate value to calculate pretax adjusted rates of return, so if you do not want to calculate pretax adjusted rates of return, you do not need to enter this value. And you use the After-Tax Reinvestment Rate value to calculate after-tax adjusted rates of return, so if you do not want to calculate after-tax adjusted rates of return, you do not need to enter this value.*

4. Enter the Pretax and After-Tax Discount Rate values.

The Pretax and After-Tax Discount Rate figures apply to the net present value calculations. Generally, the pretax discount rate approximates the pretax internal rate of return delivered on assets and investments with a similar level of risk, and the after-tax discount rate approximates the after-tax internal rate of return delivered by similarly risky assets and investments. However, wide diversity continues to exist in both the theory and practice of developing and using appropriate discount rates for net present value analysis.

NOTE   *You use the Pretax Discount Rate value to calculate pretax net present values, so if you do not want to calculate pretax net present values, you do not need to enter this value. And you use the After-Tax Discount Rate value to calculate after-tax net present values, so if you do not want to calculate after-tax net present values, you do not need to enter this value.*

5. Enter the Gross Sales value forecasted for each period of the forecasting horizon.

The Gross Sales values represent the forecasted sales generated by the asset or investment over each of the periods of the forecasting horizon. You use these forecasts to estimate the income tax expense and the cash flows. Accordingly, implicit in the construction of the workbook is the assumption that you use cash-basis accounting for income tax purposes and for development of the sales forecasts.

Enter cash inflows as positive amounts and cash outflows as negative amounts. (If you are analyzing the cash flows from financial assets, this amount might be the investment revenue forecasted for each period. If you are analyzing the cash flows from assets that deliver productivity or efficiency gains, this amount might be the cost savings forecasted for each period.)

6. **Enter the Cost of Sales values forecasted for each period of the forecasting horizon.**

The Cost of Sales values represent the forecasted costs that are tied to sales generated over the forecasting horizon. These values might include cost of goods sold, selling costs, and perhaps other variable sales costs, such as commissions owed salespeople. You use these forecasts to estimate the taxable income and the cash flows.

Enter cash outflows as positive amounts and cash inflows as negative amounts. (If you are analyzing the cash flows from a financial asset or an asset that delivers productivity gains, this amount might be zero for each period.)

7. **Enter the Cost Center costs for Cost Centers 1, 2, and 3.**

The operating expenses for Cost Centers 1, 2, and 3 represent the cash basis operating expenses for the forecasting horizon. These values might be three expense classifications related to holding the asset or investment, or they might be the total expenses for three groups of expenses. You use these forecasts to estimate the taxable income and the cash flows.

In the Cost Center 1 Costs row, enter those costs that fall into the first classification or category. In the Cost Center 2 Costs row, enter those costs that fall into the second classification or category. In the Cost Center 3 Costs row, enter those costs that fall into the third classification or category. Be sure to enter cash outflows as positive amounts and cash inflows as negative amounts.

8. **Enter the Interest Expense value, the cost of carrying any debt used to fund a portion of the asset or investment purchase.**

The Interest Expense values represent the period interest expense of carrying any debt related to the asset purchase. The interest expense equals zero when you use no debt in the asset or investment purchase. You use these forecasts to estimate the taxable income and the cash flows.

9. **Enter the Marginal Income Tax Rate values.**

The Marginal Income Tax Rate value is the percentage that, when multiplied by the operating profit (or loss) for the period, calculates the income tax expense (or savings). If you are interested only in calculating pretax profit measures, enter zero as this amount.

10. **Enter the Depreciation expenses included in the expense categories 1, 2, or 3 of the forecasting horizon.**

The Depreciation expenses represent the amounts of depreciation included in operating expenses for Cost Centers 1, 2, and 3 for the forecasting horizon. When no depreciation is included in the operating expenses for Cost Centers 1, 2, and 3, this amount equals zero.

11. **Enter the Other Noncash Expenses values for the forecasting horizon.**

The Other Noncash Expenses values represent the amounts of noncash expenses other than depreciation, included in operating expenses for Cost Centers 1, 2, and 3 for the forecasting horizon. Examples of such noncash expenses include the depletion of natural resource assets and the amortization of intangible assets. When no other noncash expenses exist in the operating expenses for Cost Centers 1, 2, and 3, these amounts equal zero.

12. **Enter the Debt Principal Payments values.**

The Debt Principal Payments values represent the cash paid out to reduce any debt used to fund any portions of the asset or investment purchase. If you use no debt in the asset or investment purchase or you use debt for which the payments you made include only interest, these amounts equal zero.

13. **Enter the Other Cash Nonexpenses values.**

The Other Cash Nonexpenses values represent the amounts of cash nonexpenses, other than debt principal payments, that affect cash flows but not profits. Examples of such noncash expenses include the expenses that are not deductible for calculation of taxable profits, such as life insurance on key employees, and expenditures that are not expenses, such as deposits paid to vendors and suppliers.

14. **Enter the Gross Residual value forecasted for each period of the forecasting horizon.**

The Gross Residual values represent the figures at which you can dispose of the asset or investment on the forecasting horizon. You use these amounts to calculate the capital gains (or losses) and the liquidation cash flows. If the asset or investment cannot be liquidated except at the end of the holding period, you need to enter only the final residual forecast.

15. **Enter the Transaction/Disposal Costs values.**

The Transaction/Disposal costs values represent any incidental expenses or costs of disposing of the asset or investment. Examples include removal costs and brokerage fees. You use these amounts to calculate the capital gains (or losses) and the liquidation cash flows. You need only enter Transaction/Disposal Costs figures for those periods for which you forecast a gross residual.

16. **Enter the Outstanding Debt on Asset(s) values.**

The Outstanding Debt on Asset(s) values represent the debt that you will pay off as a result of disposing of the asset. You need to enter outstanding debt figures only for those periods for which you forecast a gross residual.

17. **Enter the Nontaxable Portion of Residual values.**

The Nontaxable Portion of Residual values represent those amounts of the cash received upon disposal that are not subject to capital gains taxes. You use these amounts to calculate the capital gains (or losses) and the liquidation cash flows. Typically, the nontaxable portion of the residual is the net book value of the asset or investment. If no depreciation has been charged, this means the nontaxable portion equals the original cost. You need to enter the Nontaxable Portion of Residual figures only for those periods for which you forecast a gross residual.

18. **Enter the Marginal Tax Rate on Residual value.**

The Marginal Tax Rate on Residual, or capital gains rate, represents the percentage that, when multiplied by the net gain or loss stemming from the disposal of the asset, calculates the capital gains tax expense (or savings). You need to enter Marginal Tax Rate on Residual figures only for those periods for which you forecast a gross residual.

After you enter the required inputs, the workbook makes the calculations necessary to construct pro forma cash flow forecasts and calculate a standard set of investment measures.

Understanding the Workbook's Calculations

The cash flow forecast and analysis workbook has eight parts: the inputs area, the Profit and Loss Statement, the Gain and Loss Statement, the Operating Cash Flows Statement, the Liquidation Cash Flows Statement, the Cash Flow Analysis, the Pretax Cash Flow Scenarios, and the After-Tax Cash Flow Scenarios.

Cash Flow Forecasting Inputs

Only one set of formulas exists in the inputs area of the cash flow forecast and analysis workbook: the one in the second row that identifies the period for which the results are calculated. The rest of the rows contain input cells where you can enter your own data. Unless you turn off cell protection, these are the only cells in which you can enter data.

The period identifier simply numbers the periods forecasted. The start of the first period is stored as the integer 0. (Using zero as the starting balance is the traditional way to identify those cash flows that are not discounted because they occur at the beginning of the forecasting horizon.) Periods that follow are stored as the previous period plus one.

NOTE   *The period identifiers are formatted with a custom format that places the word* period *in front of the period identifier. If you want to change this, simply use another number format.*

Profit and Loss Statement

The Profit and Loss Statement schedule has 12 rows that contain calculated data, as shown in Figure 21-2.

	Period 1	Period 2	Period 3	Period 4	Period 5	Period 6	Period 7	Period 8	Period 9	Period 10
Profit and Loss Statement										
Gross Sales	$10,000	$10,000	$10,000	$10,000	$10,000	$10,000	$10,000	$10,000	$10,000	$10,000
Less: Cost of Sales	(2,500)	(2,500)	(2,500)	(2,500)	(2,500)	(2,500)	(2,500)	(2,500)	(2,500)	(2,500)
Gross Margin	7,500	7,500	7,500	7,500	7,500	7,500	7,500	7,500	7,500	7,500
Operating Expenses										
Cost Center 1	3,000	3,000	3,000	3,000	3,000	3,000	3,000	3,000	3,000	3,000
Cost Center 2	1,000	1,000	1,000	1,000	1,000	1,000	1,000	1,000	1,000	1,000
Cost Center 3	1,000	1,000	1,000	1,000	1,000	1,000	1,000	1,000	1,000	1,000
Total Operating Expenses	5,000	5,000	5,000	5,000	5,000	5,000	5,000	5,000	5,000	5,000
Operating Income	2,500	2,500	2,500	2,500	2,500	2,500	2,500	2,500	2,500	2,500
Interest Expense	1,000	1,000	1,000	1,000	1,000	1,000	1,000	1,000	1,000	1,000
Net Income (Loss) Before Taxes	1,500	1,500	1,500	1,500	1,500	1,500	1,500	1,500	1,500	1,500
Income Tax Expenses (Savings)	495	495	495	495	495	495	495	495	495	495
Net Income (Loss) After Taxes	$1,005	$1,005	$1,005	$1,005	$1,005	$1,005	$1,005	$1,005	$1,005	$1,005
Gain and Loss Statement	Period 1	Period 2	Period 3	Period 4	Period 5	Period 6	Period 7	Period 8	Period 9	Period 10
Gross Residual	$25,000	$25,000	$25,000	$25,000	$25,000	$25,000	$25,000	$25,000	$25,000	$25,000
Less: Transaction/Disposal Costs	(1,250)	(1,250)	(1,250)	(1,250)	(1,250)	(1,250)	(1,250)	(1,250)	(1,250)	(1,250)
Net Residual	23,750	23,750	23,750	23,750	23,750	23,750	23,750	23,750	23,750	23,750
Nontaxable Portion of Residual	22,500	20,000	17,500	15,000	12,500	10,000	7,500	5,000	2,500	0
Pretax Gain (Loss) on Disposal	1,250	3,750	6,250	8,750	11,250	13,750	16,250	18,750	21,250	23,750
Income Tax Expenses (Savings)	350	1,050	1,750	2,450	3,150	3,850	4,550	5,250	5,950	6,650
After-Tax Gain (Loss) on Disposal	$900	$2,700	$4,500	$6,300	$8,100	$9,900	$11,700	$13,500	$15,300	$17,100

Figure 21-2   The Profit and Loss Statement schedule of the cash flow forecast and analysis workbook.

Gross Sales

The Gross Sales figures show the sales estimates. You enter this amount in the inputs area of the workbook. The Profit and Loss Statement simply references the input value you supply.

Less: Cost of Sales

The Cost of Sales figures show the cost of sales estimates. You enter this amount in the inputs area of the workbook. Again, the Profit and Loss Statement simply references the input value you supply.

Gross Margin

The Gross Margin figures show the amounts left over from the sales proceeds after paying for the cost of sales. The Gross Margin figures represent the amount of cash that goes toward paying your other expenses and your profits.

The Gross Margin value for each period is the Gross Sales figure for the period less the Cost of Sales figure. But because the Cost of Sales figures are pulled into the Profit and Loss Statement as negative amounts, the Gross Margin formula simply adds the positive Gross Sales figure to the negative Cost of Sales figure. For example, the formula for the first period is:

```
=C26+C27
```

The formula for the second period is:

```
=D26+D27
```

and so on.

Operating Expenses – Cost Centers 1, 2, and 3

The figures in these three rows show the amounts of the operating expenses for the three categories entered in the inputs area of the workbook.

Total Operating Expenses

The Total Operating Expenses figures show the sums of the operating expenses entered in the inputs area of the workbook for the three expense categories. For example, the formula for the first period is:

```
=SUM(C31:C33)
```

The formula for the second period is:

```
=SUM(D31:D33)
```

and so on.

Operating Income

The Operating Income figures show the amounts of sales dollars left after paying the cost of sales and the operating expenses. The Operating Income figures represent the amounts that go toward paying you financing expenses, income taxes, and profits.

The Operating Income value for each period is the Gross Margin figure for the period minus the Total Operating Expenses figure. For example, the formula for the first period is:

```
=C28-C34
```

The formula for the second period is:

```
=D28-D34
```

and so on.

Interest Expense

The Interest Expense figures show the amounts required to carry any debt used to fund portions of your asset or investment purchase. If you used no debt to fund the purchase, these amounts are zero.

The Interest Expense value for each period is the value you enter in the inputs area of the workbook.

Net Income (Loss) Before Taxes

The Net Income (Loss) Before Taxes figures represent the amounts of operating income left after paying any interest expense. These amounts represent your taxable operating profits.

The Net Income (Loss) Before Taxes figure for each period is the Operating Income figure minus the Interest Expense figure. For example, the formula for the first period is:

```
=C35-C37
```

The formula for the second period is:

`=D35-D37`

and so on.

Income Tax Expenses (Savings)

The Income Tax Expenses (Savings) figures show the forecasted income tax expenses (or savings) using the pretax operating profits calculated and the marginal income tax rates entered in the inputs area of the workbook.

The Income Tax Expenses (Savings) figure for each period is the Net Income (Loss) Before Taxes figure multiplied by the Marginal Income Tax Rate figure. For example, the formula for the first period is:

`=C14*C38`

The formula for the second period is:

`=D14*D38`

and so on.

Net Income (Loss) After Taxes

The Net Income (Loss) After Taxes figures show the after-tax profits of holding the asset or investment.

The Net Income (Loss) After Taxes value for each period is the Net Income (Loss) Before Taxes figure minus the Income Tax Expenses (Savings) figure. For example, the formula for the first period is:

`=C38-40`

The formula for the second period is:

`=D38-D40`

and so on.

Gain and Loss Statement

The Gain and Loss Statement schedule has seven rows of calculated data (see Figure 21-2).

Gross Residual

The Gross Residual figures show the total amounts for which the asset or investment can be liquidated for each period of the forecasting horizon. You enter these figures in the inputs area of the workbook.

Less: Transaction/Disposal Costs

The Transaction/Disposal Costs figures show the costs associated with liquidating the asset or investment for each period of the forecasting horizon. You enter these figures in the inputs area of the workbook.

Net Residual

The Net Residual figures are the amounts left over from liquidating an asset or investment after paying any transaction or disposal costs, using the Gross Residual figures and the Transaction/Disposal Costs figures.

The Net Residual figure for each period is the Gross Residual figure minus the Transaction/Disposal Costs figure. But because the Transaction/Disposal Costs figure is pulled into the Gain and Loss Statement schedule as a negative amount, the Net Residual formula simply adds the positive Gross Residual figure to the negative Transaction/Disposal Costs figure. For example, the formula for the first period is:

```
=C45+C46
```

The formula for the second period is:

```
=D45+D46
```

and so on.

Nontaxable Portion of Residual

The Nontaxable Portion of Residual figures show the amounts of the residuals that are not included in capital gains or losses calculations. You enter these figures in the inputs area of the workbook.

Pretax Gain (Loss) on Disposal

The Pretax Gain (Loss) on Disposal figures are the capital gains or losses that must be included in capital gains tax calculations.

The Pretax Gain (Loss) on Disposal figure for each period is the Net Residual figure minus the Nontaxable Portion of Residual figure. For example, the formula for the first period is:

```
=C47-C49
```

The formula for the second period is:

```
=D47-D49
```

and so on.

Income Tax Expenses (Savings)

The Income Tax Expenses (Savings) figures represent the tax effect of the liquidation of the asset or investment, calculated by using the Pretax Gain (Loss) on Disposal figures and the Marginal Income Tax Rate figures entered in the inputs area of the workbook.

The Income Tax Expenses (Savings) value for each period is calculated by multiplying the Marginal Tax Rate on Residual figure by the Pretax Gain (Loss) on Disposal figure. For example, the formula for the first period is:

```
=C50*C23
```

The formula for the second period is:

```
=D50*D23
```

and so on.

After-Tax Gain (Loss) on Disposal

The After-Tax Gain (Loss) on Disposal figures show the after-tax profit (or loss) from liquidating the asset or investment.

The After-Tax Gain (Loss) on Disposal value for each period is the Pretax Gain (Loss) on Disposal figure minus the Income Tax Expenses (Savings) figure stemming from the disposal. For example, the formula for the first period is:

```
=C50-C52
```

The formula for the second period is:

```
=D50-D52
```

and so on.

Operating Cash Flows Statement

The Operating Cash Flows Statement schedule has eight rows with calculated data, as shown in Figure 21-3.

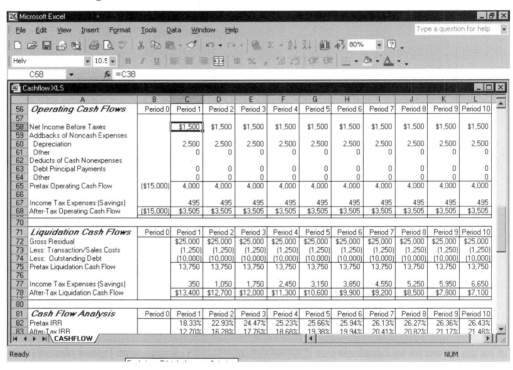

Figure 21-3 The Operating Cash Flows and Liquidation Cash Flows schedules of the cash flow forecast and analysis workbook.

Net Income Before Taxes

The Net Income Before Taxes figure shows the pretax profits calculated on the Profit and Loss Statement.

Addbacks of Noncash Expenses – Depreciation

The Depreciation figures show the depreciation expenses included in the three operating expense classifications or categories. You enter these amounts in the inputs area of the workbook.

Addbacks of Noncash Expenses – Other

The Other Noncash Expenses figures show the other noncash expenses included in the three operating expense categories. You enter these amounts in the inputs area of the workbook.

Deducts of Cash Nonexpenses – Debt Principal Payments

The Debt Principal Payments figures show the debt principal payments made to reduce the debt used to fund a portion of the asset or investment purchase. You enter these amounts in the inputs area of the workbook.

Deducts of Cash Nonexpenses – Other

The Other Cash Nonexpense figures show the other cash payments you made that were not expenses and, therefore, were not included in the three operating expense categories. You enter these amounts in the inputs area of the workbook.

Pretax Operating Cash Flow

The Pretax Operating Cash Flow figures are the pretax cash expended or received as a result of holding the asset or investment. The first cash flow figure shows the initial cash outlay needed to acquire the asset or investment. The second and subsequent cash flow figures show the pretax operating cash flow figures. The Cash Flow Analysis Statement schedule uses these pretax cash flows to calculate the pretax profitability and liquidity measures.

The Pretax Operating Cash Flow value for Period 0, the initial cash investment required to acquire the investment, is the value you enter in the inputs area of the workbook. Notice that this amount is pulled into the Operating Cash Flows Statement schedule as a negative amount because it is an outflow. The Pretax Operating Cash Flow values for subsequent periods are calculated by adding noncash expenses to the net income (Loss) Before Taxes figure and subtracting the Other Cash Nonexpenses figure from the Net Income (Loss) Before Taxes figure. For example, the formula for the first period is:

```
=C58+C60+C61-C63-C64
```

The formula for the second period is:

```
=D58+D60+D61-D63-D64
```

and so on.

Income Tax Expenses (Savings)

The Income Tax Expenses (Savings) figures show the income tax expenses (or savings) calculated in the Profit and Loss Statement schedule.

After-Tax Operating Cash Flow

The After-Tax Operating Cash Flow figures are calculated by using the Pretax Operating Cash Flow figures and the Income Tax Expenses (Savings) figures. The Cash Flow Analysis schedule uses these after-tax cash flows to calculate the after-tax profitability and liquidity measures.

The After-Tax Operating Cash Flow value for Period 0, the initial cash investment, is pulled from the cell containing the pretax operating cash flow (B65). The figures for subsequent periods are calculated as the Pretax Operating Cash Flow figure minus the Income Tax Expenses (Savings) figure. For example, the formula for the first period is:

```
=C65-C67
```

The formula for the second period is:

```
=D65-D67
```

and so on.

Liquidation Cash Flow Statement

The Liquidation Cash Flow Statement schedule has six rows with calculated data (see Figure 21-3).

Gross Residual

The Gross Residual figures show the amounts for which the asset or investment can be sold. You enter these amounts in the inputs area of the workbook.

Less: Transaction/Sales Costs

The Transaction/Sales Costs figures show the expenses of liquidating the asset or investment. You enter these amounts in the inputs area of the workbook.

Less: Outstanding Debt

The Outstanding Debt figures show the principal balances of any debt used to fund portions of the asset or investment purchase. You enter these amounts in the inputs area of the workbook.

Pretax Liquidation Cash Flow

The Pretax Liquidation Cash Flow figure is calculated as the Gross Residual figure minus the Transaction/Sales Costs figure and minus the Outstanding Debt figure. But because the Transaction/Sales Costs figure and the Outstanding Debt figure are pulled into the Liquidation Cash Flow Statement schedule as negative amounts, the Pretax Liquidation Cash Flow formula simply adds the Gross Residual figure to the negative Transaction/Sales Costs figure and the negative Outstanding Debt figure. For example, the formula for the first period is:

```
=C72+C73+C74
```

The formula for the second period is:

```
=D72+D73+D74
```

and so on.

Income Tax Expenses (Savings)

Income Tax Expenses (Savings) figures show any capital gains taxes associated with liquidating the asset or investment.

The figure for each period is the value calculated in the Gain and Loss Statement schedule.

After-Tax Liquidation Cash Flow

The After-Tax Liquidation Cash Flow figures are the after-tax cash received as a result of liquidating an asset or investment at the end of the period.

The After-Tax Liquidation Cash Flow value for each period is the Pretax Liquidation Cash Flow figure minus the Income Tax expenses (Savings) figure. For example, the formula for the first period is:

```
=C75-C77
```

The formula for the second period is:

```
=D75-D77
```

and so on.

Cash Flow Analysis

The Cash Flow Analysis schedule calculates the profitability and liquidity measures for each of the alternative holding periods, as shown in Figure 21-4. The schedule has 10 rows with calculated data. The values for Pretax IRR, After-Tax IRR, Pretax Adjusted IRR, After-Tax Adjusted IRR, Pretax Net Present Value, and After-Tax Net Present Value are similar in that the value shown in the Period 1 column assumes that the asset or investment is purchased at the beginning of the first period (Period 0), is held for one period, and then is sold at the end of the first period. Similarly, the values shown in the subsequent period columns assume that the asset or investment is purchased at the beginning of the first period and then is sold at the end of the indicated period. These values often fluctuate, depending on the holding period. By developing and examining the values delivered by the asset or investment under alternative holding periods, you can choose holding periods that enhance profits. For example, a 10% pretax internal rate of return of an asset or investment held for three years means you get back not only all your initial investment but a dime a year for every dollar invested. An 8% pretax internal rate of return for the same asset or investment held for four years means you get back all your initial investment but only eight cents for every dollar invested a year.

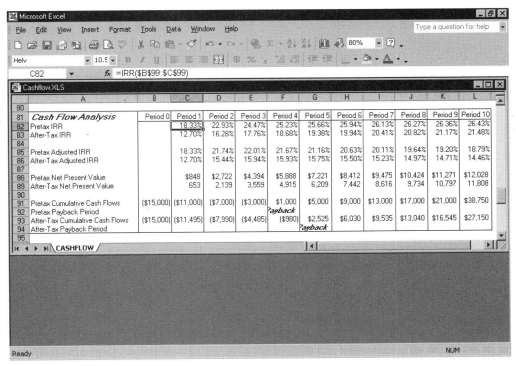

Figure 21-4 The Cash Flow Analysis schedule of the cash flow forecast and analysis workbook.

Pretax IRR

The Pretax IRR figures are the pretax internal rates of return, which are calculated by using the pretax operating and liquidation cash flows that are generated by the asset or investment, assuming the asset or investment is held through the end of the period.

The specific Pretax IRR (internal rate of return) figure for each period is calculated by using the figures in the Pretax Cash Flow Scenarios schedule. The formula for the first period is:

```
=IRR($B$99:$C$99)
```

The formula for the second period is:

```
=IRR($B$100:$C$100)
```

and so on. The values in the IRR function represent the pretax cash flows forecasted if the asset or investment is held through the period.

After-Tax IRR

The After-Tax IRR figures are the after-tax internal rates of return, which are calculated by using the after-tax operating and liquidation cash flows that are generated by the asset or investment, assuming the asset or investment is held through the end of the period.

The specific After-Tax IRR (internal rate of return) figure for each period is calculated by using the figures in the After-Tax Cash Flow Scenarios schedule. The formula for the first period is:

```
=IRR($B$112:$C$112)
```

The formula for the second period is:

```
=IRR($B$113:$C$113)
```

and so on. The values in the IRR function represent the after-tax cash flows forecasted if the asset or investment is held through the period.

Note that the equation that calculates the internal rates of return for an asset or investment held 10 periods is, by definition, a tenth root polynomial equation with up to 10 correct solutions. Accordingly, several internal rates of return can be correct for any investment you analyze. Be particularly careful in applying the internal rate of return measure to those assets or investments for which cash flows fluctuate between positive and negative amounts. Generally, an asset or investment has as many correct IRRs as sign changes in the cash flow. If there is only one sign change—for example, if the initial investment is negative and all the cash flows that follow are positive—you have only one IRR. However, if the first cash flow and fourth cash flows are negative, there are three sign changes and up to three correct IRRs. (The first sign change is the initial negative cash flow changing to positive, the second is the third-period changing to the fourth-period negative, and the third is the fourth-period negative changing to the fifth-period positive cash flow.) For this reason, you might want to use the adjusted rate of return or the net present value profit measure instead of the internal rate of return measure.

Pretax Adjusted IRR

The Pretax Adjusted IRR figures are the pretax internal rates of return, which are calculated by using the pretax operating and liquidation cash flows that are generated by the asset or investment, assuming that the asset or investment is held through the end of the period and assuming that any interim cash flows are reinvested at the pretax reinvestment rate specified in the inputs area of the workbook. (Notice that in Period 1, because there would be no interim cash flows—both the operating and liquidation cash flows occur at the end of the first period—the pretax adjusted IRR equals the pretax IRR.) This schedule assumes that when you buy an asset or make an investment at the beginning of the first period and sell at the end of the second period, you reinvest the operating cash flow generated by the investment in the first period at the pretax reinvestment rate specified in the inputs area of the workbook until the end of the second period.

The figure for each period's Pretax Adjusted IRR (internal rate of return adjusted for reinvestment of the interim cash flows) is calculated by using the figures in the Pretax Cash Flow Scenarios schedule and the Pretax Reinvestment Rate figure specified in the inputs area of the workbook. The formula for the first period is:

```
=MIRR($B$99:$C$99,,$B$4)
```

The formula for the second period is:

```
=MIRR($B$100:$C$100,,$B$4)
```

and so on. The values used in the MIRR function represent the pretax cash flows forecasted if the asset or investment is held through the period. The contents of the cell referenced by $B$4 is the pretax reinvestment rate.

After-Tax Adjusted IRR

The After-Tax Adjusted IRR figures are the after-tax internal rates of return, which are calculated by using the after-tax operating and liquidation cash flows that are generated by the asset or investment, assuming the asset or investment is held through the end of the period and assuming that any interim cash flows are reinvested at the after-tax reinvestment rate specified in the inputs area of the workbook. (Notice that in Period 1, because there would be no interim cash flows—both the operating and liquidation cash flows occur at the end of the first period—the after-tax adjusted IRR equals the after-tax IRR.) This schedule assumes that when you buy an asset or make an investment at the beginning of the first period and sell at the end of the second period, you reinvest the operating cash flow generated by the investment in the first period at the after-tax reinvestment rate specified in the inputs area of the workbook until the end of the second period.

The figure for each period's After-Tax Adjusted IRR (internal rate of return adjusted for reinvestment of the interim cash flows) is calculated by using the figures in the After-Tax Cash Flow Scenarios schedule and the After-Tax Reinvestment Rate figure specified in the inputs area of the workbook. The formula for the first period is:

```
=MIRR($B$112:$C$112,,$B$5)
```

The formula for the second period is:

```
=MIRR($B$113:$C$113,,$B$5)
```

and so on. The values in the MIRR function represent the after-tax cash flows forecasted if the asset or investment is held through the period. The contents of the cell referenced by $B$5 is the after-tax reinvestment rate.

Pretax Net Present Value

The Pretax Net Present Value figures are calculated by using the pretax operating and liquidation cash flows generated by the asset or investment, assuming the asset or investment is held through the end of the period, and by using the pretax discount rate specified in the inputs area of the workbook. Pretax net present values are significant in that they express in current cash the amount by which the investment falls short of or exceeds the time value of money specified by the pretax discount rate. For example, a $1,000 net present value of an asset or investment held for three years means that holding the investment for three years returns $1,000 more (in the current dollar value) than the pretax discount rate specifies. A negative $500 net present value for the same asset or investment held four years means that holding the asset or investment for four years returns $500 less (in current dollar value) than the pretax discount rate specifies. The pretax net present values often fluctuate, depending on the holding period. By developing and examining the pretax net present values delivered by the asset or investment under alternative holding periods, you can choose holding periods to enhance pretax profits.

For instance, in the example introduced in the preceding sentences, you actually lose $1,500 by holding the investment an additional (fourth) year. (The $1,500 of loss is the difference between making $1,000, which is what happens if you hold the investment for three years, and losing $500, which is what happens if you hold the investment for four years.)

The Pretax Net Present Value figure for each period is calculated by using the figures in the Pretax Cash Flow Scenarios schedule and the Pretax Discount Rate figure specified in the inputs area of the workbook. The formula for the first period is:

```
=NPV($B$6,$C$99:$C$99)+$B$99
```

The formula for the second period is:

```
=NPV($B$6,$C$100:$C$100)+$B$100
```

and so on. The values in the NPV function represent the pretax cash flows forecasted if the asset or investment is held through the period. The contents of the cell referenced by $B$6 is the pretax discount rate. The amount added to the NPV function is the initial investment.

After-Tax Net Present Value

The After-Tax Net Present Value figures are calculated by using the after-tax operating and liquidation cash flows generated by the asset or investment, assuming the asset or investment is held through the end of the period, and by using the after-tax discount rate specified in the inputs area of the workbook. After-tax net present values are significant in that they express in current cash the amount by which the investment falls short of or exceeds the time value of money specified by the after-tax discount rate. For example, a $1,000 net present value of an asset or investment held for three years means that holding the investment for three years returns $1,000 more (in current dollar value) than the after-tax discount rate specifies. A negative $500 net present value for the same asset or investment held four years means that holding the asset or investment for four years returns $500 less (in current dollar value) than the after-tax discount rate specifies. The after-tax net present value often fluctuates, depending on the holding period. By developing and examining the after-tax net present values delivered by the asset or investment under alternative holding periods, you can choose holding periods to enhance after-tax profits. For example, in the example introduced in the preceding sentences, you lose $1,500 by holding the investment an additional (fourth) year.

The After-Tax Net Present Value figure for each period is calculated by using the figures in the After-Tax Cash Flow Scenarios schedule and the After-Tax Discount Rate figure specified in the inputs area of the workbook. The formula for the first period is:

```
=NPV($B$7,$C$112:$C$112)+$B$112
```

The formula for the second period is:

```
=NPV($B$7,$C$113:$C$113)+$B$113
```

and so on. The values in the NPV function represent the after-tax cash flows forecasted if the asset or investment is held through the period. The contents of the cell referenced by $B$7 is the after-tax reinvestment rate. The amount added to the NPV function is the initial investment.

Pretax Cumulative Cash Flows

The Pretax Cumulative Cash Flows figures represent the cumulative cash flows that result from holding the asset or investment, which are calculated by using the pretax cash flows from the Pretax Cash Flows Scenarios schedule, assuming the investment is held for 10 periods. The period during which the cumulative cash flow figure turns from a negative amount to a positive amount indicates the period in which the investment pays back the original cash invested—a common measure of liquidity.

The Pretax Cumulative Cash Flows figure for each period is calculated by using the 10-period holding scenario in the Pretax Cash Flow Scenarios schedule. The formula in the Period 0 column for the initial investment is:

```
=SUM($B$108:B108)
```

The formula for the first period is:

```
=SUM($B$108:C108)
```

The formula for the second period is:

```
=SUM($B$108:D108)
```

and so on. The results represent the cumulative pretax cash flows through the period.

Pretax Payback Period

The Pretax Payback Period is a text flag (the word *Payback*) that identifies the period during which the initial investment and any negative operating cash flows are finally paid back. The text flag appears in the column for the period in which the cumulative cash flow changes from negative to positive.

The Pretax Payback Period formulas determine whether the cumulative pretax cash flow has turned from a negative amount, indicating that the initial investment has not been fully paid back, to a positive amount, indicating that the initial investment has been paid back. The formula for the first period is:

```
=IF((AND(B91<0,C91>0=))=TRUE(),"Payback","")
```

The formula for the second period is:

```
=IF((AND(C91<0,D91>0=))=TRUE(),"Payback","")
```

and so on. For the period during which the initial investment is finally paid back, the text flag *Payback* appears in the column.

After-Tax Cumulative Cash Flows

The After-Tax Cumulative Cash Flows figures represent the cumulative cash flows that result from holding the asset or investment calculated by using the after-tax cash flows as calculated in the After-Tax Cash Flow Scenarios schedule, assuming the investment is held for 10 periods. The period during which the cumulative cash flow figure turns from a negative amount to a positive amount indicates the period in which the investment pays back the original cash invested—a common measure of liquidity.

The After-Tax Cumulative Cash Flows figure for each period is calculated by using the 10-year holding period scenario in the After-Tax Cash Flow Scenarios schedule. The formula for the initial investment is:

```
=SUM($B$121:B121)
```

The formula for the first period is:

```
=SUM($B$121:C121)
```

The formula for the second period is:

```
=SUM($B$121:D121)
```

and so on. The results represent the cumulative after-tax cash flows through the period.

After-Tax Payback Period

The After-Tax Payback Period is a text flag (the word *Payback*) that identifies the period during which the initial investment and any negative operating cash flows are finally paid back. The text flag appears in the column for the period in which the cumulative cash flow moves from a negative amount to a positive amount.

The After-Tax Payback Period formulas determine whether the cumulative after-tax cash flow has turned from a negative amount, indicating that the initial investment has not been fully paid back, to a positive amount, indicating that the initial investment has been paid back. The formula for the first period is:

```
=IF((AND(B93<0,C93>=0))=TRUE(),"Payback"," ")
```

The formula for the second period is:

```
=IF((AND(C93<0,D93>=0))=TRUE(),"Payback"," ")
```

and so on. For the period during which the initial investment is finally paid back, the text flag *Payback* appears in the column.

Pretax Cash Flow Scenarios

The Pretax Cash Flow Scenarios schedule has 12 rows, as shown in Figure 21-5. These are the forecasted cash flows for the alternative holding periods and are used to calculate the profitability and liquidity measures in the Cash Flow Analysis schedule. You will probably use this schedule only indirectly because it provides the raw data used to calculate the profitability measures. However, to read the schedule, you simply look down column A, which describes the various lengths of time you can hold the asset or investment, until you come to the number of periods held that you want to examine—that row then shows the cash flows occurring each period for the number-of-periods-held scenario. For example, suppose you want to view the pretax cash flows if the investment is held for five periods. You first look down the first column of the Pretax Cash Flow Scenarios column. When you come to 5, you're at the row that shows the cash flows that assume you hold the asset or investment for five periods. The negative amount in column B shows the Period 0 cash flow ($15,000 in Figure 21-5). The positive amounts in columns C through F in Figure 21-5 show the operating cash flow of $4,000. The positive cash flow in column G shows the combined operating and liquidation cash flows as $17,750. Notice that in columns H and beyond, representing periods and beyond, the amounts appear as 0 because the asset or investment has been disposed of and, therefore, no longer results in cash flows.

C82 = IRR($B$99:$C$99)

Pretax Cash Flow Scenarios

Number of Periods Held:	Period 0	Period 1	Period 2	Period 3	Period 4	Period 5	Period 6	Period 7	Period 8	Period 9	Period 10
1	($15,000)	$17,750	$0	$0	$0	$0	$0	$0	$0	$0	$0
2	(15,000)	4,000	17,750	0	0	0	0	0	0	0	0
3	(15,000)	4,000	4,000	17,750	0	0	0	0	0	0	0
4	(15,000)	4,000	4,000	4,000	17,750	0	0	0	0	0	0
5	(15,000)	4,000	4,000	4,000	4,000	17,750	0	0	0	0	0
6	(15,000)	4,000	4,000	4,000	4,000	4,000	17,750	0	0	0	0
7	(15,000)	4,000	4,000	4,000	4,000	4,000	4,000	17,750	0	0	0
8	(15,000)	4,000	4,000	4,000	4,000	4,000	4,000	4,000	17,750	0	0
9	(15,000)	4,000	4,000	4,000	4,000	4,000	4,000	4,000	4,000	17,750	0
10	(15,000)	4,000	4,000	4,000	4,000	4,000	4,000	4,000	4,000	4,000	17,750

After-Tax Cash Flow Scenarios

Number of Periods Held:	Period 0	Period 1	Period 2	Period 3	Period 4	Period 5	Period 6	Period 7	Period 8	Period 9	Period 10
1	($15,000)	$16,905	$0	$0	$0	$0	$0	$0	$0	$0	$0
2	(15,000)	3,505	16,205	0	0	0	0	0	0	0	0
3	(15,000)	3,505	3,505	15,505	0	0	0	0	0	0	0
4	(15,000)	3,505	3,505	3,505	14,805	0	0	0	0	0	0
5	(15,000)	3,505	3,505	3,505	3,505	14,105	0	0	0	0	0
6	(15,000)	3,505	3,505	3,505	3,505	3,505	13,405	0	0	0	0
7	(15,000)	3,505	3,505	3,505	3,505	3,505	3,505	12,705	0	0	0
8	(15,000)	3,505	3,505	3,505	3,505	3,505	3,505	3,505	12,005	0	0
9	(15,000)	3,505	3,505	3,505	3,505	3,505	3,505	3,505	3,505	11,305	0
10	(15,000)	3,505	3,505	3,505	3,505	3,505	3,505	3,505	3,505	3,505	10,605

Figure 21-5 The Pretax and After-Tax Cash Flow Scenarios schedules of the cash flow forecast and analysis workbook.

Period 0

The values in the Period 0 cash flows column show the initial cash outlay to acquire the asset or investment and are the same for each of the alternative holding periods.

The Period 0 cash flow, which is the initial cash outlay to acquire the asset or investment, is the same for each of the holding periods in the Pretax Cash Flow Scenarios schedule.

Period 1 Through 10

The period cash flows show the forecasted pretax cash flow stemming from holding and perhaps disposing of an asset or investment for each of 10 periods. For example, the Period 1 pretax cash flow for holding period 1 equals the sum of both the pretax operating cash flow and the pretax liquidation cash flow for the first period; cash flows beyond the first period equal zero, signifying that asset or investment has been liquidated. Similarly, the Period 2 pretax cash flow for holding period 2 equals the sum of the pretax operating cash flow and the pretax liquidation cash flow for the second period; cash flows for Period 3 and beyond for holding period 2 equal zero. The Period 1 pretax cash flow for holding period 2 equals the pretax operating cash flow for the first period. This schedule provides the alternative pretax cash flows used in the pretax profitability and liquidity measures shown in the Cash Flow Analysis schedule.

The same basic formula calculates the period cash flows for any of the periods in each of the alternative holding period scenarios. The basic formula uses a nested IF statement with the following structure:

```
IF the period is before the period the asset or investment is
liquidated,

THEN assume that the period cash flow equals the pretax operating cash
flow for the period,

ELSE IF the period is the same as the period the asset or investment
is liquidated,

THEN assume the period cash flow equals the sum of the pretax
operating cash flow and the pretax liquidation cash flow,

ELSE assume the period cash flow is 0 because the period is after the
period the asset or investment was liquidated.
```

For example, the formula to calculate the first-period cash flow when you hold the asset or investment for one period is:

```
=IF(C$98<$A99,C$65,IF(C$98=$A99,C$65+C$75,0))
```

The formula to calculate the second-period cash flow when you hold the asset or investment for one period is:

```
=IF(D$98<$A99,D$65,IF(D$98=$A99,D$65+D$75,0))
```

The formula to calculate the first-period cash flow when you hold the asset or investment for two periods is:

```
=IF(C$98<$A100,C$65,IF(C$98=$A100,C$65+C$75,0))
```

The formula to calculate the second-period cash flow when you hold the asset or investment for two periods is:

```
=IF(D$98<$A100,D$65,IF(D$98=$A100,D$65+D$75,0))
```

and so on.

After-Tax Cash Flow Scenarios

The After-Tax Cash Flow Scenarios schedule has 12 rows (see Figure 21-5). These are the forecasted cash flows for the alternative holding periods and are used to calculate the profitability and liquidity measures in the Cash Flow Analysis schedule.

Period 0

The values in the Period 0 cash flow column show the initial cash outlay to acquire the asset or investment and are the same for each of the alternative holding periods.

The Period 0 cash flow, which is the initial cash outlay to acquire the asset or investment, is the same for each of the holding periods in the After-Tax Cash Flow Scenarios schedule.

Period 1 Through 10

The period cash flows show the forecasted after-tax cash flow stemming from holding and perhaps disposing of an asset or investment for each of 10 periods. For example, the Period 1 after-tax cash flow for holding period 1 equals the sum of both the after-tax operating cash flow and the after-tax liquidation cash flow for the first period; cash flows beyond the first period equal zero, signifying that the asset or investment has been liquidated. Similarly, the Period 2 after-tax cash flow for holding period 2 equals the sum of the after-tax liquidation cash flow for the second period; cash flows for Period 3 and beyond for holding period 2 equal zero. The Period 1 after-tax cash flow for holding period 2 equals the after-tax operating cash flow for the first period. This schedule provides the alternative after-tax cash flows used in the after-tax profitability and liquidity measures shown in the Cash Flow Analysis schedule.

The same basic formula calculates the period cash flows for any of the periods in each of the alternative holding period scenarios. The basic formula uses a compound IF function statement with the following structure:

```
IF the period is before the period the asset or investment is
liquidated,
```

THEN assume that the period cash flow equals the after-tax operating cash flow for the period,

ELSE IF the period is the same as the period the asset or investment is liquidated,

THEN assume the period cash flow equals the sum of the after-tax operating cash flow and the after-tax liquidation cash flow,

ELSE assume the period cash flow is 0 because the period is after the period the asset or investment was liquidated.

For example, the formula to calculate the first-period cash flow when you hold the asset or investment for one period is:

```
=IF(C$111<$A112,C$68,IF(C$111=$A112,C$68+C$78,0))
```

The formula to calculate the second-period cash flow when you hold the asset or investment for one period is:

```
=IF(D$111<$A112,D$68,IF(D$111=$A112,D$68+D$78,0))
```

The formula to calculate the first-period cash flow when you hold the asset or investment for one period is:

```
=IF(C$111<$A113,C$68,IF(C$111=$A113,C$68+C$78,0))
```

The formula to calculate the second-period cash flow when you hold the asset or investment for two periods is:

```
=IF(D$111<$A113,D$68,IF(D$111=$A113,D$68+D$78,0))
```

and so on.

Customizing the Workbook

You can use the cash flow forecast and analysis workbook without modification for many cash flow forecasts and analyses. However, you might want to change the workbook so that it more closely matches your requirements. For example, you can add text that describes the asset or investment for which cash flows are forecasted and analyzed. You can increase or decrease the number of periods. For example, you can increase the number of periods to 12 if your periods are months and you want to forecast an entire year. You might also want to remove either the pretax or the after-tax profitability and liquidity measures if you don't consider one or the other in your decision making. Before you change anything in the workbook other than the forecasting inputs, unprotect the document.

Changing the Number of Forecasting Periods

You can easily increase and decrease the number of forecasting periods shown in the cash flow forecast and analysis workbook. To increase the number of periods, follow these steps:

1. **Make room for more columns.**

   Remove the border from the last column of the cash flow forecast and analysis schedules to make room for more columns.

2. **Create more columns.**

   Copy the current last column of the cash flow forecast and analysis schedules to the right to create more columns as needed.

3. **Replace the border.**

   Replace the border on the right of the cash flow forecast and analysis schedules.

4. **Make room for more rows.**

   Remove the bottom borders of the Pretax Cash Flow Scenarios and After-Tax Cash Flow Scenarios schedules.

5. **Create more rows.**

   Copy the last row of both the Pretax Cash Flow Scenarios and After-Tax Cash Flow Scenarios into the same number of rows in the same way that you added columns to the cash flow forecast and analysis summary.

6. **Replace the bottom borders.**

   Replace the bottom borders on both the Pretax Cash Flow Scenarios and the After-Tax Cash Flow Scenarios schedules.

7. **Adjust formulas to account for the new columns and rows.**

   Adjust the pretax and after-tax internal rate of return, adjusted rate of return, and net present value formulas for the new columns so that the cash flow value arguments in the IRR, MIRR, and NPV functions use the correct row of the Pretax Cash Flow Scenarios or After-Tax Cash Flow Scenarios.

To decrease the number of periods, follow these steps:

1. **Delete columns.**

   Delete any unneeded columns from the right side of the schedule.

2. Delete rows.

In the Pretax Cash Flow Scenarios and After-Tax Cash Flow Scenarios schedules, delete the rows that correspond to the columns you deleted.

Removing the Pretax Profitability and Liquidity Measures

To remove the pretax profitability and liquidity measures from the spreadsheet, follow these steps:

1. Delete the Pretax Cash Flow Scenarios schedule.

2. From the Cash Flow Analysis schedule, delete the Pretax IRR, the Pretax Adjusted IRR, the Pretax Net Present Value, the Pretax Cumulative Cash Flows, and the Pretax Payback Period rows.

Removing the After-Tax Profitability and Liquidity Measures

To remove the after-tax profitability and liquidity measures from the spreadsheet, follow these steps:

1. Delete the After-Tax Cash Flow Scenarios schedule.

2. From the Cash Flow Analysis schedule, delete the After-Tax IRR, the After-Tax Adjusted IRR, the After-Tax Net Present Value, the After-Tax Cumulative Cash Flows, and the After-Tax Payback Period rows.

Summary

Cash flow forecasting and discounted cash flow analysis is basic to investment analysis. For most capital investments, there's no way to objectively assess an investment until cash flows and the time value of money are considered. The workbook described and the techniques discussed in this chapter will help you perform just this type of analysis.

Part 4

APPENDIX AND GLOSSARY

Appendix

WRITING A BUSINESS PLAN

Featuring:

- Defining Three Types of Business Plans
- Writing a White Paper Business Plan
- Writing a New Venture Business Plan

If you use the BIZPLAN.XLS workbook described in Chapter 18, there's a good chance you'll also want to draft a written business plan to accompany that workbook. To help you with this task, in this short appendix we clarify what business people really mean when they use the term *business plan* and then provide some suggestions and point you to resources that you can use to make the work of writing a business plan easier and more successful.

Defining Three Types of Business Plans

In our experience, people use the term *business plan* to refer to three distinct items: a firm's overall strategy and roadmap (which we'll call here a *strategic plan*), the 10- to 20-page document that entrepreneurs use to promote a new venture to investors and other key stakeholders (which we'll call here a *new venture plan*), and the 20- or 50- or even 100-page document that a new business owner uses to prove to him- or herself and others that he or she has thought carefully about starting or growing a business (which we'll call here a *white paper plan*).

Unfortunately, we aren't equipped to provide you with useful advice about writing a strategic plan. Writing such a plan requires industry expertise and experience, unique insight about a firm and its place, and the perspective of top management. We can offer some useful information about writing white paper plans and new venture plans, however.

Writing a White Paper Business Plan

If you want to write a white paper plan, know that this process is well documented elsewhere. You can get a detailed outline for a white paper plan (in both English and Spanish), for example, from the United States federal government's Small Business Administration Web site at *http://www.sba.gov/starting/indexbusplans.html*, as shown in Figure A-1.

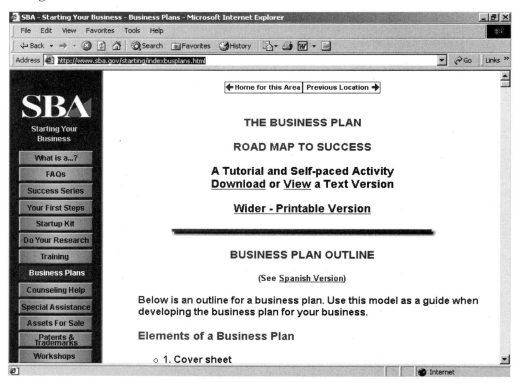

Figure A-1   The Small Business Administration's Business Plan outline lets you create a white paper business plan.

PowerPoint's AutoContent Wizard supplies a detailed template for creating a white-paper-style business plan presentation, as shown in Figure A-2. (For more information about PowerPoint's AutoContent Wizard, refer to Chapter 5.)

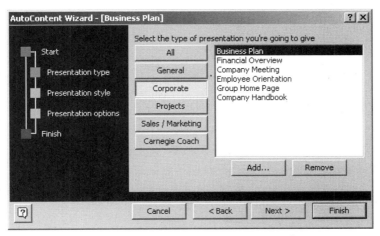

Figure A-2   PowerPoint's AutoContent Wizard lets you create a white paper business plan presentation.

NOTE   *White paper plans would need to include a business pro forma such as you might produce with the BIZPLAN.XLS workbook described in Chapter 18.*

Writing a New Venture Business Plan

If you want to write a new venture plan, you take a different approach. New venture plans, boiled down to their very essence, answer the following five questions that prospective investors need to answer in order to decide whether they should invest:

1. Is a firm's product or service feasible?

For example, can the technology really be developed? Is the necessary legal and regulatory approval obtainable? Does the process work in practice? Obviously, if a firm is already operating, this question doesn't need to be asked and answered. But for many types of new ventures—especially technology companies—the question does need to be discussed.

2. Do customers want the product or service?

In other words, is there true demand? This might sound like a silly question, but potential customers ignore many interesting and seemingly useful products and services.

3. Is the basic transaction profitable?

In other words, will people pay a price that produces a profit? Customers might want products and services that firms can't afford to provide.

4. Is the return on investment adequate?

Even profitable businesses might not be feasible if they require too much capital relative to the profits they generate. New ventures not only need to be profitable but they also need to produce acceptable returns on investments. This return on investment measurement might be measured with either an internal rate of return, which is probably most common, or a net present value, which is most accurate. Note that an input to any return on investment calculation—the investment required to start the venture—is also an important factor in any prospective investor's deliberations.

5. Can the management team operate the business?

Even if you can answer yes to the first four questions, that's not really enough. A new venture will probably fail if the management team lacks the skills to successfully run the business. So the last part of a new venture plan needs to describe the management team and why they're likely to succeed. The ideal answer to this question is, of course, to be able to show through past performance that the management team has successfully run a similar business.

NOTE   *We think you could use these questions as the highest level headings in a new venture plan. The only other headings you might want to add to such a new venture plan would be for an introduction and an executive summary.*

Here are three final observations about new venture plans: First, it's very unlikely that an entrepreneur can honestly answer yes to all five questions. Many new venture plans do, of course, give yes answers to all five questions. But we suggest that an honest answer such as, "we don't yet know," or "it depends on future developments," will attract better and more sophisticated venture investors and increase your chances of success. We also note here that in the recent dot-com hysteria, many new ventures were funded even though they could honestly answer yes to only the first question. (Of course, many shouldn't have been funded, but that's another topic.)

Second, answering no to any of the five questions means the new venture won't work. Each of the five questions is a link in the chain of success. Break a link and the chain breaks, too.

Third, a business pro forma, such as you might build using the BIZPLAN.XLS workbook described in Chapter 18, needs to be part of or an appendix to your new venture plan. By creating a detailed five- or ten-year forecast, you back up your answers and provide more detail to the people reading, and potentially funding, your new venture plan.

GLOSSARY

absolute cell reference

A **cell reference** that isn't adjusted by Excel as it's copied.

active cell

The currently selected **cell** on an Excel **worksheet.**

Active Server Pages

Abbreviated ASP. Dynamically created pages from a Microsoft Access or SQL database.

active sheet

The currently selected (and usually visible) sheet in an Excel worksheet.

ActiveX

A Microsoft technology that is typically used to create small programs that run inside a **Web page.** ActiveX components work in **Internet Explorer** 4 or later, and do not work in Netscape Navigator without an additional **plug-in.**

alignment

How Excel positions **labels** and **values** in **cells.** Typically, labels are left-aligned and values are right-aligned.

animated gif

An image file that shows movement. You commonly see animated gif images on **Web pages.** Many of the motion clips available from the PowerPoint Motion Clip Gallery are animated gifs.

animation

Animation simply means movement. You can add animation to many of the **objects** that appear on a PowerPoint **slide,** including slide text.

applet

A miniature program that is built into an Office program. Examples include **WordArt,** Microsoft Draw, and **Organization Chart.**

application

A program that is designed for a specific task, for example, a **word processor** or a **database.**

application window

The window that opens when you start an Office program.

appointment

In Outlook, a scheduling **item** that has a start time and an end time and that may last less than a day or more than a day.

area chart

An area **chart** plots **data point** values using lines. Optimally, the lines are stacked so they show cumulative data point **values,** and the areas between the lines are colored.

argument

The input **value** supplied to an Excel **function.** Functions can use values, **formulas,** and even other functions as arguments.

attachment

A file that travels along with an **e-mail** message.

AutoContent Wizard

A PowerPoint guide that displays dialog boxes that ask about the **presentation** you want to create. Based on your answers, the **wizard** creates a rough-draft version of the presentation.

AutoText

A feature that lets you quickly and easily type a character or two to insert text or graphics that are stored.

backup

An up-to-date copy of the files on your system.

banner ad

A rectangular-shaped advertisement on a **Web page.**

bar chart

A bar **chart** plots **data point** values in individual bars but arranges the bars so you calibrate them using a horizontal **values** axis.

bookmark

A named location in a document; also a placeholder within a Web page that allows **hyperlinks** to refer to this location within the **Web page.** A bookmark in a Web page is also known as a named anchor.

bubble chart

Treats the horizontal axis as a second **values** axis, thereby plotting pairs of **data points** just **XY charts** do. Bubble **charts** differ from XY charts, however, in that Excel sizes the bubbles using the values of a third data point.

Calendar

In Outlook, the **module** you use to schedule **appointments**.

Cascading Style Sheets

Abbreviated CSS. A standard for applying formatting and positioning information to a **Web page.** CSS information can be used within a Web page or placed in an external style sheet file. Web pages that are linked to external style sheets obtain text-formatting information from the style sheet.

cell

The space at the intersection of a row and column in a table or a **worksheet.**

cell protection

Formatting that prevents a user from entering information into a **cell** or changing the contents of a cell.

cell reference

Each **cell** in an Excel **worksheet** has an address, called a reference, consisting of the column letter and row number. For example, the cell in the top left corner of the worksheet is cell A1.

cell selector

A dark outline that identifies the active **cell** in an Excel **worksheet.** The reference of the **active cell** also appears on the left side of the **formula bar** in the Name box. If you type a number and press the Enter key, Excel places the number in the active cell.

CGI scripts

A standard for running small programs on a **Web server.** Typically used on UNIX Web servers.

character spacing

Expanding or condensing the spaces between letters in a word.

chart

A picture that shows quantitative information. Examples include **pie charts, line charts, bar charts,** and **column charts.**

chart area

The area in a **chart** that includes plot area, any **chart text,** and a **legend.**

chart text

A description of a **chart** or some part of a chart.

chart type

Excel supplies 14 types of **charts: area, bar, bubble, column, cone, cylinder, doughnut, line, pie, pyramid, radar, stock, surface,** and **XY (scatter).** Each chart type uses unique **data markers.**

Chart Wizard

The Excel tool used to quickly and easily create professional, presentation-quality **chart**s based on **worksheet** data.

Click-and-Type

A feature that lets you move the insertion point to any location on the page of a Word document and begin typing.

clip art

Graphics, photographs, line art, video, and so on that can be used to provide visual enhancement to a document or presentation. The Microsoft Clip Gallery is included with Office applications.

Clipboard

An area in memory that temporarily stores material that you cut or copy.

color scheme

In PowerPoint, a set of eight compatible colors that are used for the parts of the **slides** in a **presentation**.

column chart

A column **chart** plots **data point** values in individual bars but arrange the bars so you calibrate them using a vertical **values** axis.

cone chart

A cone **chart** plots **data point values** in individual three-dimensional cones. Cone charts use either horizontal or vertical category axes.

Contacts

In Outlook, the **module** you use to create and maintain a **database** of contacts.

content editing

Reviewing a document for reading level, logic, omissions, repetition, factual accuracy and consistency, and clarity.

copy editing

Reviewing a document for style, **grammar,** punctuation, spelling, capitalization, logic, organization, and diction.

crawler-based search engine

A **search engine** that automatically "crawls" the Web searching for **Web sites** to examine and include in the search engine's database of Web sites.

criteria

Conditions you specify for **filtering** and **sorting database.**

cross-reference

A phrase that points the reader to more information or related information about the topic at hand.

custom slide show

A list, or subset, of **slides** you want to display as a separate, customized **presentation.**

cylinder chart

A cylinder **chart** plots **data point values** in individual three-dimensional cylinders. Cylinder charts use either horizontal or vertical category axes.

data category

Organizes the **data values** in the **data series** in a **chart.** On any chart that shows how data values change over time, the data category is time, which means that the data category names are time-period identifiers: years, quarters, months, or some other time interval.

Data map

A **chart** that maps geographic data. Excel doesn't create data maps, but the MapPoint program, which comes with Excel, will.

data marker

Graphical elements used to represent individual **data point values** in a **chart,** such as a symbol or point in a **line chart.**

data-marker description

An explanation of **data markers** such as axis scales and data labels.

data point

Individual **values** of a **chart** created from an Excel **worksheet.**

data series

Identifies the information you plot on a **chart.** If you ask the question "What does my chart show?" every one-word answer generally identifies a data series.

data source

A document that contains contact information or a catalog.

data table

A **table** of data that calculates results based on changing one input variable of one or more **formulas** or changing two input variables in a formula.

data value

The number, or numeric value, that Microsoft **Graph** uses to create bars, columns, or lines that visually represent the data on a chart.

database

A range of common information, arranged in consecutive rows and columns. Each **cell** in a row in a **database** contains unique data, while each cell in a column contains similar data.

date values

Values that represent dates. Typically, one formats date values so they look like recognizable dates and not values. By convention, the number 1 represents January 1, 1900.

design template

Provides a **color scheme** in PowerPoint that is used for all the **presentation's slides**; a Title Master slide, which shows how your title slide looks; a Slide Master slide, which shows how the nontitle slides in your presentation look; and a set of slide layouts.

desktop publishing

Using software to combine text and graphics into a document that can be printed on a printer attached to a personal computer or on a typesetting machine at a commercial printer.

digital certificate

An electronic credential that verifies that you are who you say you are when connected to the **Internet**.

discussion group

A part of a **Web site** that emulates **newsgroups,** allowing visitors to post messages and read and reply to other visitors' messages.

DNS

An abbreviation for Domain Name Service. Translates numerical **IP addresses** into user-friendly **domain names,** and vice versa.

Document Map view

Displays a task pane that contains the styles used in a Word document.

document window

The portion of an Office window that displays the current document.

domain

A group of computers on a **network** that all use a central **server** to handle users and security policies. The server must run either Microsoft Windows NT Server or Windows 2000 Server.

domain name

The main part of a **Web** address. Domain names usually represent companies, organizations, or individuals and must be registered with an accredited domain name registrar.

doughnut chart

Similar to a **pie chart**; plots **data series** in concentric rings and shows each **data point value** as a segment, or bite, of the ring.

drag-and-drop

A technique for copying and moving information using the mouse. You drag your selection to the desired new location and when you release the mouse, it drops into place.

drawn object

An **object** you create using the drawing tools in an Office application.

drop cap

A character that is enlarged to set off the first lines in a document.

Dynamic HTML

A version of **HTML** that introduces movement and the ability to react to a user's actions on a **Web page**.

electronic postage

U.S. postage stamps that you can download from the **Internet.**

e-mail

A form of communication that involves sending mail-like messages across a **network** (typically the **Internet**).

e-mail account

An **e-mail** address that has its own mailbox, that is, mail isn't forwarded to another account as is the case with **e-mail aliases.**

e-mail alias

An **e-mail** alias works like a sort of virtual e-mail address that forwards received mail to another address.

encryption

Encoding information so that unauthorized persons cannot access it.

endnote

A reference that appears at the end of a Word document.

event

In Outlook, a scheduling **item** that does not have a start time or an end time and that can last an entire day or several days.

field

A column of similar data in a **database.**

filter

A process where only the **records** based on **criteria** you specify are displayed in a **database**.

Flesch-Kincaid formula

An equation used to test the readability level of a document.

folder

The container for files on your system. In early versions of Microsoft Windows and in some other operating systems, a folder is called a directory.

font

A particular typeface that has size, style, and effects such as italic, boldface, and so on.

footer

Also called a running foot. An area inside the bottom margin of the page that typically includes the page number, chapter number, chapter title, and so on.

footnote

A reference that appears at the bottom of a page.

form

A dialog box you use to enter **database records** into a database.

form handler

The software that gathers data from a **form**. Form handlers are either a part of **FrontPage Server Extensions**, **CGI scripts**, or **Active Server Pages**.

Formatting toolbar

The **toolbar** that contains buttons that correspond to the commands for formatting text, paragraphs, lists, and the like.

formula

An equation you create and enter into Excel. Formulas begin with an equal sign (=) and include standard mathematical operators and parentheses as appropriate.

formula bar

The bar directly above the Excel **worksheet** window that displays the **label, value, function,** or **formula** in the selected worksheet **cell.**

formula errors

It's possible to build an illogical or unsolvable **formula.** When you do, Excel displays an error message in the **cell** rather than calculating the result. The error message, which begins with the # symbol, describes the error.

frames

An **HTML** feature that permits splitting a **Web page** into multiple areas (frames) within which separate Web pages are displayed. Not supported by all **Web browsers.**

FrontPage

An application you can use to create **Web pages.**

FrontPage Server Extensions

A set of extensions to **Web servers** that enables FrontPage to easily accomplish advanced **server**-based tasks, such as handling submitted form data.

FrontPage web

A **Web site** that is created with **FrontPage** and contains special FrontPage information. Typically, once a web is published to the **Internet,** it is referred to as a Web site.

Full Screen view

Clears everything from the screen except the document itself.

function

A predefined **formula** in Excel, such as SUM.

GIF

An abbreviation for Graphics Interchange Format. A file format used most commonly for small graphics on **Web pages.** A GIF contains a maximum of 256 colors and can be made partially transparent or into a short **animation.**

grammar

The rules whereby language is constructed.

grammar checker

A tool that verifies the grammar in a document, suggests changes and corrections, and explains the associated rules.

Graph

An **applet** that's included with PowerPoint. You use it to create **charts** and graphs for a **presentation.**

handouts

Printed copies of your **slides** that you distribute either before your **presentation** so that people can take notes or after your presentation so that people have a record of what you said.

header

Also called a running head. An area inside the top margin of the page that typically includes the page number, chapter number, chapter title, and so on.

home page

Also called a front page. The first page that is displayed on a **Web site,** typically named *index.html, index.htm,* or *Default.htm.*

host name

The name of an individual computer on the **Internet** or an **intranet.** It is the leftmost part of a **Web** address. For example, for the address *wks1.microsoft.com,* the host name is *wks1.*

HTML

An abbreviation for HyperText Markup Language, the language used to create **Web pages.**

HTTP

An abbreviation for Hypertext Transfer Protocol, the rules that specify how a **Web browser** and a **Web server** communicate.

hyperlink

A word, a phrase, an image, or a symbol that forms a connection with a resource that can be in the same document, on your local computer, on your local **network,** or on the **Internet.**

image map

An image that contains multiple hyperlinks—each corresponding to a different region or **hotspot** of the image.

Inbox

In Outlook, the **module** you use to send and receive **e-mail** messages.

Instant Messaging

A form of communication that is roughly a cross between chat and telephone. Users run an Instant Messaging program that notifies them when people they know are online. Users can then conduct a text-based "conversation."

Internet

The world's largest computer **network,** connecting tens of millions of users.

Internet Explorer

The **Web browser** that's included with recent versions of Microsoft Windows.

Internet Merchant account

An account with a bank or financial institution for the purpose of processing online credit card transactions.

Internet service provider

Abbreviated ISP. A company that provides access to the **Internet** via dial-up connections, DSL, leased lines, or other connection methods.

IP address

A unique number that identifies a computer on a **network** or on the **Internet.**

item

In Outlook, every **record** is an **item,** including every **e-mail** message, appointment, note, and task.

JPEG

An abbreviation for Joint Photographic Experts Group. A file format used for photos and other high-quality images on **Web pages** that uses image compression to reduce file size.

keyword

A word or term that you enter in a field in a search service. Multiple keywords form a search string, a phrase that the search service compares with information it finds in its **database. Keywords** are also important in résumé building and job descriptions. Job seekers and recruiters can search on them to identify positions and potential candidates.

kiosk

An unattended computer that you can set up to display a PowerPoint **presentation** that automatically advances from **slide** to slide based on rehearsal timing data.

label

A text entry in an Excel **worksheet** that describes quantitative data.

legend

Names and identifies the **data series** in an Excel **chart.**

line chart

Plots individual **data points** in a line, using either different **data marker** symbols or different colored lines to distinguish the **data series,** and using a horizontal **data category** axis.

link

Short for **hyperlink.** A word, a phrase, an image, or a symbol that forms a connection with a resource that can be located on your local computer, your local **network,** or the **Internet.**

mailing list

A list to which users can subscribe that allows them to receive **e-mail** messages on a particular topic sent by a company or organization.

Master Slide

A blueprint for creating individual **slides.**

message rule

A filter that you can apply to block mail from certain senders and route mail to specific folders.

Microsoft Office User Specialist (MOUS)

A person who has passed the Microsoft Office User Specialist (MOUS) certification test at either the proficient user level or the expert user level.

module

In Outlook, a part of the application that serves a particular purpose. The Outlook modules are **Inbox, Calendar, Tasks, Notes,** and **Contacts.**

motion clip

A movie, video, or **animation** file.

My Documents folder

The default storage container for all Word documents.

natural language query

A plain English question.

navigation bars

A series of buttons or **hyperlinks** that help visitors quickly access the most important pages on a **Web site**.

network

A group of computers and peripheral devices (such as printers, modems, and so on) that are connected in some way so that their users can share files and other resources.

newsgroups

Electronic bulletin boards on the **Internet** where users can post messages, read other users' posts, and reply to them.

Normal template

The pattern that contains the default styles used to format a document.

Normal view

Does not display **headers** and **footers**, graphics, and certain formatting and is best used for entering and editing text.

Notes

In Outlook, the **module** you use to keep track of odd bits of information.

object

A **table,** a **chart,** a picture—anything you can create or store on your computer that you can then insert into an Office program.

OCR program

An optical character recognition program that can convert a scanned document into text that can be used in a **word-processing** program or a **Web page** editor.

Office Assistant

A little animated creature, intended to be helpful, that appears on your screen when you first access Help in an Office program.

offline file

A file that is stored on the **network** but that you make available to you while not connected to the network.

OLE

A Microsoft Windows tool for sharing data. With OLE, or Object Linking and Embedding, you can transfer data between Windows programs by copying and pasting.

online meeting

Sharing and exchanging information with people at different computers over a **network** or the **Internet** in real time. You can initiate an online meeting from within any Office application.

operator precedence

The set of mathematical rules that specify in which order mathematical operations should occur in a **formula.** Excel follows standard rules of operator precedence and first performs exponential operations, then multiplication and division operations, and finally, addition and subtraction. (To override these rules, you must use parentheses.)

Organization Chart

An Office **applet** that you can use to create organization **charts** in your documents.

orphan

The first line of a paragraph that appears by itself as the last line of a printed page or a column.

Outline view

Displays an outline of your Word document if it was created using Word styles. In PowerPoint, Outline view is a list of **slides** in your **presentation.**

Outlook

Personal information management software that is part of the Office suite. You can also use Outlook to send and receive **e-mail.**

Pack And Go Wizard

A PowerPoint tool that creates a standalone version of a **presentation** that includes all the slides in your presentation and a PowerPoint browser program that lets you show these slides. You use the **wizard** to create a copy of a presentation you can show on a computer that doesn't have the PowerPoint program installed.

page banner

An automatically created heading that displays the title of the **Web page.**

paragraph

A chunk of text that ends when you press the Enter key.

parallel construction

In writing, a technique that grammatically coordinates similar items. For example, the items in a list might all be sentences or all noun phrases or might all begin with an "ing" verb.

password

A combination of characters you enter to access a protected document.

permissions

The level of access given to a user or group for a particular file or folder.

personal information database

A huge file that contains data about individuals and that can be searched on the **Internet,** sometimes for free and sometimes for a fee.

personalized menu

A menu that displays only the commands you most often use. Personalized menus are a feature of Office that you can enable or disable.

pie chart

A pie chart shows a single **data series** and depicts individual **data points** as segments of the circle, or slices of the pie.

PIM

Abbreviation for personal information manager. Software that typically includes an address and phone book, a scheduler, a to-do list manager, and the ability to keep notes and track interactions with contacts.

PivotChart

A chart based on **PivotTable** data. You manipulate PivotCharts in much the same way as you manipulate PivotTables—by dragging field buttons to different axes.

PivotTable

An Excel feature that enables you to **sort, filter,** and pivot data in a manner that displays important information more clearly.

pixel

A single dot on a computer screen. Everything displayed on a computer monitor is made up of pixels. Common screen resolutions are 640x480 or 800x600—800 pixels wide and 600 pixels high.

placeholder

In PowerPoint, a box or an area you use to affix **objects** or text to a **slide**.

Places bar

The list of icons on the left of Open, New, and Save dialog boxes. Clicking the icons quickly opens the associated place, such as **My Documents**.

plain text

A document format that includes no formatting and only the basic ASCII character set.

plug-in

A program that plugs into another program to provide it with enhanced functionality. Adobe Acrobat Reader, Macromedia Flash, and Shockwave are examples of **Web browser** plug-ins.

PNG

An abbreviation for Portable Network Graphic. A newer file format designed for high-quality images with optional transparency. Not supported by all **Web browsers.**

point

The measuring unit for a font. One point equals 1/72 inch.

POP

An abbreviation for Post Office Protocol, which retrieves messages from an **e-mail** server.

presentation

The PowerPoint **slides** you create and store in the same file on your computer. A presentation is also a document file.

presentation broadcast

A **slide show** that you deliver over a **network.** PowerPoint comes with tools and software you need to deliver a presentation broadcast to as many as 15 people over a network.

presentation window

The portion of the screen used to display the **presentation** you've opened or are creating.

Print Layout view

Shows how the document will appear on the printed page.

Print Preview

Displays your document at various sizes as mocked-up printed pages.

properties

Characteristics of an **object** or a device, such as a picture or a document.

protocol

A formal specification that defines the rules whereby data is transmitted and received.

proxy server

A **network server** that sits in between the local network and the **Internet,** protecting the local network from attacks as well as caching **Web pages** to improve **Web-browsing** performance for local clients.

Query Wizard

An Excel tool that retrieveS data from an external **database** for analysis inside Excel.

radar chart

Plots each data category's **data point** values on separate **value** axes and connects the data point values of each **data series** with a line.

range

A rectangular area of an Excel **worksheet,** such as a two-**cell** by two-cell square, a five-cell by nine-cell rectangle, or even an entire worksheet. Excel uses opposite corner **cell references** and a colon to define ranges.

range name

A single **cell** or group of cells in an Excel **worksheet** that you designate with a name. Range names simplify the process of creating **formulas.**

record

A row of data in a **database.**

recto

The right-hand page in a two-page spread.

recurring task

In Outlook, an activity that occurs periodically, such as a monthly meeting, a quarterly report, and so on.

Rehearsal Timing tool

In PowerPoint, the tool you use to practice and time a **presentation.** You can use the timing information collected by this tool to automatically advance through the **slides** in a presentation.

relational database

A more complex **database** with multiple **tables** linked together. You can't build a relational database using Excel. You need to use a relational database program such as Access.

relative cell reference

A **cell reference** that, if copied, gets adjusted by Excel.

rich text

A document format that was originally developed to transfer documents between applications running on different operating systems. You can save a Word document as rich text, and you can create an **e-mail** message in rich text.

right-clicking

The process of using the right mouse button rather than the left. In Office programs, right-clicking opens a **shortcut menu.**

scientific notation

A method used to express very large or very small numbers in an abbreviated form. For example, if a value is too large to fit into a single **cell,** Excel either increases the cell width or displays the cell contents using scientific notation. The number 123456789, for example, may appear as something like 1.2E+08 or 1.235E+08, depending on the width of the cell. Likewise, the number .0000001 may appear as something like 1E-07.

search engine

A program contained on a **Web site** that allows visitors to search for **Web pages** on the **Internet.**

serif

Any of the short lines that extend from the upper or lower parts of a letter.

server

A **network** computer that provides services, such as printing, storage, and communications.

sharing

Making a resource available to others on the **network.**

shortcut

An icon on the desktop that represents an application, a file, a document, a printer, or any other **object** in Microsoft Windows.

shortcut key

A series of keystrokes that can substitute for the actions associated with selecting from menus.

shortcut menu

A menu of related commands that appears when you **right-click** an object; also sometimes referred to as a context menu or a right-click menu.

signature

A file that you can append to the close of your **e-mail** messages. A typical business signature contains your name, title, the name of your organization, perhaps its physical address, and your phone number.

slide

The basic PowerPoint building block.

slide show

All the **slides** you want to present to an audience.

Slide Sorter

In PowerPoint, a view that displays small pictures of each **slide** in your **presentation**. You use the Slide Sorter to verify that both the slides and their order are correct.

slide transition

In PowerPoint, a specification that makes the change from one **slide** to the next noticeable. For example, you can tell PowerPoint that the current slide should be wiped away to reveal the next slide underneath.

sort

Arranging data in a **database** in ascending or descending order.

sound clip

A file that contains audio.

speaker's notes

Comments you want to use as you talk about the displayed **slide**. You enter and store speaker's notes in the Speaker's Notes pane.

special effects

Garnishments, such as **slide transitions, animation,** sound, and video, that you add to a **presentation** to enhance its impact and value.

speech recognition

Sometimes called voice recognition. A program that can understand the spoken word and transform it into the written word.

spelling checker

A tool that verifies the spelling in a document, either as you type or when you indicate that it should do so.

SSL

An abbreviation for Secure Sockets Layer. A way of **encrypting** data that is transferred to and from a **Web site** and is typically used for **Web stores** that process credit card transactions.

Standard toolbar

The **toolbar** that contains buttons that correspond to the commands for such operations as opening, saving, viewing, and printing files.

status bar

The bar directly above the Microsoft Windows taskbar that displays information about a command or a process that is running.

stock chart

A stock **chart** plots security prices in a common open-high-low-close format.

style

A collection of formatting information that can include the font type, font size, attributes, alignment, character spacing, paragraph spacing, and so on.

stylesheet

A list of the available styles for a document.

subdomain

A **domain** that is a child of another domain. For example, *support.microsoft.com* is a subdomain of *microsoft.com*.

surface chart

A surface **chart** plots **data series** in a three-dimensional grid, generally using color not to identify data series but rather to indicate **value** axis ranges.

table

An element that consists of rows and columns and concisely presents information at a glance.

table of contents

A listing that includes part names, chapter names, section names, and so on and their associated page reference.

Tasks

The Outlook **module** that you use to manage your to-do list.

template

A collection of styles that provides the basic pattern for a document. Also a **Web page** that acts as a starting point for new Web pages. Any content or formatting information on a template is automatically applied to new pages created with the template, streamlining the process of making pages.

thesaurus

A dictionary of synonyms (words that mean the same or nearly the same).

thumbnail image

A small version of an image that is **hyperlinked** to the full-size version.

title bar

Appears at the top of an Office program window, just above the menu bar, and displays the file name of the document.

toolbar

The toolbar or toolbars, located just below the menu bar, provide a series of buttons that allow for faster selection of frequently used menu commands.

TrueType

A type of font whose printed output is identical to its screen display.

underscore

The "_" character. It is often used to represent a space in filenames on the **Internet** because it is compatible with both the Microsoft Windows naming scheme and the UNIX naming scheme.

URL

An abbreviation for Uniform Resource Locator, an address for a resource on the **Internet.**

value

A value in a **worksheet** that can be used in **formulas** to calculate a result.

vector-based graphics

Computer-based line drawings. Vector-based (line) graphics are usually much smaller than an equivalent raster-based (bitmap) graphic, such as a **GIF,** or **JPEG** file, and the lines can also be edited at a later time.

verso

The left-hand page in a two-page spread.

view

A way of displaying information in a document.

virtual domains

The ability to make a single computer host multiple **domain names.** When discussing **Web hosting** plans, virtual domain support means that you can use your own **domain name.**

VML

An abbreviation for Vector Markup Language. A Microsoft-proposed extension to the XML standard that permits **vector-based graphics** to be created using a small amount of text-based code, permitting quick downloads and the ability to edit the image in the future. **Internet Explorer** 5 and later can natively display VML images.

Web

The World Wide Web, an area of the **Internet** containing linked **Web sites.**

Web browser

A program used to display **Web pages.**

Web component

A small program that runs in a **Web page.** FrontPage provides a number of Web components that you can insert, including Microsoft Office Web Components, a series of **ActiveX** components that provide visitors with the ability to interact with and manipulate spreadsheet data.

Web hosting

To store a **Web site** and make it available for others to view on the **Internet.**

Web Layout view

Shows how the document will display in a **Web browser.**

Web page

A document using the **HTML** file format. A Web page can be stored on the **Web,** a company intranet, or locally on your computer's hard drive or floppy disk.

Web presentation

A PowerPoint **presentation** that you publish to a **Web site.** Anyone that can view that Web site can view the presentation.

Web Query

An Excel tool you can use to retrieve tabular data from a **Web page.**

Web ring

A collection of **Web sites** that all cover the same topic and that post a Web ring **banner ad** on their sites, allowing visitors to easily view other sites in the Web ring.

Web server

A computer that is running a Web server program, enabling it to serve **Web pages** to other hosts on the **Internet** or a local area **network.**

Web site

A collection of **Web pages** that are connected by means of **hyperlinks.**

Web store

A **Web site** that visitors can browse and then purchase products or services.

what-if analysis

The process of changing one or more input variables to determine the effect on a calculated result.

widow

A single last line of a paragraph that becomes separated from the related text and lands at the top of a printed page or column.

wizard

A guide that steps you through the creation of a specific kind of document.

WordArt

An Office **applet** that you can use to turn chunks of text into colorful, interesting graphics **objects.**

word processor

A computer program that transforms written, verbal, and recorded information into electronic and print format.

workbook

An Excel file that contains at least one **worksheet.** The standard Excel workbook contains three worksheets. An Excel workbook file extension is .xls.

worksheet

A grid of **cells** in which you enter **labels, values,** and **formulas** in Excel. One or more worksheets comprise an Excel workbook.

XY (Scatter) chart

An XY (scatter) **chart** lets you visually explore the relationships between **data series** by treating the horizontal axis as a second **values** axis. To accomplish this, XY charts actually plot pairs of **data points.**

Index

ways to create, 35–37

working (*See* working folders)

Font button, Formatting toolbar, 30

Font Color button, Formatting toolbar, 30

fonts

    applying effects using Formatting toolbar, 30

    changing in Word documents, 30

    changing in worksheets, 104–5

    changing size in Word documents, 30

    changing size in worksheets, 104–5

    for chart text, 347

    glossary definition, 613

Font Size button, Formatting toolbar, 30

footers, 613. *See also* headers and footers

footnotes, 613

forecasting

    break-even analysis forecast, profit-volume-cost and break-even analysis workbook, 545–48

    business planning workbook, 479–514

    cash flow forecast and analysis workbook, 563–96

    profit volume forecast, profit-volume-cost and break-even analysis workbook, 548–54

Format Cells dialog box, 103–4

Format Painter feature, 27

formatting. *See also* Formatting toolbar

    copying, 27, 84

    drawn objects, 360

    Excel charts, 346–47

    finding and replacing, 29

    text in Word tables, 273

    Web page text, 233

    Word documents, 30, 269–96

    Word tables using AutoFormat feature, 278–81

    worksheets, 102–10

Formatting toolbar

    adding buttons to, 70–71

    glossary definition, 613

    list of buttons, 30

    removing buttons from, 70

    ways to display, 24–25

    in Word, 24, 25, 30, 70–72

form handlers, 613

form letters

    creating, 370–76

    merged, printing, 376

    printing envelopes, 377–78

    tips for creating, 376–77

Form Page Wizard, FrontPage, 467–72

forms, database

    creating, 198–201

    entering data, 198

    glossary definition, 613

    layouts for, 199–200

    naming, 201

    overview, 192

    styles for, 200

forms, Web page. *See also* order forms; Web stores

    adding fields, 250–51

    creating, overview, 249–50

    creating for order-taking, 467–75

    creating for visitor searches, 263–65

    making changes to field properties, 251–54

    modifying, 254–56

    processing results, 256–63, 471, 476–77

    responding to data requests using Outlook, 258–63

formula bar, worksheet, 91, 614

formula errors, 98, 614

formulas, worksheet

    cell references in, 96–97

    copying, 112–14

    entering, 94–98

    errors in, 98

    glossary definition, 614

    modifying, 98

    moving, 114

    operators in, 94–96

    overview, 94–96

    parentheses in, 95–96

    recalculating, 97

Form Wizard, Access, 198–201

forwarding e-mail messages, 178

frames, 614

FreeMerchant.com Web site, 477

FrontPage Server Extensions, 263, 440, 471, 614

FrontPage webs, 222–27, 614. *See also* Microsoft FrontPage
Full Screen view, 62, 614
functions, worksheet, 98–101, 614

G

gain and loss statement schedule, cash flow forecast and analysis workbook
    after-tax gain (loss) on disposal, 577–78
    gross residual, 576
    illustrated, 572
    income tax expenses (savings), 577
    net residual, 576
    nontaxable portion of residual, 576
    overview, 576
    pretax gain (loss) on disposal, 577
    transaction/disposal costs, 576
geographic data comparisons, 329, 330
GIFs, 615
Go (Infoseek), 455
Google, 455
Go to feature, in Excel, 92
grammar, defined, 615
grammar checker, 77–78, 615
Graph applet, 615
graphic images. *See also* clip art
    adding to presentation slides, 129–37
    adding to Web pages, 235–36
    AutoShapes, 133–37
    clip art, 130–33
    creating thumbnails for Web pages, 239–40
    digital, 445
    inserting from files, 363–64
    resizing, 237–38, 362
    scanning directly into Web pages, 236–37
    tips for presentations, 154
    wrapping text around, 238, 364
Greeting Line dialog box, 375
groups, sending personalized e-mail messages using Mail Merge Wizard, 382–84

H

handouts, presentation
    creating, 532–34
    glossary definition, 615
    printing, 58, 533–34
headers and footers
    adding to Outlook contacts lists, 416–17
    adding to Word documents, 285–88
    different on first page, 288
    different on left and right pages, 287
    glossary definitions, 613, 615
Help system. *See also* Office Assistant
    disabling Office Assistant, 67
    getting Help from within dialog boxes, 69
    overview, 4
    searching for topics, 68
    using Answer Wizard, 68
    using Help Contents, 5–6, 68
    using Help Index, 6–7, 68
    in Word, 67–69
home pages, 615. *See also* Web pages
horizontal lines, in Web pages, 236
horizontal scroll bar, Word, 64
host names, 438, 615
HotBot, 455
HTML
    in e-mail messages, 181
    for e-mail newsletters, 422, 424
    glossary definition, 616
HTTP (Hypertext Transfer Protocol), 616
hyperlinks
    creating, 233–35
    exchanges as form of advertising, 456–57
    glossary definition, 616
    verifying, 447
    between Web pages, 233–34
    within Web pages, 234–35
hyphenation, adjusting in Word documents, 293–95

I

icons. *See* shortcuts, defined
image maps, 616
images. *See* graphic images
Import And Export Wizard, Outlook, 394–95
importing
    address books into Contacts folder, 394–95
    Excel worksheet data into Access, 213–17
    text for Web pages, 229–30
    Word outlines into PowerPoint, 127
Import Spreadsheet Wizard, Access, 214–17
Inbox
    glossary definition, 616
    illustrated, 171
    moving e-mail messages to folders, 186–87
    receiving e-mail messages, 171–74
income statements, business planning workbook
    common size, 501–2
    cost of sales, 498
    gross margin, 498–99
    illustrated, 498
    income tax expenses (savings), 500–501
    interest expense, 500
    interest income, 500
    net income (loss) after taxes, 501
    net income (loss) before taxes, 500
    operating expenses, 499
    operating income, 499
    overview, 480, 497
    sales revenue, 498
    total operating expenses, 499
income tax expenses (savings)
    in gain and loss statement schedule, cash flow forecast and analysis workbook, 577
    in income statements, business planning workbook, 500–501
    in liquidation cash flow statement schedule, cash flow forecast and analysis workbook, 581
    in operating cash flows statement schedule, cash flow forecast and analysis workbook, 580
    in profit and loss statement schedule, cash flow forecast and analysis workbook, 575

Increase Indent button, Formatting toolbar, 30
information collection, as reason
  to have Web site, 435
input values, in functions. *See* arguments, function
Insert Address Block dialog box, 375
Insert Clip Art pane, 130–31
Insert Function dialog box, 99–100
Insert Picture dialog box, 133, 363–64
Insert Table dialog box, 271–72
Instant Messaging, 616
interactive Web stores, 466–77
Internet, 616
Internet Explorer, 448, 449, 616
Internet Merchant accounts, 617
Internet service providers, 617
inventory databases, 464
IP addresses, 617
italics
    using Formatting toolbar, 30
    in Word documents, 30
    in worksheets, 105
items, 159, 617. *See also* Microsoft Outlook

J

JPEG files, 617
JumboStore.com Web site, 477

K

keyboard shortcuts. *See* shortcut keys
keywords, 617
kiosks, 617

L

Label Options dialog box, 385
labels, address, 385–87
labels, chart, 345, 346
labels, worksheet
    aligning, 102
    copying, 110–12

O

objects
- assigning macros to, 313–14
- drawing, 357–58
- glossary definition, 620
- role in PowerPoint, 118
- selecting, 25, 82

OCR programs, 445, 620

Office. *See* Microsoft Office

Office Assistant
- changing character, 69
- disabling, 67
- glossary definition, 620
- hiding Clippit, 67
- hiding/showing, 4
- overview, 4–5
- in Word, 67

offline files, 620

offline Web site publicity, 458

OLE (Object Linking and Embedding), 620. *See also* objects

online advertising, 455–57

online meetings, 620

online presentations. *See* slide shows

Open Directory, 455

opening Office documents, 52–53

operating cash flows statement schedule, cash flow forecast and analysis workbook
- addbacks of noncash expenses, 579
- after-tax operating cash flow, 580
- debt principal payments, 579
- deducts of cash nonexpenses, 579
- depreciation, 579
- illustrated, 578
- income tax expenses (savings), 580
- net income before taxes, 578
- overview, 578
- pretax operating cash flow, 579–80

operator precedence, 95–96, 620

operators
- addition (+), 94, 95
- division (/), 94, 95
- exponentiation (^), 94, 95
- multiplication (*), 94, 95
- order of precedence, 95–96
- role of parentheses, 95–96
- subtraction (-), 94, 95

Opera Web browser, 449, 450

order forms
- creating for Web stores, 467–75
- filling out, 475–76
- Form Page Wizard, 467–72
- modifying draft, 472–75
- processing orders, 476–77

Organization Chart applet, 620

organization charts
- adding details to, 366
- adding to documents, 364–65
- customizing, 366
- as type of diagram, 139, 364

.org top-level domain, 438

orientation, page, 56

orphans, 295–96, 621

outlines
- creating in PowerPoint, 124–26, 525–26
- developing for sales presentations, 516–21
- for e-mail newsletters, 428–29
- importing to PowerPoint from Word, 127

Outline view, 62, 621

Outlook. *See* Microsoft Outlook

P

Pack And Go Wizard, 621

page banners, 242–43, 621

page numbers, adding to Word documents, 285, 286, 289–90

page orientation, 56

paragraphs, 621

parallel construction, 621

Parameters feature, FrontPage, 232

parentheses, 95–96

passwords
- for Access databases, 52
- for Excel workbooks, 49–50

X

Y

The manuscript for this book was prepared and submitted to Redmond Technology Press in electronic form. Text files were prepared using Microsoft Word 2000. Pages were composed using PageMaker 6.5 for Windows, with text in Frutiger and Caslon. Composed files were delivered to the printer as electronic prepress files.

Project Editor
Paula Thurman

Layout
Minh-Tam S. Le

Indexer
Julie Kawabata